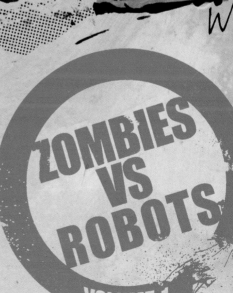

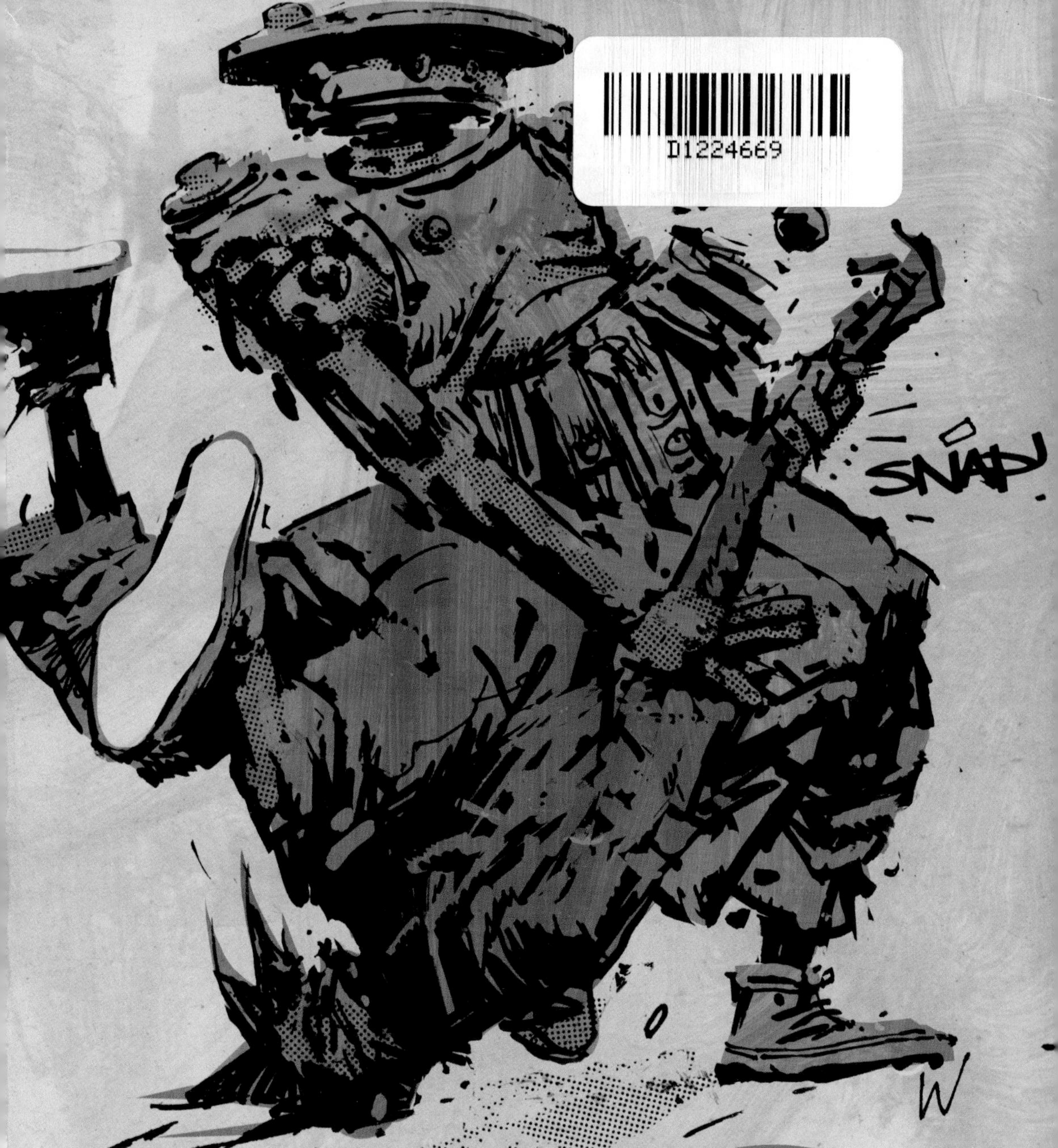
SNAP

ZOMBIES
VS
ROBOTS

VOLUME 1

ISBN: 978-1-63140-414-6

18 17 16 15   2 3 4 5

®

www.IDWPUBLISHING.com
IDW founded by Ted Adams, Alex Garner, Kris Oprisko, and Robbie Robbins

Ted Adams, CEO & Publisher
Greg Goldstein, President & COO
Robbie Robbins, EVP/Sr. Graphic Artist
Chris Ryall, Chief Creative Officer/Editor-in-Chief
Matthew Ruzicka, CPA, Chief Financial Officer
Alan Payne, VP of Sales
Dirk Wood, VP of Marketing
Lorelei Bunjes, VP of Digital Services
Jeff Webber, VP of Digital Publishing & Business Development

Facebook: facebook.com/idwpublishing
Twitter: @idwpublishing
YouTube: youtube.com/idwpublishing
Tumblr: tumblr.idwpublishing.com
Instagram: instagram.com/idwpublishing

Inherit The Earth
Writer: Chris Ryall
Artist: Anthony Diecidue

The Orphan
Writer: Steve Niles
Artist: Val Mayerik
Colorist: Jay Fotos

Tales of ZvR
Writer/Artist: Ashley Wood
Dialogue/Lettering: Chris Ryall

Zombies vs. Robots created by Chris Ryall & Ashley Wood

Series Editor: Chris Ryall
Editorial Assist: Michael Benedetto
Letterer: Shawn Lee

Cover by Ashley Wood
Collection Edits by Justin Eisinger & Alonzo Simon
Collection Design by Clyde Grapa

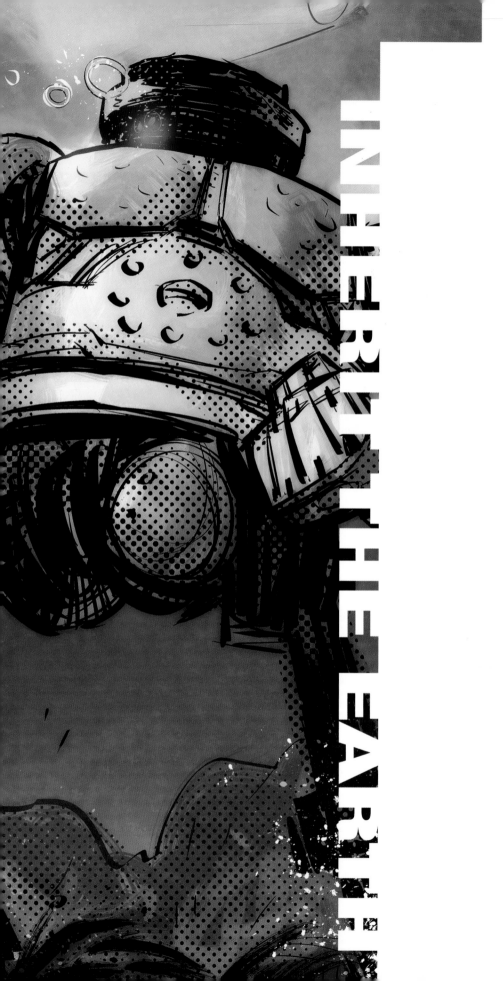

INHERIT THE EARTH

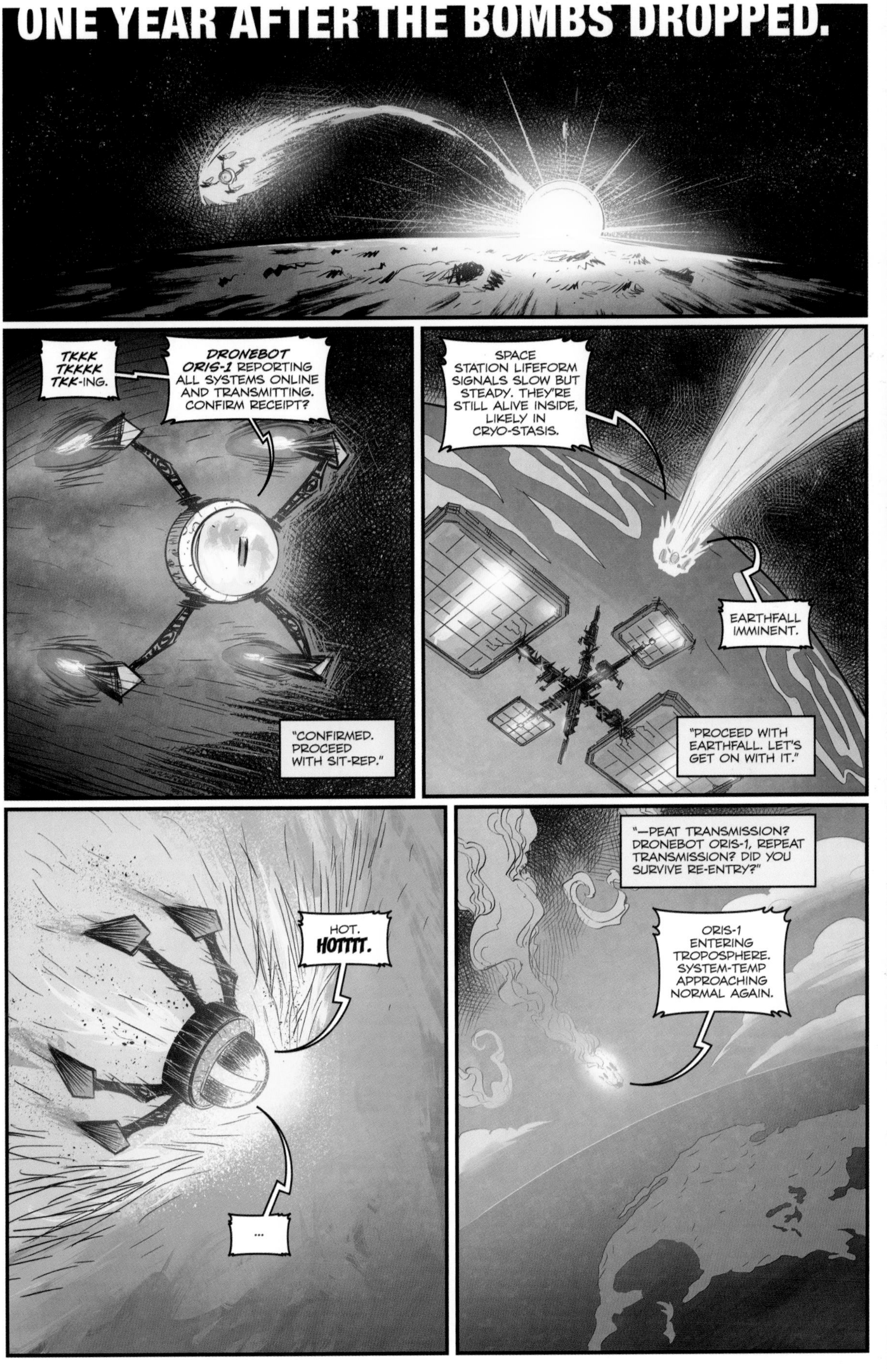
ONE YEAR AFTER THE BOMBS DROPPED.
TKKK TKKKK TKK-ING.
DRONEBOT ORIS-1 REPORTING ALL SYSTEMS ONLINE AND TRANSMITTING. CONFIRM RECEIPT?
"CONFIRMED. PROCEED WITH SIT-REP."
SPACE STATION LIFEFORM SIGNALS SLOW BUT STEADY. THEY'RE STILL ALIVE INSIDE, LIKELY IN CRYO-STASIS.
EARTHFALL IMMINENT.
"PROCEED WITH EARTHFALL. LET'S GET ON WITH IT."
HOT. HOTTTT.
...
"—PEAT TRANSMISSION? DRONEBOT ORIS-1, REPEAT TRANSMISSION? DID YOU SURVIVE RE-ENTRY?"
ORIS-1 ENTERING TROPOSPHERE. SYSTEM-TEMP APPROACHING NORMAL AGAIN.

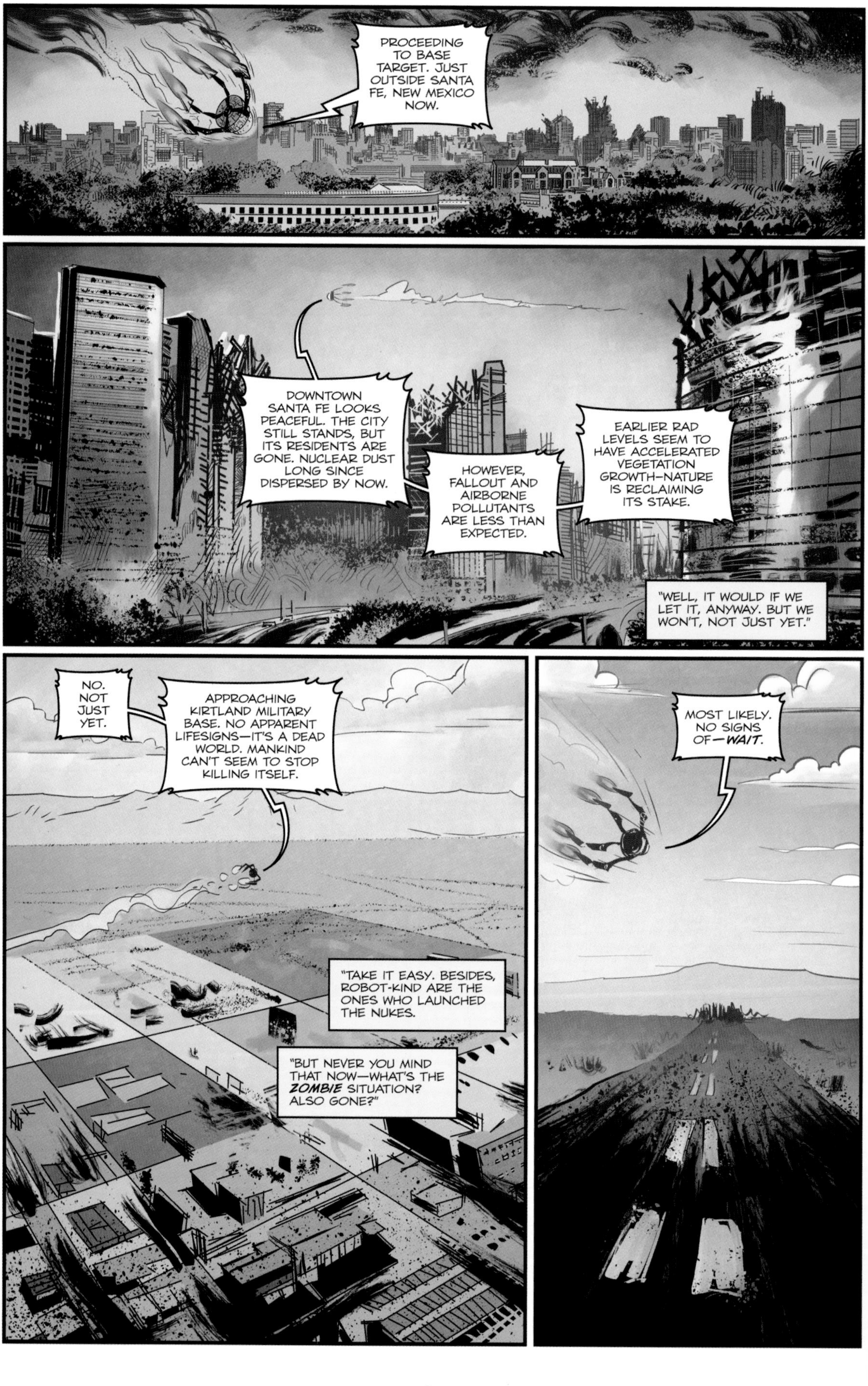

PROCEEDING TO BASE TARGET. JUST OUTSIDE SANTA FE, NEW MEXICO NOW.
DOWNTOWN SANTA FE LOOKS PEACEFUL. THE CITY STILL STANDS, BUT ITS RESIDENTS ARE GONE. NUCLEAR DUST LONG SINCE DISPERSED BY NOW.
HOWEVER, FALLOUT AND AIRBORNE POLLUTANTS ARE LESS THAN EXPECTED.
EARLIER RAD LEVELS SEEM TO HAVE ACCELERATED VEGETATION GROWTH—NATURE IS RECLAIMING ITS STAKE.
"WELL, IT WOULD IF WE LET IT, ANYWAY. BUT WE WON'T, NOT JUST YET."
NO. NOT JUST YET.
APPROACHING KIRTLAND MILITARY BASE. NO APPARENT LIFESIGNS—IT'S A DEAD WORLD. MANKIND CAN'T SEEM TO STOP KILLING ITSELF.
"TAKE IT EASY. BESIDES, ROBOT-KIND ARE THE ONES WHO LAUNCHED THE NUKES.
"BUT NEVER YOU MIND THAT NOW—WHAT'S THE *ZOMBIE* SITUATION? ALSO GONE?"
MOST LIKELY. NO SIGNS OF—*WAIT*.

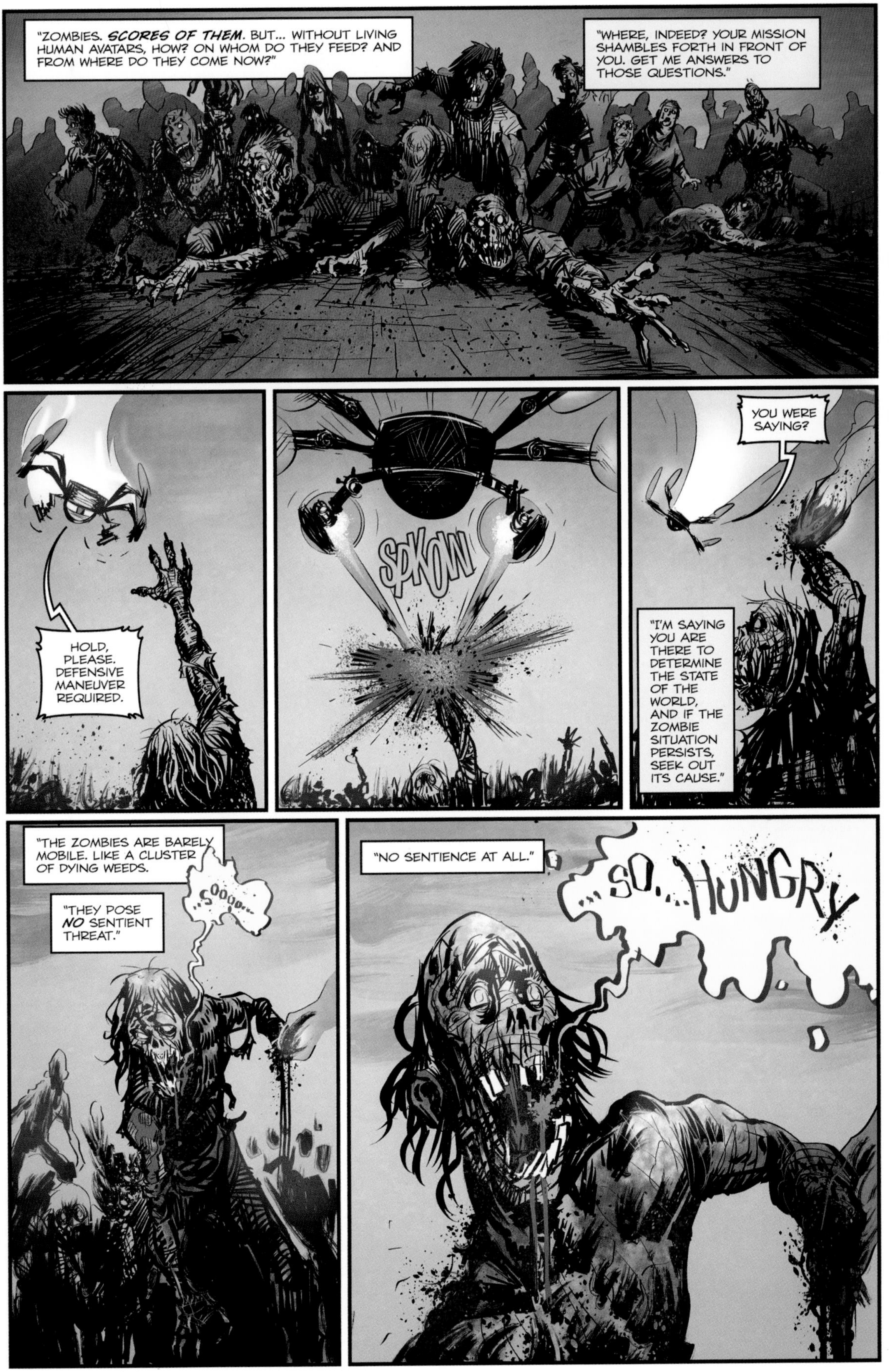
"ZOMBIES. SCORES OF THEM. BUT... WITHOUT LIVING HUMAN AVATARS, HOW? ON WHOM DO THEY FEED? AND FROM WHERE DO THEY COME NOW?"
"WHERE, INDEED? YOUR MISSION SHAMBLES FORTH IN FRONT OF YOU. GET ME ANSWERS TO THOSE QUESTIONS."
HOLD, PLEASE. DEFENSIVE MANEUVER REQUIRED.
SPKOW
YOU WERE SAYING?
"I'M SAYING YOU ARE THERE TO DETERMINE THE STATE OF THE WORLD, AND IF THE ZOMBIE SITUATION PERSISTS, SEEK OUT ITS CAUSE."
"THE ZOMBIES ARE BARELY MOBILE. LIKE A CLUSTER OF DYING WEEDS.
"THEY POSE NO SENTIENT THREAT."
..SOOOO...
"NO SENTIENCE AT ALL."
...SO....HUNGRY

THE INTERNATIONAL SPACE STATION.

CRYO-STASIS TUBES INSIDE THE ISS.

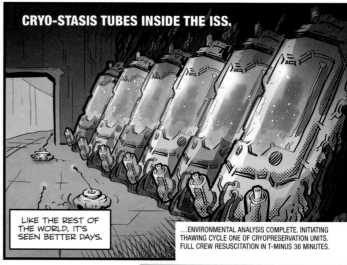

LIKE THE REST OF THE WORLD, IT'S SEEN BETTER DAYS.

...ENVIRONMENTAL ANALYSIS COMPLETE. INITIATING THAWING CYCLE ONE OF CRYOPRESERVATION UNITS. FULL CREW RESUSCITATION IN T-MINUS 36 MINUTES.

INITIATING THAWING CYCLE TWO OF CRYOPRESERVATION UNITS. FULL CREW RESUSCITATION IN T-MINUS 24 MINUTES...

SSSSSSSSSSSS

BACK ON EARTH, AT THE KIRTLAND BASE WHERE THE ZVR STORY BEGAN...

THIS IS HOW IT LOOKED BEFORE.

NOW.

THE KIRTLAND BASE IS AS TRASHED AS THE REST OF THE CITY.

ENTERING THE LABORATORY COMPLEX NOW.

"ANY SIGN OF MORE ZOMBIES? ANY OF THE BASE'S ROBOT GUARDS STILL STANDING?"

"ANSWERS BEGIN TO COALESCE. A HUMAN CORPSE ON THE GROUND, LONG SINCE DEAD. THE INTER-DIMENSIONAL GATEWAY ACTIVE AND GENERATING.

"THAT'S NOT A PARADOX. BUT IT IS A DILEMMA. GO ON."

"GENERATING WHAT?"

ZOMBIES. A HORDE OF TRANSFIGURED HUMANS COMING FORWARD FROM A FUTURE TIMELINE. THE FINAL FOLLY OF THE FOUNDING SCIENTISTS—QUITE THE PARADOX.

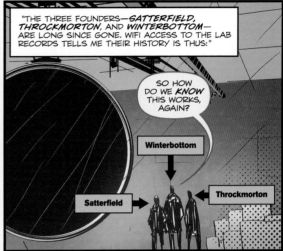

"THE THREE FOUNDERS—*SATTERFIELD, THROCKMORTON,* AND *WINTERBOTTOM*—ARE LONG SINCE GONE. WIFI ACCESS TO THE LAB RECORDS TELLS ME THEIR HISTORY IS THUS:"

SO HOW DO WE *KNOW* THIS WORKS, AGAIN?

Winterbottom

Satterfield

Throckmorton

"PHILLIPPE SATTERFIELD'S GATEWAY WAS A BRILLIANT INTERDIMENSIONAL DOORWAY TO OTHER TIMES AND PLACES."

THERE'S ONE SIMPLE ANSWER TO YOUR EVEN MORE SIMPLISTIC QUESTION:

IT WORKS BECAUSE I BUILT IT TO WORK.

"A GATEWAY THROUGH WHICH AN IMPROPERLY-OUTFITTED HUMAN DID NOT SURVIVE. AND THUS DID THE INFECTION BEGIN.

"WHEREAS FRITZ WINTERBOTTOM'S SUIT ENABLED HIM TO SAFELY ENTER ANOTHER TIME AND PLACE AND ENGAGE ITS CITIZENS."

ALL THE SAME TO YOU, I WILL TRUST YOUR GATEWAY ONLY FROM INSIDE MY IMPREGNABLE BATTLE-ARMOR.

"UNFORTUITOUSLY, THOSE HUMANS WERE ACTUALLY THE INFECTED UNDEAD. AND THE HUMAN PROVED FAR MORE FRAGILE THAN THE SUIT THAT HOUSED HIM."

YAHHHH!

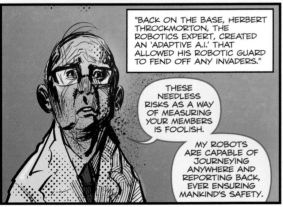

"BACK ON THE BASE, HERBERT THROCKMORTON, THE ROBOTICS EXPERT, CREATED AN 'ADAPTIVE A.I.' THAT ALLOWED HIS ROBOTIC GUARD TO FEND OFF ANY INVADERS."

THESE NEEDLESS RISKS AS A WAY OF MEASURING YOUR MEMBERS IS FOOLISH.

MY ROBOTS ARE CAPABLE OF JOURNEYING ANYWHERE AND REPORTING BACK, EVER ENSURING MANKIND'S SAFETY.

"WOULD THAT HIS CREATIONS HAD BEEN ABLE TO DISTINGUISH BETWEEN INFECTED HUMANS AND NON—."

SAY GOODBYE, PINKY.

ULP.

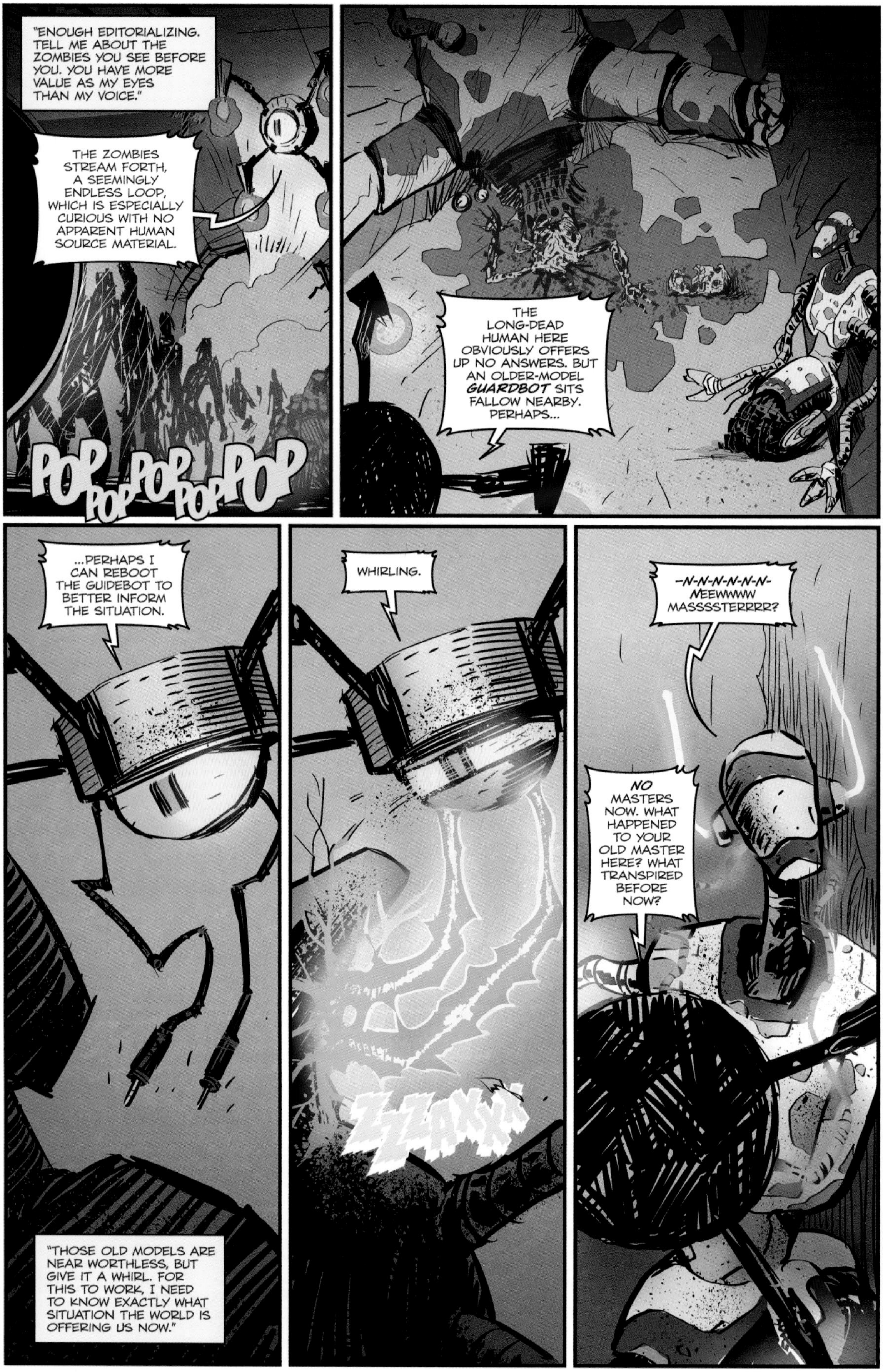
"ENOUGH EDITORIALIZING. TELL ME ABOUT THE ZOMBIES YOU SEE BEFORE YOU. YOU HAVE MORE VALUE AS MY EYES THAN MY VOICE."
THE ZOMBIES STREAM FORTH, A SEEMINGLY ENDLESS LOOP, WHICH IS ESPECIALLY CURIOUS WITH NO APPARENT HUMAN SOURCE MATERIAL.
POP POP POP POP POP
THE LONG-DEAD HUMAN HERE OBVIOUSLY OFFERS UP NO ANSWERS. BUT AN OLDER-MODEL GUARDBOT SITS FALLOW NEARBY. PERHAPS...
...PERHAPS I CAN REBOOT THE GUIDEBOT TO BETTER INFORM THE SITUATION.
"THOSE OLD MODELS ARE NEAR WORTHLESS, BUT GIVE IT A WHIRL. FOR THIS TO WORK, I NEED TO KNOW EXACTLY WHAT SITUATION THE WORLD IS OFFERING US NOW."
WHIRLING.
ZZZAXX
-N-N-N-N-N-N-NEEWWWW MASSSSTERRRR?
NO MASTERS NOW. WHAT HAPPENED TO YOUR OLD MASTER HERE? WHAT TRANSPIRED BEFORE NOW?

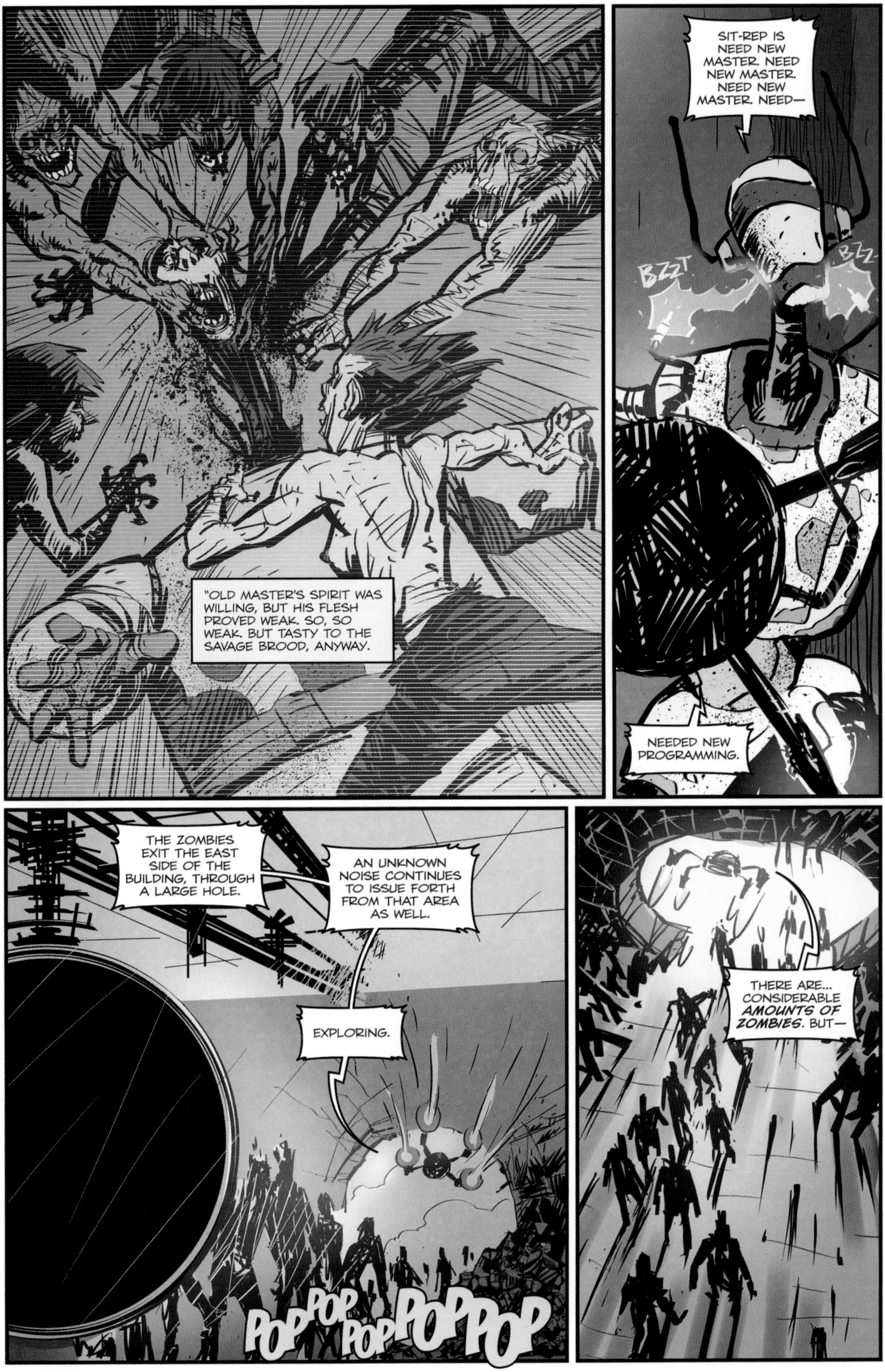
"OLD MASTER'S SPIRIT WAS WILLING, BUT HIS FLESH PROVED WEAK. SO, SO WEAK. BUT TASTY TO THE SAVAGE BROOD, ANYWAY.
SIT-REP IS NEED NEW MASTER. NEED NEW MASTER. NEED NEW MASTER. NEED—
BZZT
BZZ-
NEEDED NEW PROGRAMMING.
THE ZOMBIES EXIT THE EAST SIDE OF THE BUILDING, THROUGH A LARGE HOLE.
AN UNKNOWN NOISE CONTINUES TO ISSUE FORTH FROM THAT AREA AS WELL.
EXPLORING.
POP POP POP POP POP POP
THERE ARE... CONSIDERABLE AMOUNTS OF ZOMBIES. BUT—

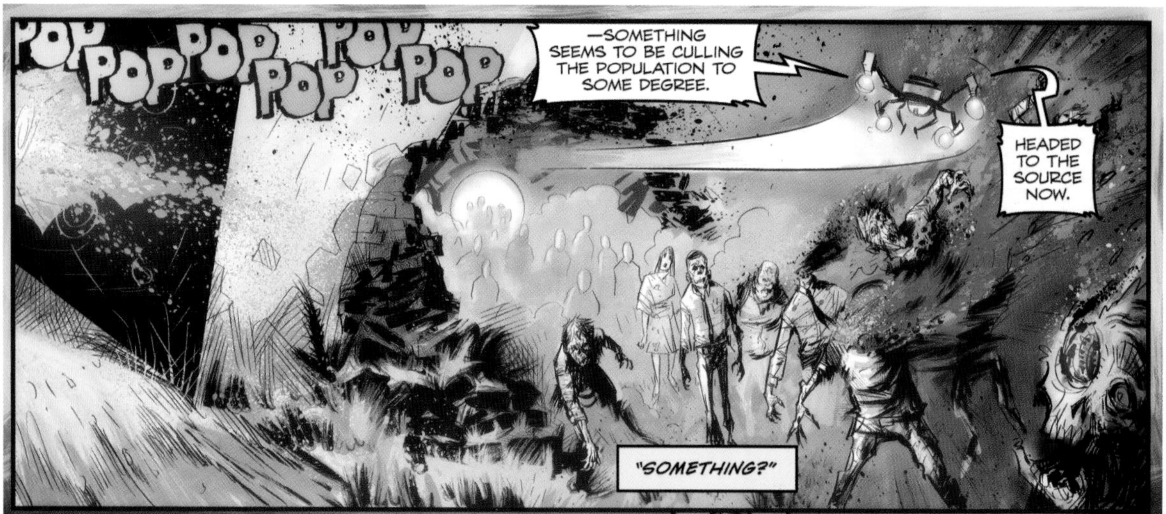
POP POP POP POP POP POP POP POP
—SOMETHING SEEMS TO BE CULLING THE POPULATION TO SOME DEGREE.
HEADED TO THE SOURCE NOW.
"SOMETHING?"

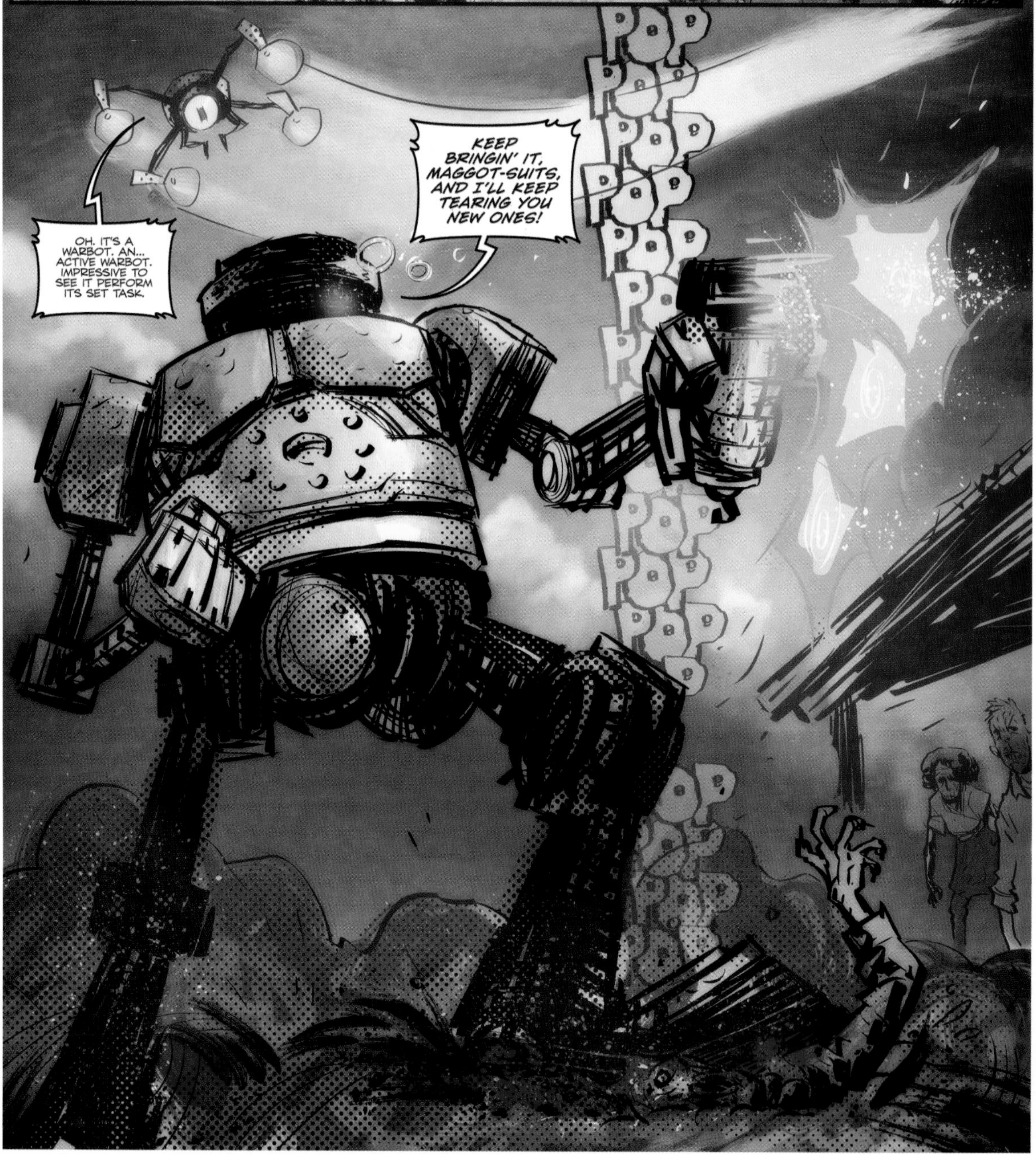
OH. IT'S A WARBOT. AN... ACTIVE WARBOT. IMPRESSIVE TO SEE IT PERFORM ITS SET TASK.
KEEP BRINGIN' IT, MAGGOT-SUITS, AND I'LL KEEP TEARING YOU NEW ONES!
POP POP POP POP POP POP POP POP
POP POP POP POP POP
POP

"AN ACTUAL WARBOT IS *UP* AND *OPERATING? IMPOSSIBLE.*"

AND, YET SO. INFRA-SENSOR IDS IT AS *WARBOT 7G.*

WARRIOR-CLASS BOT, WITH ENDLESS AMMO-GENERATING CAPABILITIES. THE FIRST OF ITS KIND, ACTUALLY—THROCKMORTON'S PRIME ACHIEVEMENT.

IT HAS ADAPTIVE A.I. PROGRAMMING, PROVIDING HUMAN-LIKE REACTION TIME BUT FAULTLESS PROGRAMMING. IN SHORT, WARBOT 7G IS EFFECTIVE AS A WAR MACHINE DUE TO ITS PROGRAMMING TO NEVER ALLOW HARM TO COME TO HUMAN— OR ROBOT-KIND.

HMM?

DID YOU SAY "THROCKMORTON"?

"DRONEBOT ORIS-1, REPORT?"

WARBOT 7G HAS, *ER,* CEASED FIRE.

"IT'S NOT PROGRAMMED TO DO THAT IF THE THREAT REMAINS. WHY DID IT CEASE—IS IT DAMAGED?"

N-NO. WARBOT 7G SEEMS TO HAVE TAKEN NOTICE OF THIS DRONEBOT UNIT.

MOST FORTUNATE THAT WARBOTS CAN NEVER BRING HARM TO ANOTHER RO—

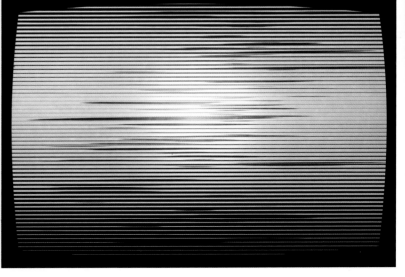

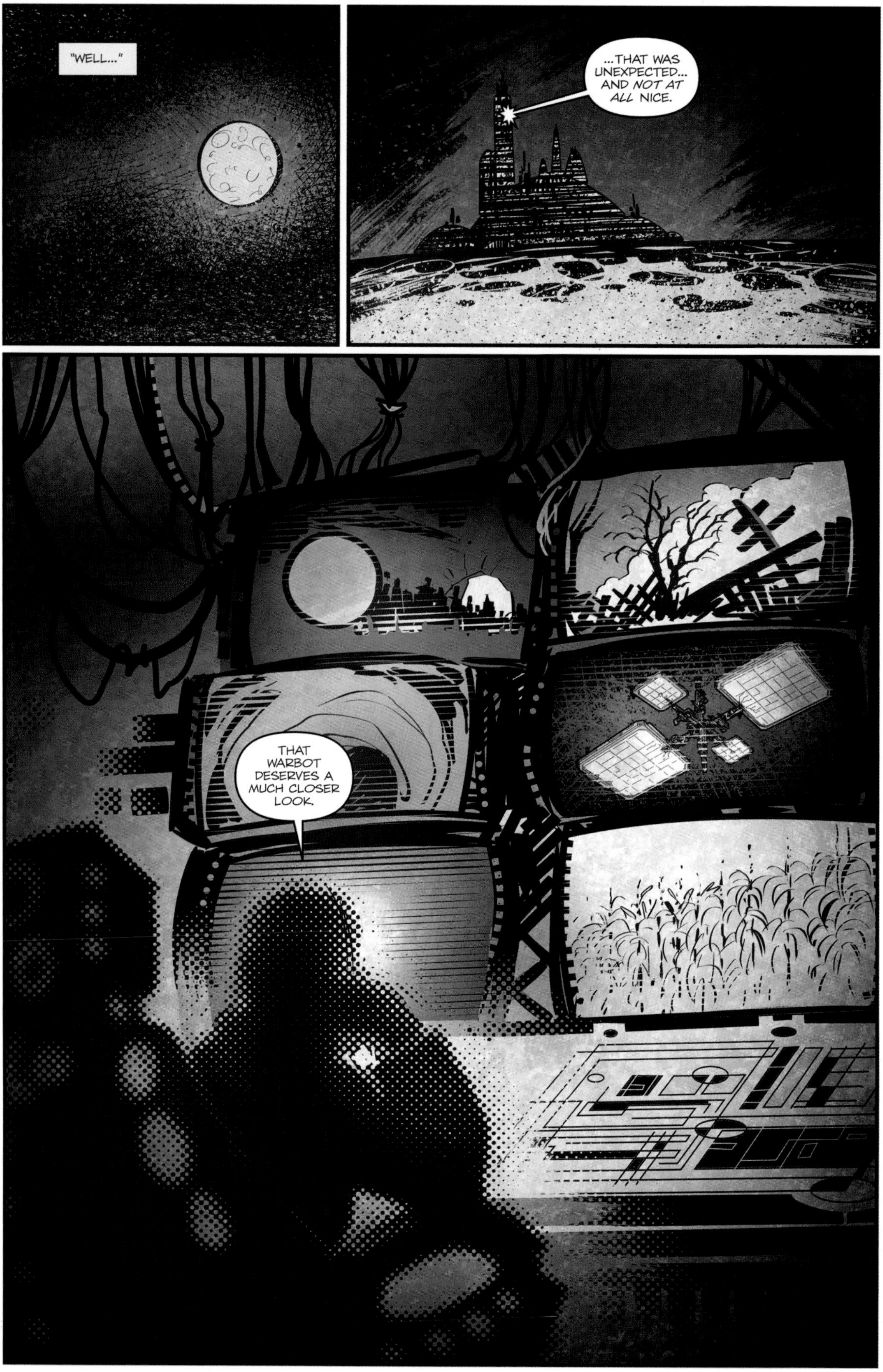
"WELL..."
...THAT WAS UNEXPECTED... AND NOT AT ALL NICE.
THAT WARBOT DESERVES A MUCH CLOSER LOOK.

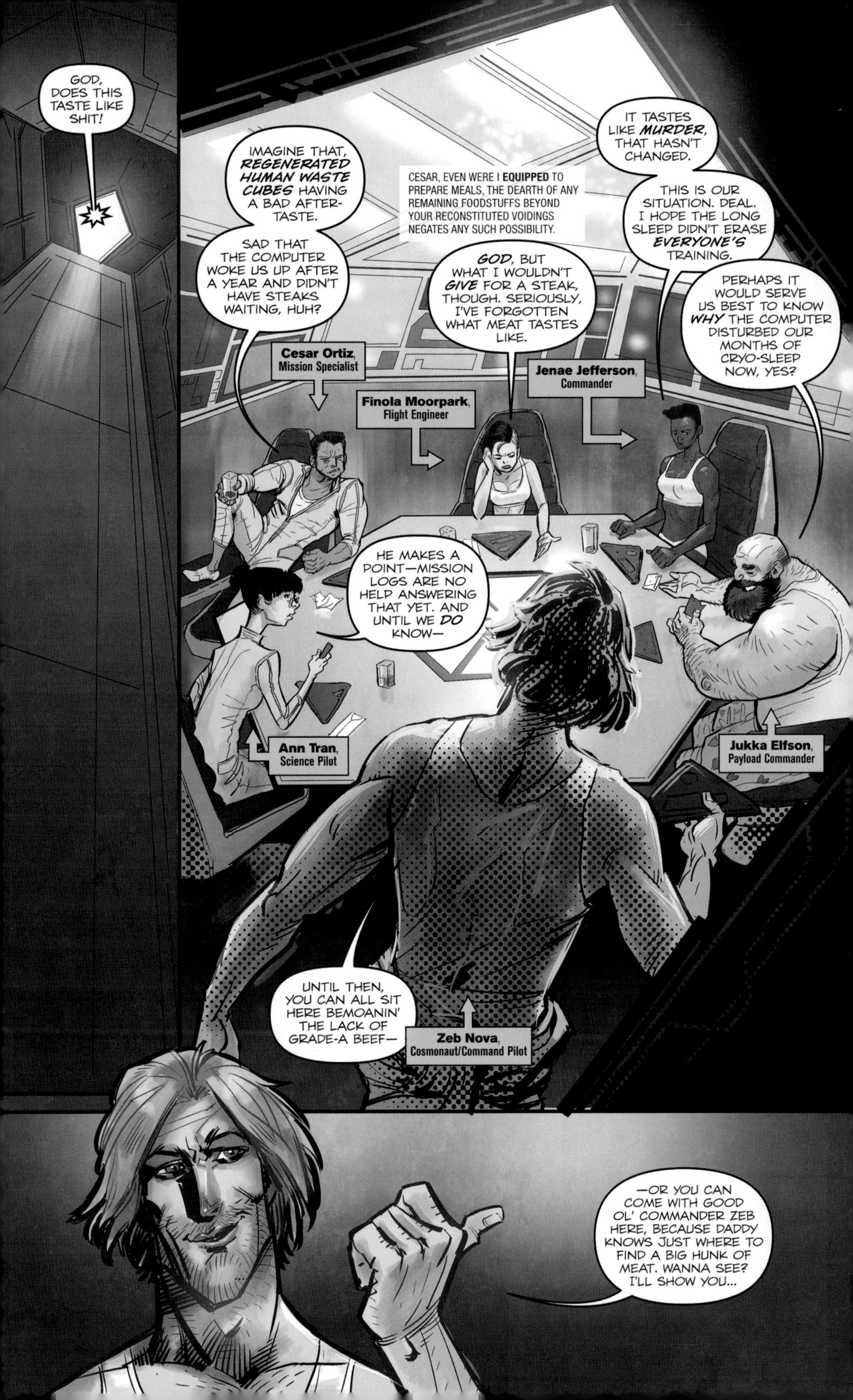
GOD, DOES THIS TASTE LIKE SHIT!
IMAGINE THAT, REGENERATED HUMAN WASTE CUBES HAVING A BAD AFTER-TASTE.
SAD THAT THE COMPUTER WOKE US UP AFTER A YEAR AND DIDN'T HAVE STEAKS WAITING, HUH?
CESAR, EVEN WERE I EQUIPPED TO PREPARE MEALS, THE DEARTH OF ANY REMAINING FOODSTUFFS BEYOND YOUR RECONSTITUTED VOIDINGS NEGATES ANY SUCH POSSIBILITY.
GOD, BUT WHAT I WOULDN'T GIVE FOR A STEAK, THOUGH. SERIOUSLY, I'VE FORGOTTEN WHAT MEAT TASTES LIKE.
IT TASTES LIKE MURDER, THAT HASN'T CHANGED.
THIS IS OUR SITUATION. DEAL. I HOPE THE LONG SLEEP DIDN'T ERASE EVERYONE'S TRAINING.
PERHAPS IT WOULD SERVE US BEST TO KNOW WHY THE COMPUTER DISTURBED OUR MONTHS OF CRYO-SLEEP NOW, YES?
Cesar Ortiz, Mission Specialist
Finola Moorpark, Flight Engineer
Jenae Jefferson, Commander
HE MAKES A POINT—MISSION LOGS ARE NO HELP ANSWERING THAT YET. AND UNTIL WE DO KNOW—
Ann Tran, Science Pilot
Jukka Elfson, Payload Commander
UNTIL THEN, YOU CAN ALL SIT HERE BEMOANIN' THE LACK OF GRADE-A BEEF—
Zeb Nova, Cosmonaut/Command Pilot
—OR YOU CAN COME WITH GOOD OL' COMMANDER ZEB HERE, BECAUSE DADDY KNOWS JUST WHERE TO FIND A BIG HUNK OF MEAT. WANNA SEE? I'LL SHOW YOU...

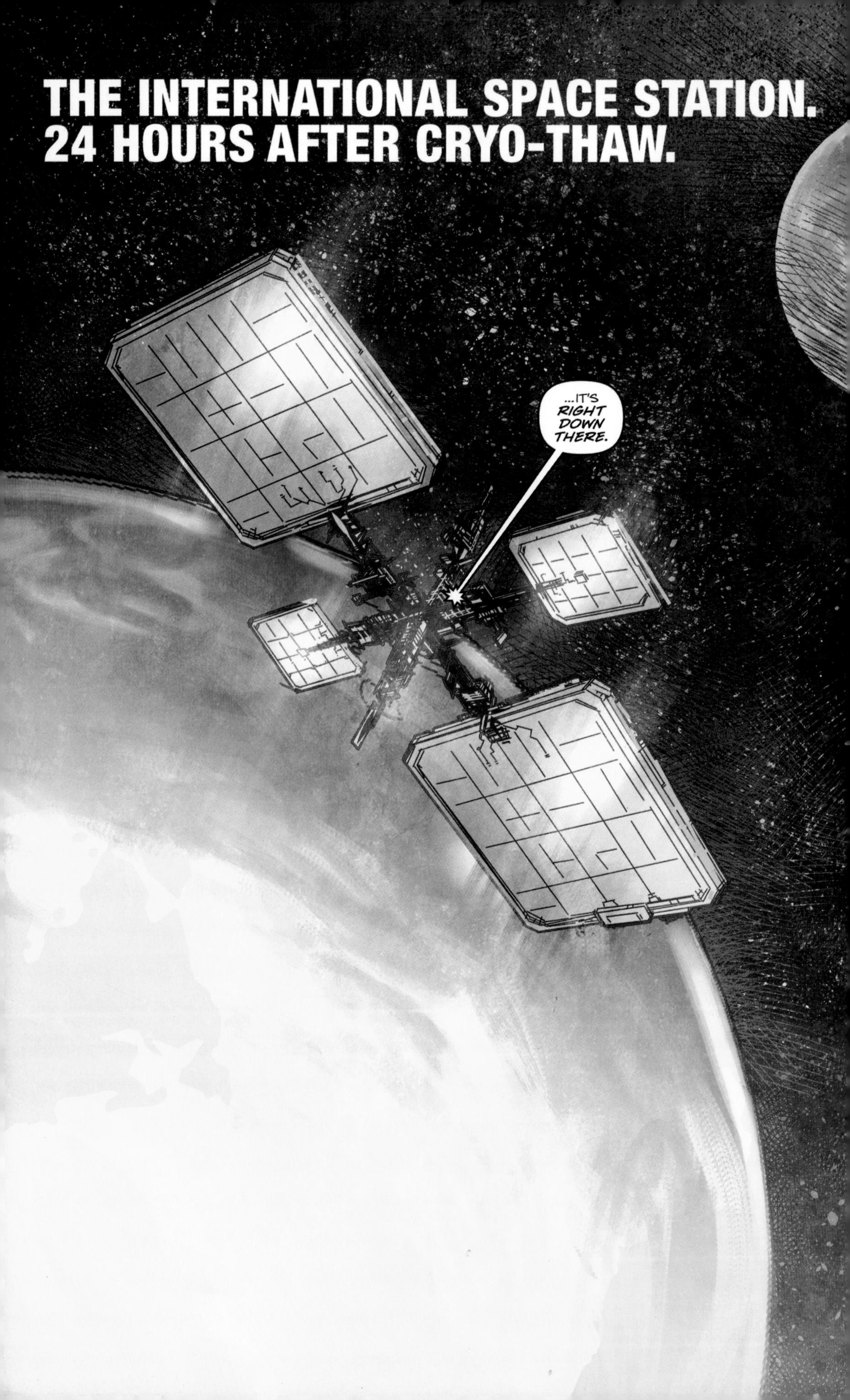
THE INTERNATIONAL SPACE STATION.
24 HOURS AFTER CRYO-THAW.
...IT'S RIGHT DOWN THERE.

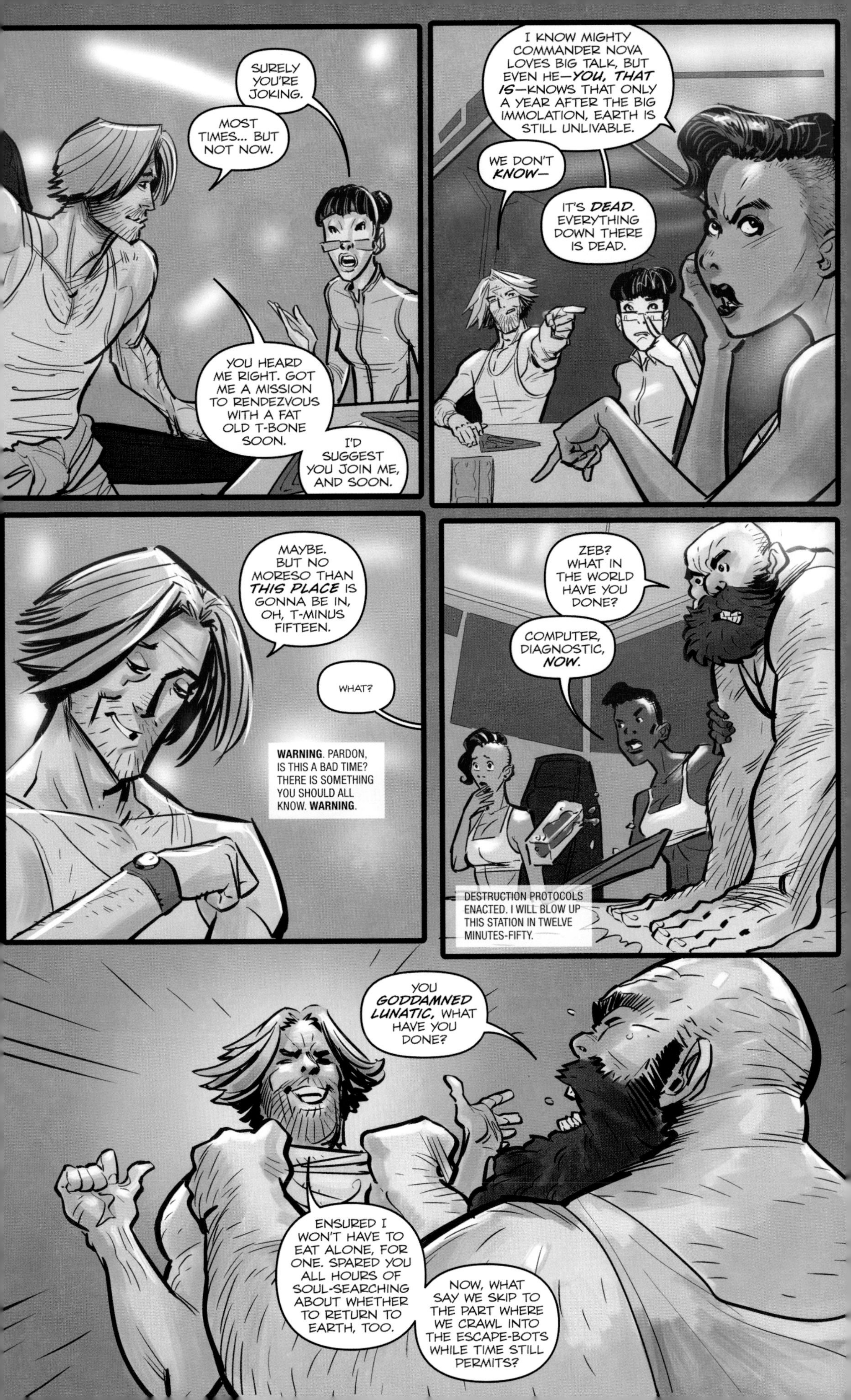

SURELY YOU'RE JOKING.
MOST TIMES... BUT NOT NOW.
YOU HEARD ME RIGHT. GOT ME A MISSION TO RENDEZVOUS WITH A FAT OLD T-BONE SOON.
I'D SUGGEST YOU JOIN ME, AND SOON.
I KNOW MIGHTY COMMANDER NOVA LOVES BIG TALK, BUT EVEN HE—YOU, THAT IS—KNOWS THAT ONLY A YEAR AFTER THE BIG IMMOLATION, EARTH IS STILL UNLIVABLE.
WE DON'T KNOW—
IT'S DEAD. EVERYTHING DOWN THERE IS DEAD.
MAYBE. BUT NO MORESO THAN THIS PLACE IS GONNA BE IN, OH, T-MINUS FIFTEEN.
WHAT?
WARNING. PARDON, IS THIS A BAD TIME? THERE IS SOMETHING YOU SHOULD ALL KNOW. WARNING.
ZEB? WHAT IN THE WORLD HAVE YOU DONE?
COMPUTER, DIAGNOSTIC, NOW.
DESTRUCTION PROTOCOLS ENACTED. I WILL BLOW UP THIS STATION IN TWELVE MINUTES-FIFTY.
YOU GODDAMNED LUNATIC, WHAT HAVE YOU DONE?
ENSURED I WON'T HAVE TO EAT ALONE, FOR ONE. SPARED YOU ALL HOURS OF SOUL-SEARCHING ABOUT WHETHER TO RETURN TO EARTH, TOO.
NOW, WHAT SAY WE SKIP TO THE PART WHERE WE CRAWL INTO THE ESCAPE-BOTS WHILE TIME STILL PERMITS?

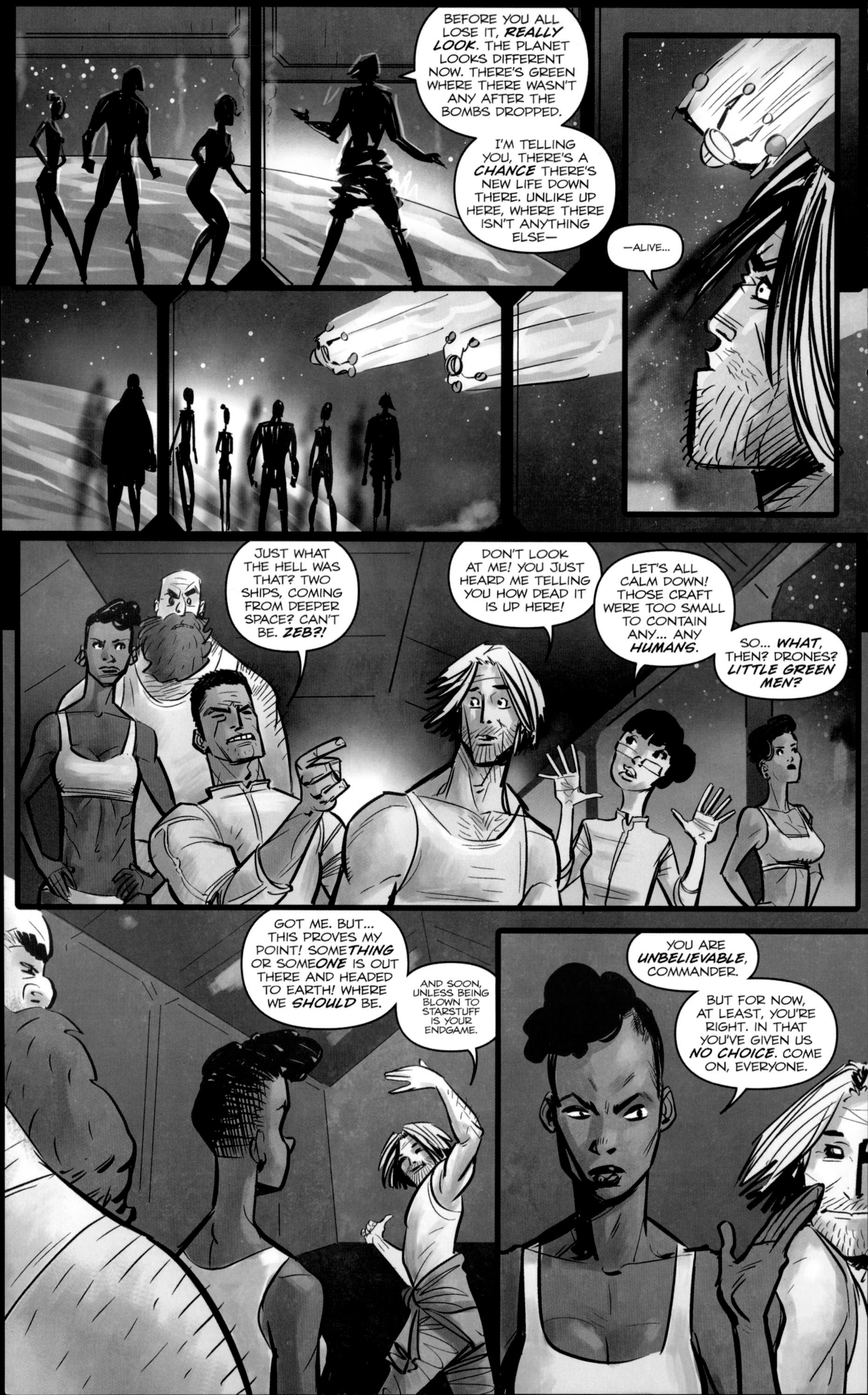
BEFORE YOU ALL LOSE IT, REALLY LOOK. THE PLANET LOOKS DIFFERENT NOW. THERE'S GREEN WHERE THERE WASN'T ANY AFTER THE BOMBS DROPPED.
I'M TELLING YOU, THERE'S A CHANCE THERE'S NEW LIFE DOWN THERE. UNLIKE UP HERE, WHERE THERE ISN'T ANYTHING ELSE—
—ALIVE...
JUST WHAT THE HELL WAS THAT? TWO SHIPS, COMING FROM DEEPER SPACE? CAN'T BE. ZEB?!
DON'T LOOK AT ME! YOU JUST HEARD ME TELLING YOU HOW DEAD IT IS UP HERE!
LET'S ALL CALM DOWN! THOSE CRAFT WERE TOO SMALL TO CONTAIN ANY... ANY HUMANS.
SO... WHAT, THEN? DRONES? LITTLE GREEN MEN?
GOT ME. BUT... THIS PROVES MY POINT! SOMETHING OR SOMEONE IS OUT THERE AND HEADED TO EARTH! WHERE WE SHOULD BE.
AND SOON, UNLESS BEING BLOWN TO STARSTUFF IS YOUR ENDGAME.
YOU ARE UNBELIEVABLE, COMMANDER.
BUT FOR NOW, AT LEAST, YOU'RE RIGHT. IN THAT YOU'VE GIVEN US NO CHOICE. COME ON, EVERYONE.

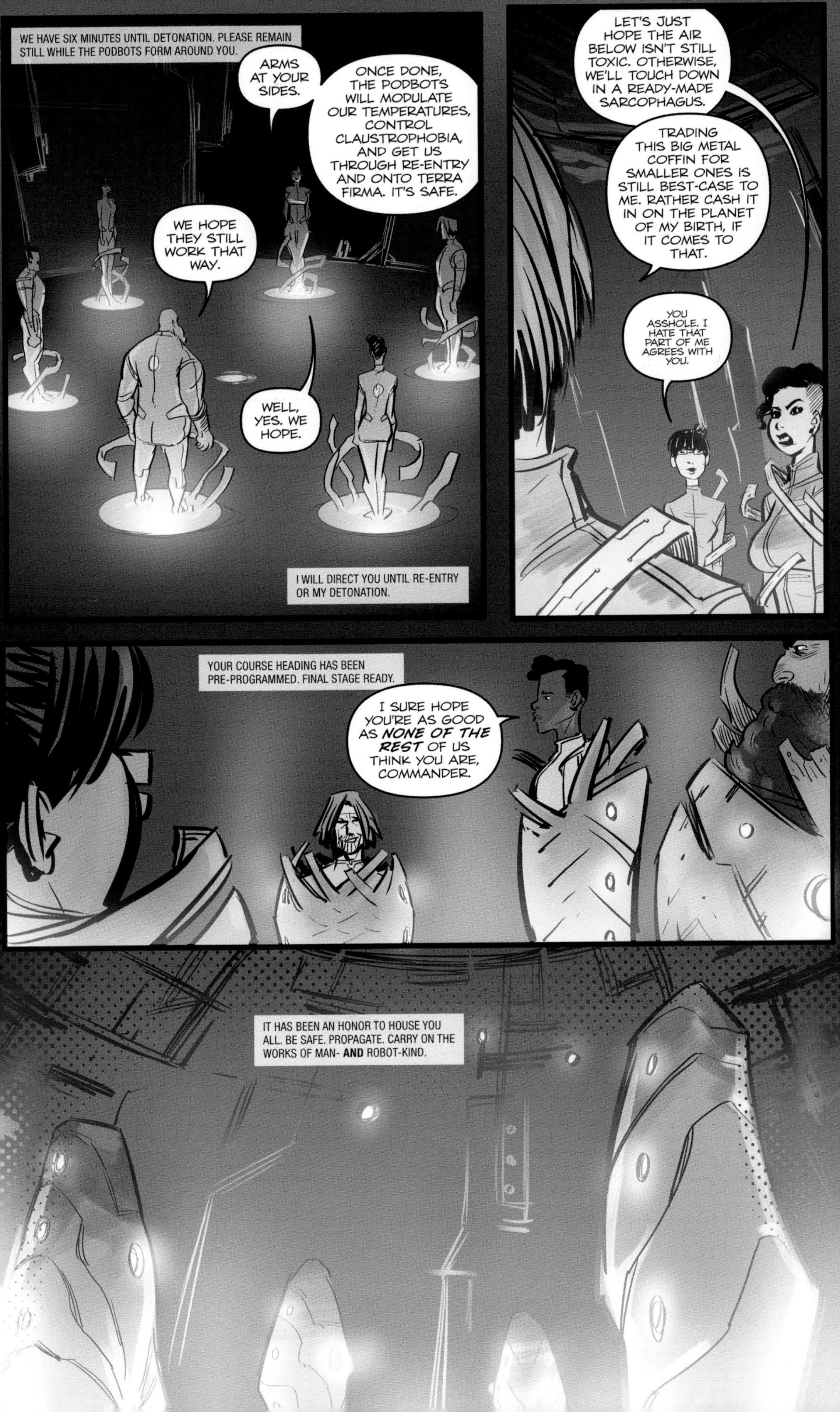
WE HAVE SIX MINUTES UNTIL DETONATION. PLEASE REMAIN STILL WHILE THE PODBOTS FORM AROUND YOU.
ARMS AT YOUR SIDES.
ONCE DONE, THE PODBOTS WILL MODULATE OUR TEMPERATURES, CONTROL CLAUSTROPHOBIA, AND GET US THROUGH RE-ENTRY AND ONTO TERRA FIRMA. IT'S SAFE.
WE HOPE THEY STILL WORK THAT WAY.
WELL, YES. WE HOPE.
I WILL DIRECT YOU UNTIL RE-ENTRY OR MY DETONATION.
LET'S JUST HOPE THE AIR BELOW ISN'T STILL TOXIC. OTHERWISE, WE'LL TOUCH DOWN IN A READY-MADE SARCOPHAGUS.
TRADING THIS BIG METAL COFFIN FOR SMALLER ONES IS STILL BEST-CASE TO ME. RATHER CASH IT IN ON THE PLANET OF MY BIRTH, IF IT COMES TO THAT.
YOU ASSHOLE. I HATE THAT PART OF ME AGREES WITH YOU.
YOUR COURSE HEADING HAS BEEN PRE-PROGRAMMED. FINAL STAGE READY.
I SURE HOPE YOU'RE AS GOOD AS ***NONE OF THE REST*** OF US THINK YOU ARE, COMMANDER.
IT HAS BEEN AN HONOR TO HOUSE YOU ALL. BE SAFE. PROPAGATE. CARRY ON THE WORKS OF MAN- **AND** ROBOT-KIND.

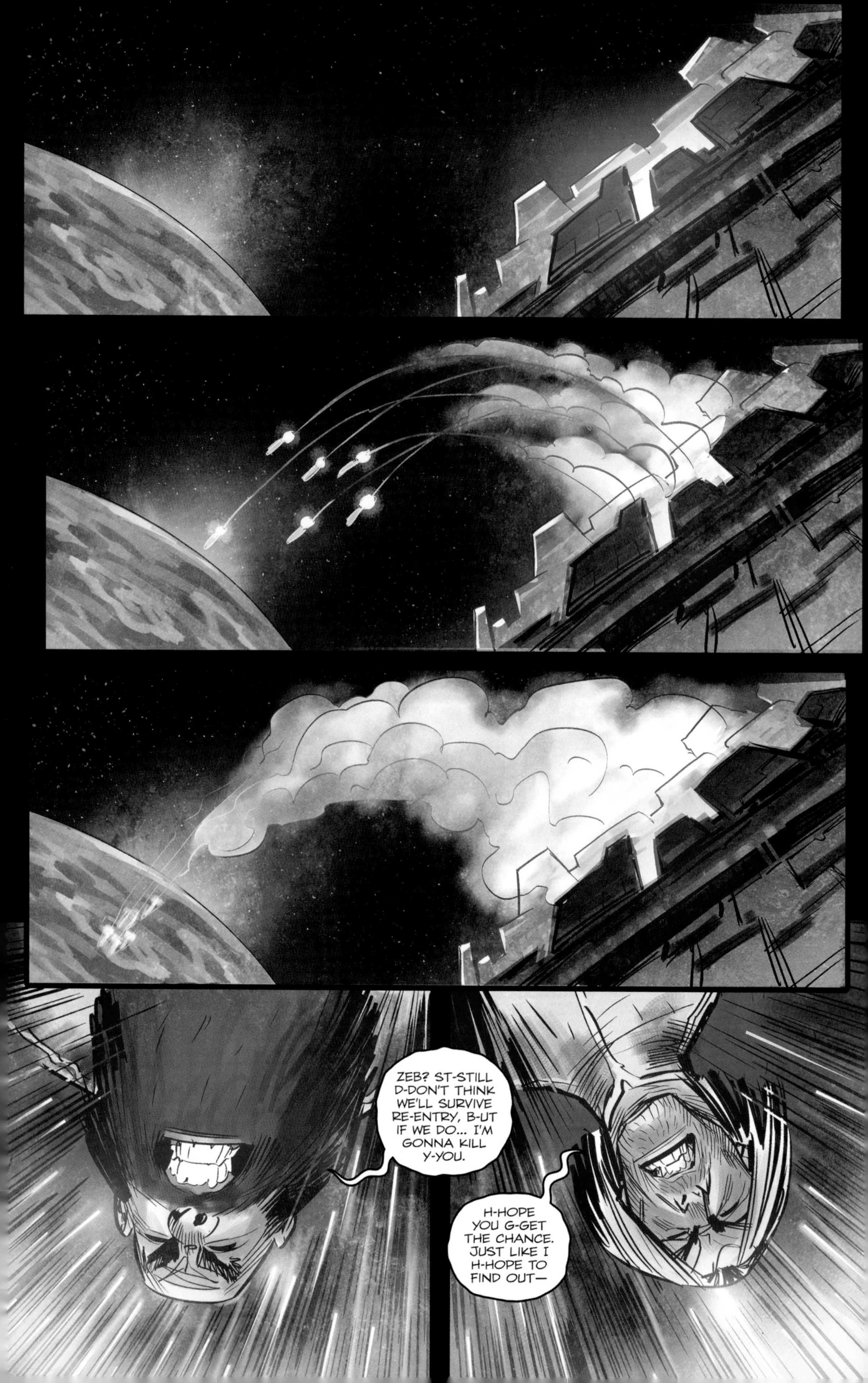
ZEB? ST-STILL D-DON'T THINK WE'LL SURVIVE RE-ENTRY, B-UT IF WE DO... I'M GONNA KILL Y-YOU.
H-HOPE YOU G-GET THE CHANCE. JUST LIKE I H-HOPE TO FIND OUT—

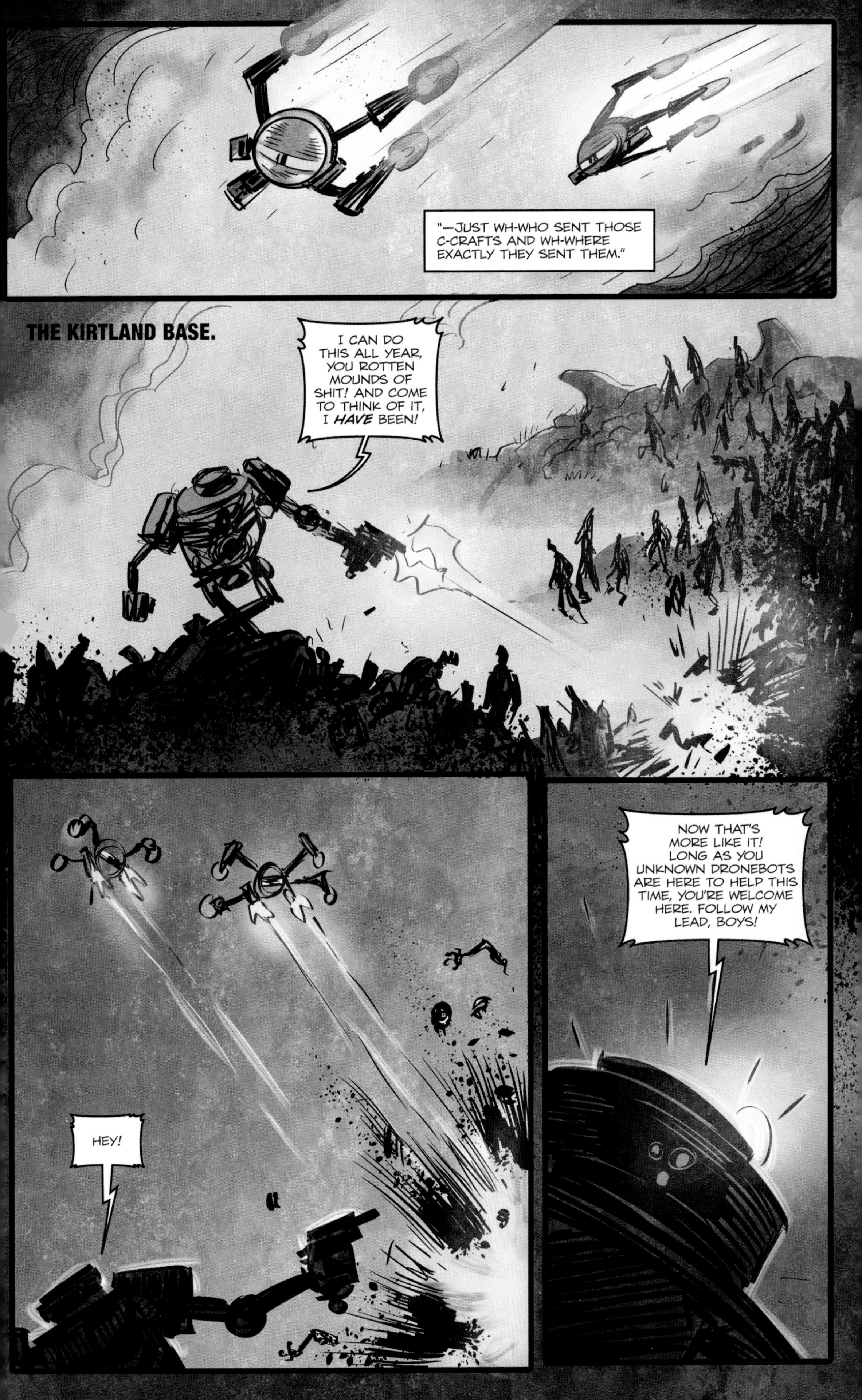
"—JUST WH-WHO SENT THOSE C-CRAFTS AND WH-WHERE EXACTLY THEY SENT THEM."
THE KIRTLAND BASE.
I CAN DO THIS ALL YEAR, YOU ROTTEN MOUNDS OF SHIT! AND COME TO THINK OF IT, I *HAVE* BEEN!
HEY!
NOW THAT'S MORE LIKE IT! LONG AS YOU UNKNOWN DRONEBOTS ARE HERE TO HELP THIS TIME, YOU'RE WELCOME HERE. FOLLOW MY LEAD, BOYS!

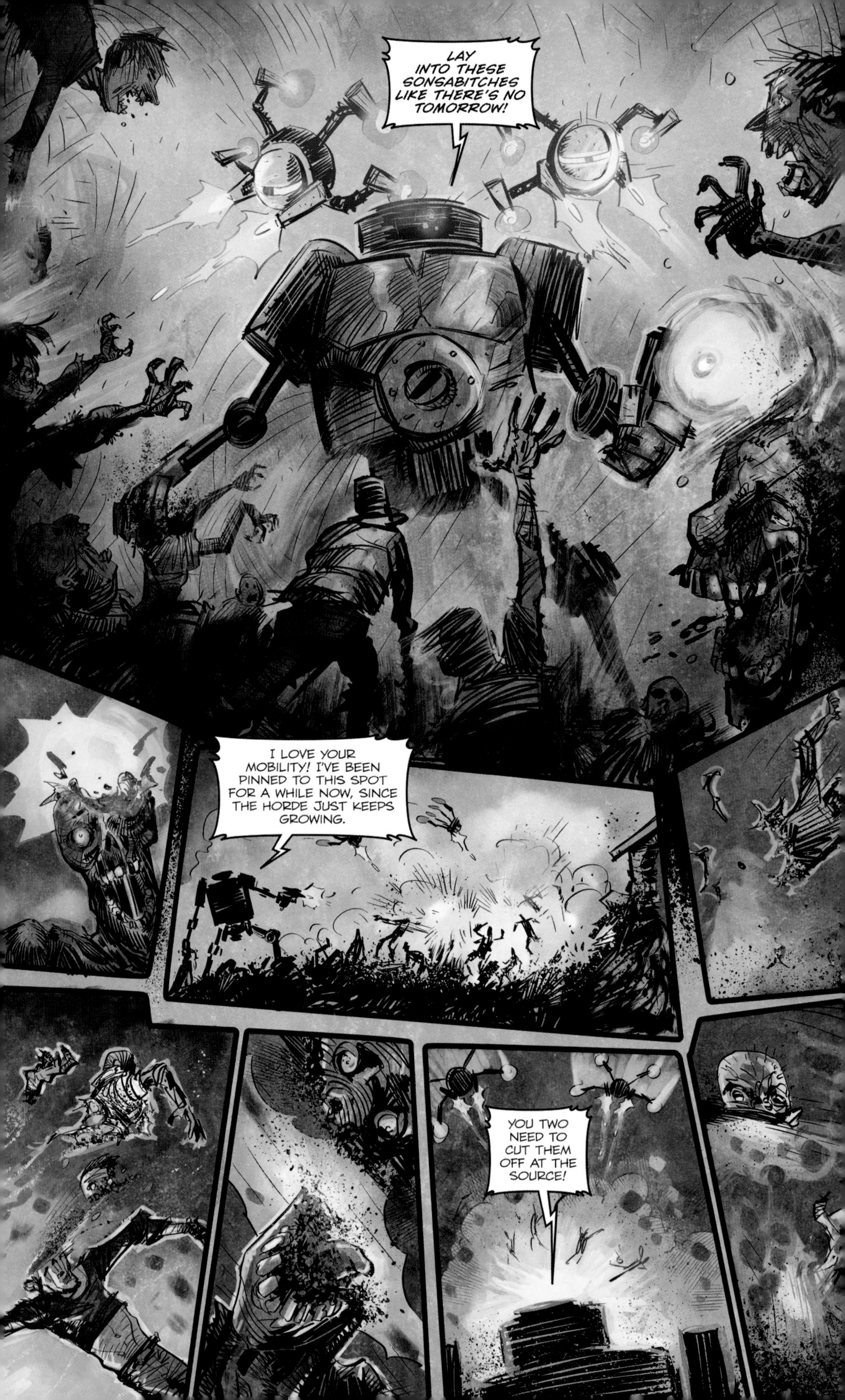
LAY INTO THESE SONSABITCHES LIKE THERE'S NO TOMORROW!
I LOVE YOUR MOBILITY! I'VE BEEN PINNED TO THIS SPOT FOR A WHILE NOW, SINCE THE HORDE JUST KEEPS GROWING.
YOU TWO NEED TO CUT THEM OFF AT THE SOURCE!

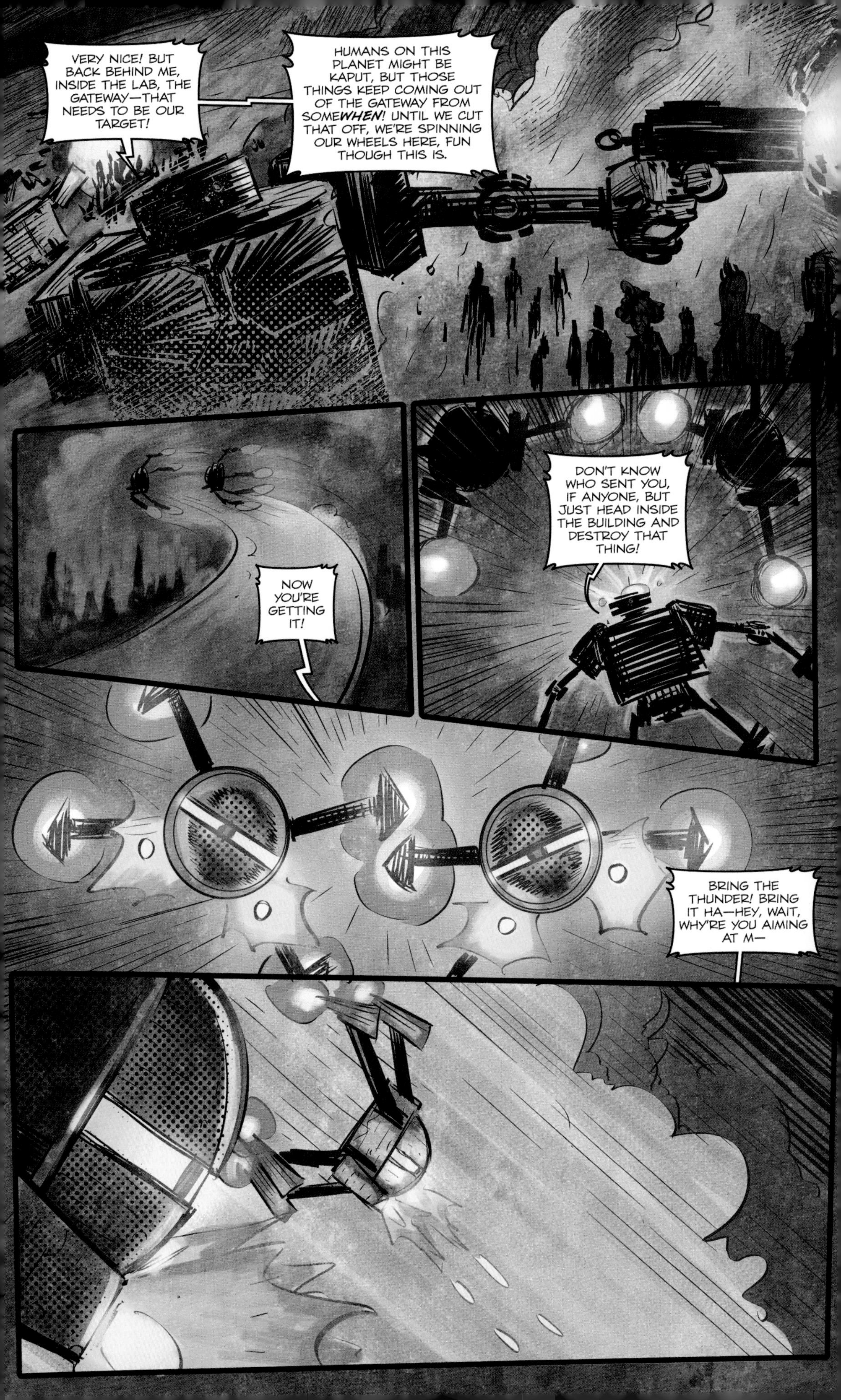
VERY NICE! BUT BACK BEHIND ME, INSIDE THE LAB, THE GATEWAY—THAT NEEDS TO BE OUR TARGET!
HUMANS ON THIS PLANET MIGHT BE KAPUT, BUT THOSE THINGS KEEP COMING OUT OF THE GATEWAY FROM SOMEWHEN! UNTIL WE CUT THAT OFF, WE'RE SPINNING OUR WHEELS HERE, FUN THOUGH THIS IS.
NOW YOU'RE GETTING IT!
DON'T KNOW WHO SENT YOU, IF ANYONE, BUT JUST HEAD INSIDE THE BUILDING AND DESTROY THAT THING!
BRING THE THUNDER! BRING IT HA—HEY, WAIT, WHY'RE YOU AIMING AT M—

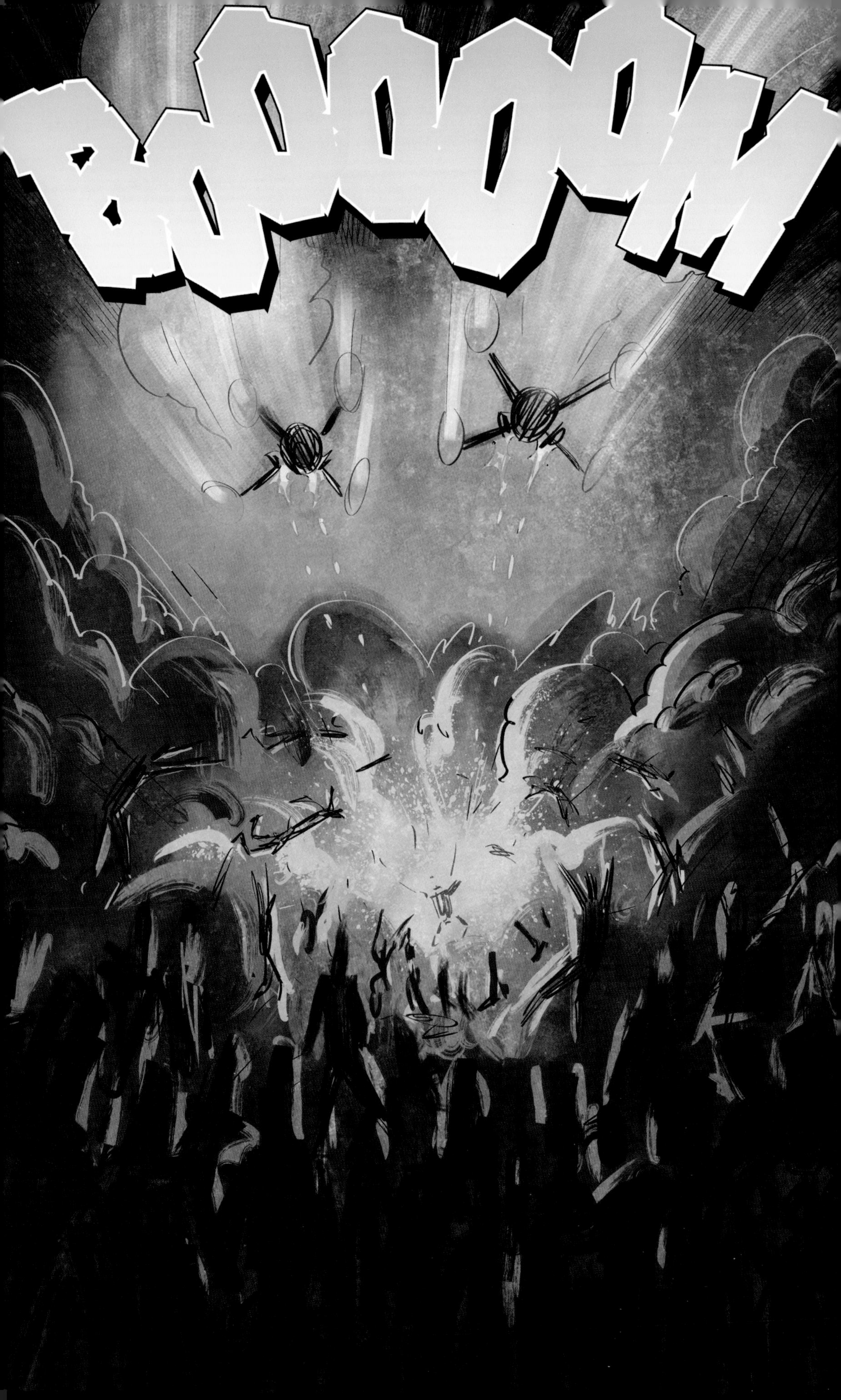
BOOOOM

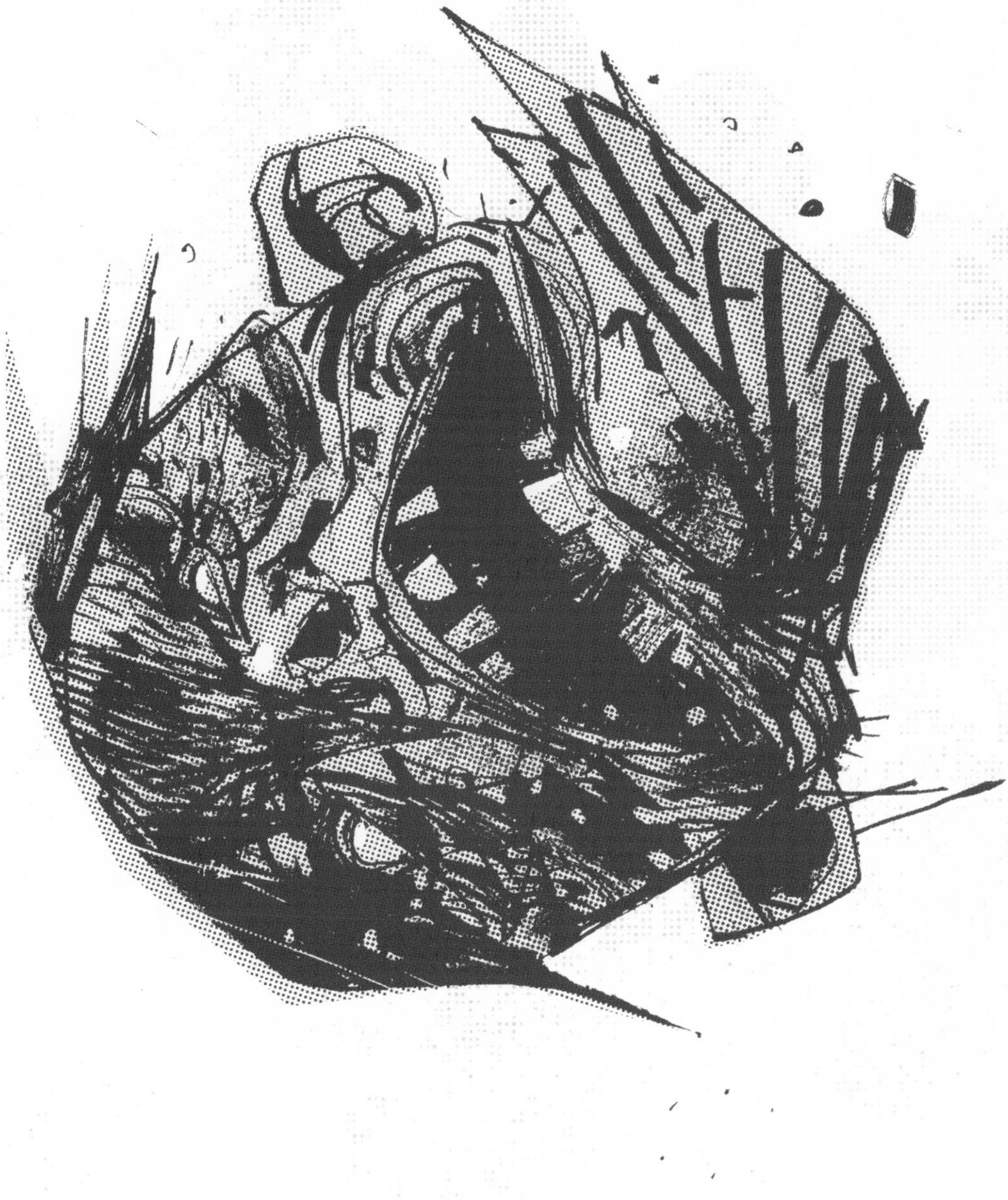

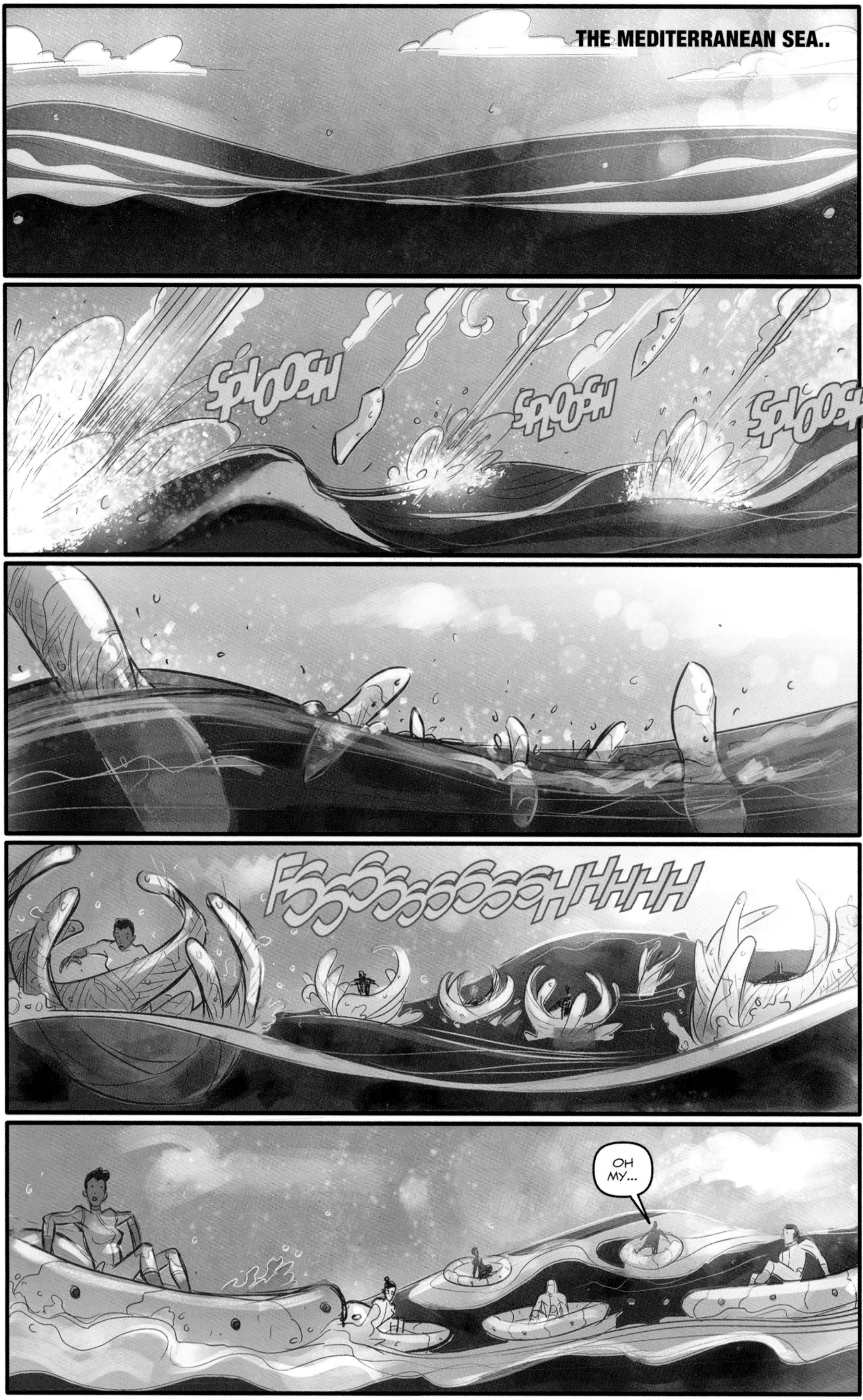
THE MEDITERRANEAN SEA..
SPLOOSH
SPLOOSH
SPLOOSH
FSSSSSSSSSHHHHH
OH MY...

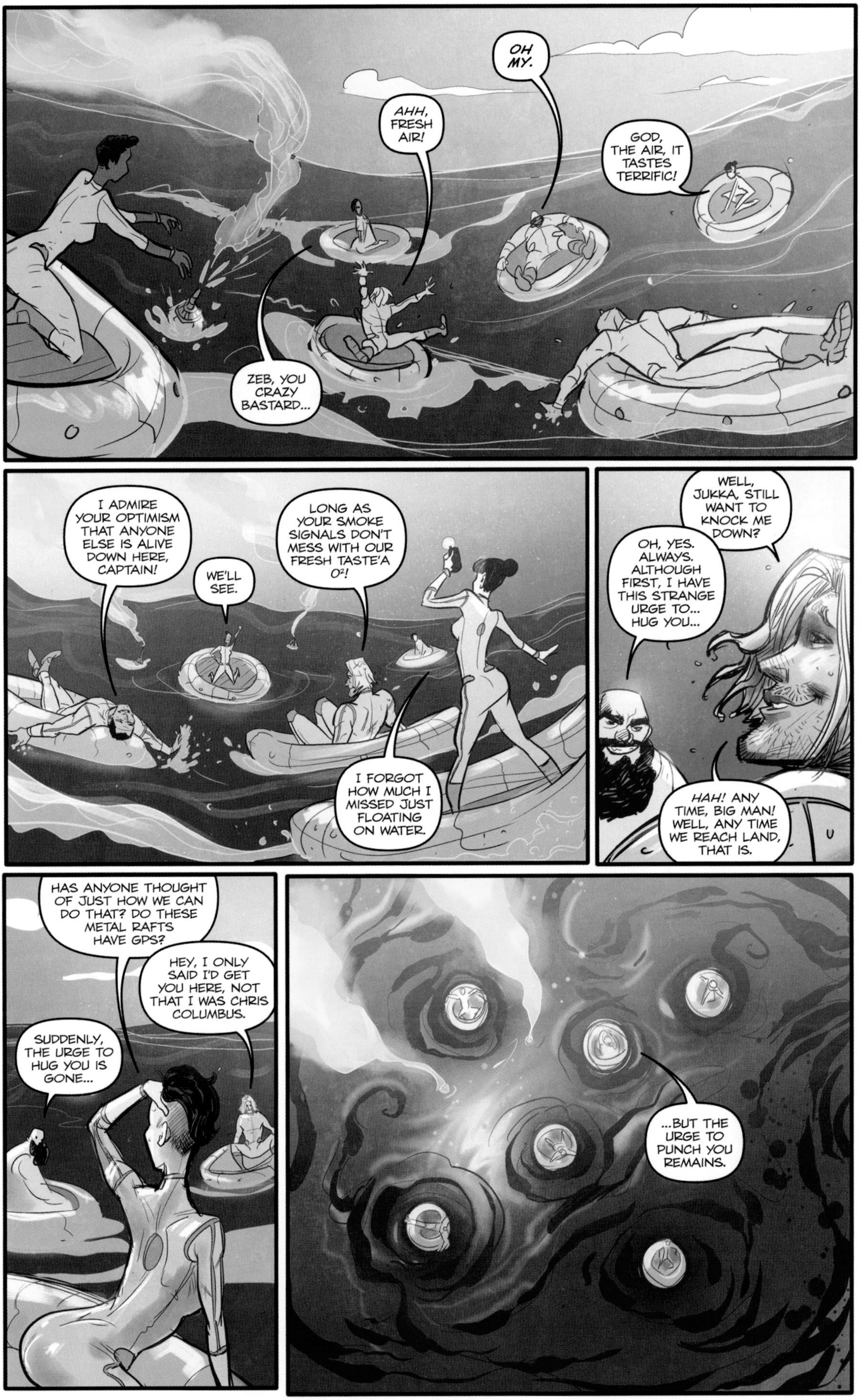
AHH, FRESH AIR!
OH MY.
GOD, THE AIR, IT TASTES TERRIFIC!
ZEB, YOU CRAZY BASTARD...
I ADMIRE YOUR OPTIMISM THAT ANYONE ELSE IS ALIVE DOWN HERE, CAPTAIN!
WE'LL SEE.
LONG AS YOUR SMOKE SIGNALS DON'T MESS WITH OUR FRESH TASTE'A O^2!
I FORGOT HOW MUCH I MISSED JUST FLOATING ON WATER.
WELL, JUKKA, STILL WANT TO KNOCK ME DOWN?
OH, YES. ALWAYS. ALTHOUGH FIRST, I HAVE THIS STRANGE URGE TO... HUG YOU...
HAH! ANY TIME, BIG MAN! WELL, ANY TIME WE REACH LAND, THAT IS.
HAS ANYONE THOUGHT OF JUST HOW WE CAN DO THAT? DO THESE METAL RAFTS HAVE GPS?
HEY, I ONLY SAID I'D GET YOU HERE, NOT THAT I WAS CHRIS COLUMBUS.
SUDDENLY, THE URGE TO HUG YOU IS GONE...
...BUT THE URGE TO PUNCH YOU REMAINS.

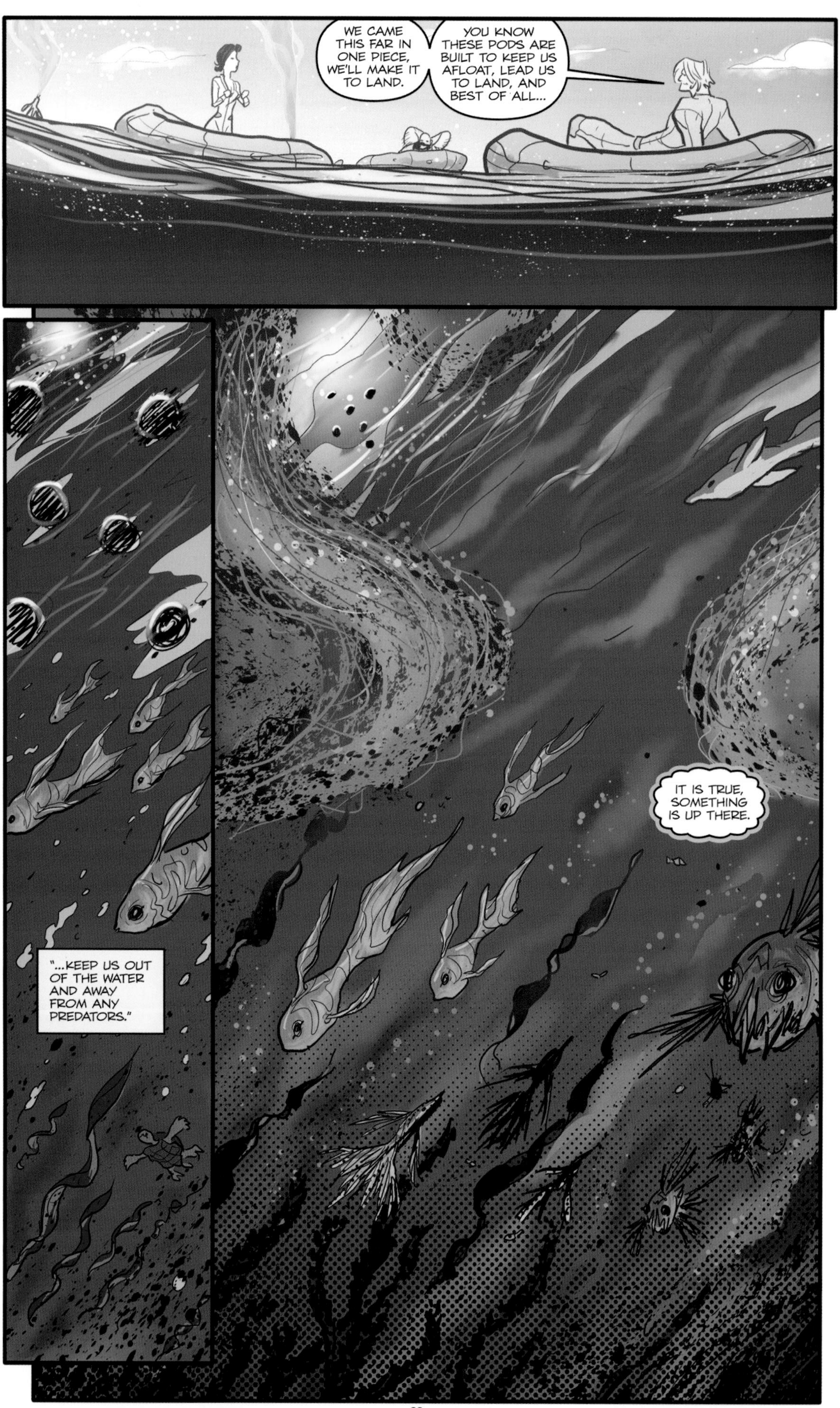
WE CAME THIS FAR IN ONE PIECE, WE'LL MAKE IT TO LAND.
YOU KNOW THESE PODS ARE BUILT TO KEEP US AFLOAT, LEAD US TO LAND, AND BEST OF ALL...
"...KEEP US OUT OF THE WATER AND AWAY FROM ANY PREDATORS."
IT IS TRUE, SOMETHING IS UP THERE.

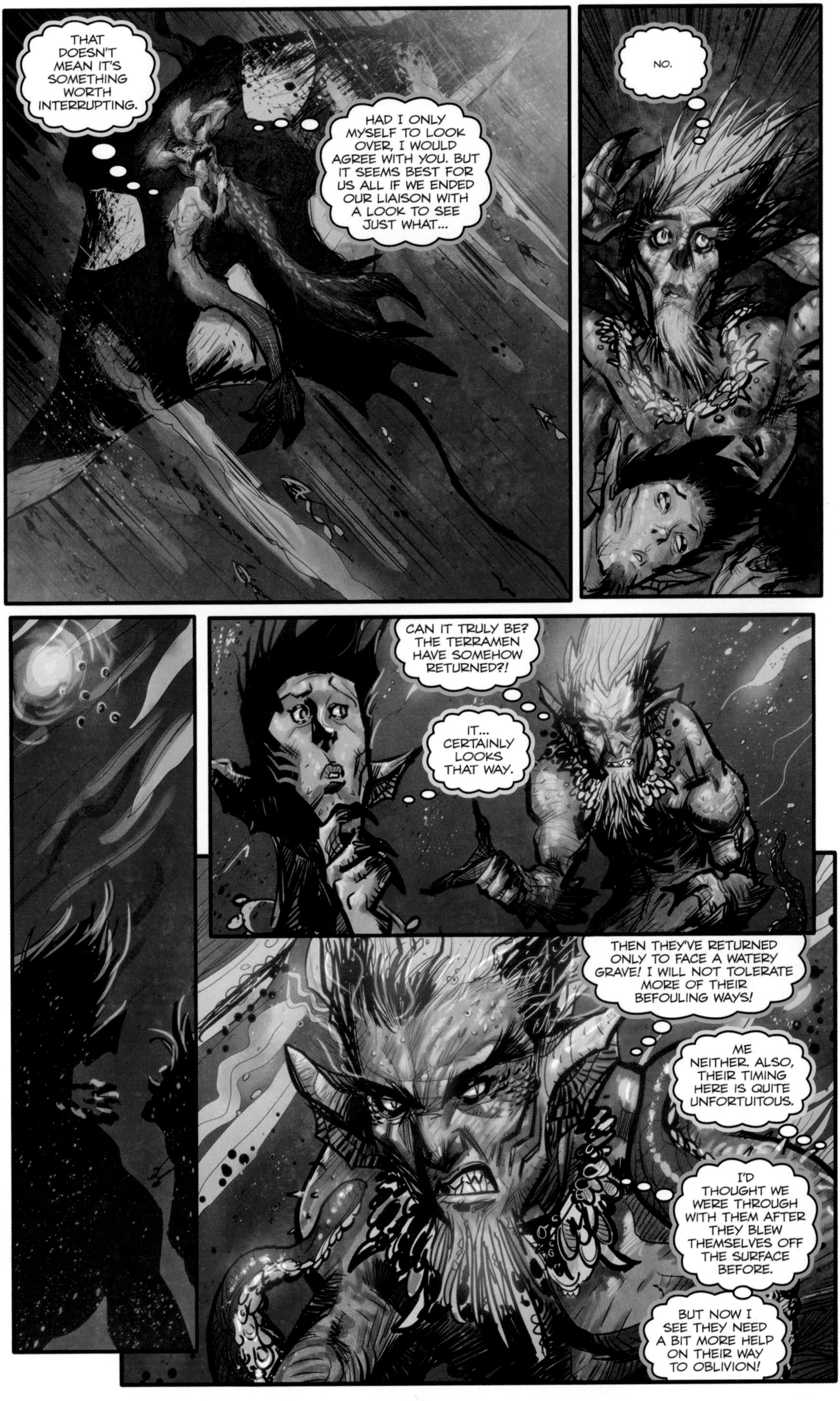
THAT DOESN'T MEAN IT'S SOMETHING WORTH INTERRUPTING.
HAD I ONLY MYSELF TO LOOK OVER, I WOULD AGREE WITH YOU. BUT IT SEEMS BEST FOR US ALL IF WE ENDED OUR LIAISON WITH A LOOK TO SEE JUST WHAT...
NO.
CAN IT TRULY BE? THE TERRAMEN HAVE SOMEHOW RETURNED?!
IT... CERTAINLY LOOKS THAT WAY.
THEN THEY'VE RETURNED ONLY TO FACE A WATERY GRAVE! I WILL NOT TOLERATE MORE OF THEIR BEFOULING WAYS!
ME NEITHER. ALSO, THEIR TIMING HERE IS QUITE UNFORTUITOUS.
I'D THOUGHT WE WERE THROUGH WITH THEM AFTER THEY BLEW THEMSELVES OFF THE SURFACE BEFORE.
BUT NOW I SEE THEY NEED A BIT MORE HELP ON THEIR WAY TO OBLIVION!

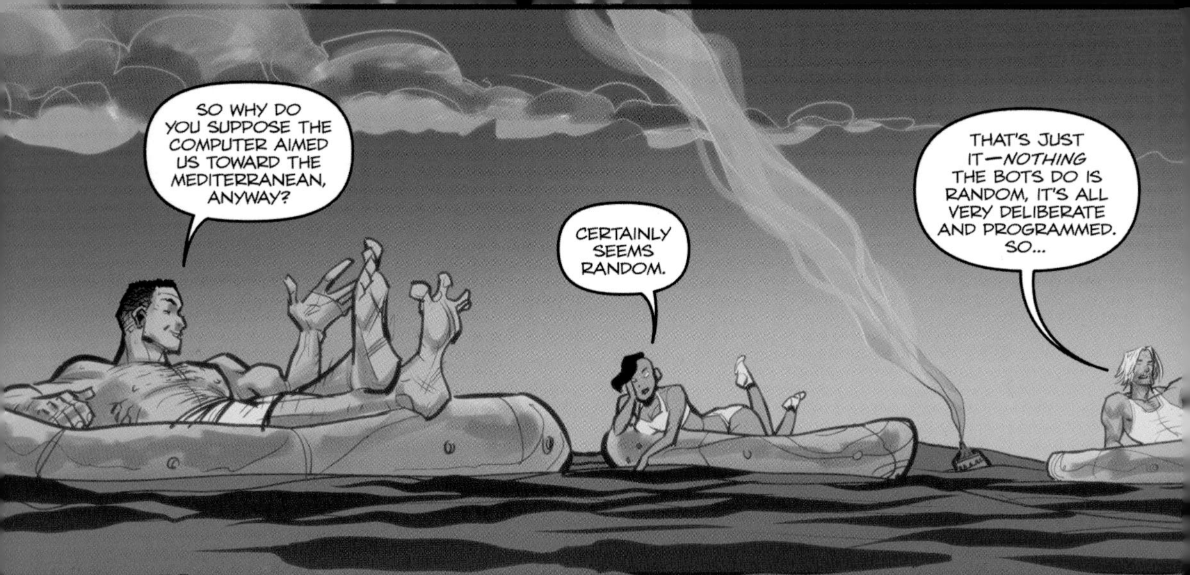
SO WHY DO YOU SUPPOSE THE COMPUTER AIMED US TOWARD THE MEDITERRANEAN, ANYWAY?
CERTAINLY SEEMS RANDOM.
THAT'S JUST IT—*NOTHING* THE BOTS DO IS RANDOM, IT'S ALL VERY DELIBERATE AND PROGRAMMED. SO...

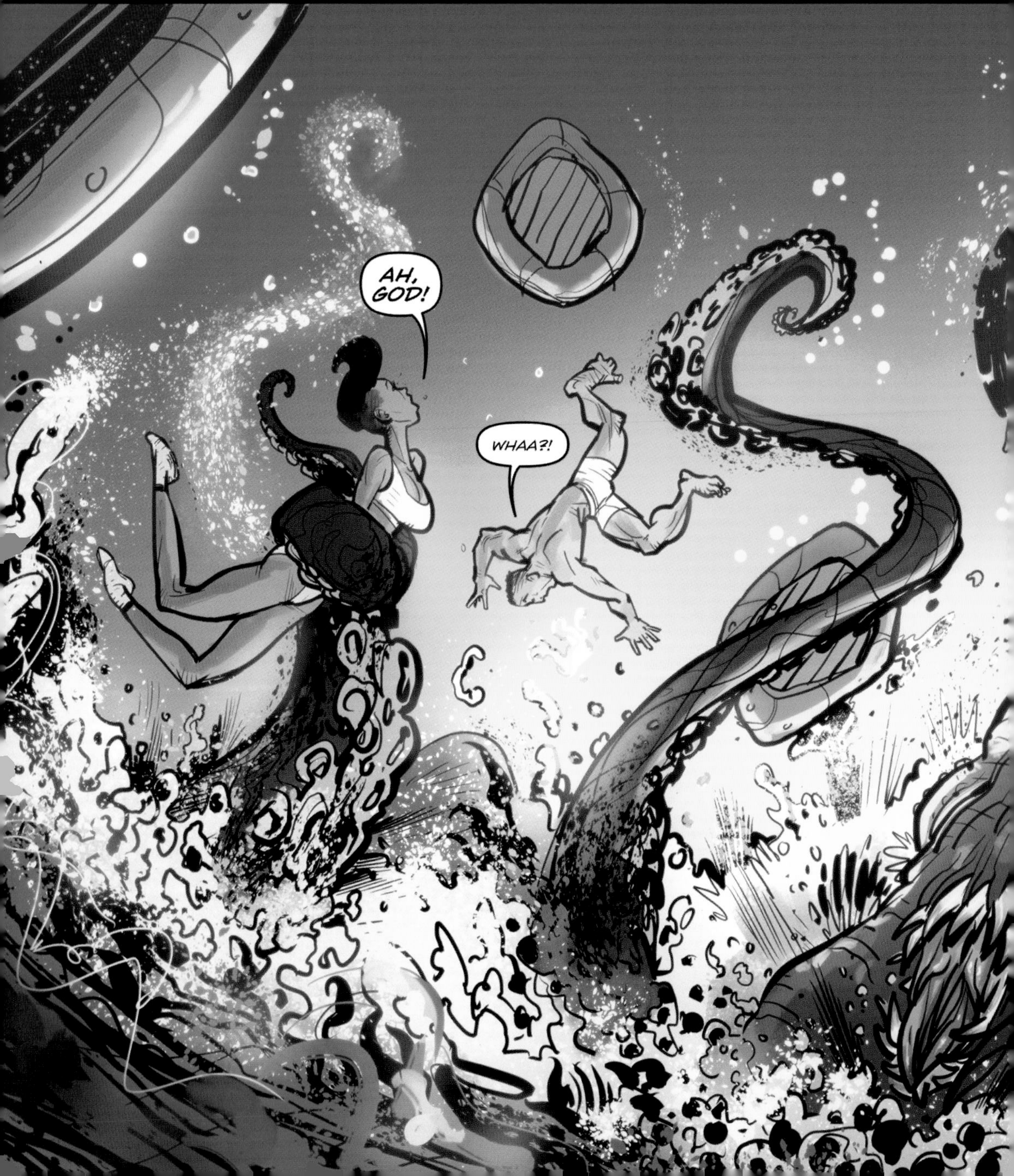
AH, GOD!
WHAA?!

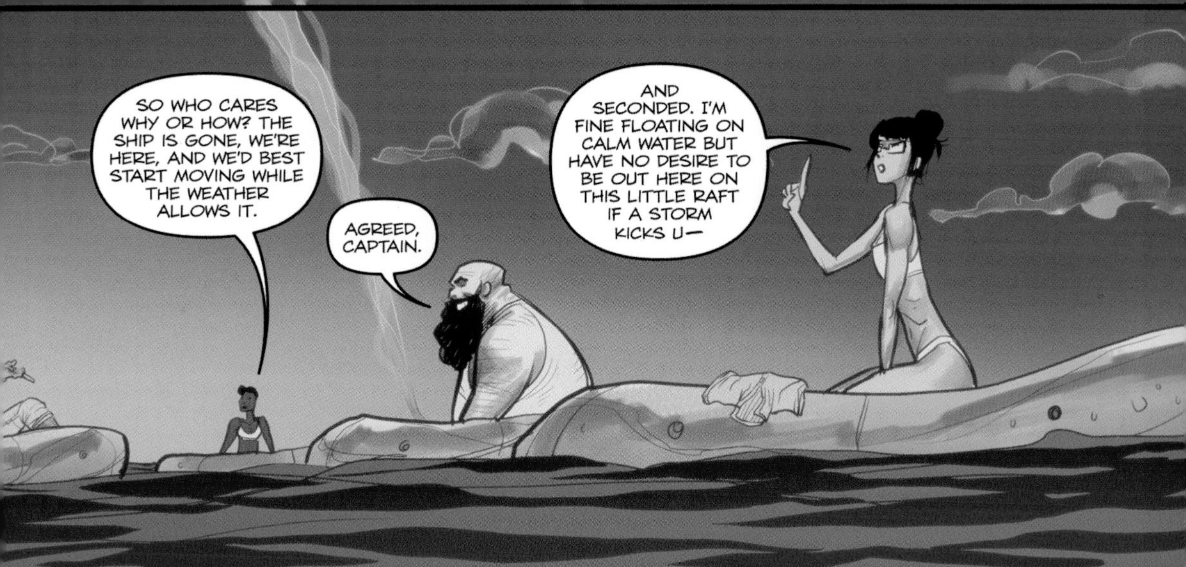
SO WHO CARES WHY OR HOW? THE SHIP IS GONE, WE'RE HERE, AND WE'D BEST START MOVING WHILE THE WEATHER ALLOWS IT.
AGREED, CAPTAIN.
AND SECONDED. I'M FINE FLOATING ON CALM WATER BUT HAVE NO DESIRE TO BE OUT HERE ON THIS LITTLE RAFT IF A STORM KICKS U—

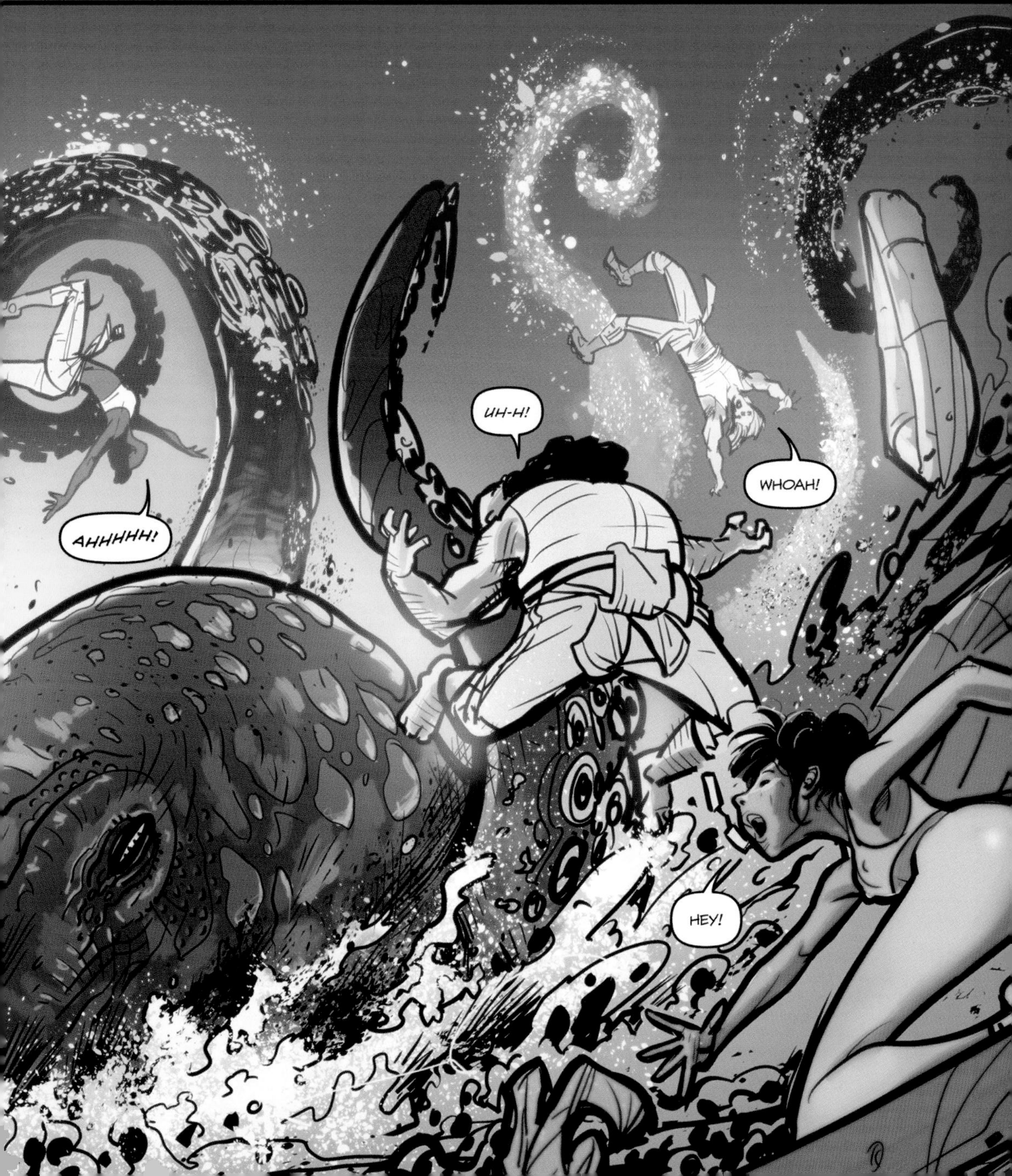
AHHHHH!
UH-H!
WHOAH!
HEY!

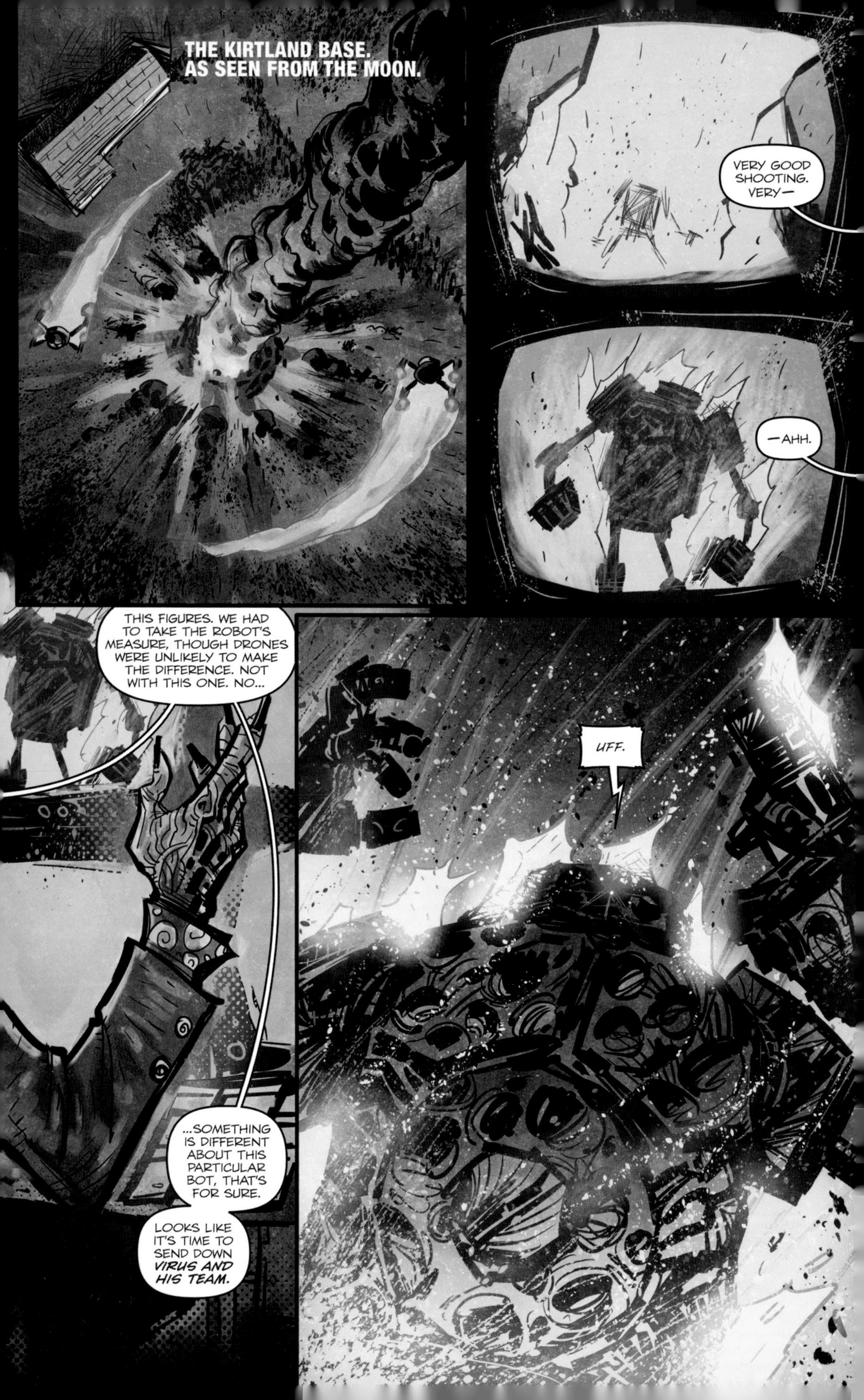
THE KIRTLAND BASE.
AS SEEN FROM THE MOON.
VERY GOOD SHOOTING. VERY—
—AHH.
THIS FIGURES. WE HAD TO TAKE THE ROBOT'S MEASURE, THOUGH DRONES WERE UNLIKELY TO MAKE THE DIFFERENCE. NOT WITH THIS ONE. NO...
...SOMETHING IS DIFFERENT ABOUT THIS PARTICULAR BOT, THAT'S FOR SURE.
LOOKS LIKE IT'S TIME TO SEND DOWN *VIRUS AND HIS TEAM.*
UFF.

WHERE'D THOSE LITTLE METAL SONSABITCHES FLY OFF TO, ANYWAY?

GOTTA PUT THEM ON THE RECEIVING END OF—

CLICK CLICK

—CRAP. BETTER AND BETTER.

AHH, THERE YOU ARE! YOU LITTLE FUCKERS THINK YOU CAN SNEAK-ATTACK ME? WHO SENT YOU, ANYWAY?!

REALLY THOUGHT I WAS ALL THAT WAS LEFT AND I LET MY MOMENTARY WEAKNESS IN SEEING OTHER ROBOTS LULL ME INTO TRUSTING THEM.

BUT I'M FRITZ WINTERBOTTOM, GODDAMMIT.

I NEED NO ONE. I TRUST NO ONE.

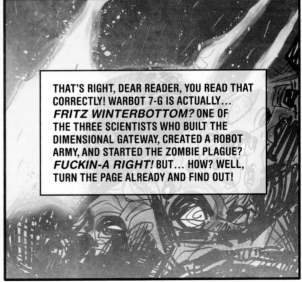

THAT'S RIGHT, DEAR READER, YOU READ THAT CORRECTLY! WARBOT 7-G IS ACTUALLY... FRITZ WINTERBOTTOM? ONE OF THE THREE SCIENTISTS WHO BUILT THE DIMENSIONAL GATEWAY, CREATED A ROBOT ARMY, AND STARTED THE ZOMBIE PLAGUE? FUCKIN-A RIGHT! BUT... HOW? WELL, TURN THE PAGE ALREADY AND FIND OUT!

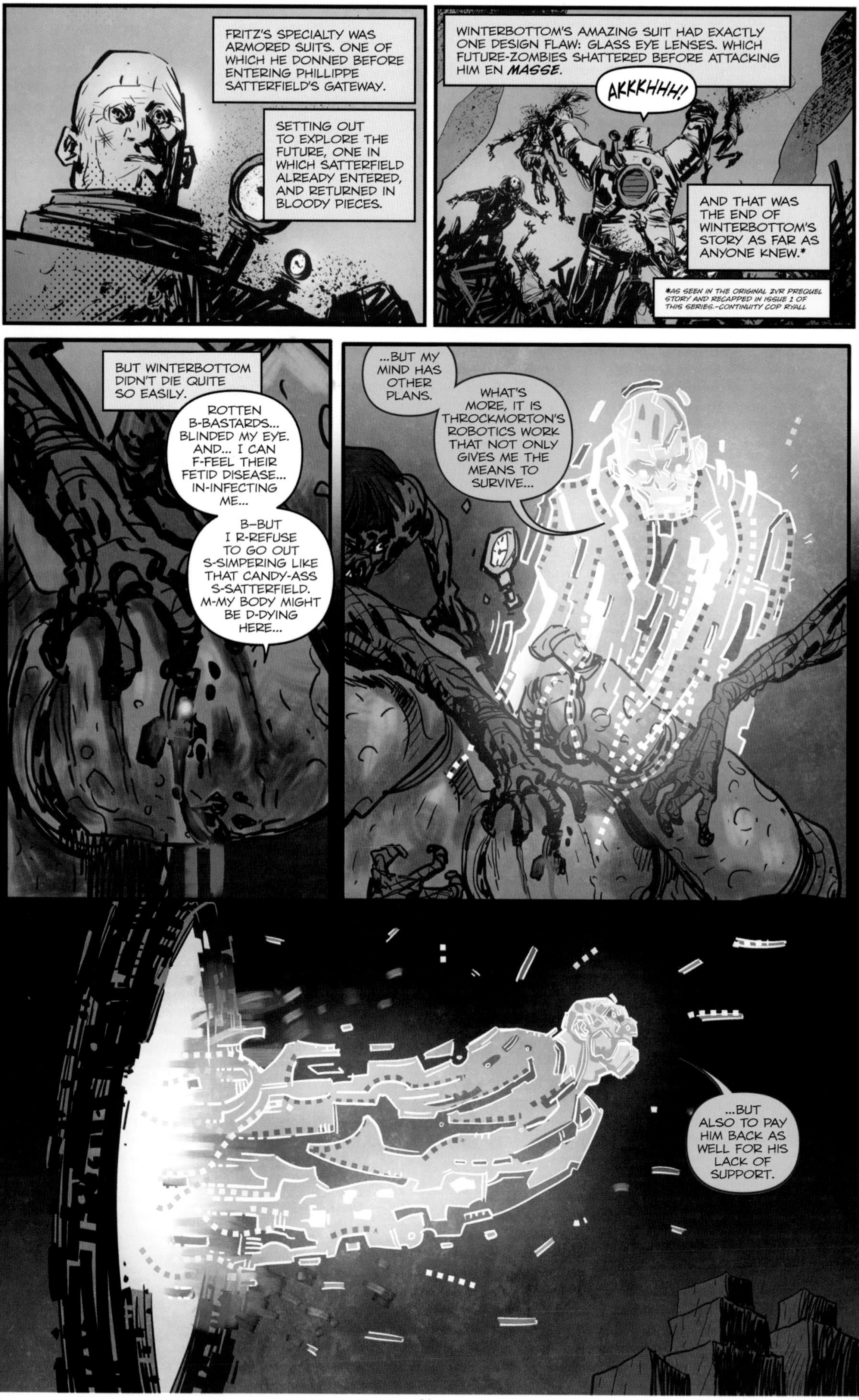

FRITZ'S SPECIALTY WAS ARMORED SUITS. ONE OF WHICH HE DONNED BEFORE ENTERING PHILLIPPE SATTERFIELD'S GATEWAY.
SETTING OUT TO EXPLORE THE FUTURE, ONE IN WHICH SATTERFIELD ALREADY ENTERED, AND RETURNED IN BLOODY PIECES.
WINTERBOTTOM'S AMAZING SUIT HAD EXACTLY ONE DESIGN FLAW: GLASS EYE LENSES. WHICH FUTURE-ZOMBIES SHATTERED BEFORE ATTACKING HIM EN ***MASSE***.
AKKKHHH!
AND THAT WAS THE END OF WINTERBOTTOM'S STORY AS FAR AS ANYONE KNEW.*
*AS SEEN IN THE ORIGINAL ZVR PREQUEL STORY AND RECAPPED IN ISSUE 1 OF THIS SERIES.-CONTINUITY COP RYALL
BUT WINTERBOTTOM DIDN'T DIE QUITE SO EASILY.
ROTTEN B-BASTARDS... BLINDED MY EYE. AND... I CAN F-FEEL THEIR FETID DISEASE... IN-INFECTING ME...
B-BUT I R-REFUSE TO GO OUT S-SIMPERING LIKE THAT CANDY-ASS S-SATTERFIELD. M-MY BODY MIGHT BE D-DYING HERE...
...BUT MY MIND HAS OTHER PLANS.
WHAT'S MORE, IT IS THROCKMORTON'S ROBOTICS WORK THAT NOT ONLY GIVES ME THE MEANS TO SURVIVE...
...BUT ALSO TO PAY HIM BACK AS WELL FOR HIS LACK OF SUPPORT.

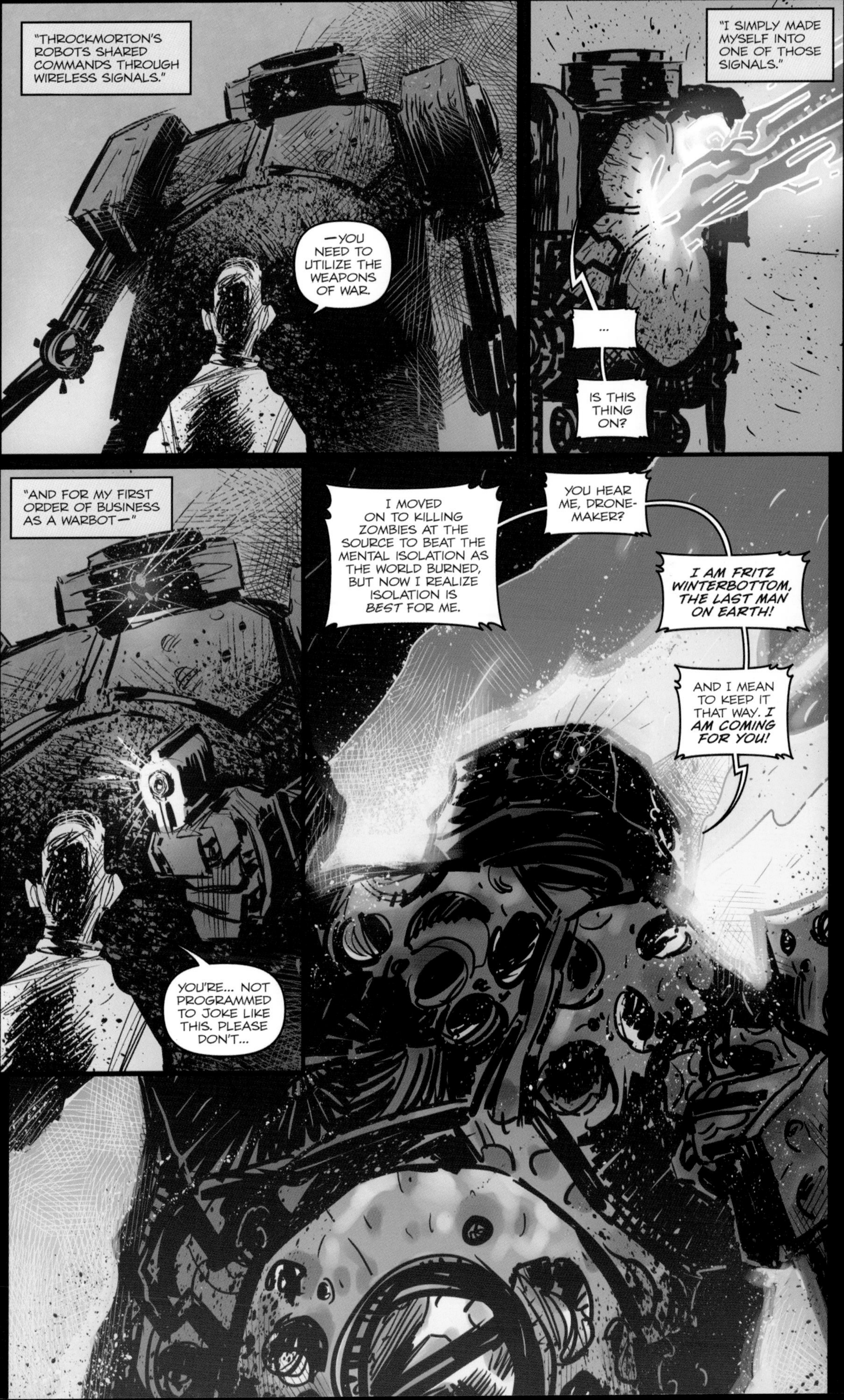
"THROCKMORTON'S ROBOTS SHARED COMMANDS THROUGH WIRELESS SIGNALS."
—YOU NEED TO UTILIZE THE WEAPONS OF WAR.
"I SIMPLY MADE MYSELF INTO ONE OF THOSE SIGNALS."
...
IS THIS THING ON?
"AND FOR MY FIRST ORDER OF BUSINESS AS A WARBOT—"
YOU'RE... NOT PROGRAMMED TO JOKE LIKE THIS. PLEASE DON'T...
I MOVED ON TO KILLING ZOMBIES AT THE SOURCE TO BEAT THE MENTAL ISOLATION AS THE WORLD BURNED, BUT NOW I REALIZE ISOLATION IS *BEST* FOR ME.
YOU HEAR ME, DRONE-MAKER?
I AM FRITZ WINTERBOTTOM, THE LAST MAN ON EARTH!
AND I MEAN TO KEEP IT THAT WAY. *I AM COMING FOR YOU!*

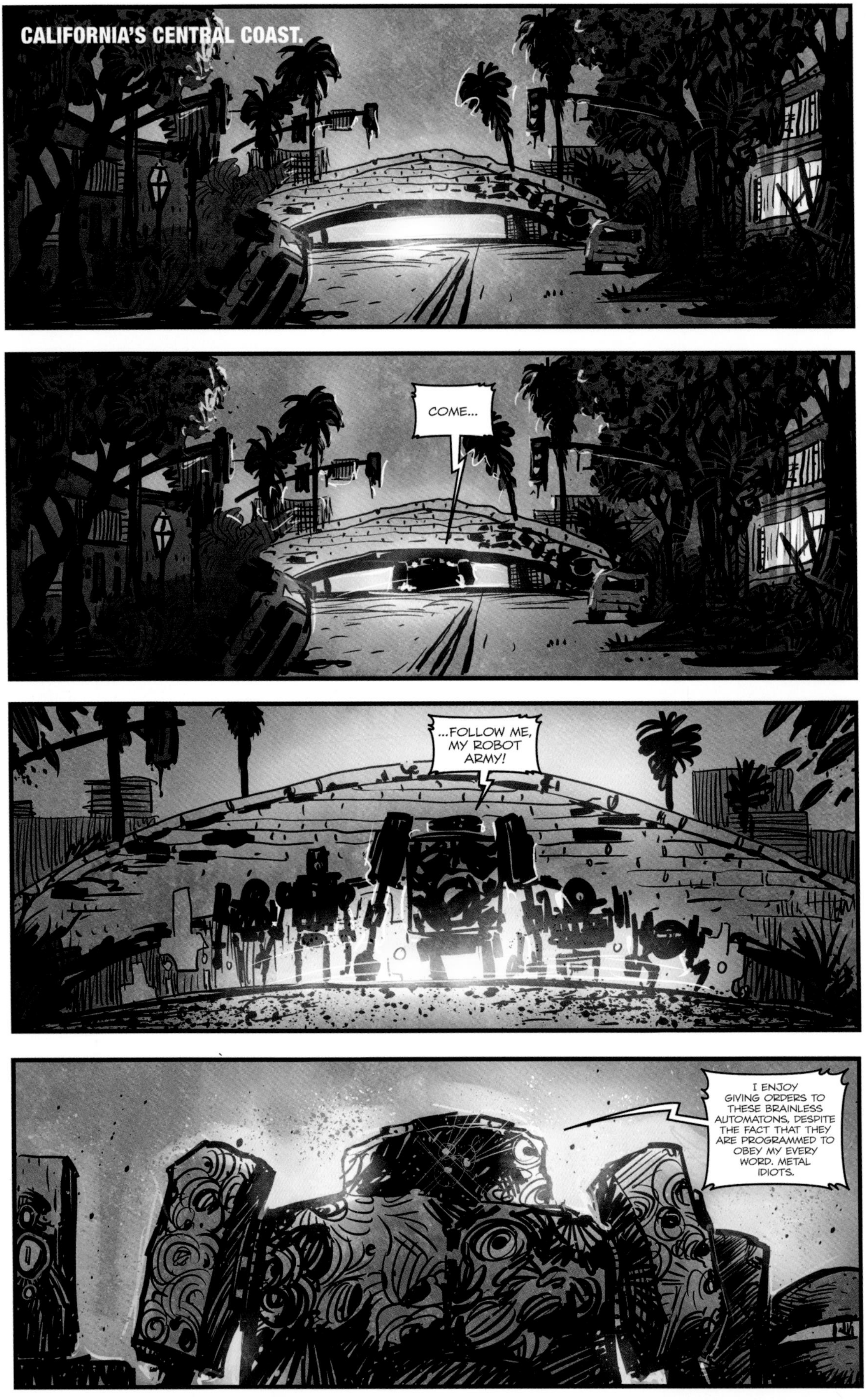
CALIFORNIA'S CENTRAL COAST.
COME...
...FOLLOW ME, MY ROBOT ARMY!
I ENJOY GIVING ORDERS TO THESE BRAINLESS AUTOMATONS, DESPITE THE FACT THAT THEY ARE PROGRAMMED TO OBEY MY EVERY WORD. METAL IDIOTS.

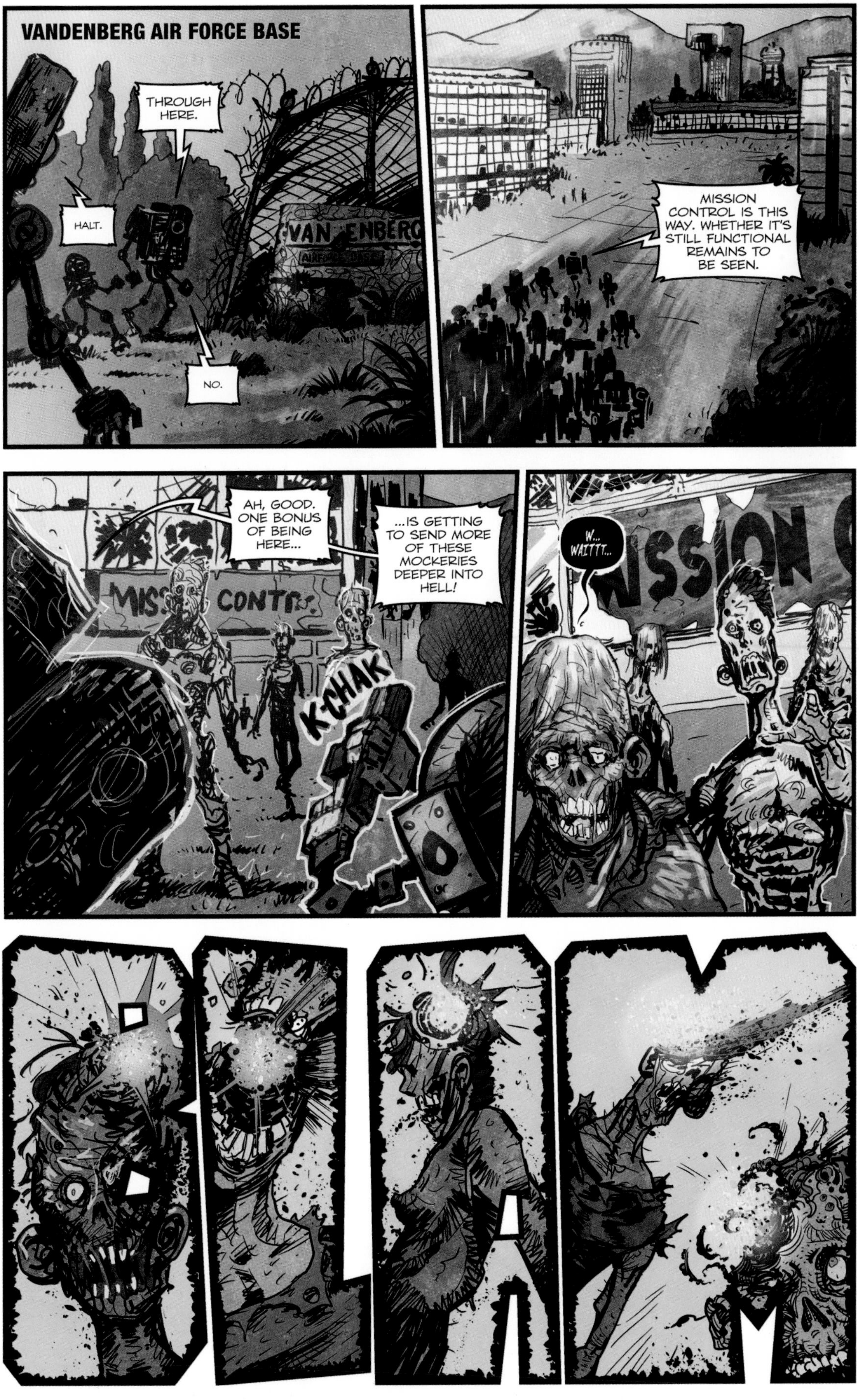
VANDENBERG AIR FORCE BASE
THROUGH HERE.
HALT.
NO.
MISSION CONTROL IS THIS WAY. WHETHER IT'S STILL FUNCTIONAL REMAINS TO BE SEEN.
AH, GOOD. ONE BONUS OF BEING HERE...
...IS GETTING TO SEND MORE OF THESE MOCKERIES DEEPER INTO HELL!
K-CHAK
W... WAITTT...
BLAM

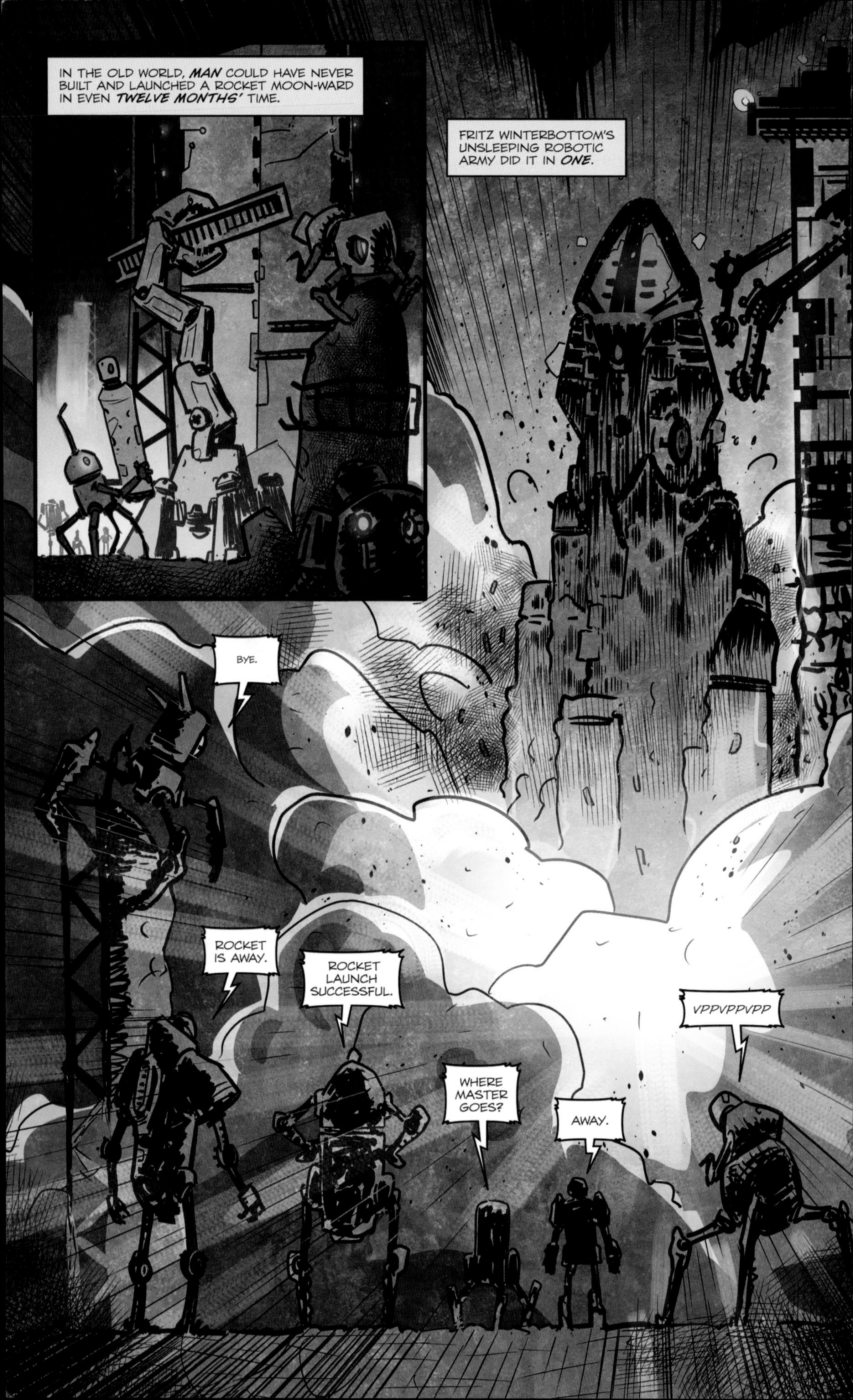
IN THE OLD WORLD, MAN COULD HAVE NEVER BUILT AND LAUNCHED A ROCKET MOON-WARD IN EVEN TWELVE MONTHS' TIME.
FRITZ WINTERBOTTOM'S UNSLEEPING ROBOTIC ARMY DID IT IN ONE.
BYE.
ROCKET IS AWAY.
ROCKET LAUNCH SUCCESSFUL.
VPPVPPVPP
WHERE MASTER GOES?
AWAY.

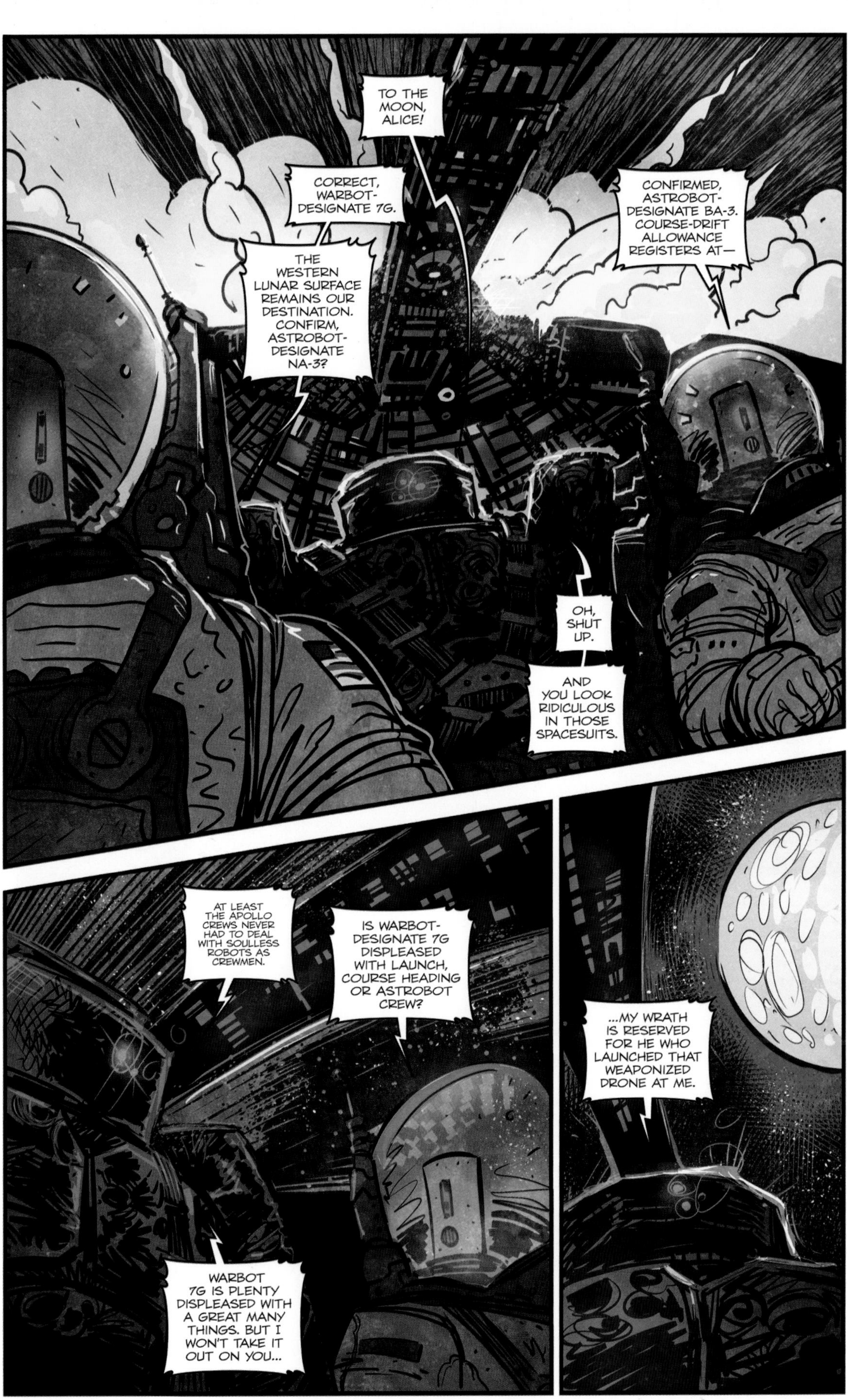
TO THE MOON, ALICE!
CORRECT, WARBOT-DESIGNATE 7G.
THE WESTERN LUNAR SURFACE REMAINS OUR DESTINATION. CONFIRM, ASTROBOT-DESIGNATE NA-3?
CONFIRMED, ASTROBOT-DESIGNATE BA-3. COURSE-DRIFT ALLOWANCE REGISTERS AT—
OH, SHUT UP.
AND YOU LOOK RIDICULOUS IN THOSE SPACESUITS.
AT LEAST THE APOLLO CREWS NEVER HAD TO DEAL WITH SOULLESS ROBOTS AS CREWMEN.
IS WARBOT-DESIGNATE 7G DISPLEASED WITH LAUNCH, COURSE HEADING OR ASTROBOT CREW?
WARBOT 7G IS PLENTY DISPLEASED WITH A GREAT MANY THINGS. BUT I WON'T TAKE IT OUT ON YOU...
...MY WRATH IS RESERVED FOR HE WHO LAUNCHED THAT WEAPONIZED DRONE AT ME.

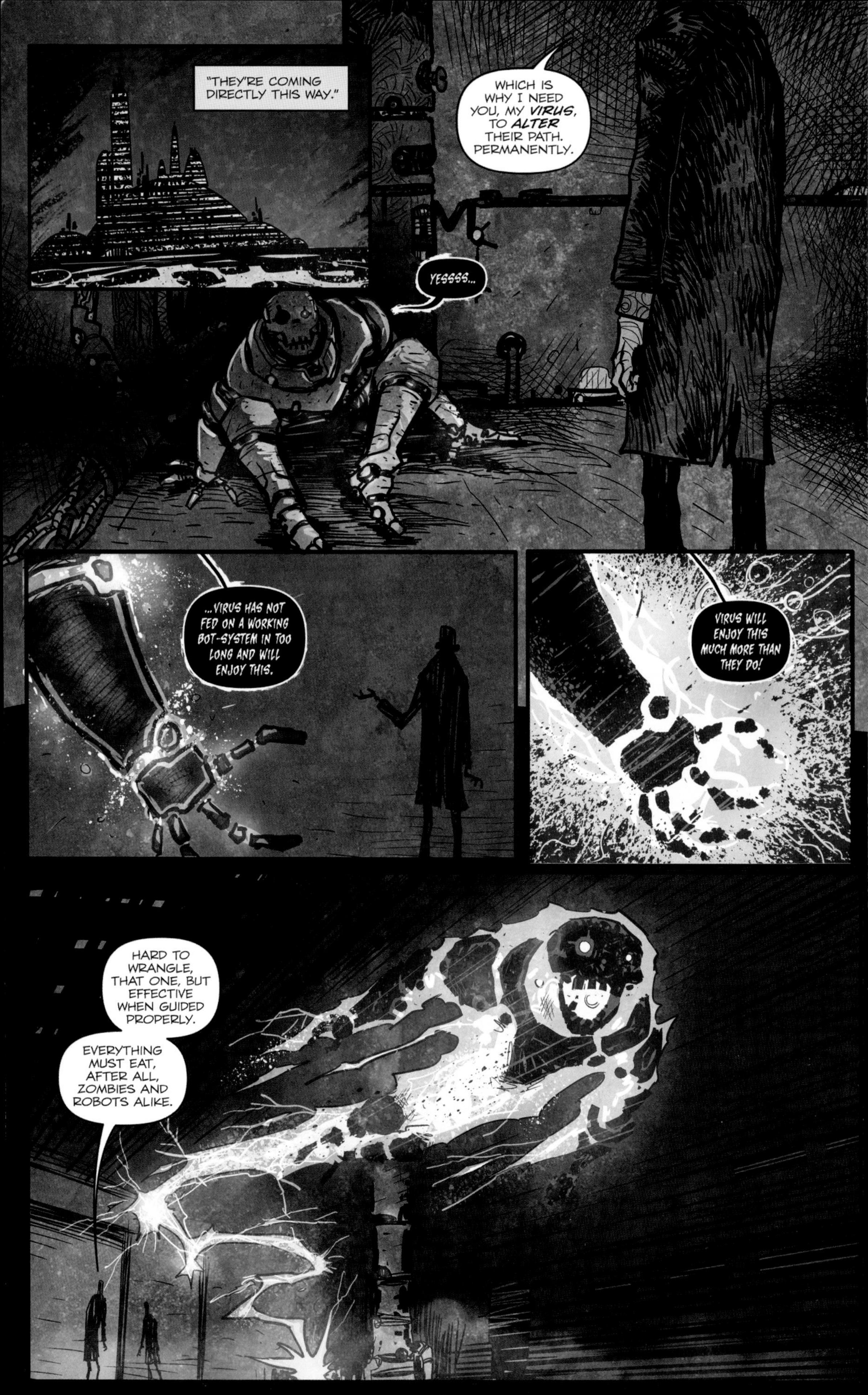
"THEY'RE COMING DIRECTLY THIS WAY."
WHICH IS WHY I NEED YOU, MY VIRUS, TO ALTER THEIR PATH. PERMANENTLY.
YESSSS...
...VIRUS HAS NOT FED ON A WORKING BOT-SYSTEM IN TOO LONG AND WILL ENJOY THIS.
VIRUS WILL ENJOY THIS MUCH MORE THAN THEY DO!
HARD TO WRANGLE, THAT ONE, BUT EFFECTIVE WHEN GUIDED PROPERLY.
EVERYTHING MUST EAT, AFTER ALL, ZOMBIES AND ROBOTS ALIKE.

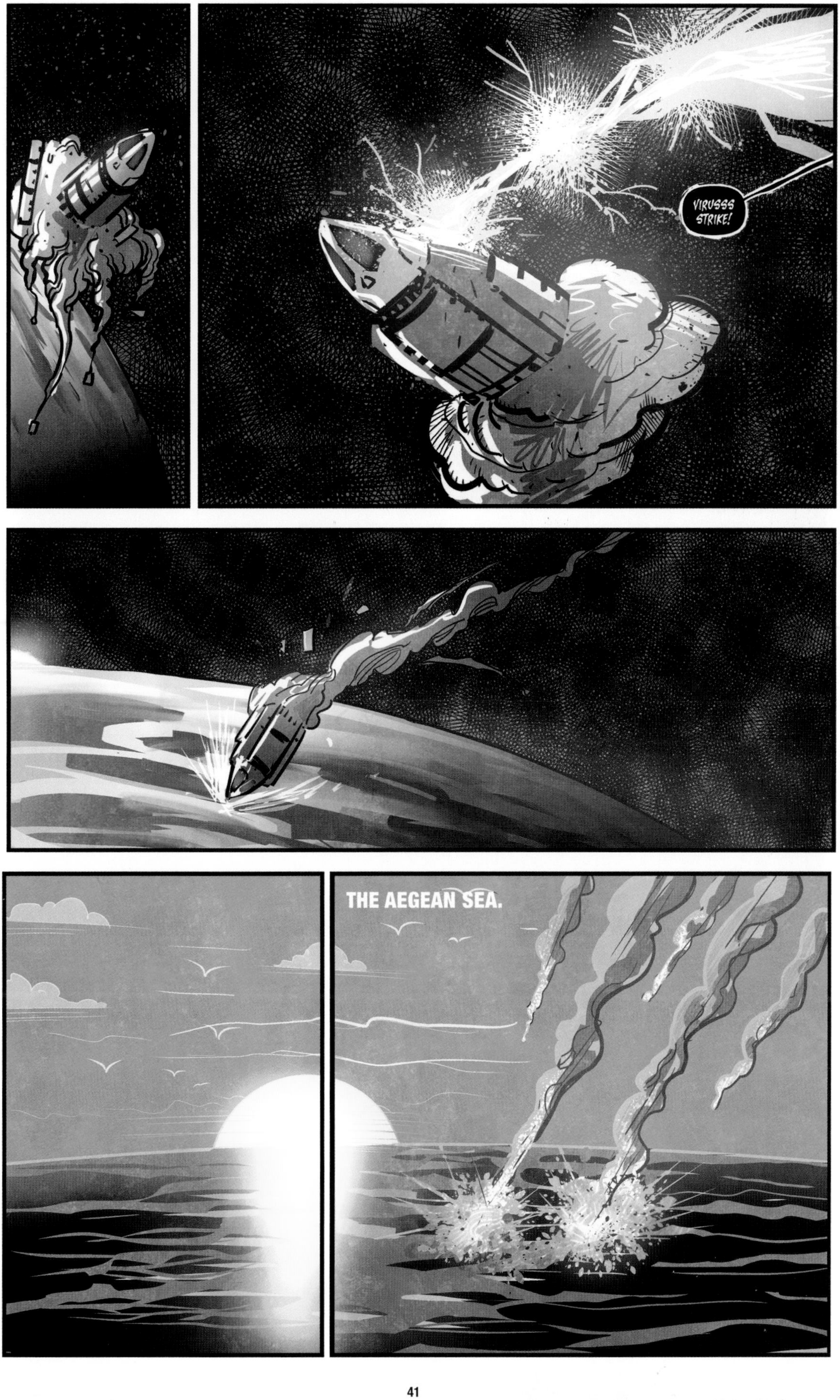
VIRUSSS STRIKE!
THE AEGEAN SEA.

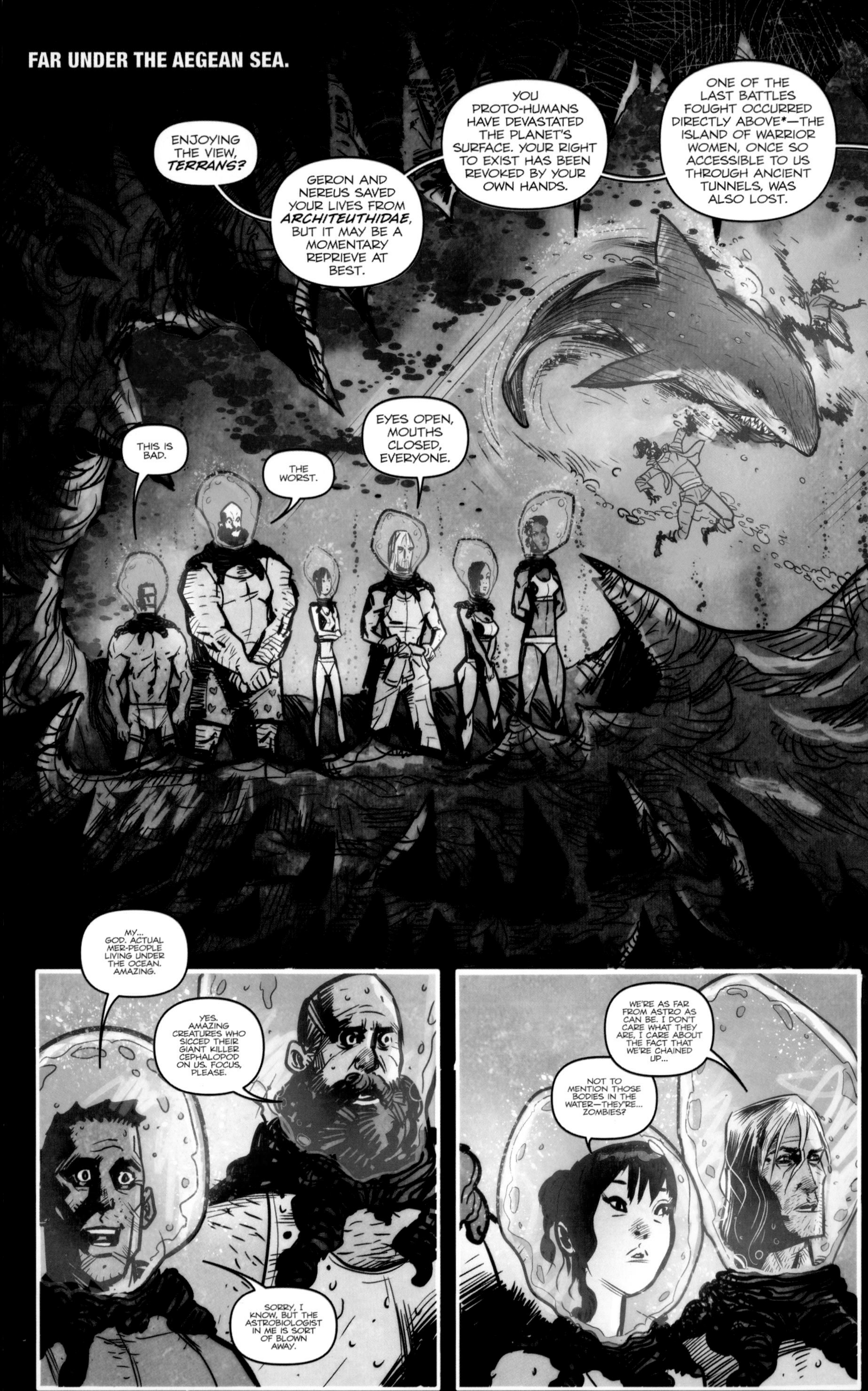
FAR UNDER THE AEGEAN SEA.
ENJOYING THE VIEW, TERRANS?
GERON AND NEREUS SAVED YOUR LIVES FROM ARCHITEUTHIDAE, BUT IT MAY BE A MOMENTARY REPRIEVE AT BEST.
YOU PROTO-HUMANS HAVE DEVASTATED THE PLANET'S SURFACE. YOUR RIGHT TO EXIST HAS BEEN REVOKED BY YOUR OWN HANDS.
ONE OF THE LAST BATTLES FOUGHT OCCURRED DIRECTLY ABOVE*—THE ISLAND OF WARRIOR WOMEN, ONCE SO ACCESSIBLE TO US THROUGH ANCIENT TUNNELS, WAS ALSO LOST.
THIS IS BAD.
THE WORST.
EYES OPEN, MOUTHS CLOSED, EVERYONE.
MY... GOD. ACTUAL MER-PEOPLE LIVING UNDER THE OCEAN. AMAZING.
YES. AMAZING CREATURES WHO SICCED THEIR GIANT KILLER CEPHALOPOD ON US. FOCUS, PLEASE.
SORRY, I KNOW, BUT THE ASTROBIOLOGIST IN ME IS SORT OF BLOWN AWAY.
WE'RE AS FAR FROM ASTRO AS CAN BE. I DON'T CARE WHAT THEY ARE, I CARE ABOUT THE FACT THAT WE'RE CHAINED UP...
NOT TO MENTION THOSE BODIES IN THE WATER—THEY'RE... ZOMBIES?

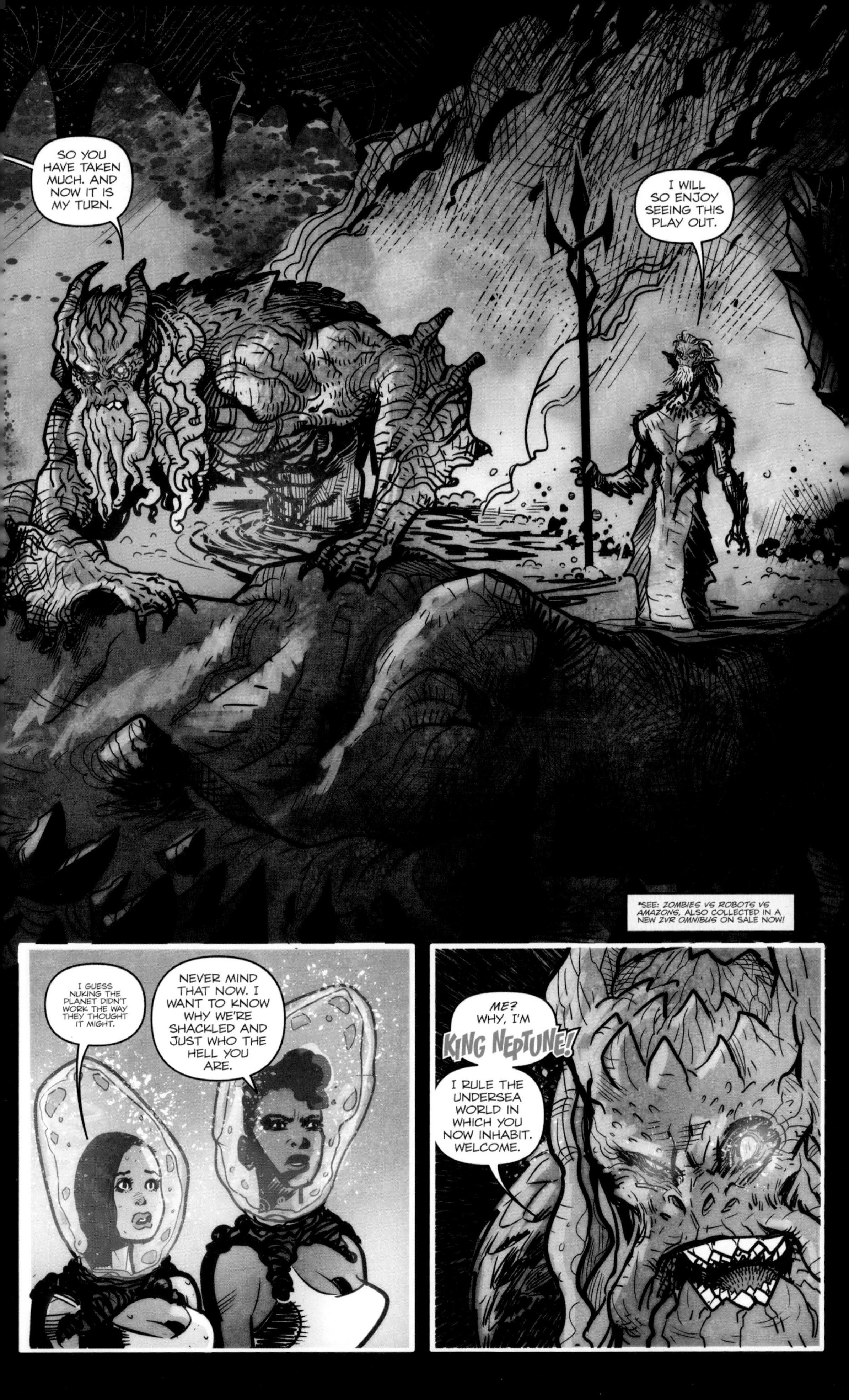
SO YOU HAVE TAKEN MUCH. AND NOW IT IS MY TURN.
I WILL SO ENJOY SEEING THIS PLAY OUT.
*SEE: ZOMBIES VS ROBOTS VS AMAZONS, ALSO COLLECTED IN A NEW ZVR OMNIBUS ON SALE NOW!
I GUESS NUKING THE PLANET DIDN'T WORK THE WAY THEY THOUGHT IT MIGHT.
NEVER MIND THAT NOW. I WANT TO KNOW WHY WE'RE SHACKLED AND JUST WHO THE HELL YOU ARE.
ME? WHY, I'M KING NEPTUNE!
I RULE THE UNDERSEA WORLD IN WHICH YOU NOW INHABIT. WELCOME.

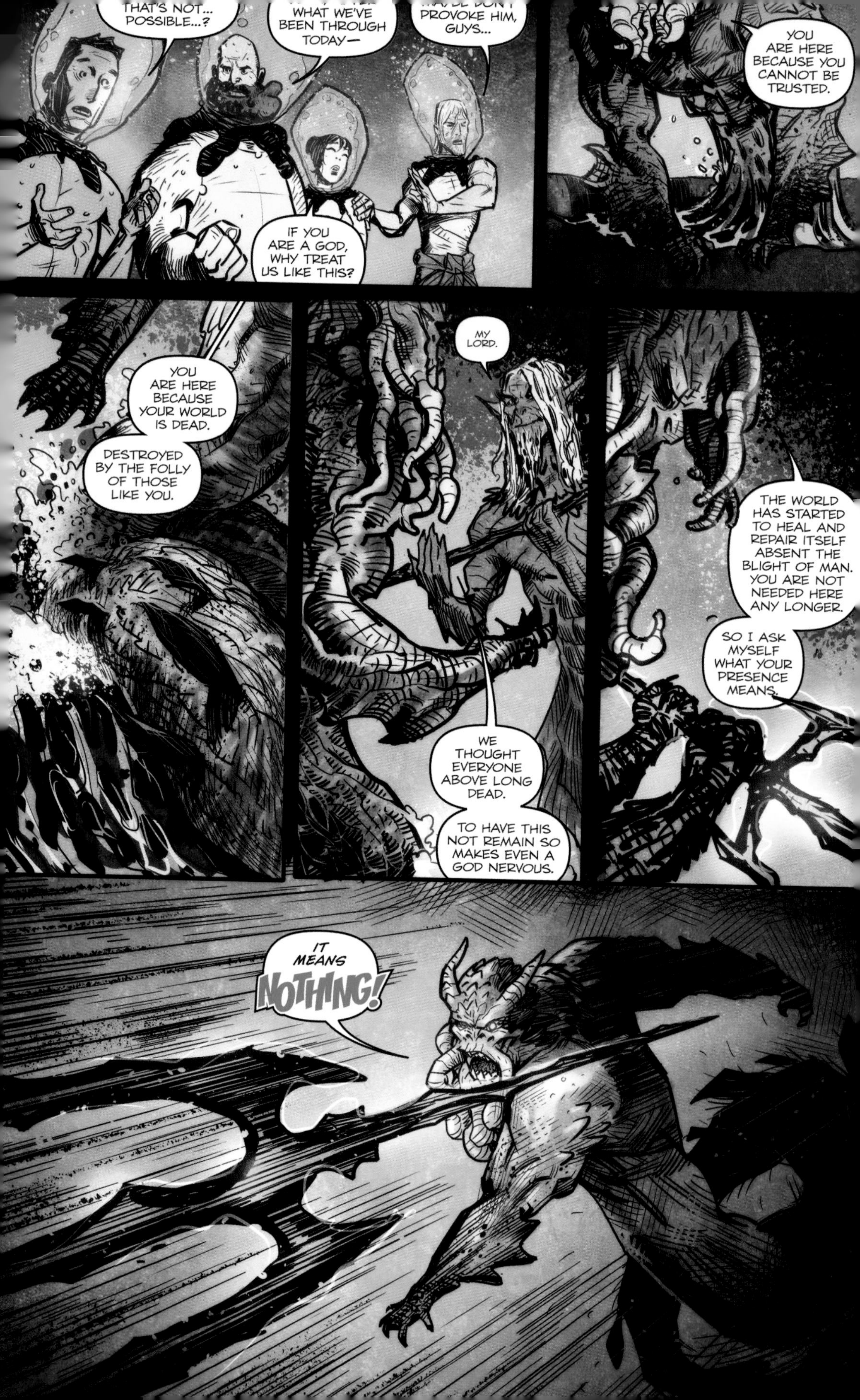
THAT'S NOT... POSSIBLE...?
WHAT WE'VE BEEN THROUGH TODAY—
PROVOKE HIM, GUYS...
IF YOU ARE A GOD, WHY TREAT US LIKE THIS?
YOU ARE HERE BECAUSE YOU CANNOT BE TRUSTED.
YOU ARE HERE BECAUSE YOUR WORLD IS DEAD.
DESTROYED BY THE FOLLY OF THOSE LIKE YOU.
MY LORD.
WE THOUGHT EVERYONE ABOVE LONG DEAD.
TO HAVE THIS NOT REMAIN SO MAKES EVEN A GOD NERVOUS.
THE WORLD HAS STARTED TO HEAL AND REPAIR ITSELF ABSENT THE BLIGHT OF MAN. YOU ARE NOT NEEDED HERE ANY LONGER.
SO I ASK MYSELF WHAT YOUR PRESENCE MEANS.
IT MEANS NOTHING!

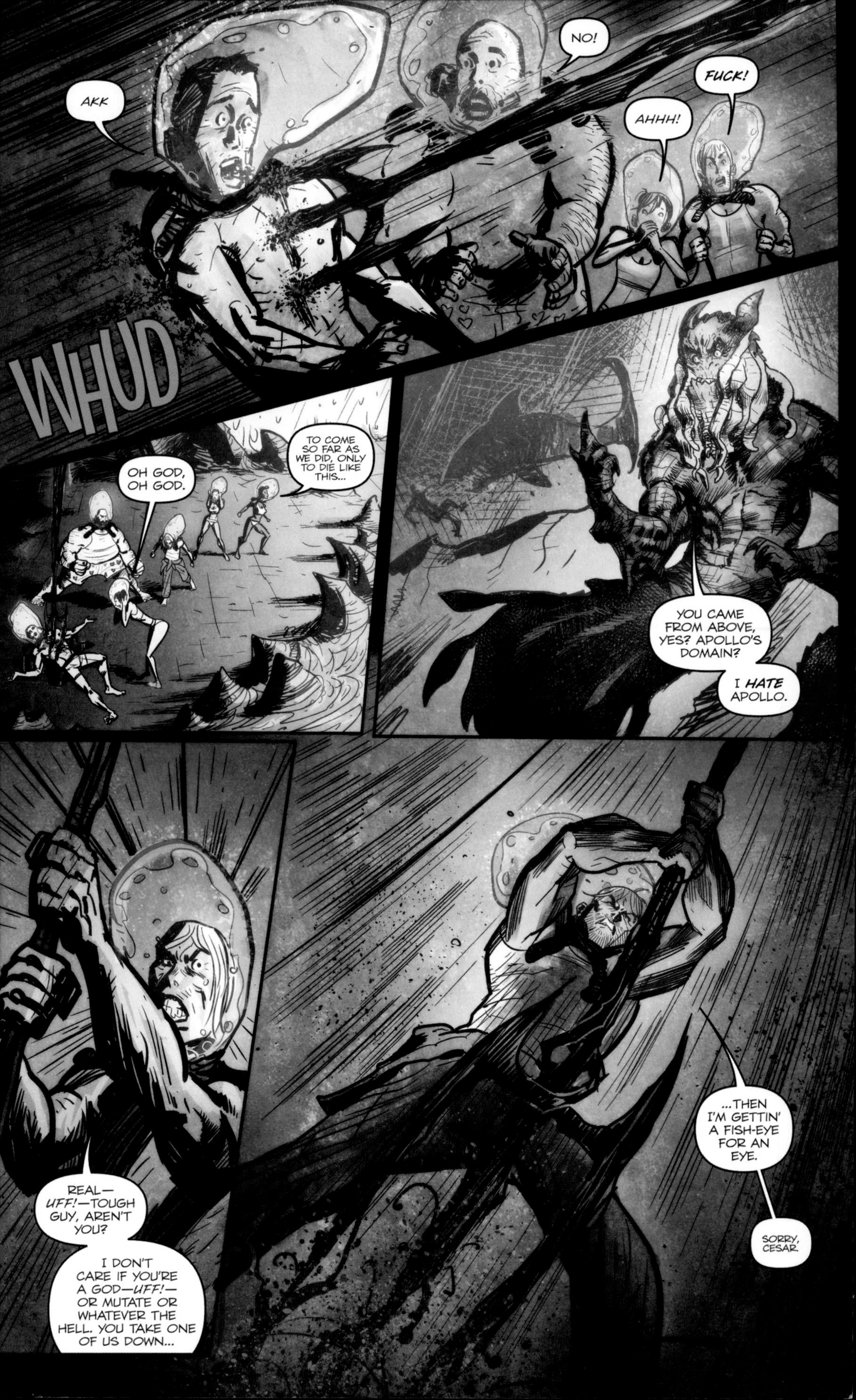
AKK
NO!
AHHH!
FUCK!
WHUD
OH GOD, OH GOD.
TO COME SO FAR AS WE DID, ONLY TO DIE LIKE THIS...
YOU CAME FROM ABOVE, YES? APOLLO'S DOMAIN?
I HATE APOLLO.
REAL— UFF!—TOUGH GUY, AREN'T YOU?
I DON'T CARE IF YOU'RE A GOD—UFF!— OR MUTATE OR WHATEVER THE HELL. YOU TAKE ONE OF US DOWN...
...THEN I'M GETTIN' A FISH-EYE FOR AN EYE.
SORRY, CESAR.

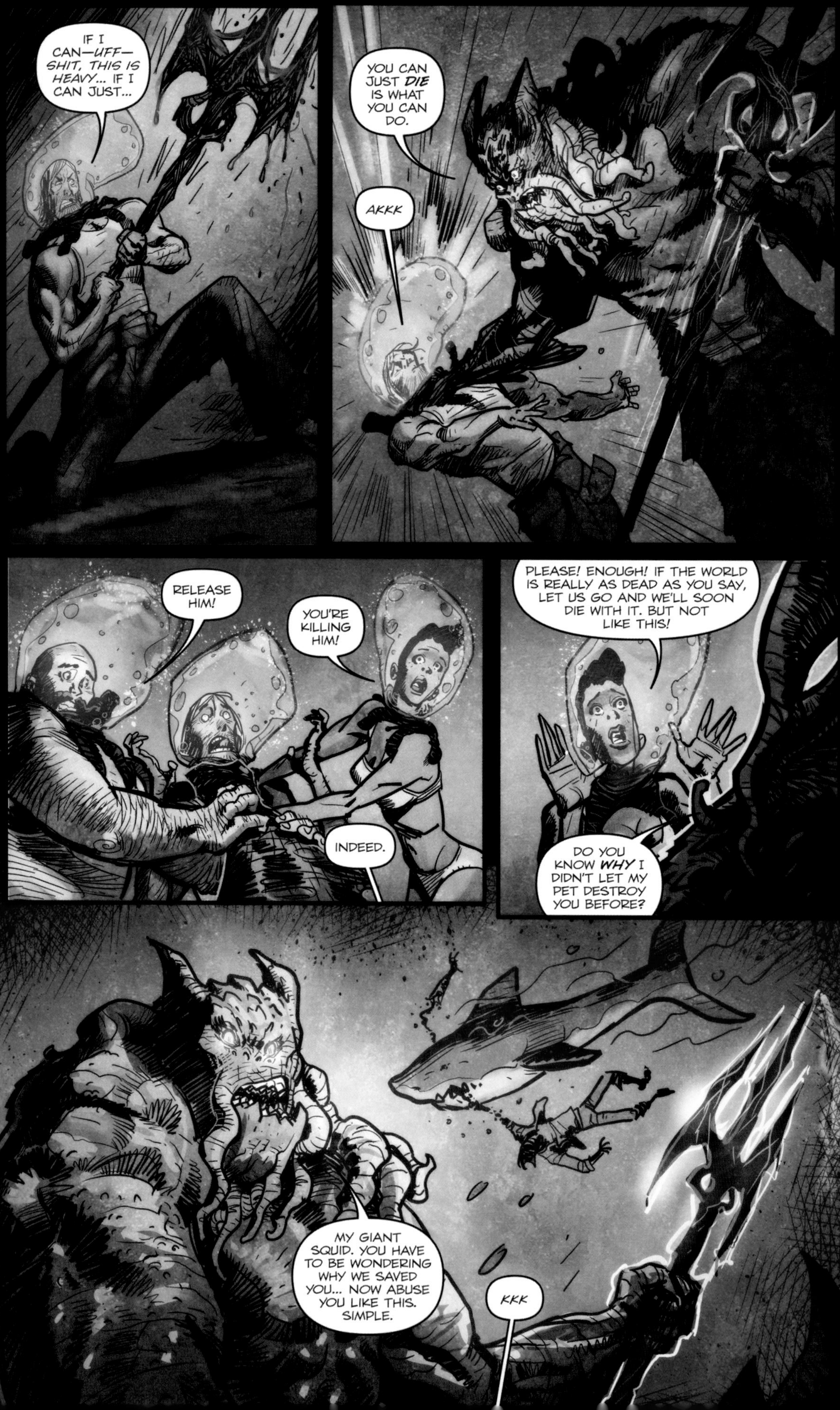
IF I CAN—UFF—SHIT, THIS IS HEAVY... IF I CAN JUST...
YOU CAN JUST DIE IS WHAT YOU CAN DO.
AKKK
RELEASE HIM!
YOU'RE KILLING HIM!
INDEED.
PLEASE! ENOUGH! IF THE WORLD IS REALLY AS DEAD AS YOU SAY, LET US GO AND WE'LL SOON DIE WITH IT. BUT NOT LIKE THIS!
DO YOU KNOW WHY I DIDN'T LET MY PET DESTROY YOU BEFORE?
MY GIANT SQUID. YOU HAVE TO BE WONDERING WHY WE SAVED YOU... NOW ABUSE YOU LIKE THIS. SIMPLE.
KKK

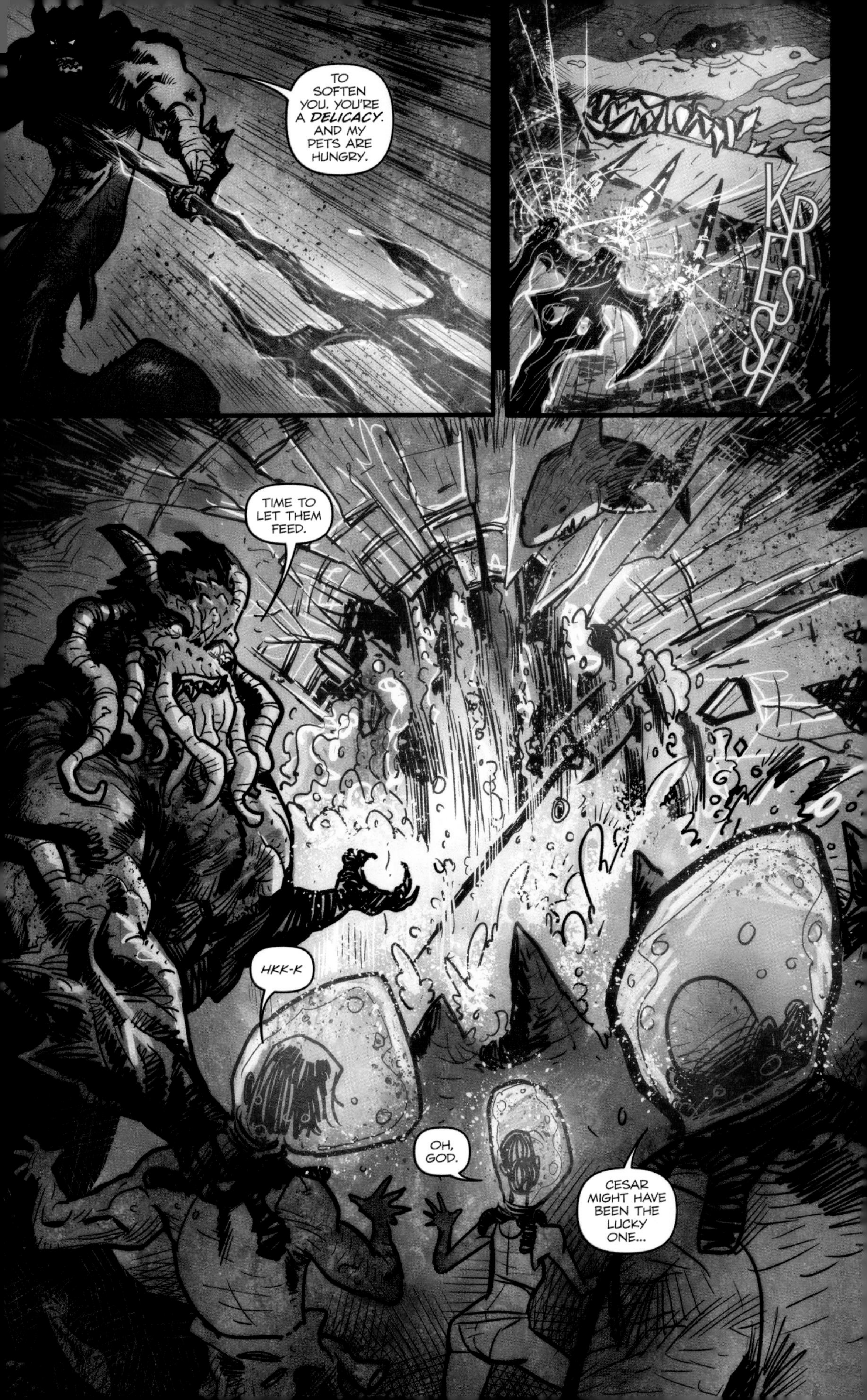
TO SOFTEN YOU. YOU'RE A DELICACY. AND MY PETS ARE HUNGRY.
KRESSH
TIME TO LET THEM FEED.
HKK-K
OH, GOD.
CESAR MIGHT HAVE BEEN THE LUCKY ONE...

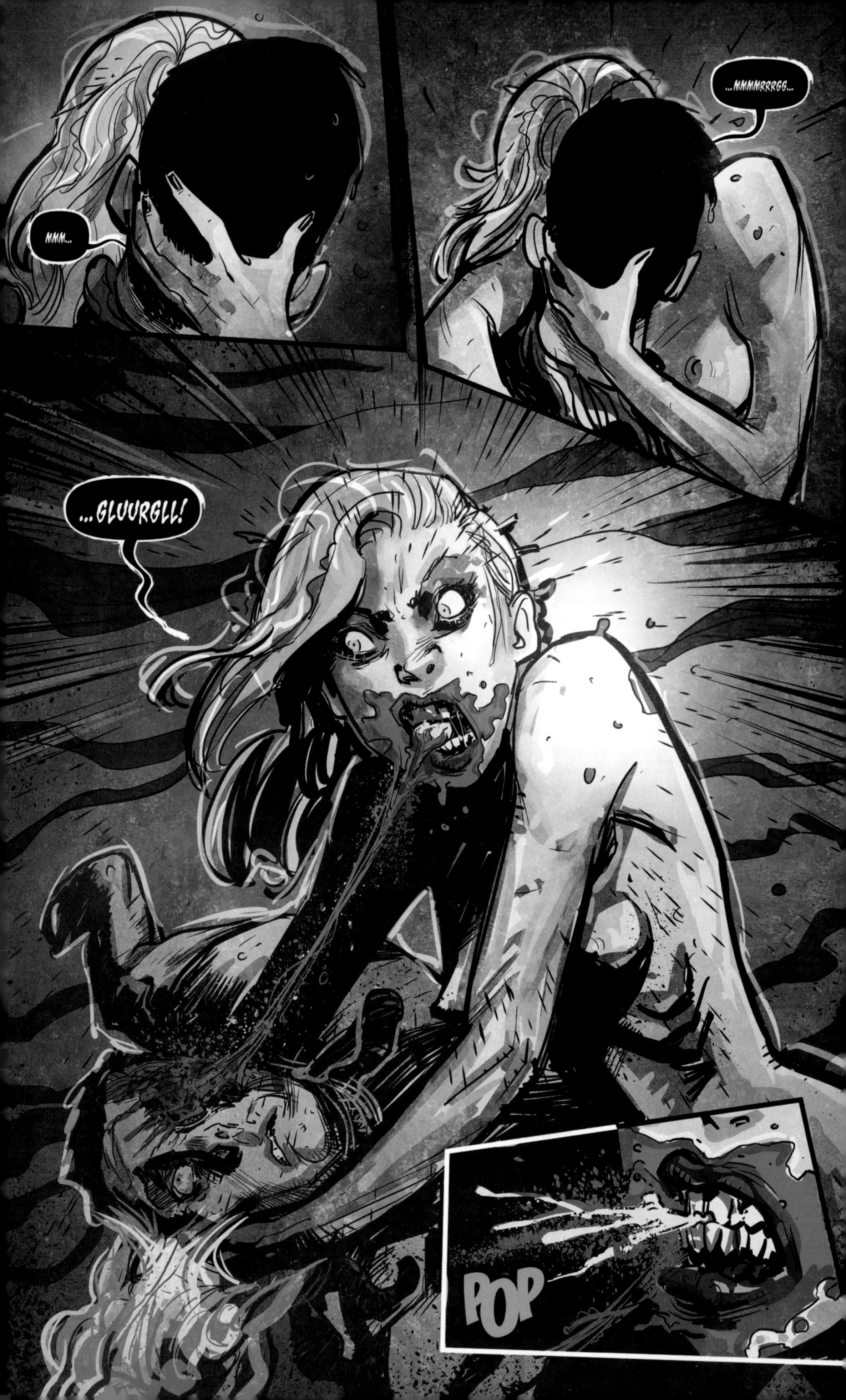
MMM...
...MMMMRRRGG...
...GLUURGLL!
POP

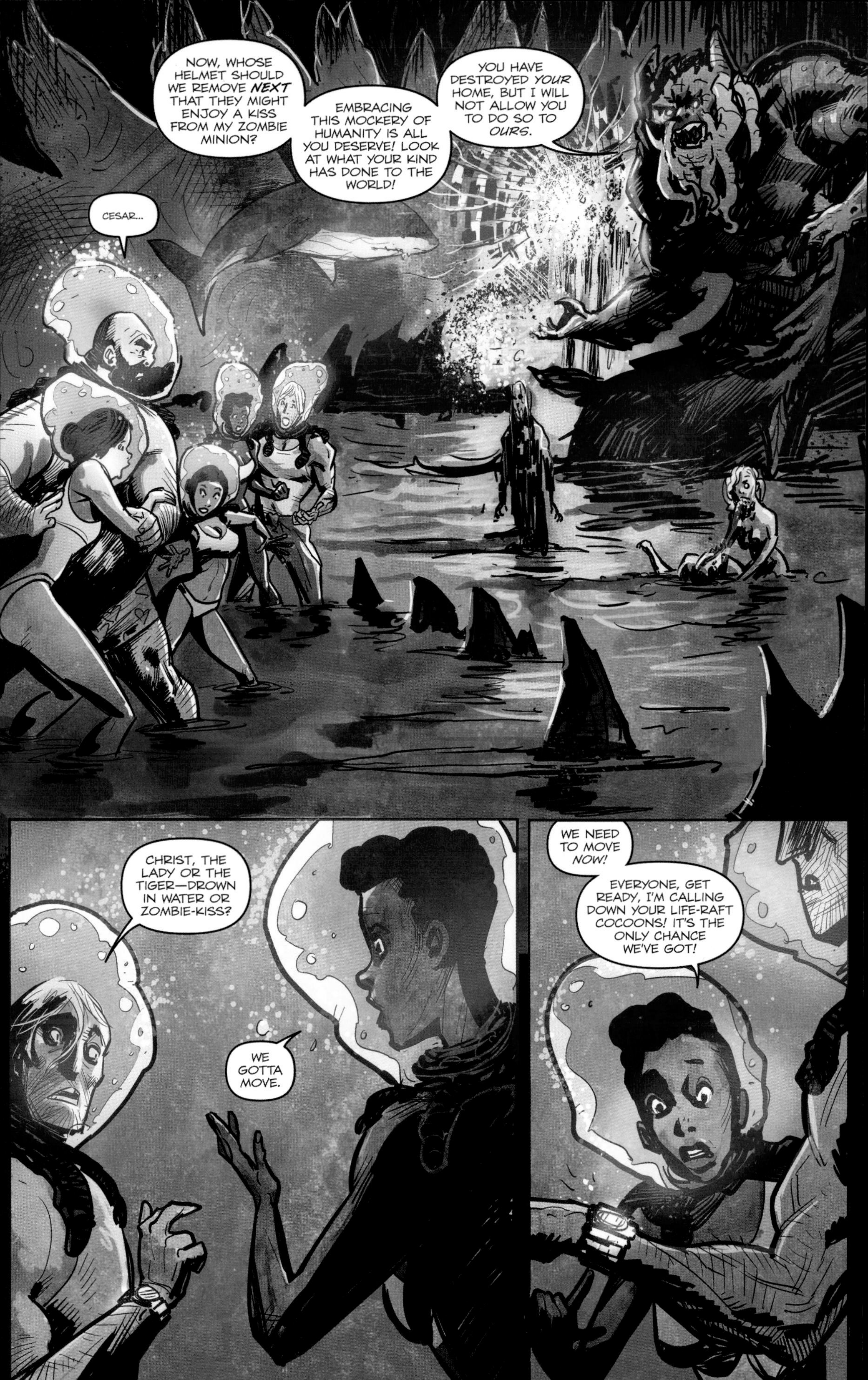
NOW, WHOSE HELMET SHOULD WE REMOVE NEXT THAT THEY MIGHT ENJOY A KISS FROM MY ZOMBIE MINION?
EMBRACING THIS MOCKERY OF HUMANITY IS ALL YOU DESERVE! LOOK AT WHAT YOUR KIND HAS DONE TO THE WORLD!
YOU HAVE DESTROYED YOUR HOME, BUT I WILL NOT ALLOW YOU TO DO SO TO OURS.
CESAR...
CHRIST, THE LADY OR THE TIGER—DROWN IN WATER OR ZOMBIE-KISS?
WE GOTTA MOVE.
WE NEED TO MOVE NOW!
EVERYONE, GET READY, I'M CALLING DOWN YOUR LIFE-RAFT COCOONS! IT'S THE ONLY CHANCE WE'VE GOT!

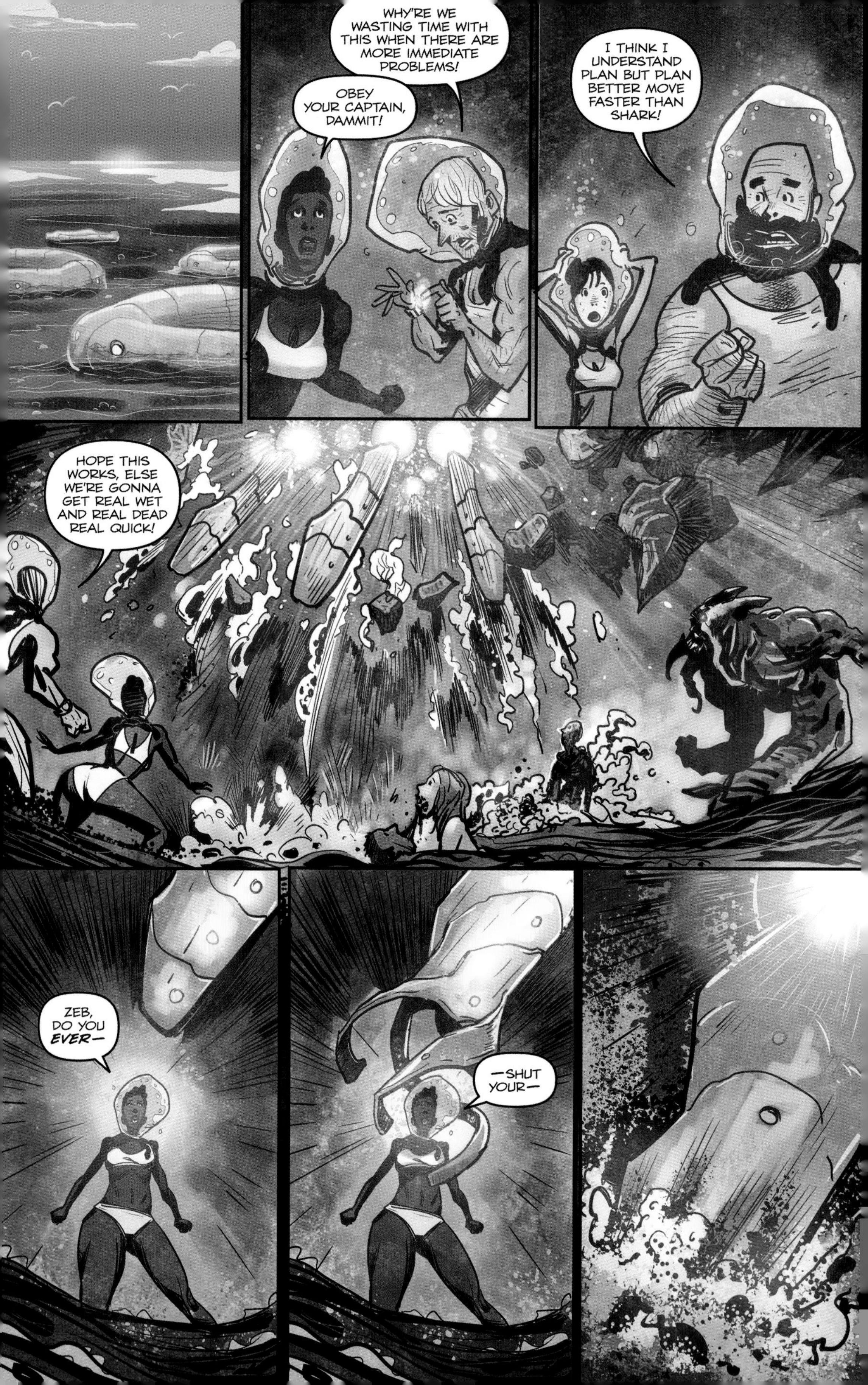
WHY'RE WE WASTING TIME WITH THIS WHEN THERE ARE MORE IMMEDIATE PROBLEMS!
OBEY YOUR CAPTAIN, DAMMIT!
I THINK I UNDERSTAND PLAN BUT PLAN BETTER MOVE FASTER THAN SHARK!
HOPE THIS WORKS, ELSE WE'RE GONNA GET REAL WET AND REAL DEAD REAL QUICK!
ZEB, DO YOU *EVER*—
—SHUT YOUR—

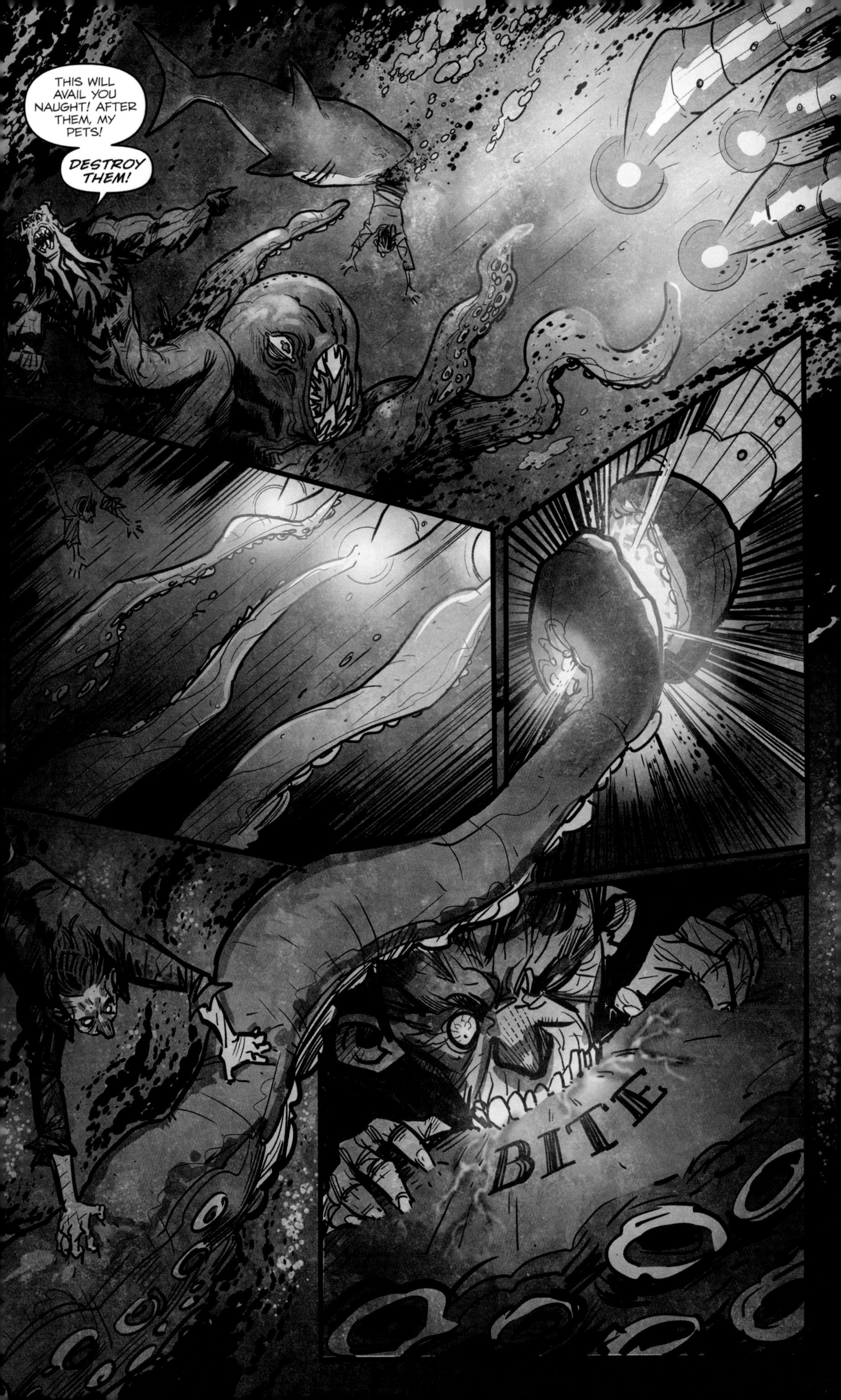
THIS WILL AVAIL YOU NAUGHT! AFTER THEM, MY PETS!
DESTROY THEM!
BITE

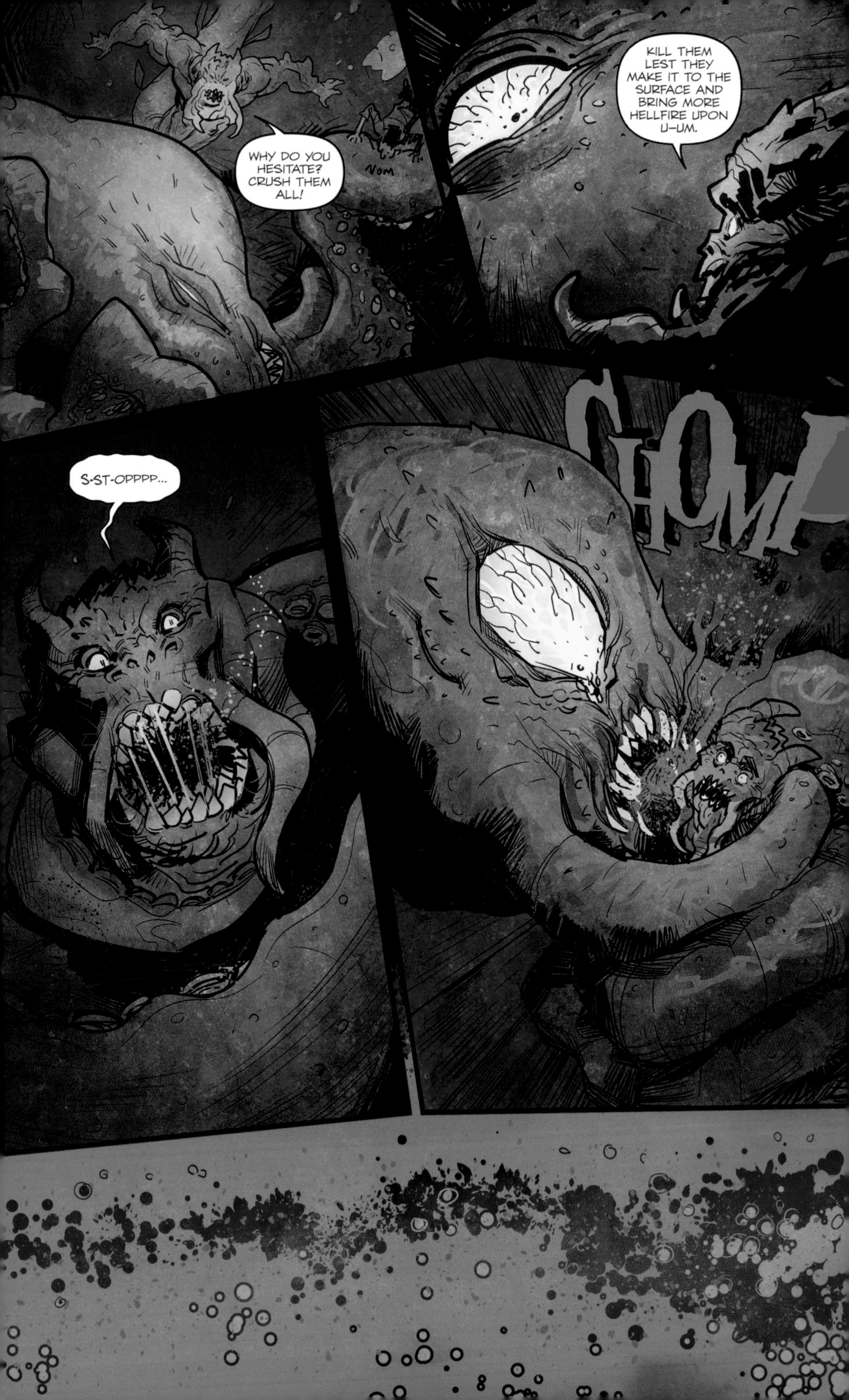
WHY DO YOU HESITATE? CRUSH THEM ALL!
NOM
KILL THEM LEST THEY MAKE IT TO THE SURFACE AND BRING MORE HELLFIRE UPON U-UM.
S-ST-OPPPP...
CHOMP

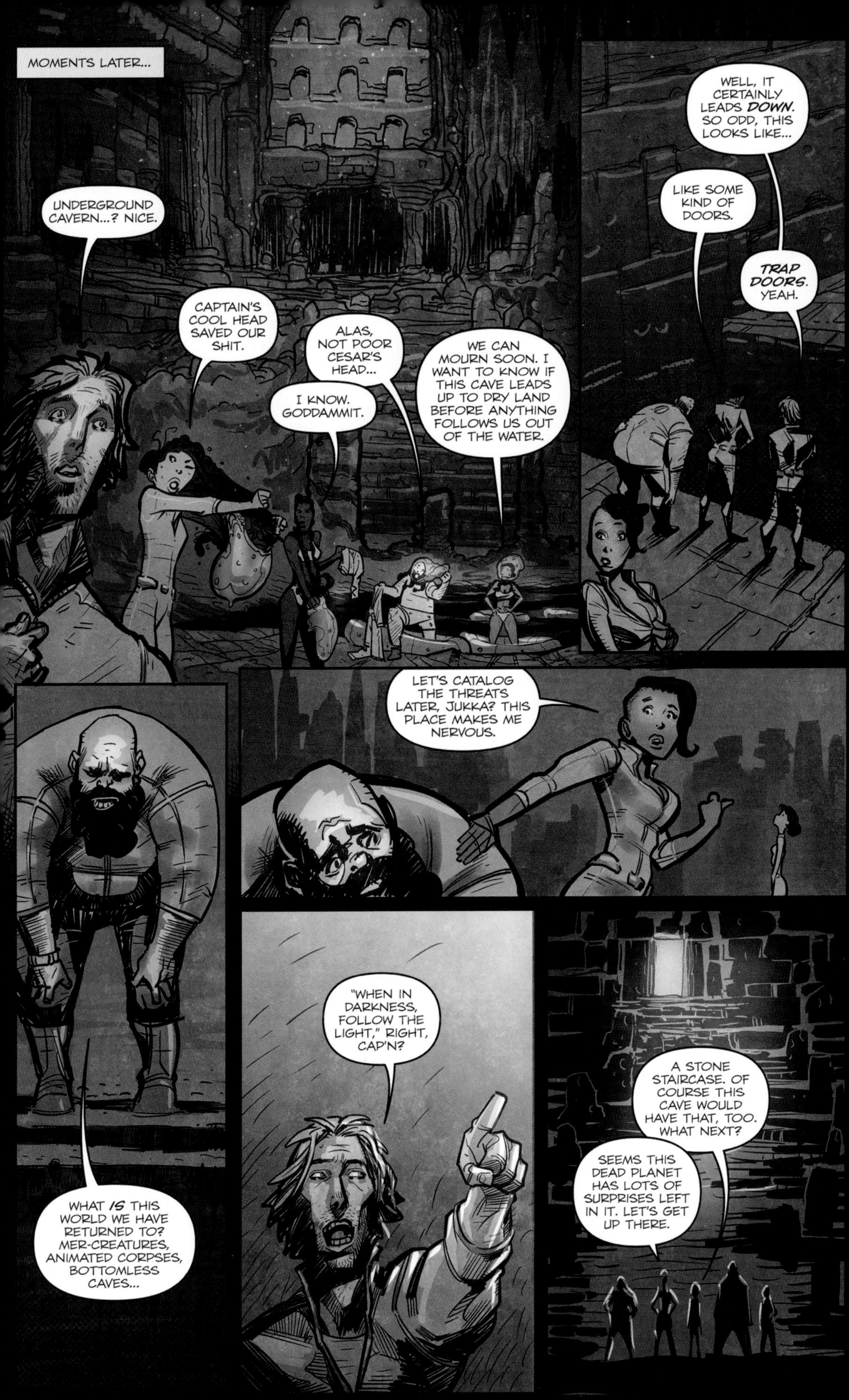
MOMENTS LATER...
UNDERGROUND CAVERN...? NICE.
CAPTAIN'S COOL HEAD SAVED OUR SHIT.
ALAS, NOT POOR CESAR'S HEAD...
I KNOW. GODDAMMIT.
WE CAN MOURN SOON. I WANT TO KNOW IF THIS CAVE LEADS UP TO DRY LAND BEFORE ANYTHING FOLLOWS US OUT OF THE WATER.
WELL, IT CERTAINLY LEADS *DOWN*. SO ODD, THIS LOOKS LIKE...
LIKE SOME KIND OF DOORS.
TRAP DOORS. YEAH.
WHAT *IS* THIS WORLD WE HAVE RETURNED TO? MER-CREATURES, ANIMATED CORPSES, BOTTOMLESS CAVES...
LET'S CATALOG THE THREATS LATER, JUKKA? THIS PLACE MAKES ME NERVOUS.
"WHEN IN DARKNESS, FOLLOW THE LIGHT," RIGHT, CAP'N?
A STONE STAIRCASE. OF COURSE THIS CAVE WOULD HAVE THAT, TOO. WHAT NEXT?
SEEMS THIS DEAD PLANET HAS LOTS OF SURPRISES LEFT IN IT. LET'S GET UP THERE.

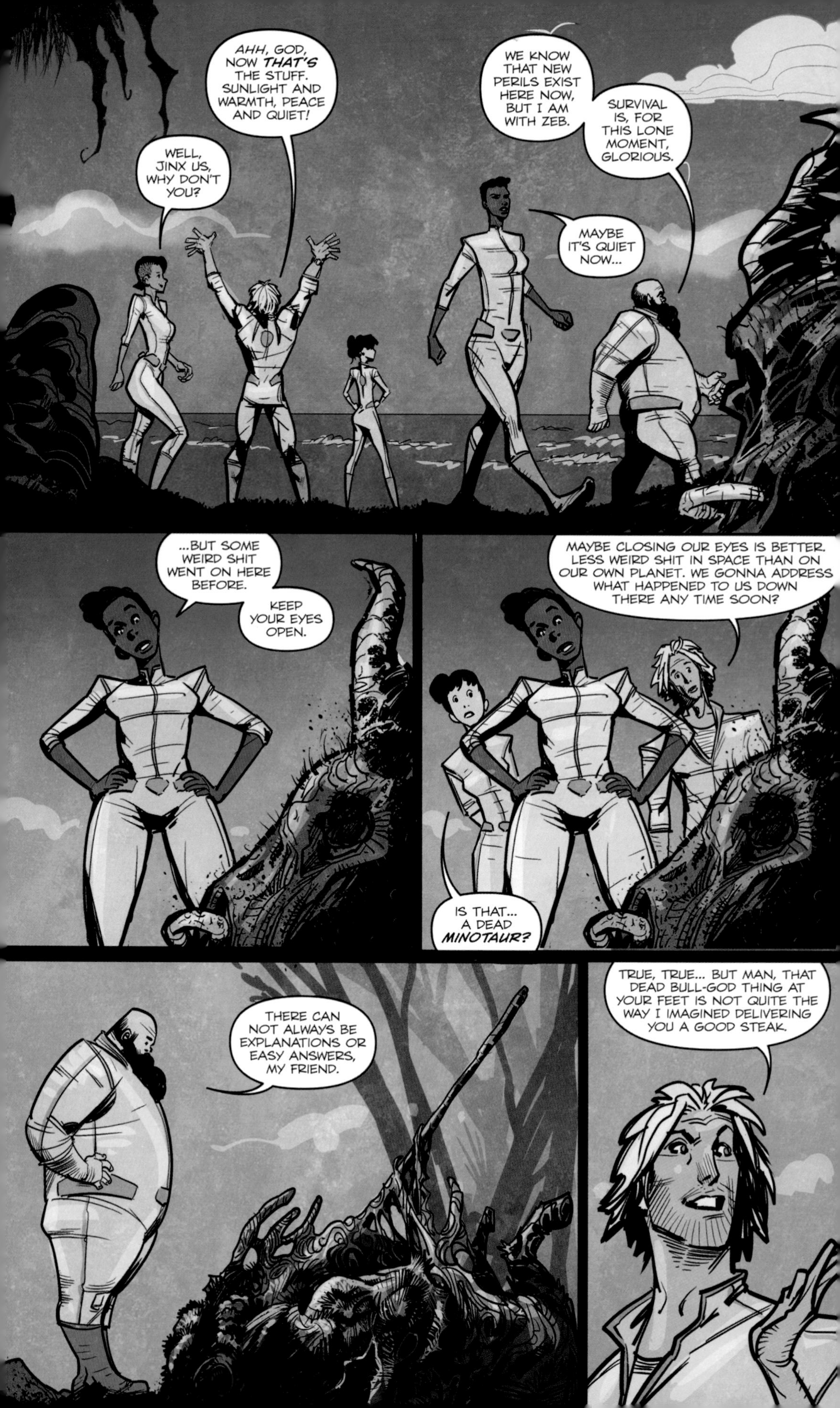
AHH, GOD, NOW THAT'S THE STUFF. SUNLIGHT AND WARMTH, PEACE AND QUIET!
WELL, JINX US, WHY DON'T YOU?
WE KNOW THAT NEW PERILS EXIST HERE NOW, BUT I AM WITH ZEB.
SURVIVAL IS, FOR THIS LONE MOMENT, GLORIOUS.
MAYBE IT'S QUIET NOW...
...BUT SOME WEIRD SHIT WENT ON HERE BEFORE.
KEEP YOUR EYES OPEN.
MAYBE CLOSING OUR EYES IS BETTER. LESS WEIRD SHIT IN SPACE THAN ON OUR OWN PLANET. WE GONNA ADDRESS WHAT HAPPENED TO US DOWN THERE ANY TIME SOON?
IS THAT... A DEAD MINOTAUR?
THERE CAN NOT ALWAYS BE EXPLANATIONS OR EASY ANSWERS, MY FRIEND.
TRUE, TRUE... BUT MAN, THAT DEAD BULL-GOD THING AT YOUR FEET IS NOT QUITE THE WAY I IMAGINED DELIVERING YOU A GOOD STEAK.

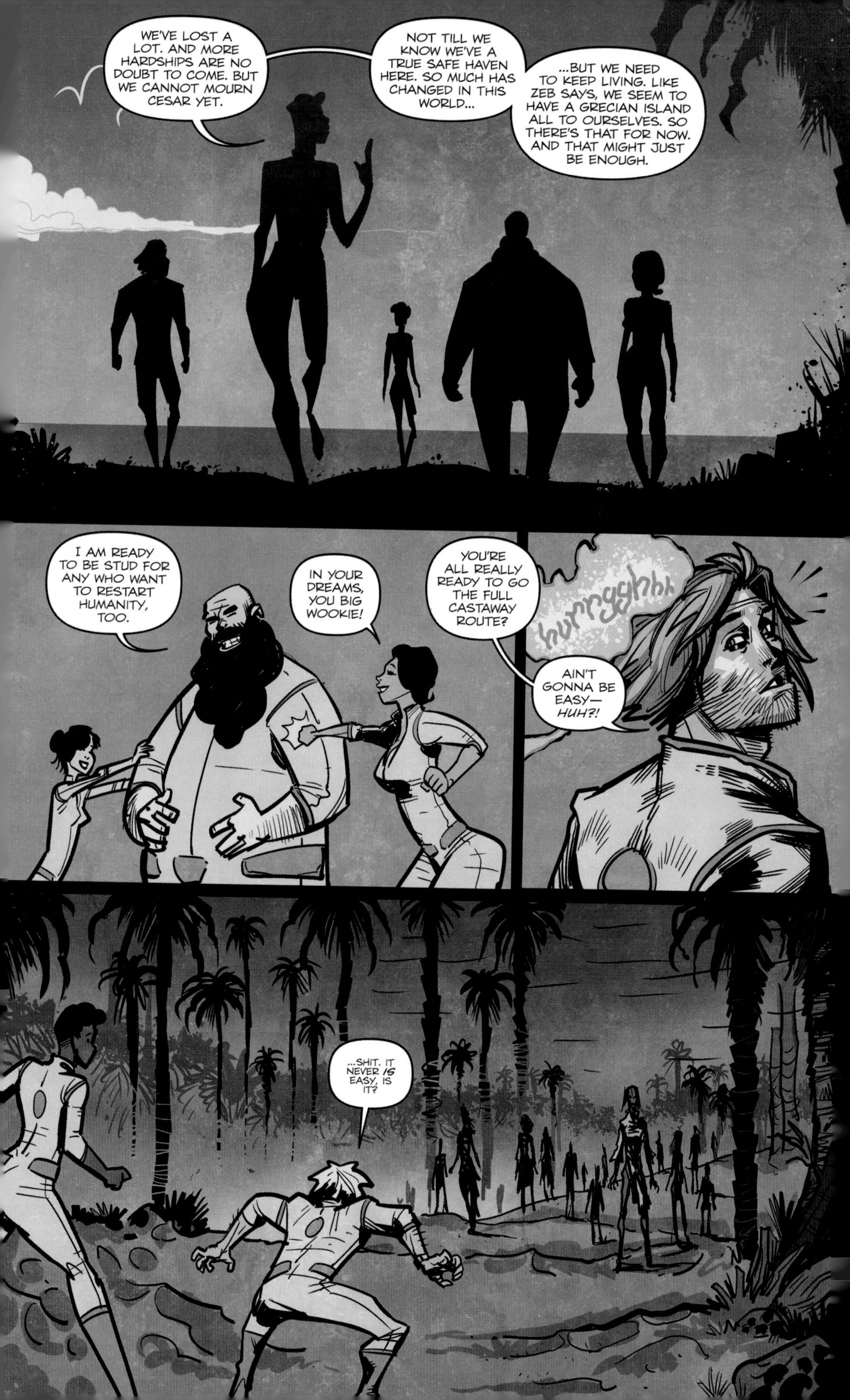
WE'VE LOST A LOT. AND MORE HARDSHIPS ARE NO DOUBT TO COME. BUT WE CANNOT MOURN CESAR YET.
NOT TILL WE KNOW WE'VE A TRUE SAFE HAVEN HERE. SO MUCH HAS CHANGED IN THIS WORLD...
...BUT WE NEED TO KEEP LIVING. LIKE ZEB SAYS, WE SEEM TO HAVE A GRECIAN ISLAND ALL TO OURSELVES. SO THERE'S THAT FOR NOW. AND THAT MIGHT JUST BE ENOUGH.
I AM READY TO BE STUD FOR ANY WHO WANT TO RESTART HUMANITY, TOO.
IN YOUR DREAMS, YOU BIG WOOKIE!
YOU'RE ALL REALLY READY TO GO THE FULL CASTAWAY ROUTE?
AIN'T GONNA BE EASY— HUH?!
...SHIT. IT NEVER IS EASY, IS IT?

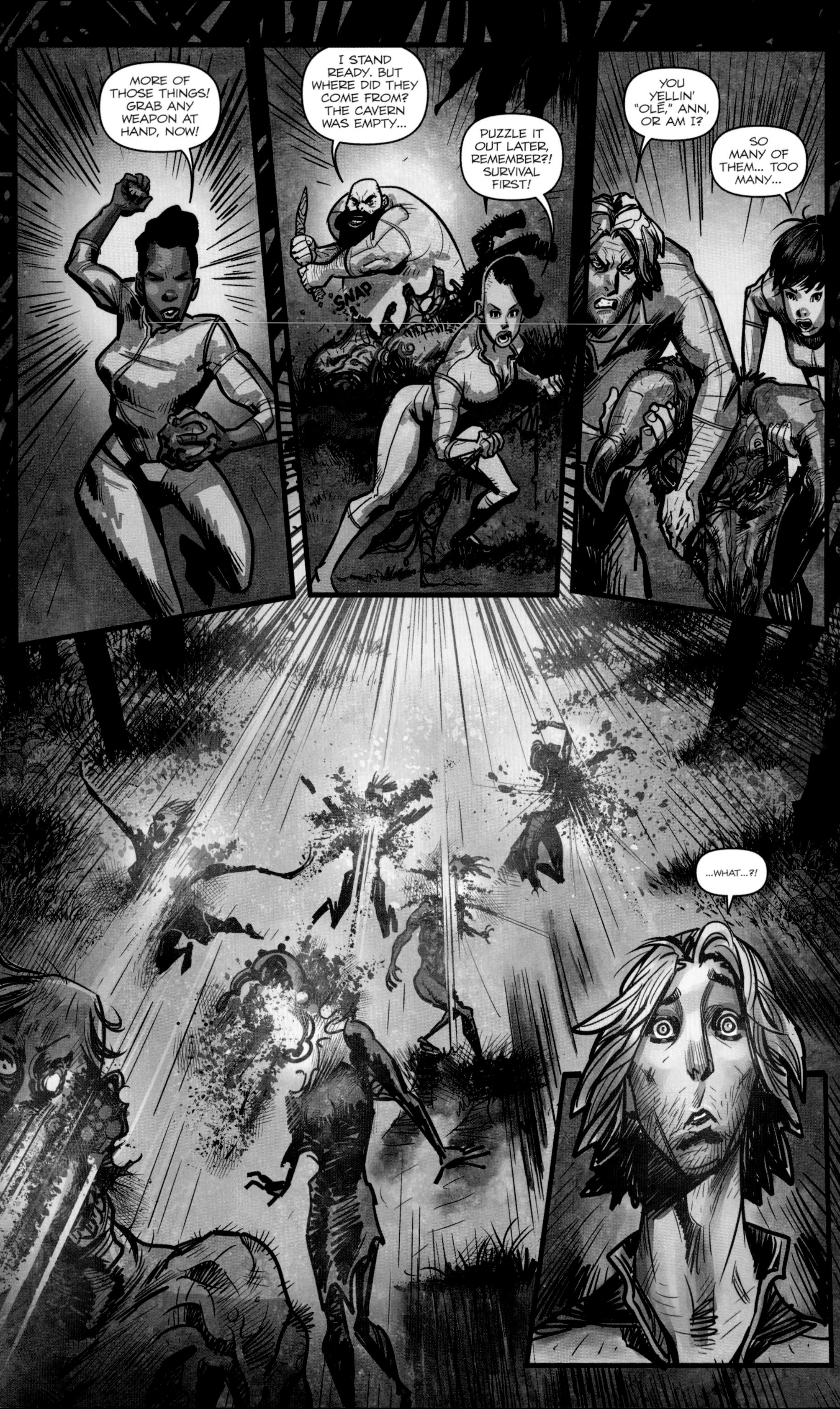

MORE OF THOSE THINGS! GRAB ANY WEAPON AT HAND, NOW!
I STAND READY. BUT WHERE DID THEY COME FROM? THE CAVERN WAS EMPTY...
SNAP
PUZZLE IT OUT LATER, REMEMBER?! SURVIVAL FIRST!
YOU YELLIN' "OLÉ," ANN, OR AM I?
SO MANY OF THEM... TOO MANY...
...WHAT...?!

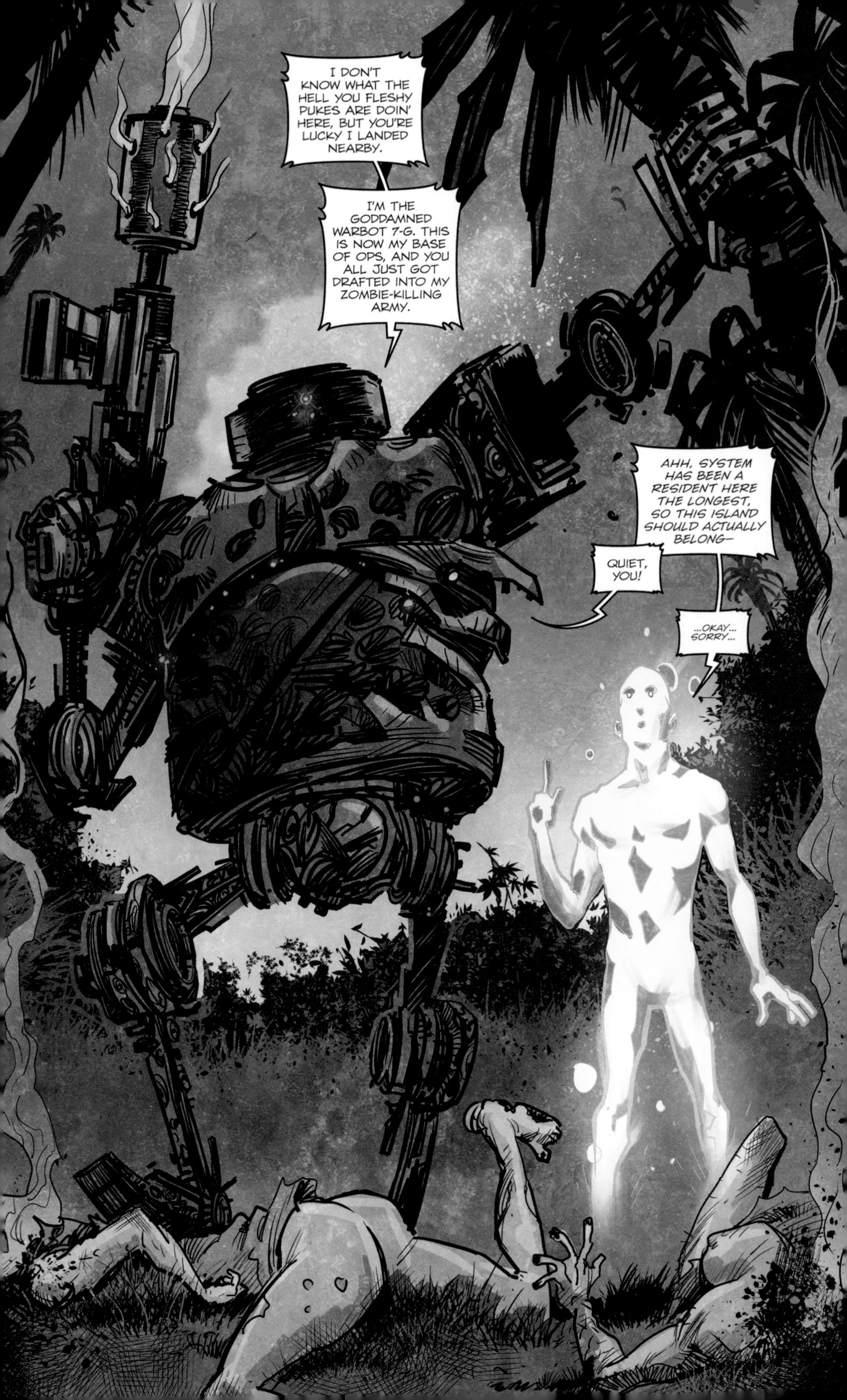
I DON'T KNOW WHAT THE HELL YOU FLESHY PUKES ARE DOIN' HERE, BUT YOU'RE LUCKY I LANDED NEARBY.
I'M THE GODDAMNED WARBOT 7-G. THIS IS NOW MY BASE OF OPS, AND YOU ALL JUST GOT DRAFTED INTO MY ZOMBIE-KILLING ARMY.
AHH, SYSTEM HAS BEEN A RESIDENT HERE THE LONGEST, SO THIS ISLAND SHOULD ACTUALLY BELONG—
QUIET, YOU!
...OKAY... SORRY...

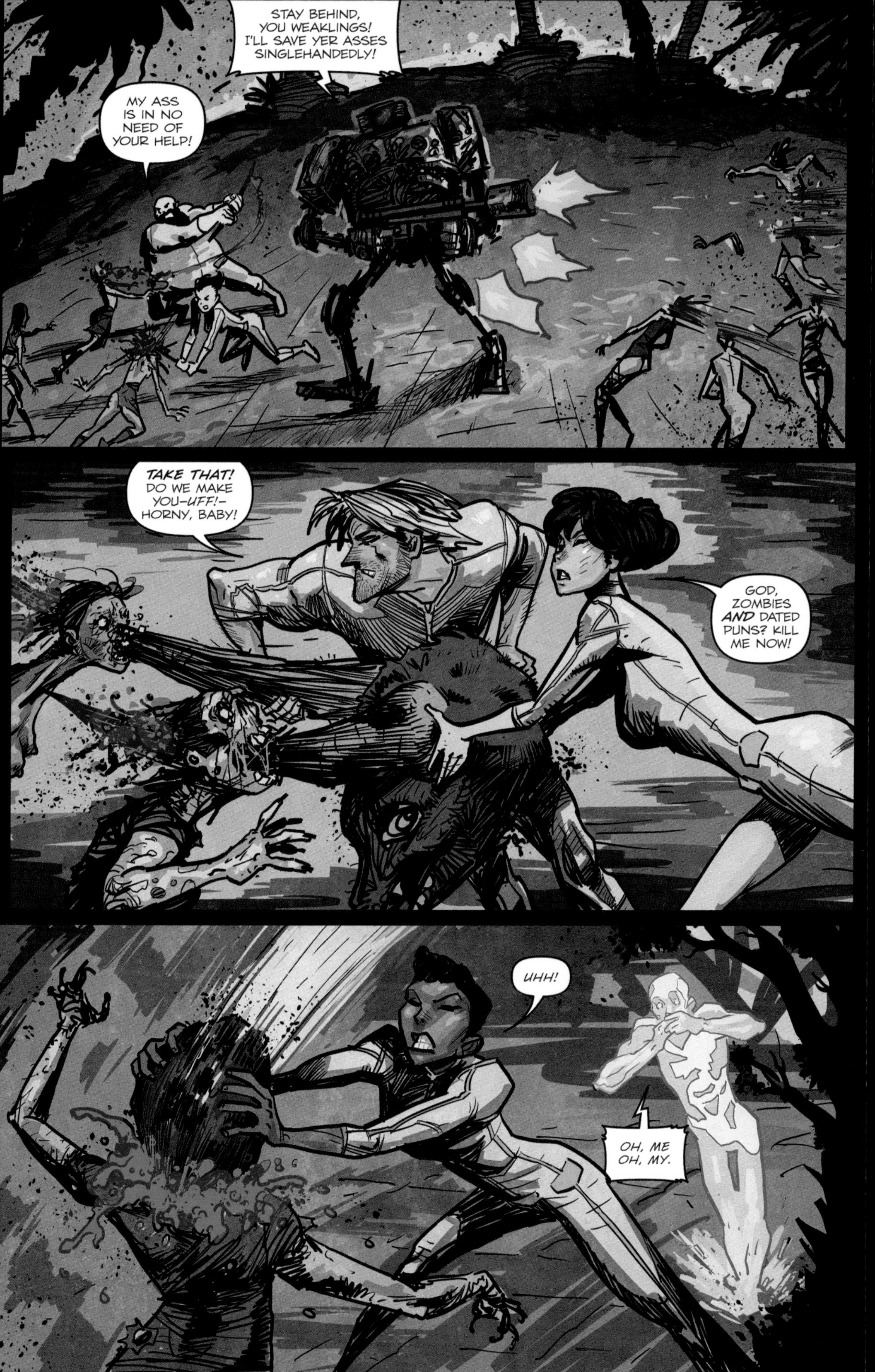
STAY BEHIND, YOU WEAKLINGS! I'LL SAVE YER ASSES SINGLEHANDEDLY!
MY ASS IS IN NO NEED OF YOUR HELP!
TAKE THAT! DO WE MAKE YOU–UFF!– HORNY, BABY!
GOD, ZOMBIES AND DATED PUNS? KILL ME NOW!
UHH!
OH, ME OH, MY.

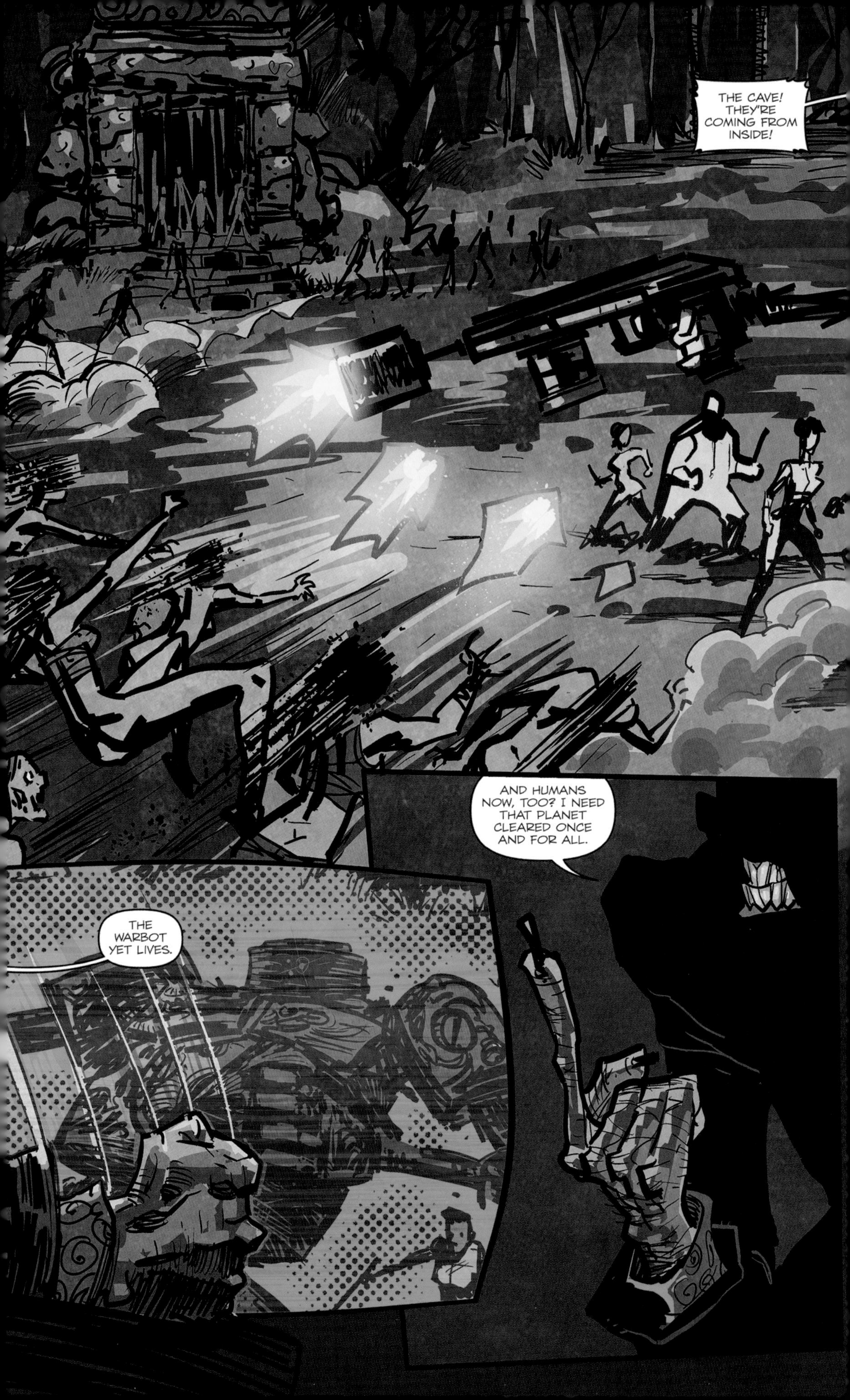
THE CAVE! THEY'RE COMING FROM INSIDE!
AND HUMANS NOW, TOO? I NEED THAT PLANET CLEARED ONCE AND FOR ALL.
THE WARBOT YET LIVES.

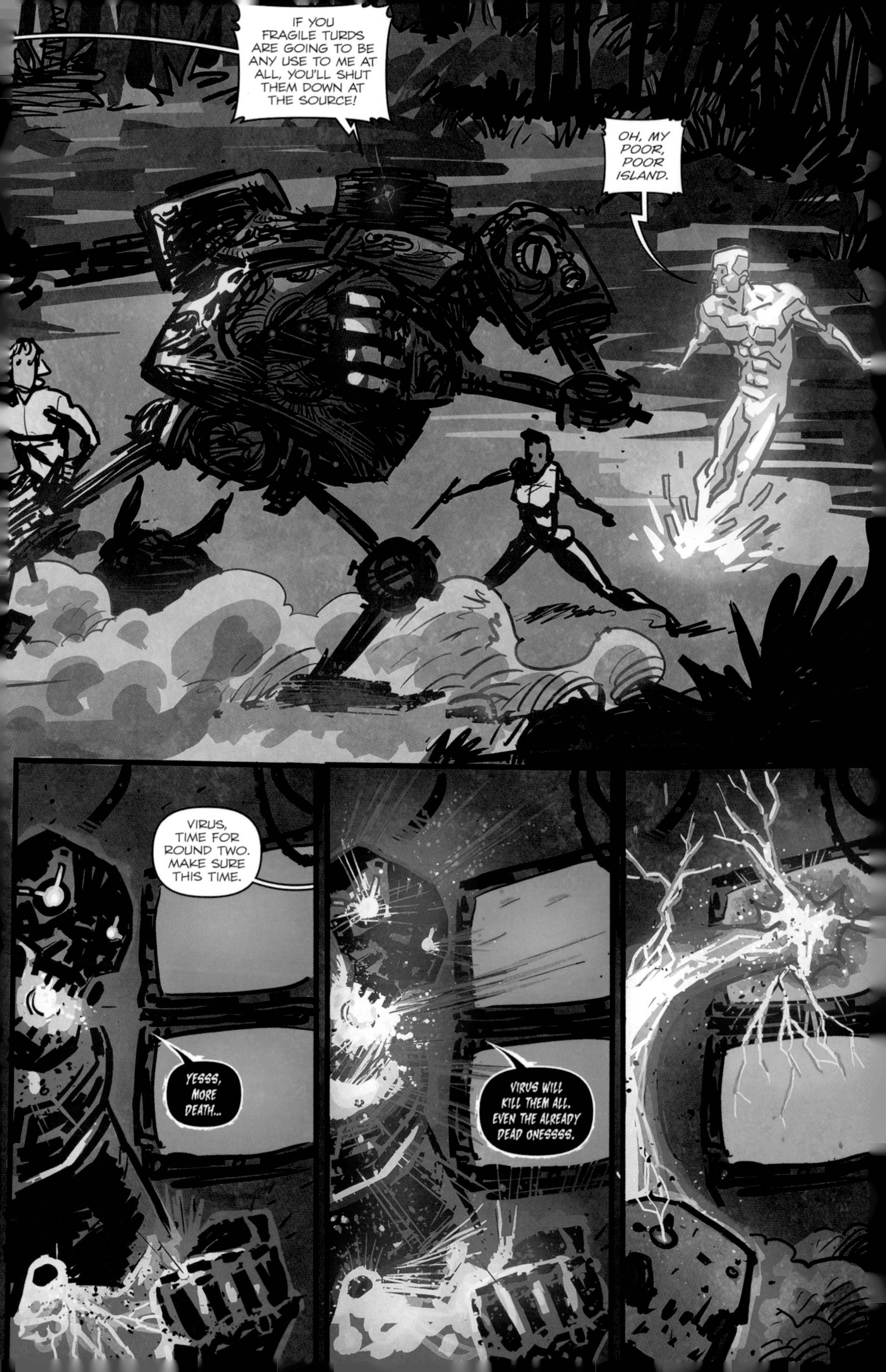
IF YOU FRAGILE TURDS ARE GOING TO BE ANY USE TO ME AT ALL, YOU'LL SHUT THEM DOWN AT THE SOURCE!
OH, MY POOR, POOR ISLAND.
VIRUS, TIME FOR ROUND TWO. MAKE SURE THIS TIME.
YESSS, MORE DEATH...
VIRUS WILL KILL THEM ALL. EVEN THE ALREADY DEAD ONESSSS.

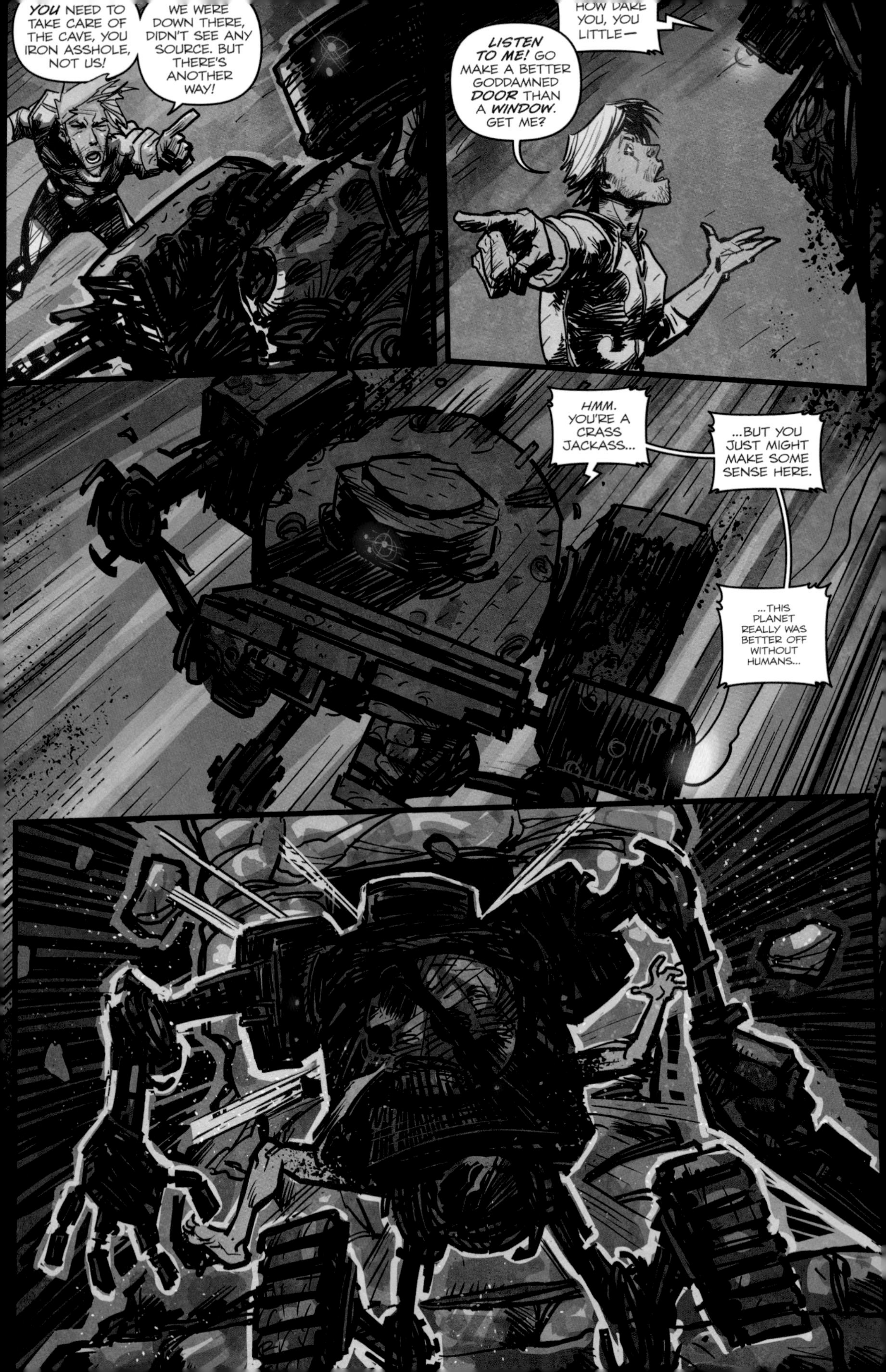
YOU NEED TO TAKE CARE OF THE CAVE, YOU IRON ASSHOLE, NOT US!
WE WERE DOWN THERE, DIDN'T SEE ANY SOURCE. BUT THERE'S ANOTHER WAY!
HOW DARE YOU, YOU LITTLE—
LISTEN TO ME! GO MAKE A BETTER GODDAMNED DOOR THAN A WINDOW. GET ME?
HMM. YOU'RE A CRASS JACKASS...
...BUT YOU JUST MIGHT MAKE SOME SENSE HERE.
...THIS PLANET REALLY WAS BETTER OFF WITHOUT HUMANS...

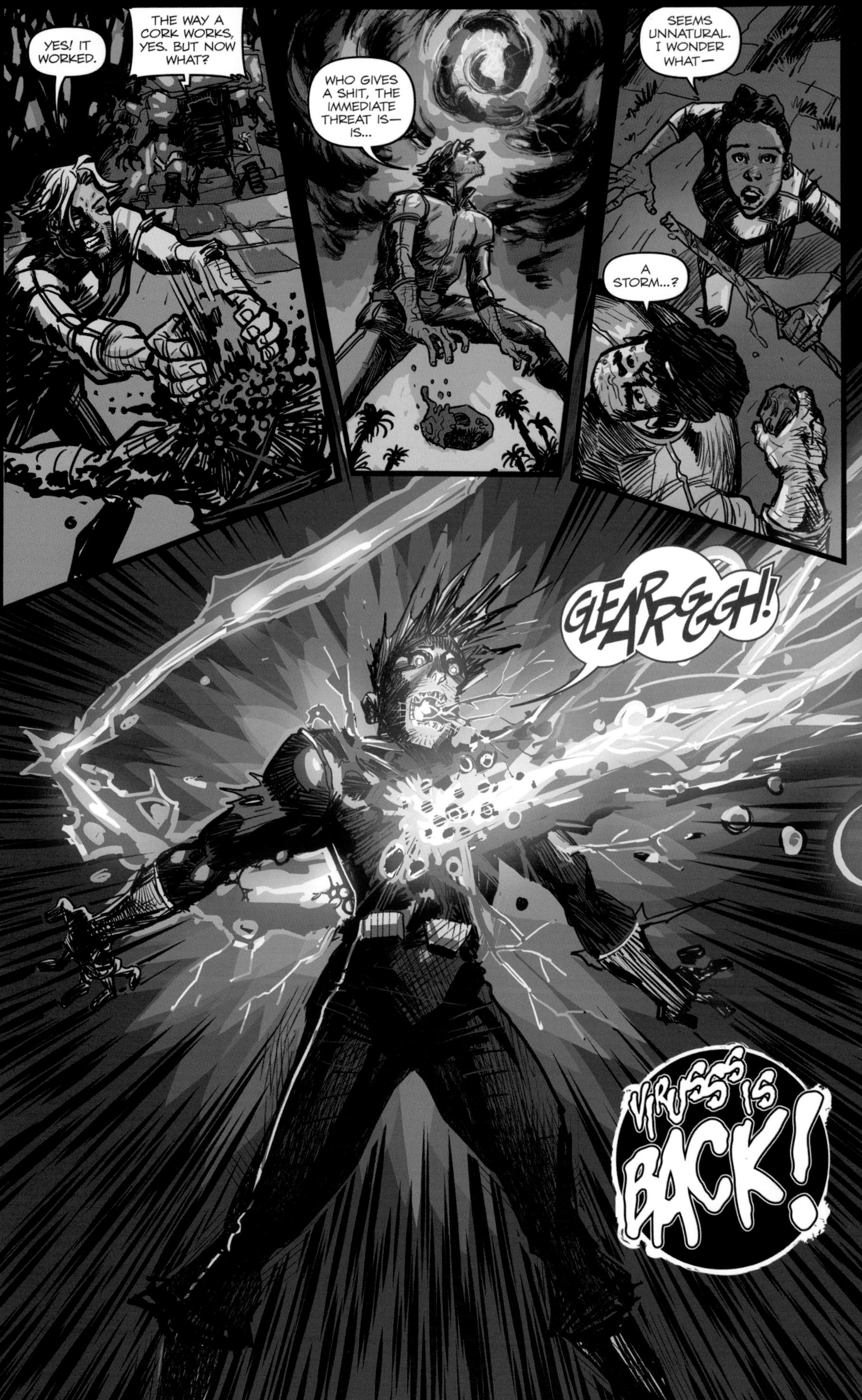
YES! IT WORKED.
THE WAY A CORK WORKS, YES. BUT NOW WHAT?
WHO GIVES A SHIT, THE IMMEDIATE THREAT IS— IS...
SEEMS UNNATURAL. I WONDER WHAT—
A STORM...?
GLEARRGGH!
VIRUSSS IS BACK!

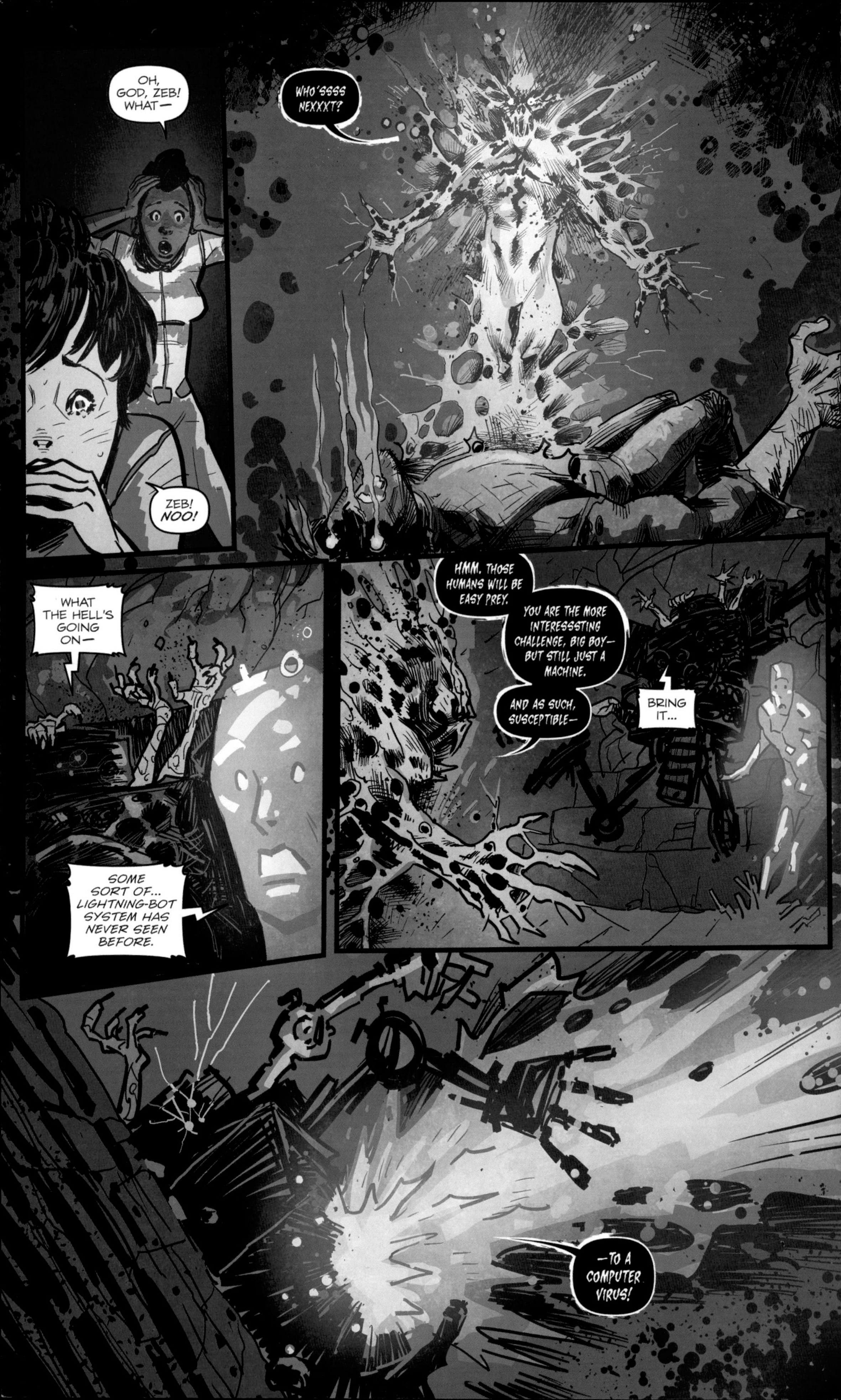

OH, GOD, ZEB! WHAT—
WHO'SSSS NEXXXT?
ZEB! NOO!
WHAT THE HELL'S GOING ON—
SOME SORT OF... LIGHTNING-BOT SYSTEM HAS NEVER SEEN BEFORE.
HMM. THOSE HUMANS WILL BE EASY PREY.
YOU ARE THE MORE INTERESSSTING CHALLENGE, BIG BOY— BUT STILL JUST A MACHINE.
AND AS SUCH, SUSCEPTIBLE—
BRING IT...
—TO A COMPUTER VIRUS!

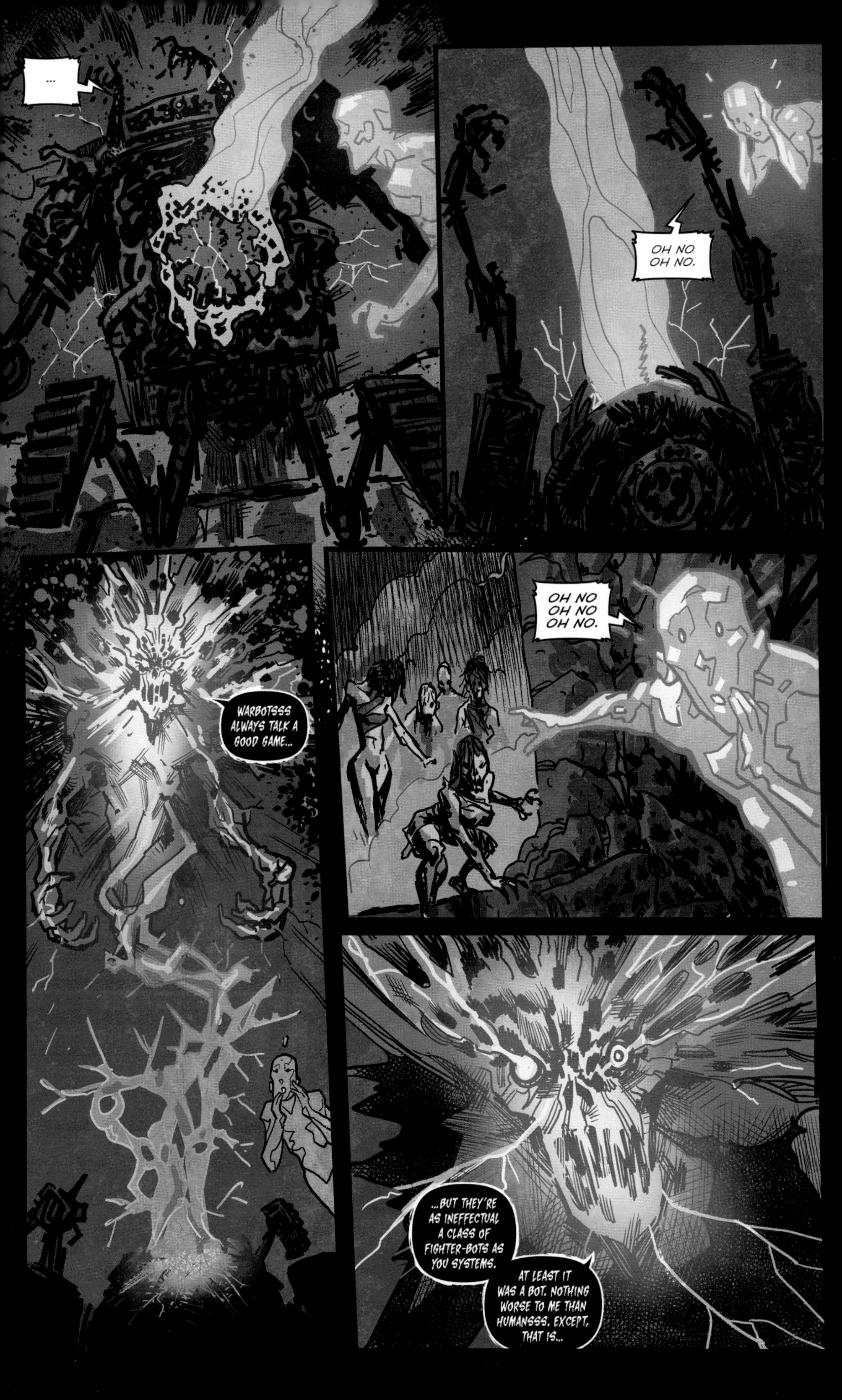
...
OH NO OH NO.
WARBOTSSS ALWAYS TALK A GOOD GAME...
OH NO OH NO OH NO.
...BUT THEY'RE AS INEFFECTUAL A CLASS OF FIGHTER-BOTS AS YOU SYSTEMS.
AT LEAST IT WAS A BOT. NOTHING WORSE TO ME THAN HUMANSSS. EXCEPT, THAT IS...

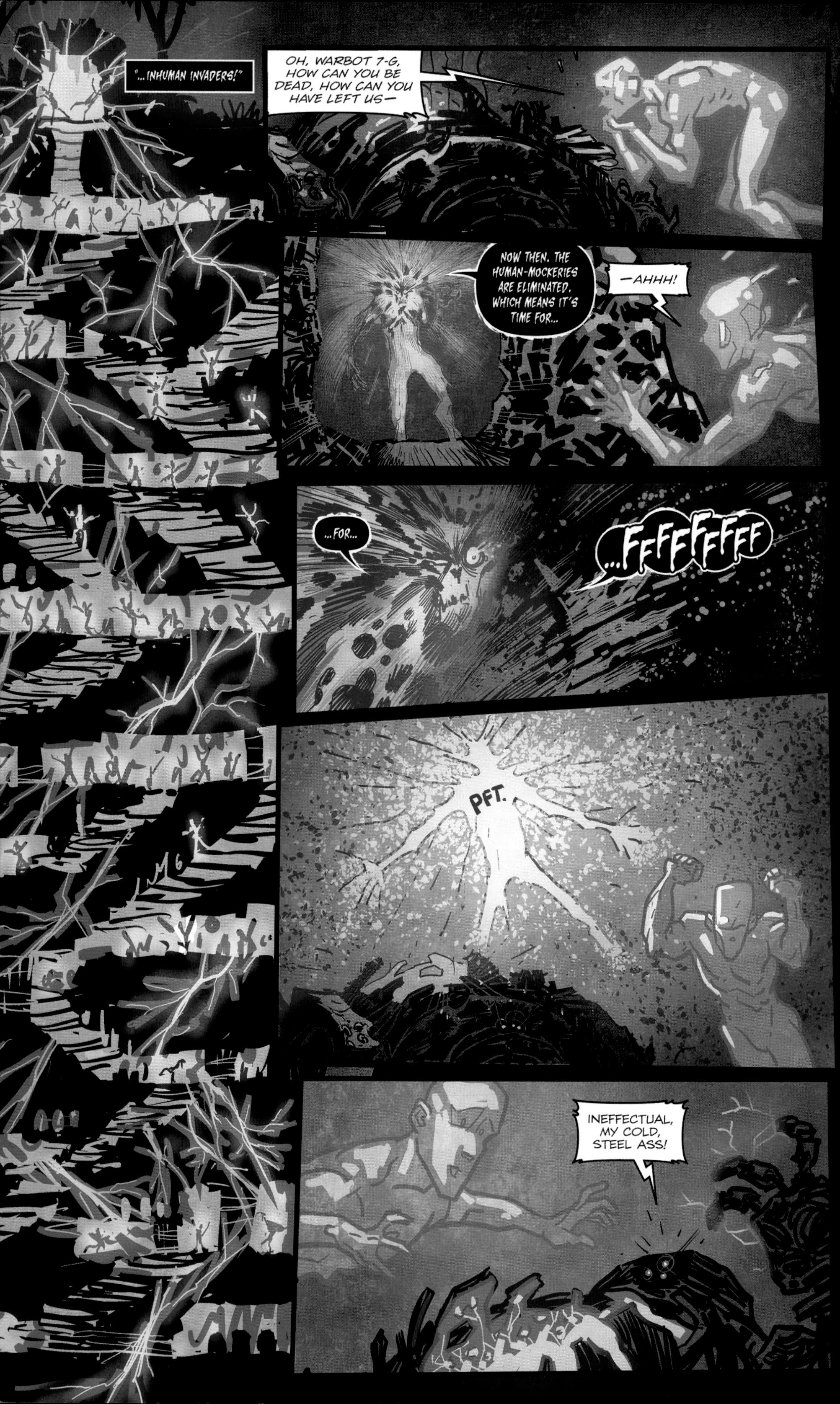
"...INHUMAN INVADERS!"
OH, WARBOT 7-G, HOW CAN YOU BE DEAD, HOW CAN YOU HAVE LEFT US—
NOW THEN. THE HUMAN-MOCKERIES ARE ELIMINATED. WHICH MEANS IT'S TIME FOR...
—AHHH!
...FOR...
...FFFFFFFF
PFT.
INEFFECTUAL, MY COLD, STEEL ASS!

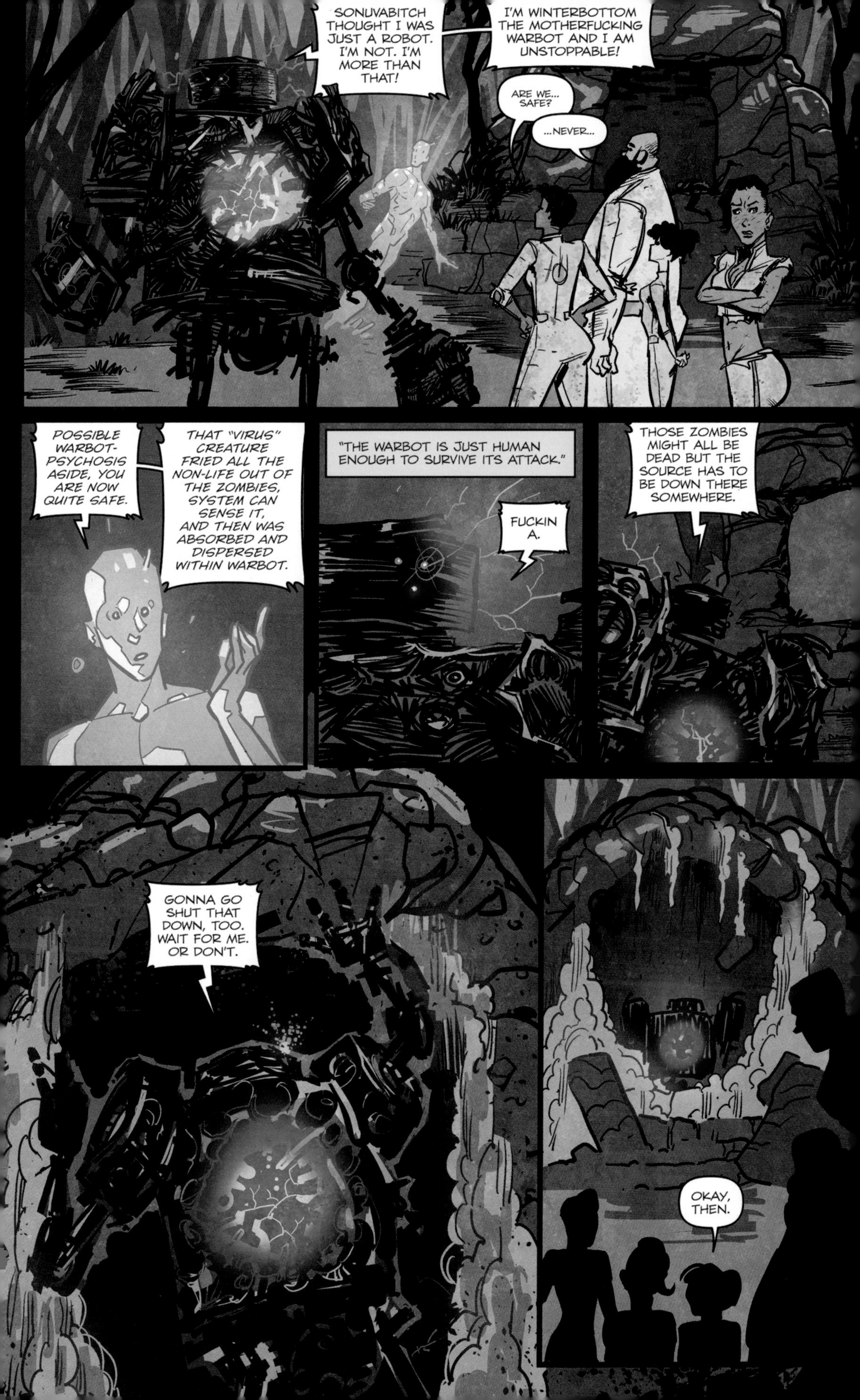
SONUVABITCH THOUGHT I WAS JUST A ROBOT. I'M NOT. I'M MORE THAN THAT!
I'M WINTERBOTTOM THE MOTHERFUCKING WARBOT AND I AM UNSTOPPABLE!
ARE WE... SAFE?
...NEVER...
POSSIBLE WARBOT-PSYCHOSIS ASIDE, YOU ARE NOW QUITE SAFE.
THAT "VIRUS" CREATURE FRIED ALL THE NON-LIFE OUT OF THE ZOMBIES, SYSTEM CAN SENSE IT, AND THEN WAS ABSORBED AND DISPERSED WITHIN WARBOT.
"THE WARBOT IS JUST HUMAN ENOUGH TO SURVIVE ITS ATTACK."
FUCKIN A.
THOSE ZOMBIES MIGHT ALL BE DEAD BUT THE SOURCE HAS TO BE DOWN THERE SOMEWHERE.
GONNA GO SHUT THAT DOWN, TOO. WAIT FOR ME. OR DON'T.
OKAY, THEN.

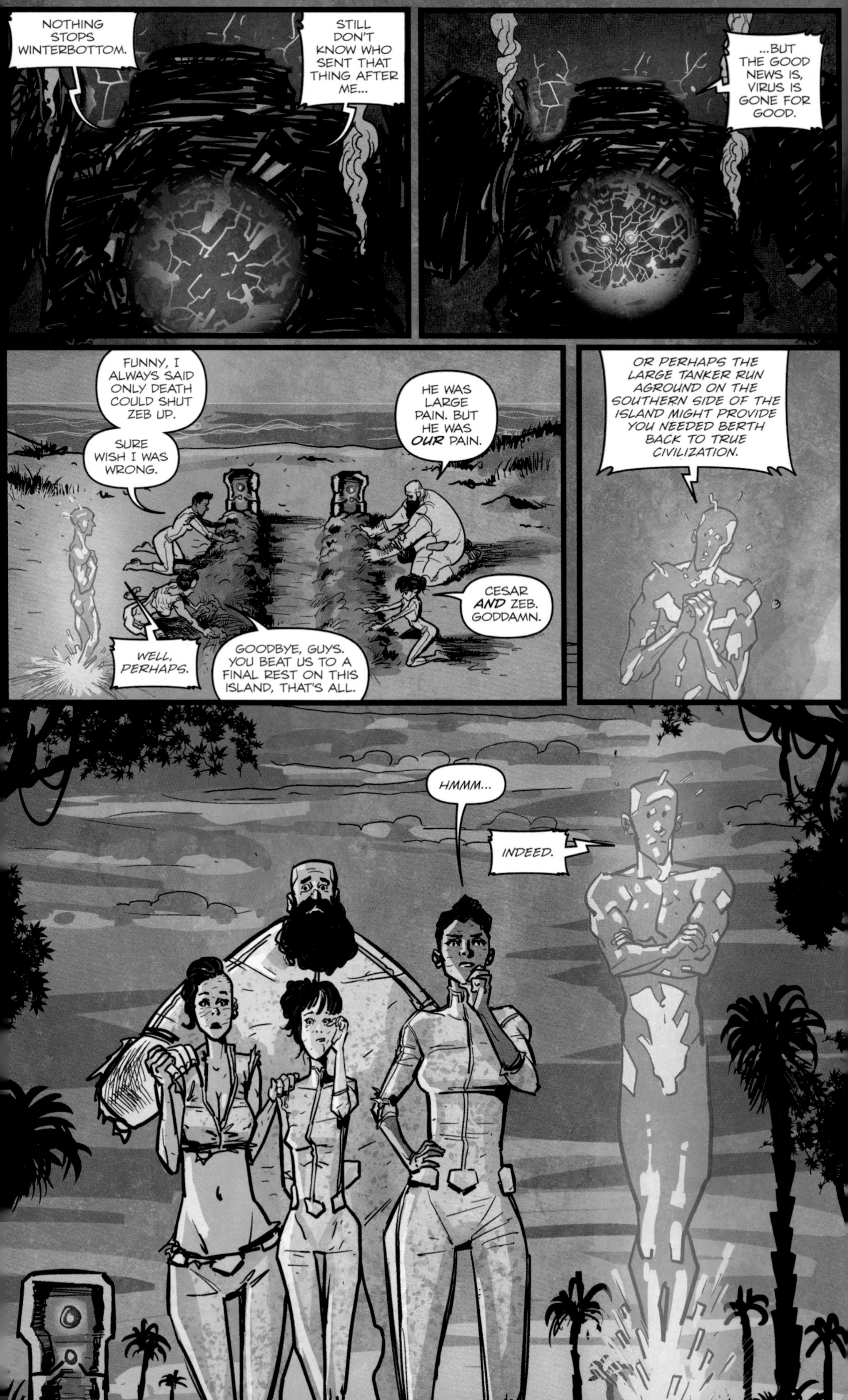
NOTHING STOPS WINTERBOTTOM.
STILL DON'T KNOW WHO SENT THAT THING AFTER ME...
...BUT THE GOOD NEWS IS, VIRUS IS GONE FOR GOOD.
FUNNY, I ALWAYS SAID ONLY DEATH COULD SHUT ZEB UP.
SURE WISH I WAS WRONG.
HE WAS LARGE PAIN. BUT HE WAS OUR PAIN.
CESAR AND ZEB. GODDAMN.
WELL, PERHAPS.
GOODBYE, GUYS. YOU BEAT US TO A FINAL REST ON THIS ISLAND, THAT'S ALL.
OR PERHAPS THE LARGE TANKER RUN AGROUND ON THE SOUTHERN SIDE OF THE ISLAND MIGHT PROVIDE YOU NEEDED BERTH BACK TO TRUE CIVILIZATION.
HMMM...
INDEED.

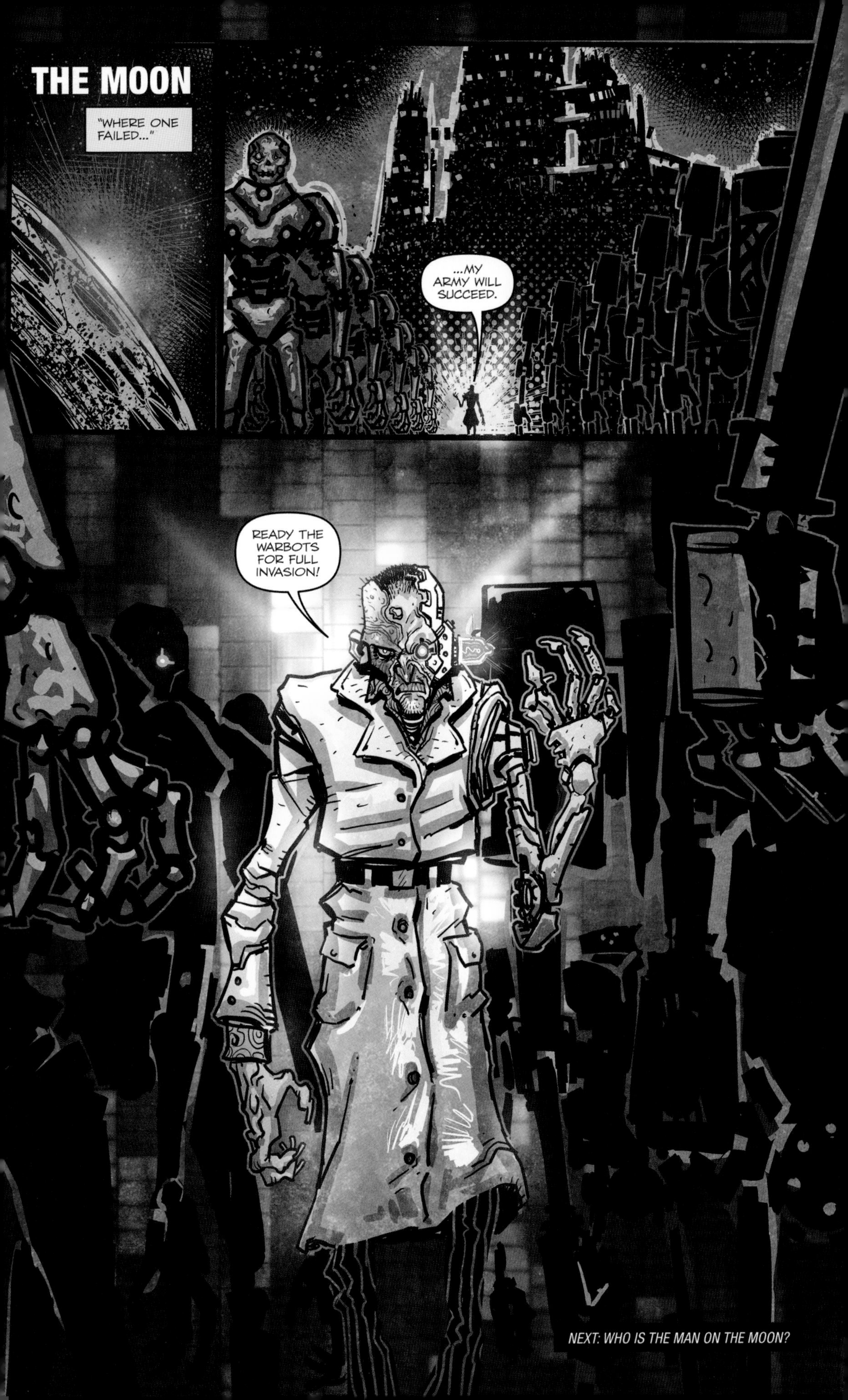
THE MOON
"WHERE ONE FAILED..."
...MY ARMY WILL SUCCEED.
READY THE WARBOTS FOR FULL INVASION!
NEXT: WHO IS THE MAN ON THE MOON?

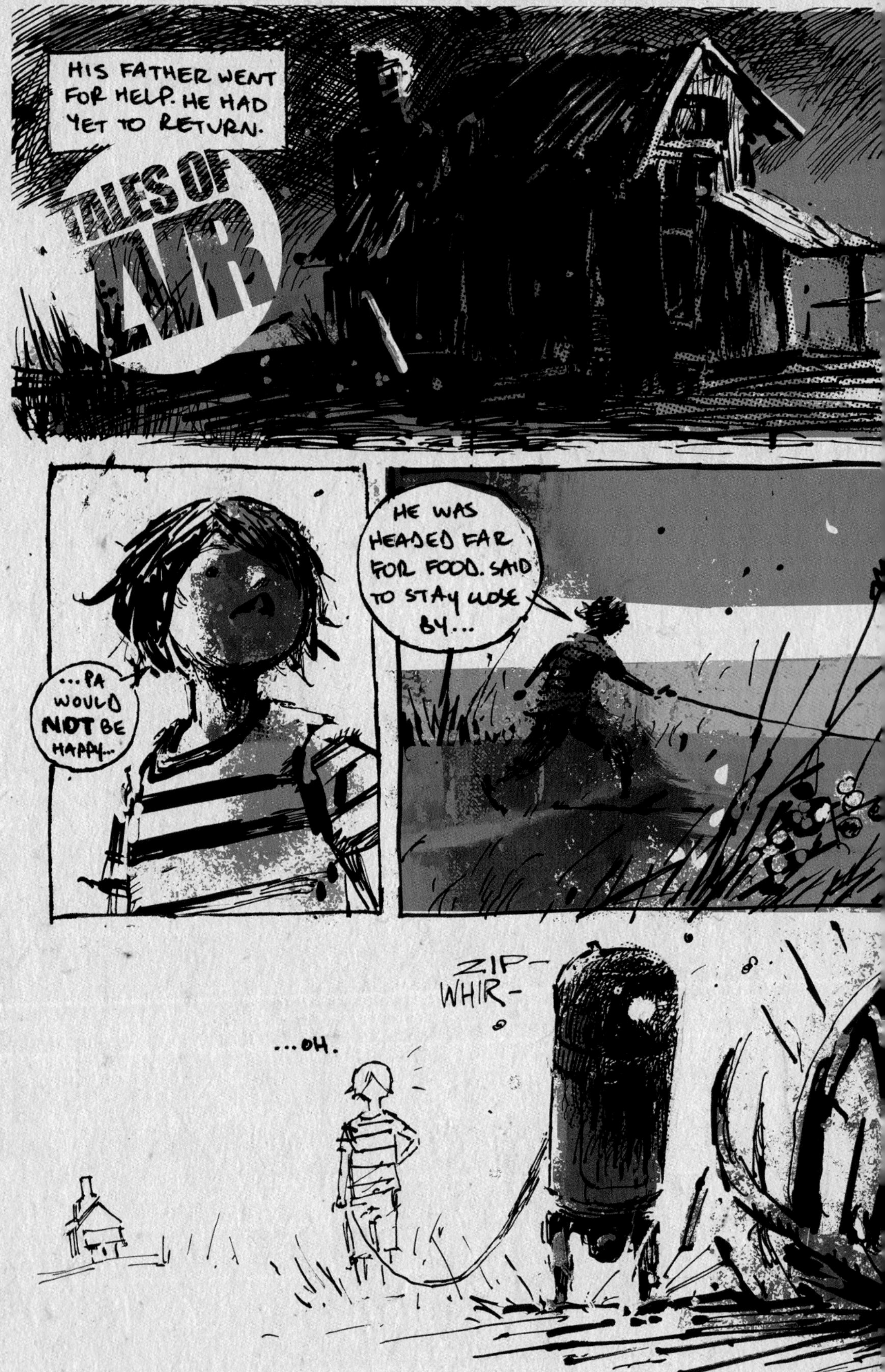
HIS FATHER WENT FOR HELP. HE HAD YET TO RETURN.
TALES OF AIR
...PA WOULD NOT BE HAPPY...
HE WAS HEADED FAR FOR FOOD. SAID TO STAY CLOSE BY...
ZIP-
WHIR-
...OH.

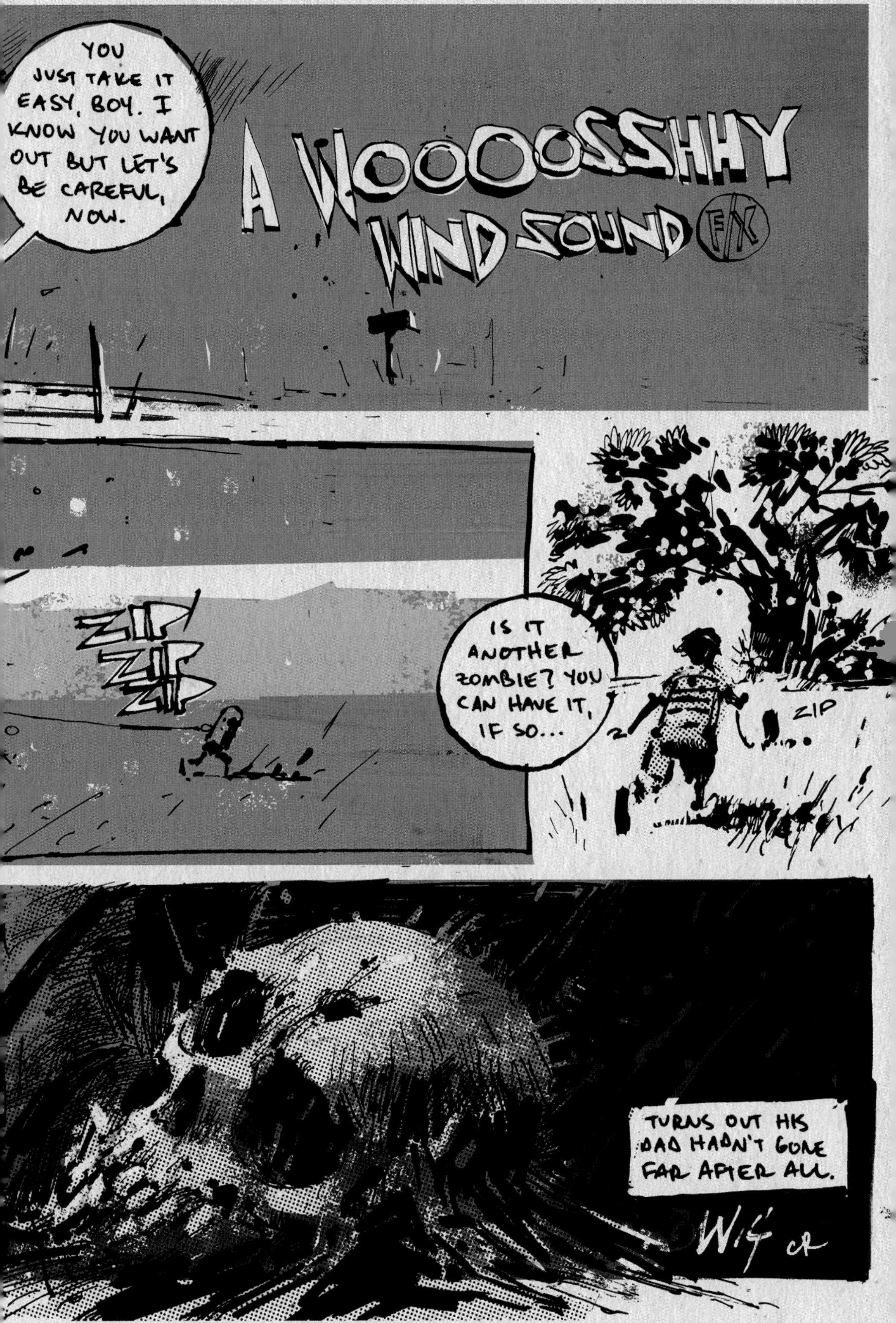
YOU JUST TAKE IT EASY, BOY. I KNOW YOU WANT OUT BUT LET'S BE CAREFUL, NOW.
A WOOOOSSHHY WIND SOUND F/X
ZIP ZIP ZIP
IS IT ANOTHER ZOMBIE? YOU CAN HAVE IT, IF SO...
ZIP
TURNS OUT HIS DAD HADN'T GONE FAR AFTER ALL.

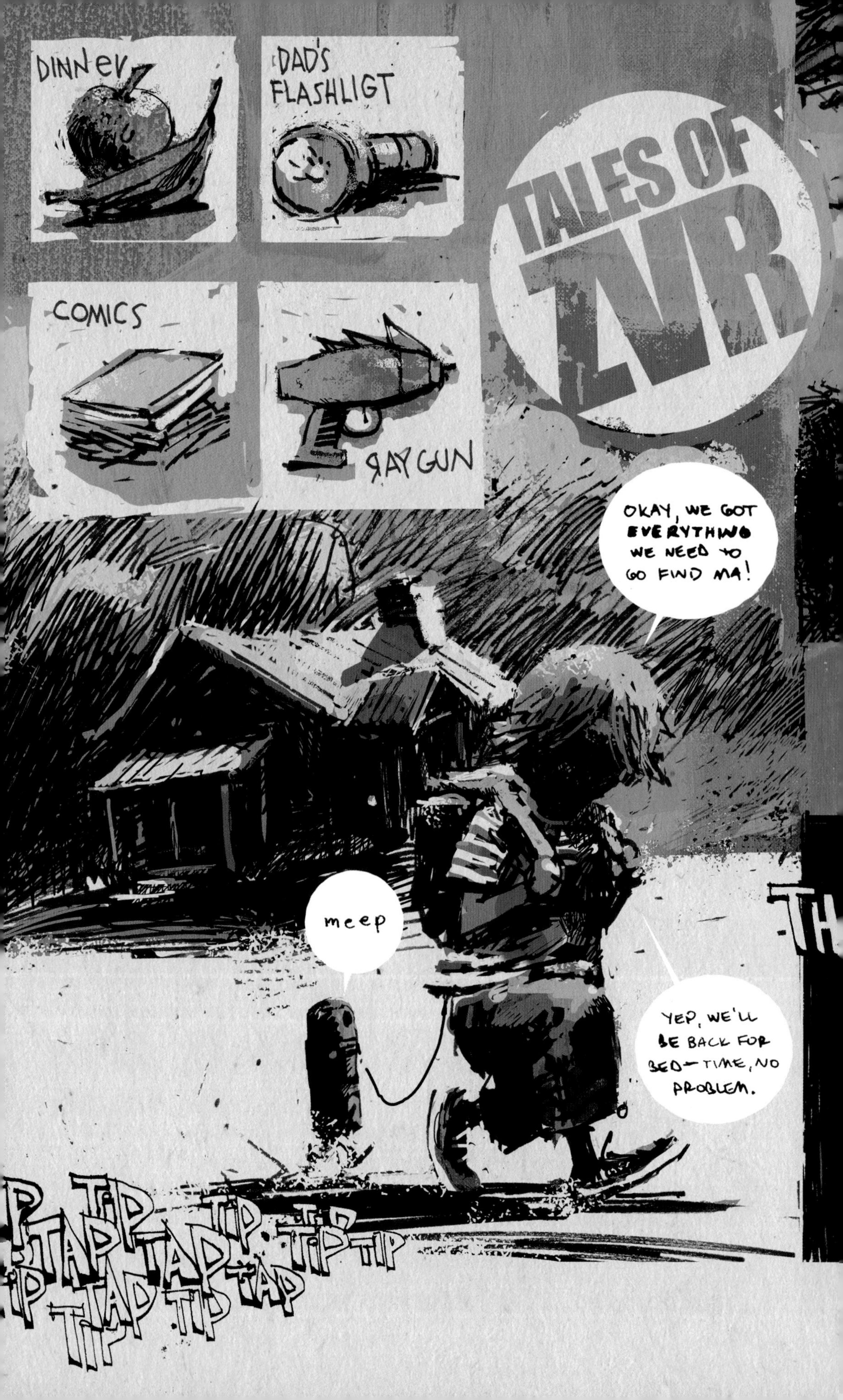
DINNer
DAD'S FLASHLIGT
COMICS
RAYGUN
TALES OF ZVR
OKAY, WE GOT EVERYTHING WE NEED TO GO FIND MA!
meep
YEP, WE'LL BE BACK FOR BED-TIME, NO PROBLEM.
TIP TAP TIP TAP TIP TAP TIP TIP TIP TAP TIP TAP

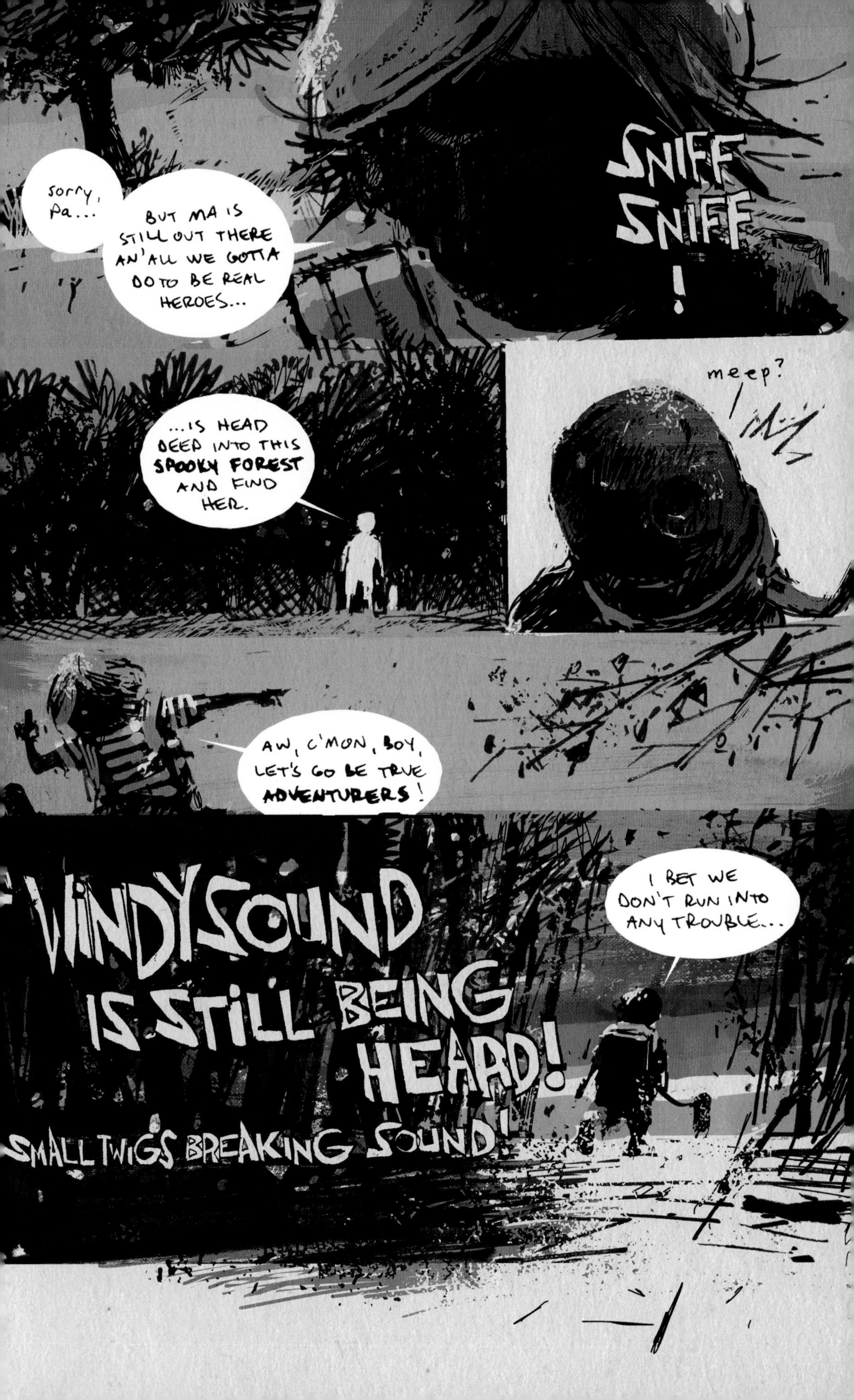
sorry, pa...
BUT MA IS STILL OUT THERE AN'ALL WE GOTTA DO TO BE REAL HEROES...
SNIFF SNIFF!
...IS HEAD DEEP INTO THIS SPOOKY FOREST AND FIND HER.
meep?
AW, C'MON, BOY, LET'S GO BE TRUE ADVENTURERS!
WINDY SOUND IS STILL BEING HEARD!
SMALL TWIGS BREAKING SOUND!
I BET WE DON'T RUN INTO ANY TROUBLE...

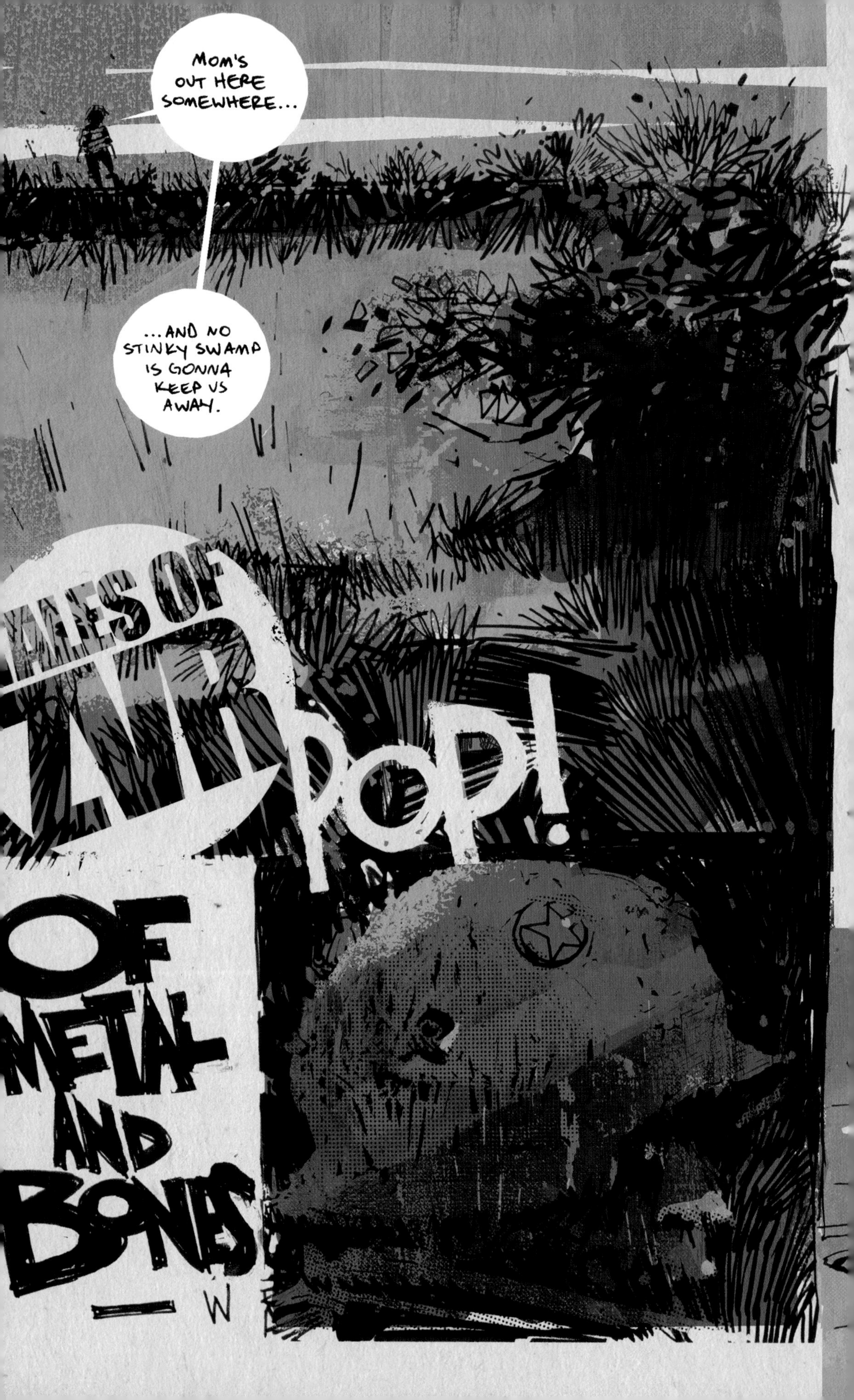
MOM'S OUT HERE SOMEWHERE...
...AND NO STINKY SWAMP IS GONNA KEEP US AWAY.
POP!
OF METAL AND BONES

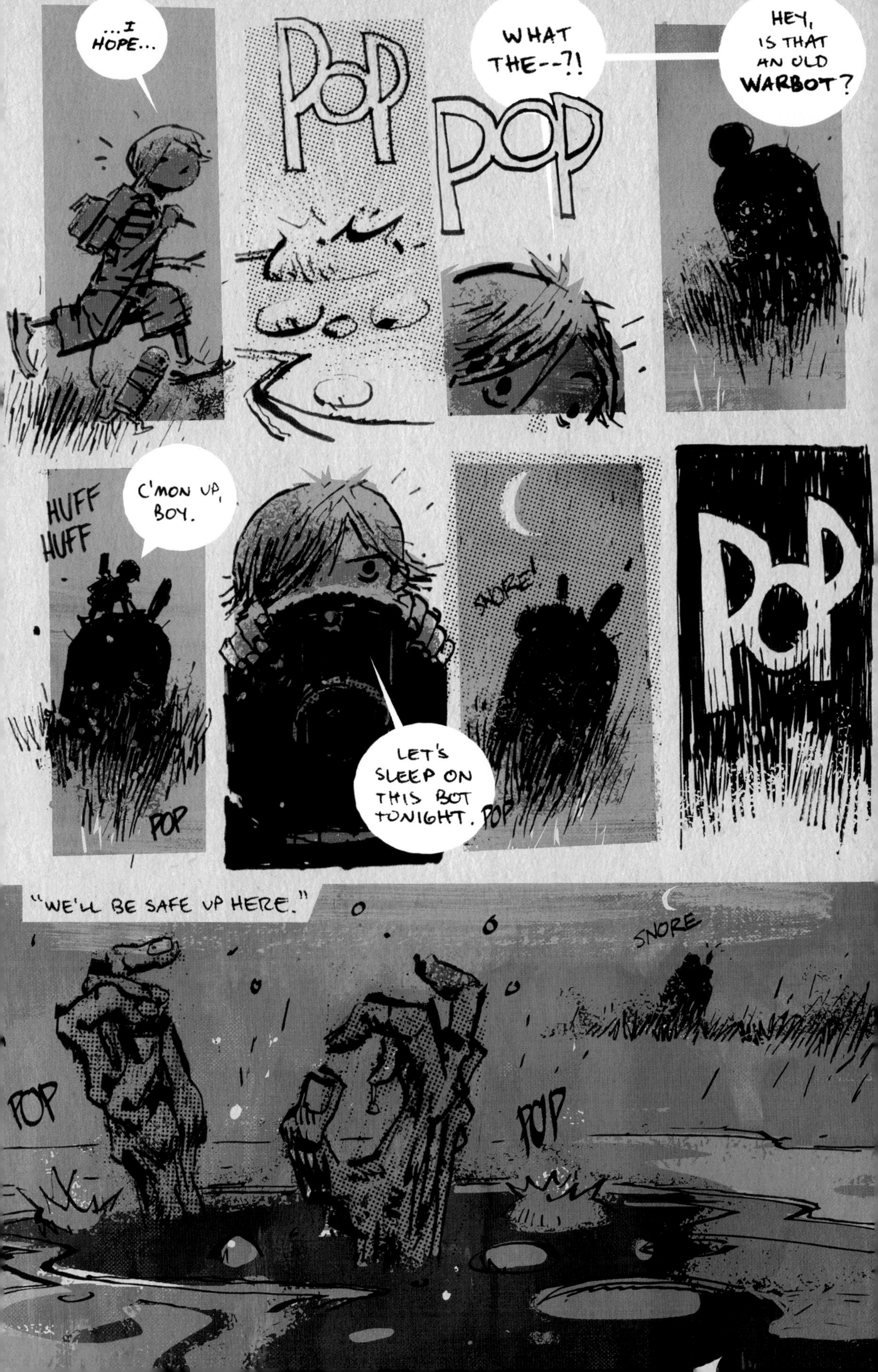
...I HOPE...
POP
WHAT THE--?!
POP
HEY, IS THAT AN OLD WARBOT?
HUFF HUFF
C'MON UP, BOY.
POP
LET'S SLEEP ON THIS BOT TONIGHT.
SNORE!
POP
POP
"WE'LL BE SAFE UP HERE."
SNORE
POP
POP

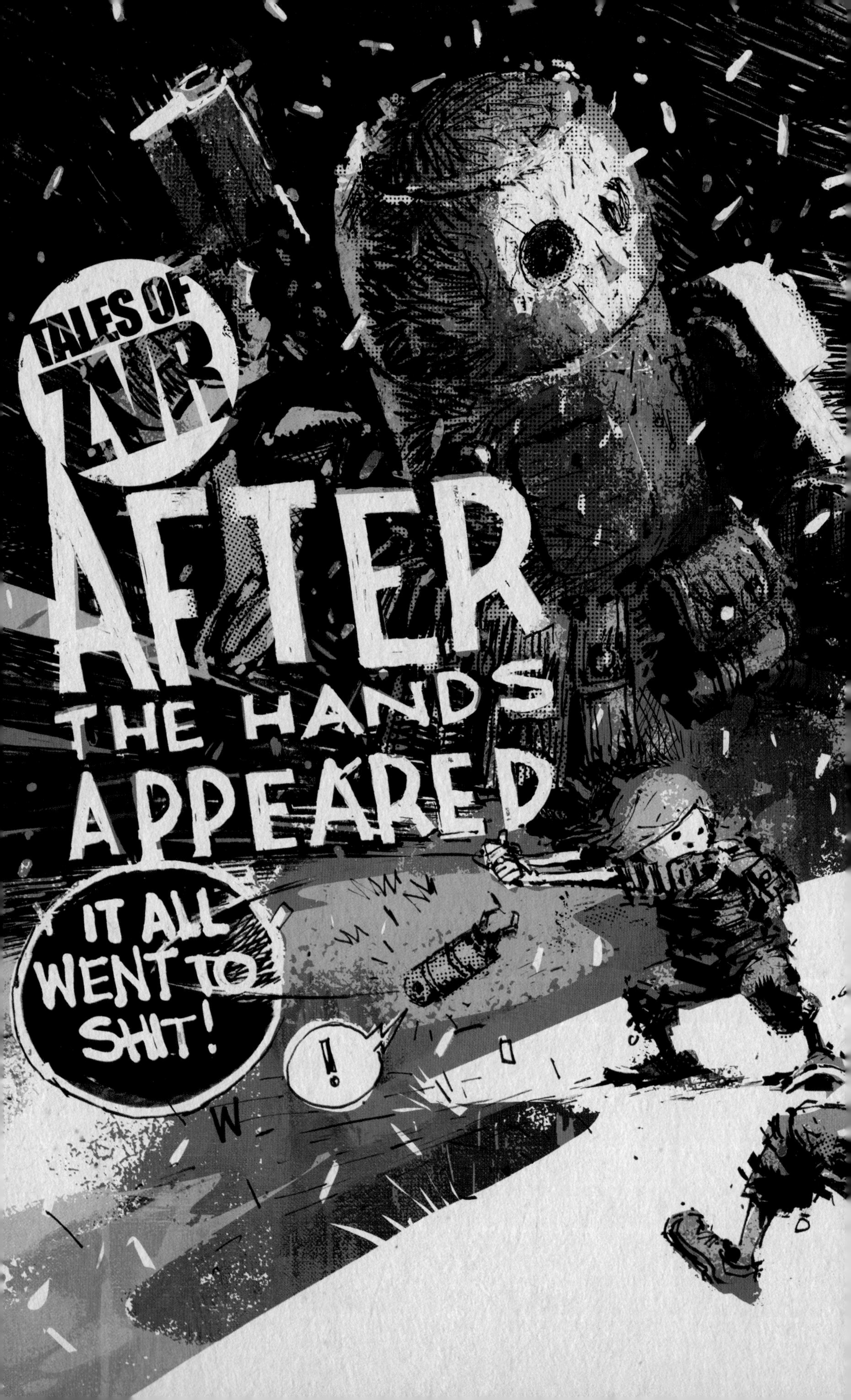
TALES OF ZAIR
AFTER THE HANDS APPEARED
IT ALL WENT TO SHIT!
!

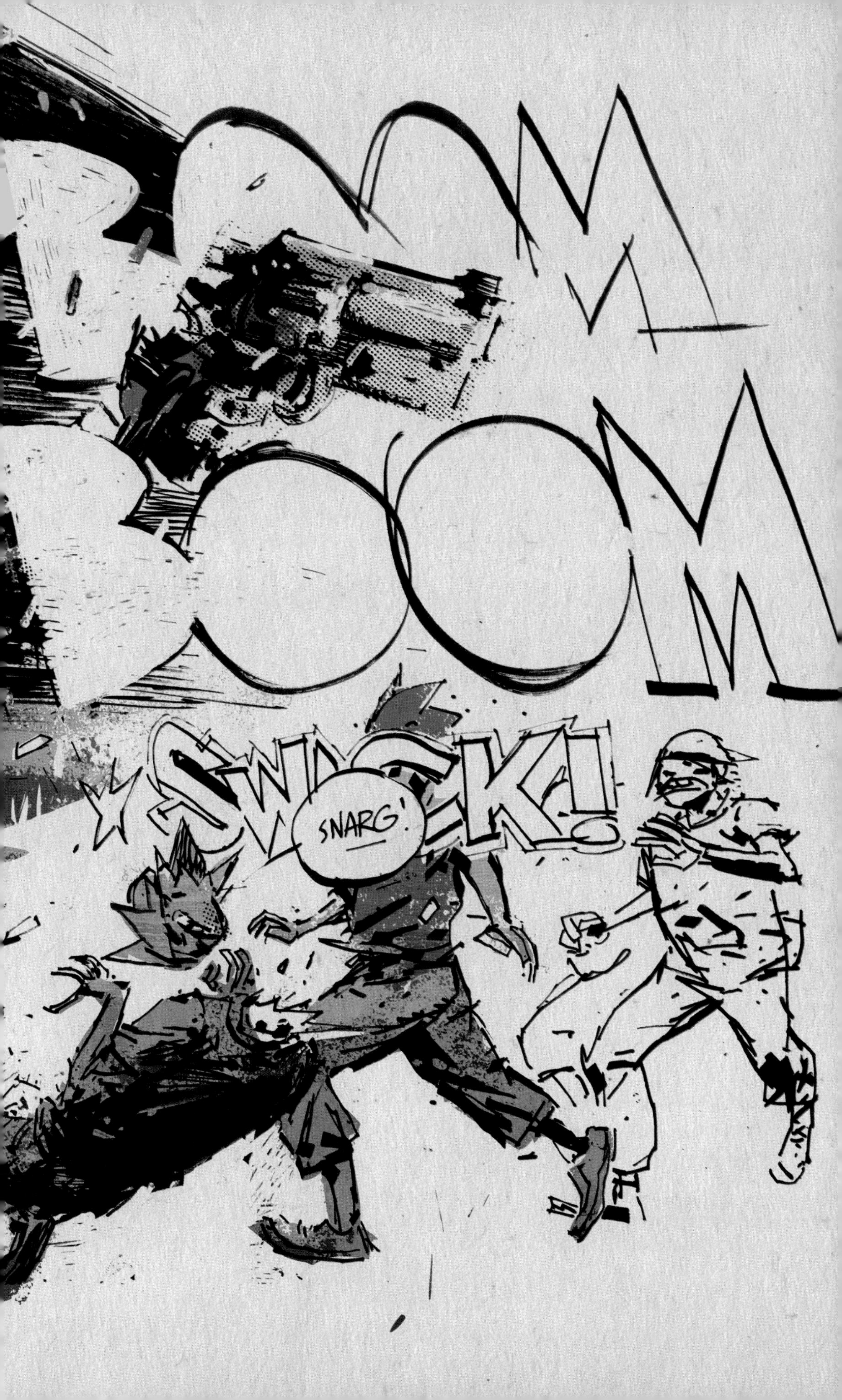
SWACK!
SNARG!

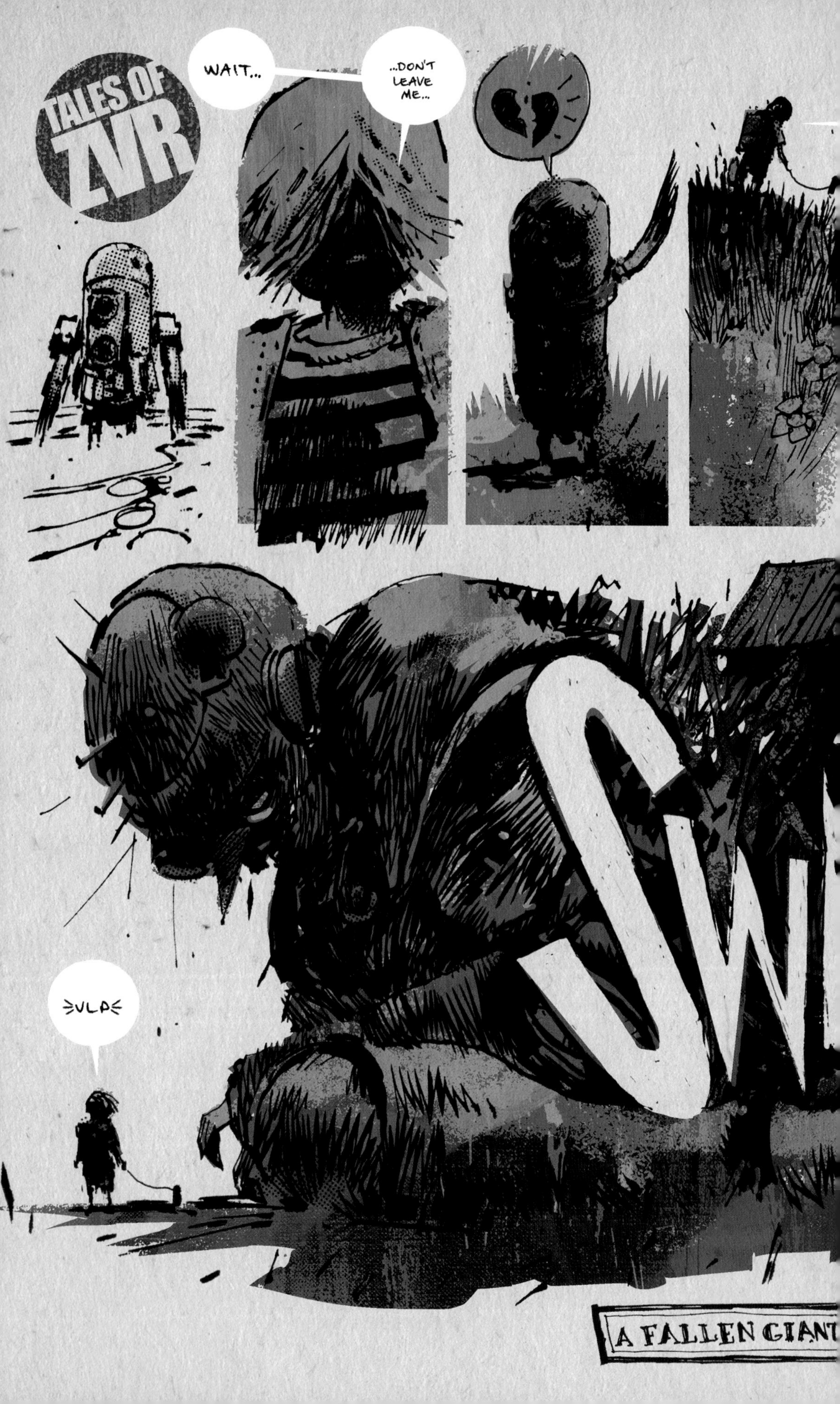
TALES OF ZVR
WAIT...
...DON'T LEAVE ME...
≶ULP≷
A FALLEN GIANT

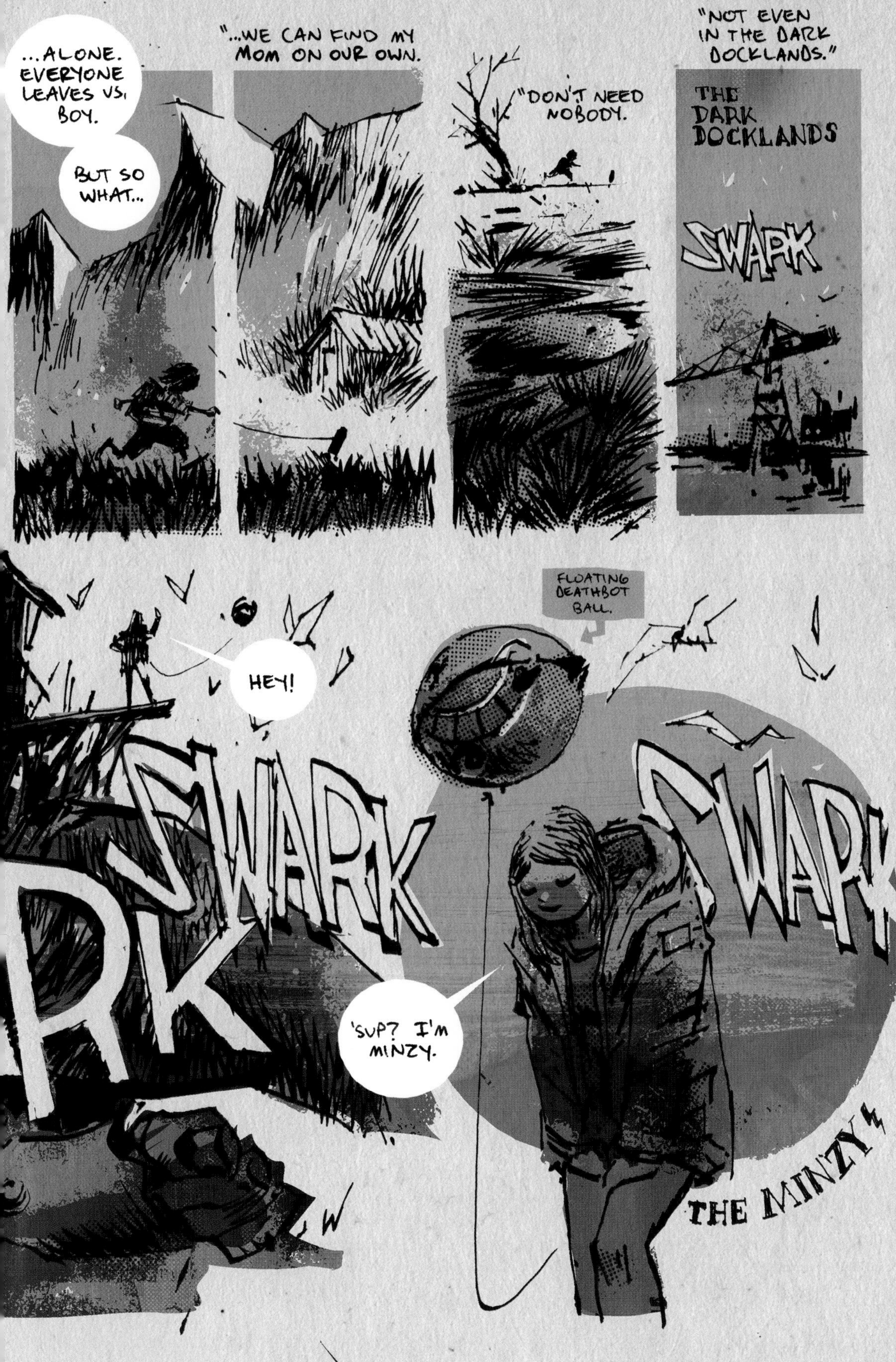

...ALONE. EVERYONE LEAVES US, BOY.
BUT SO WHAT...
"...WE CAN FIND MY MOM ON OUR OWN.
"DON'T NEED NOBODY.
"NOT EVEN IN THE DARK DOCKLANDS."
THE DARK DOCKLANDS
SWARK
FLOATING DEATHBOT BALL.
HEY!
SWARK
SWARK
RK
'SUP? I'M MINZY.
THE MINZY!

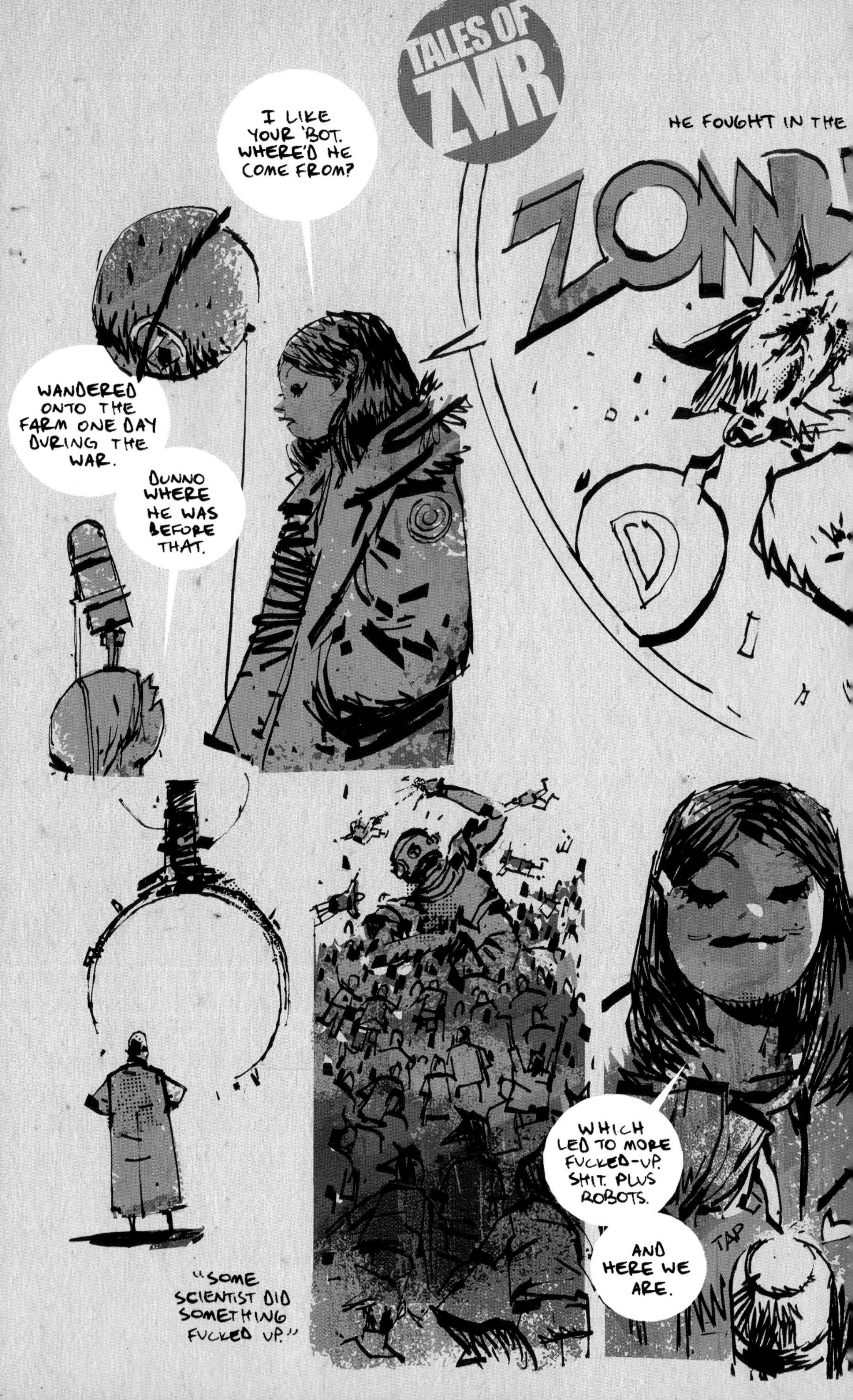
TALES OF ZVR
I LIKE YOUR 'BOT. WHERE'D HE COME FROM?
WANDERED ONTO THE FARM ONE DAY DURING THE WAR.
DUNNO WHERE HE WAS BEFORE THAT.
HE FOUGHT IN THE
ZOMB
"SOME SCIENTIST DID SOMETHING FUCKED UP."
WHICH LED TO MORE FUCKED-UP. SHIT. PLUS ROBOTS.
AND HERE WE ARE.
TAP

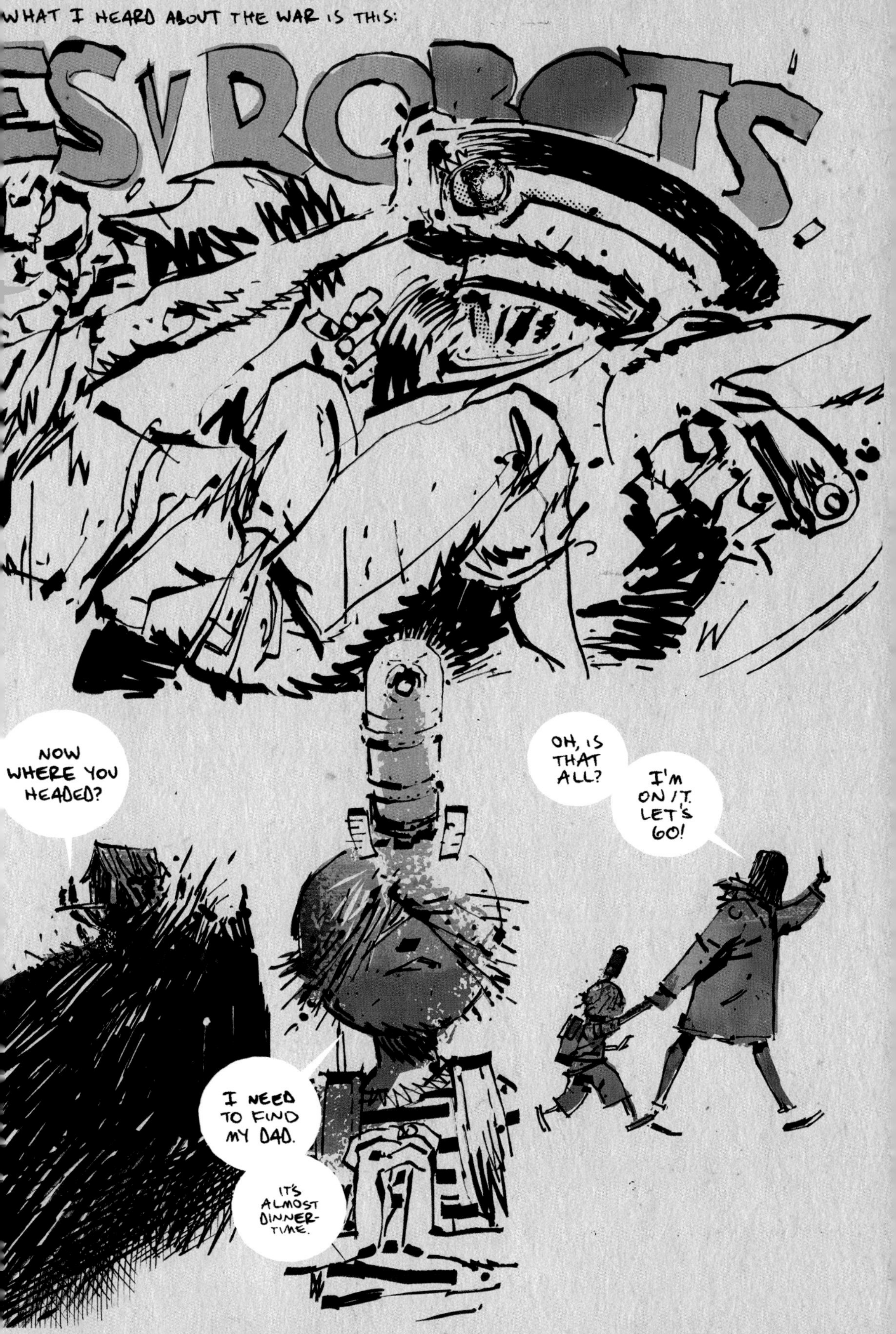
WHAT I HEARD ABOUT THE WAR IS THIS:
ES V ROBOTS!
NOW WHERE YOU HEADED?
I NEED TO FIND MY DAD.
IT'S ALMOST DINNER-TIME.
OH, IS THAT ALL?
I'M ON IT. LET'S GO!

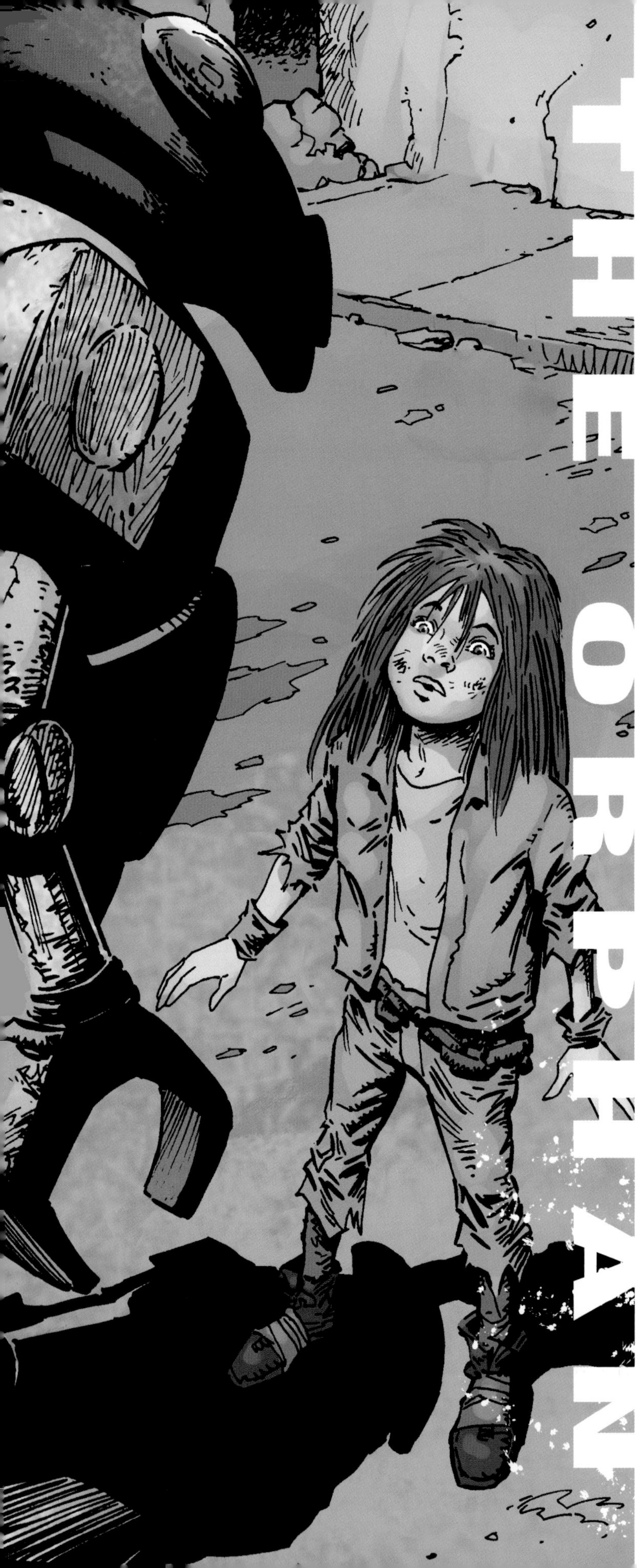
THE ORPHAN

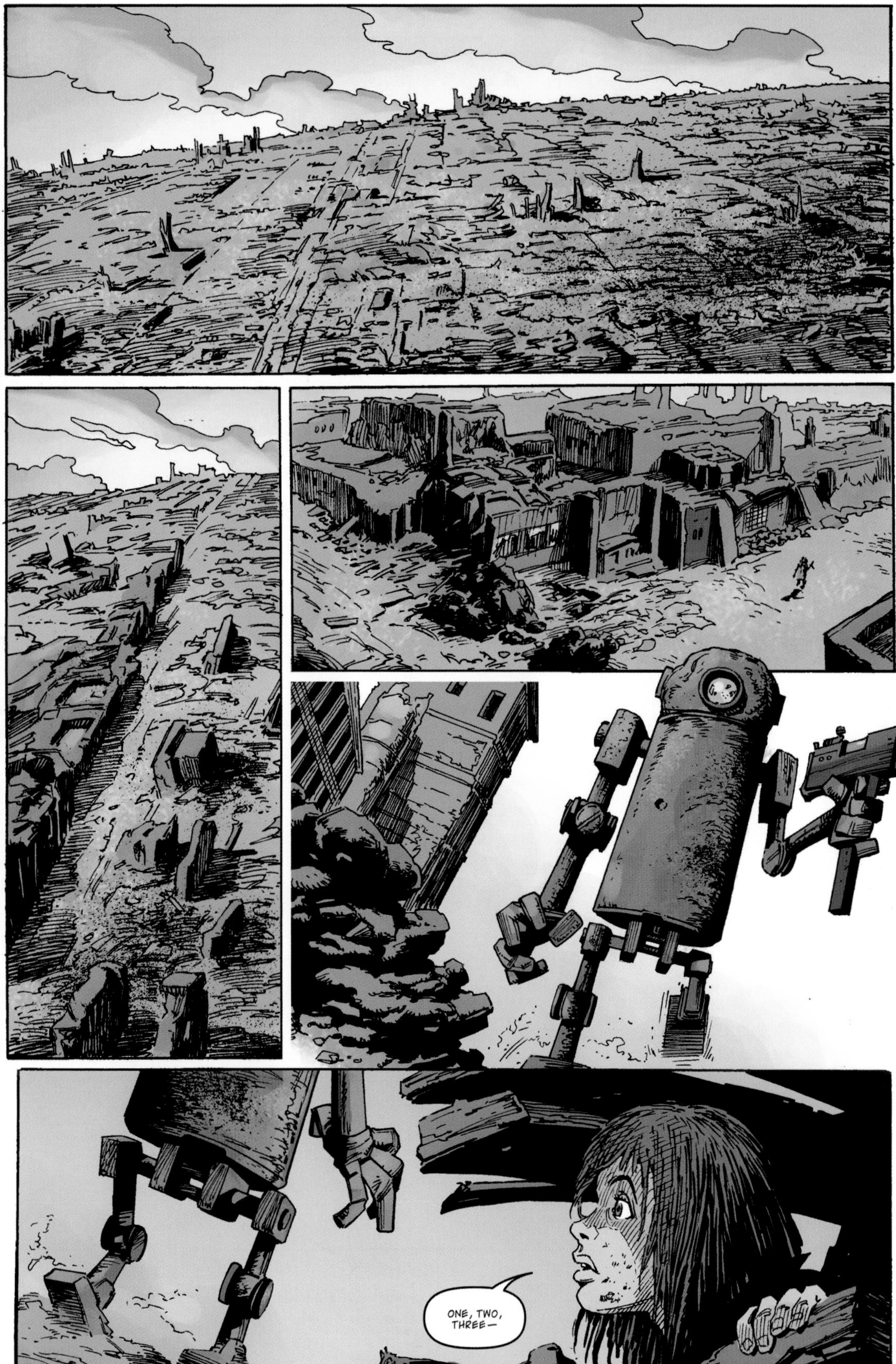
ONE, TWO, THREE—

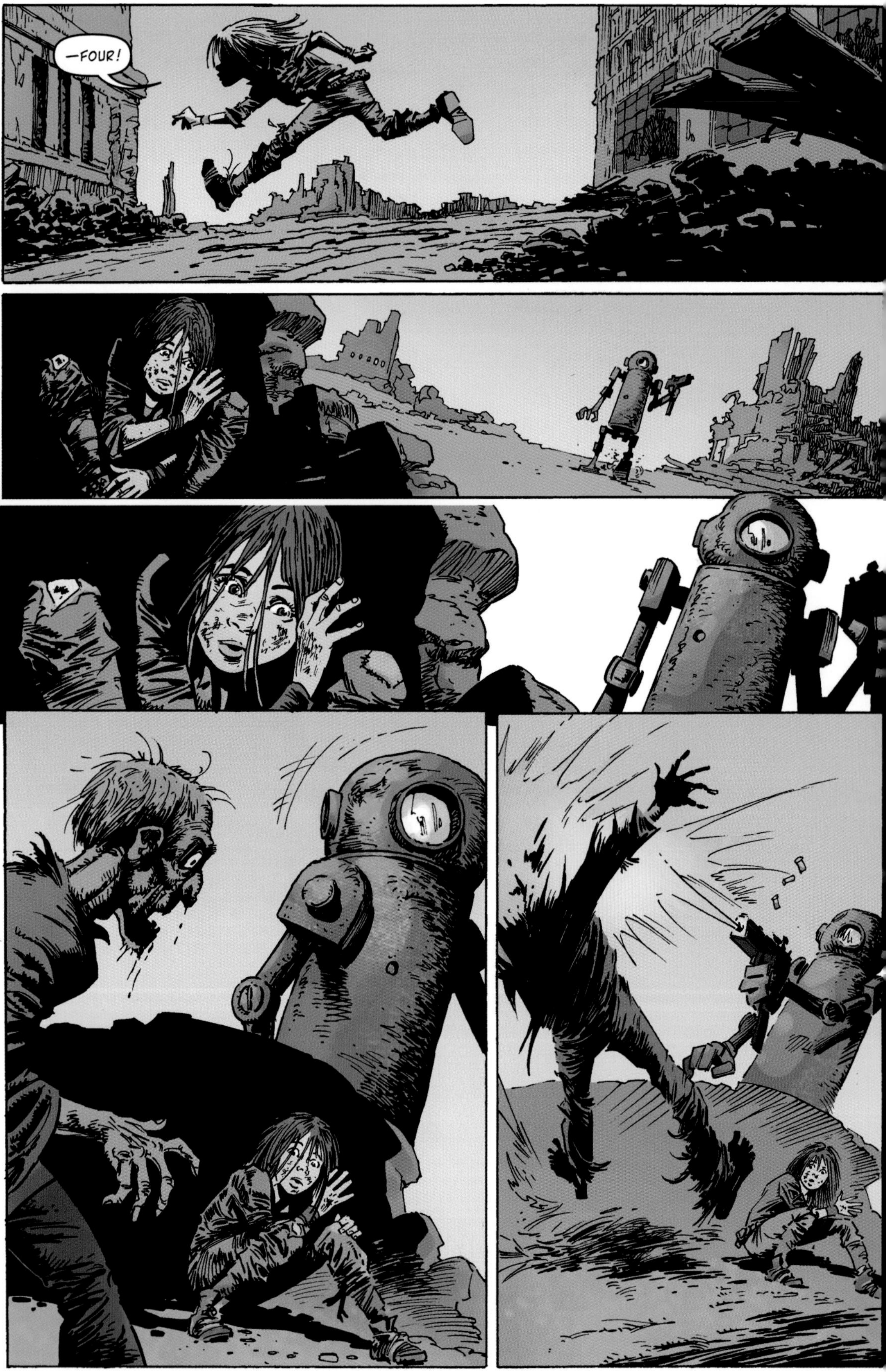
—FOUR!

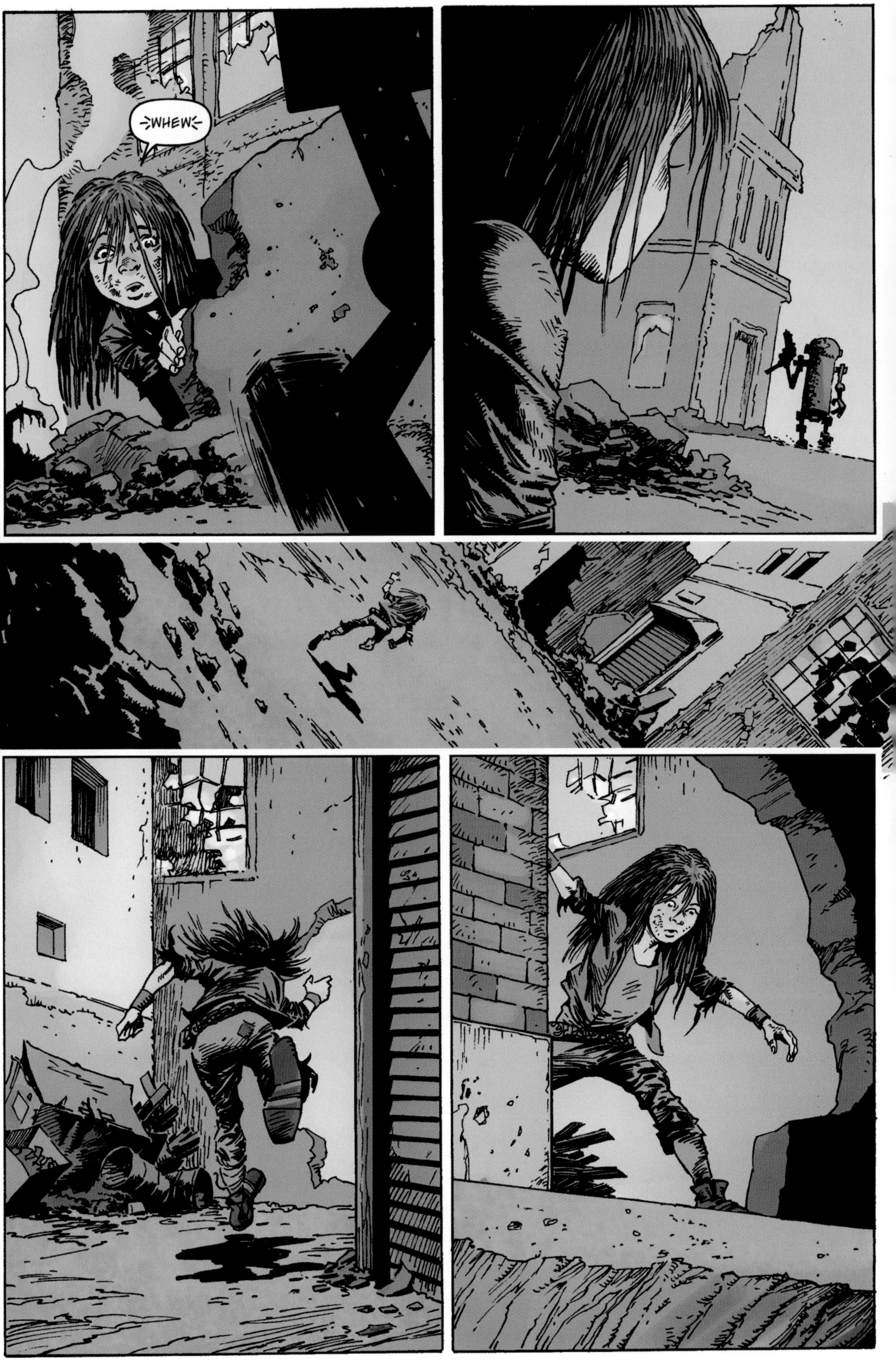
WHEW

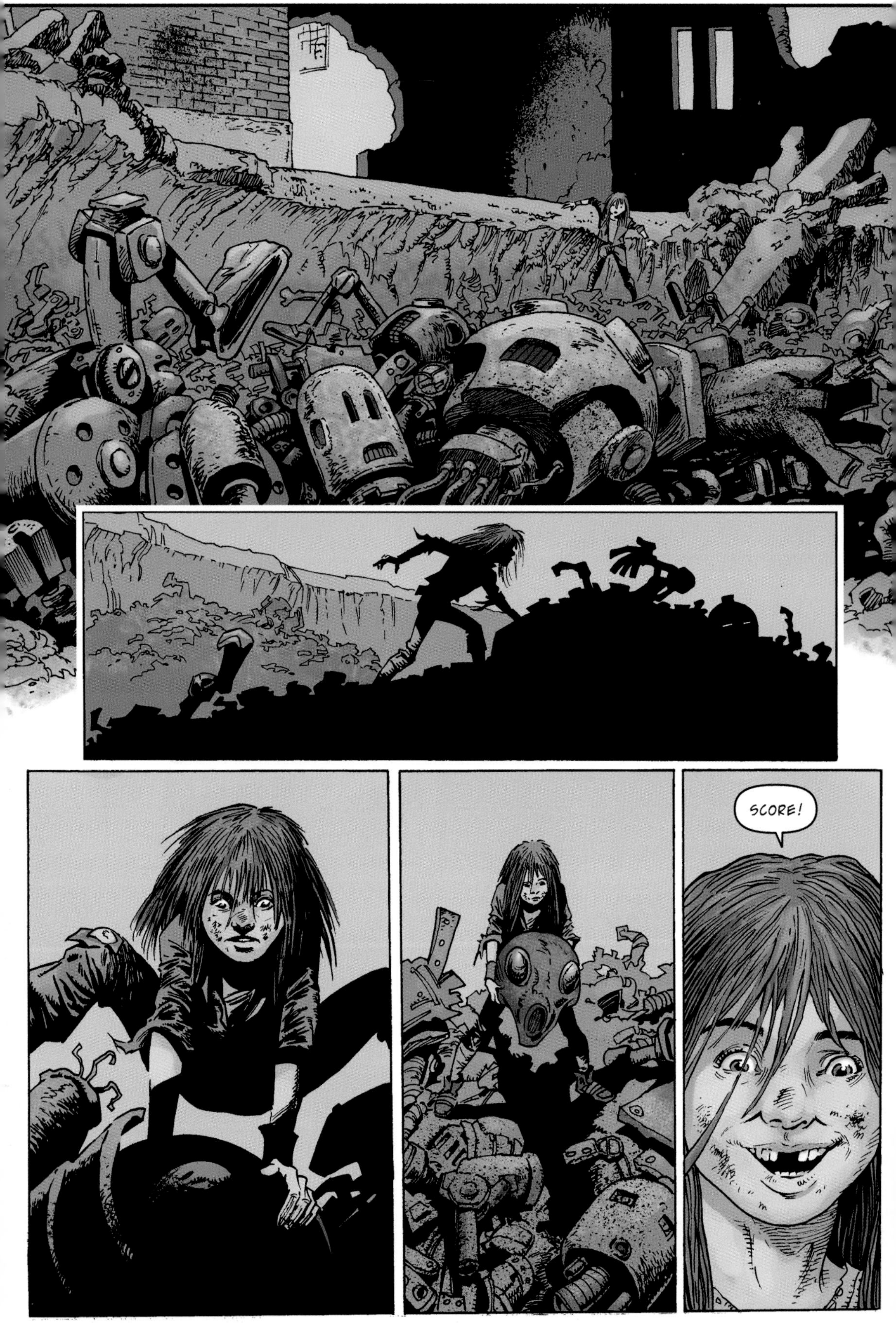
SCORE!

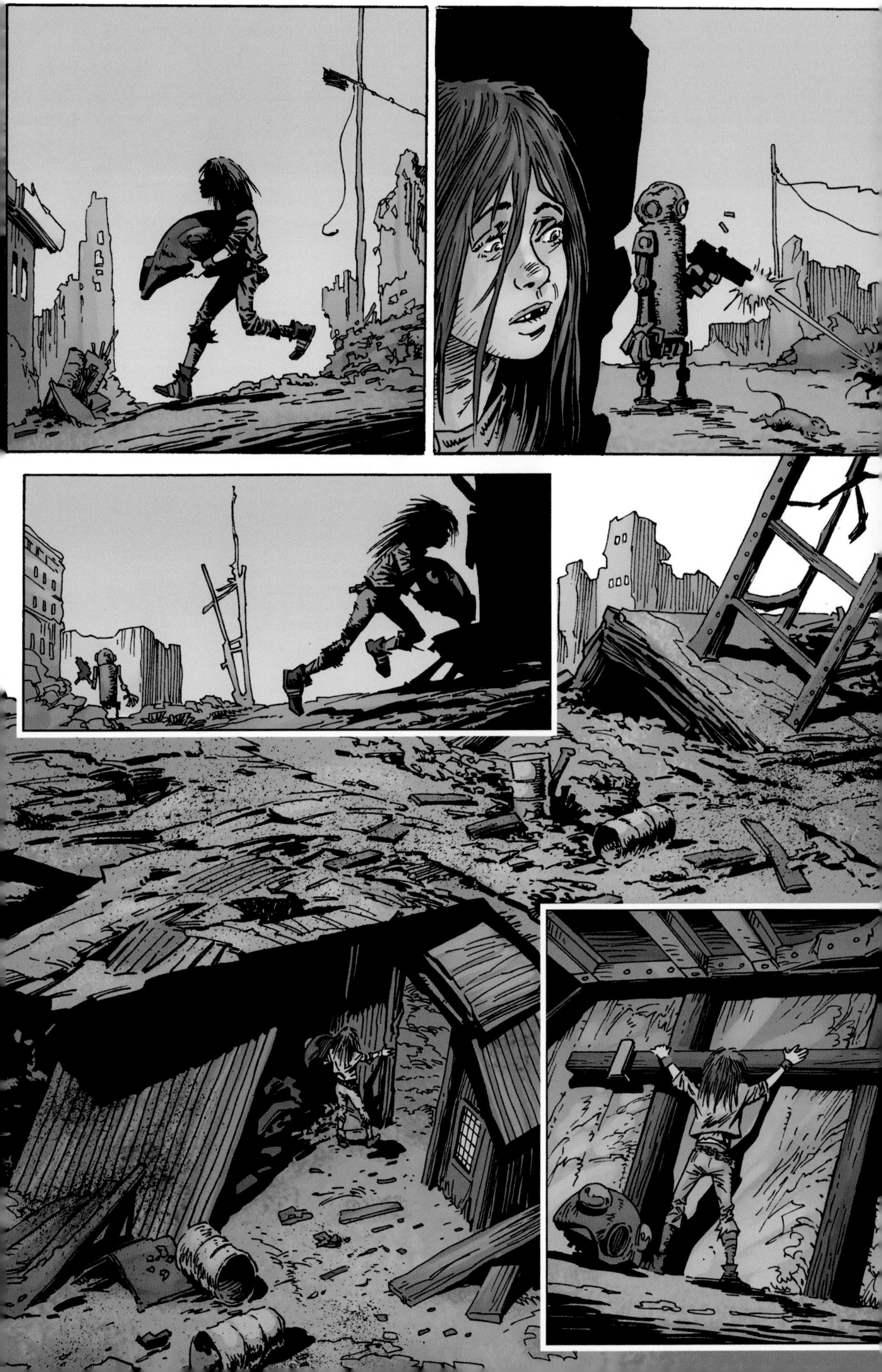

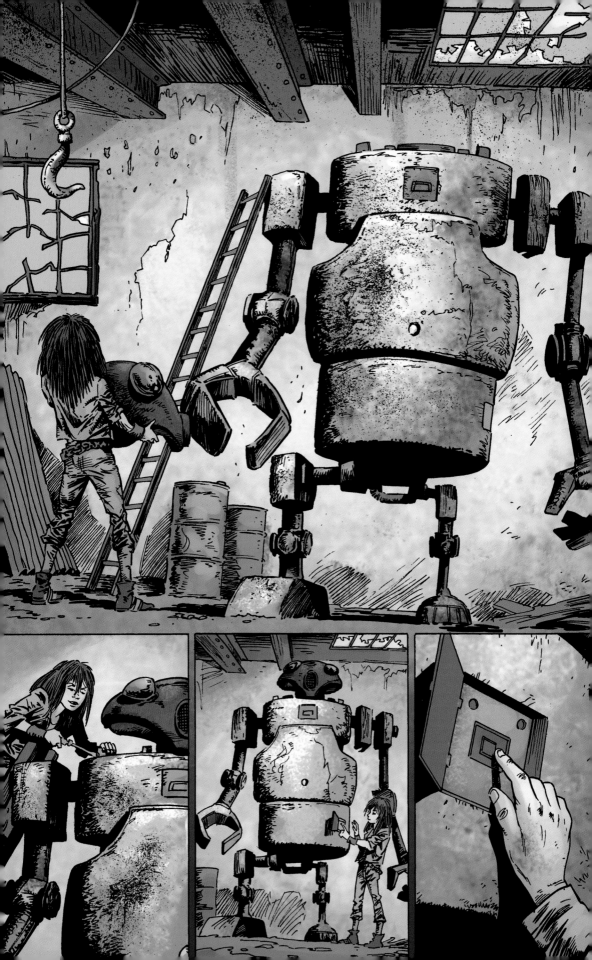

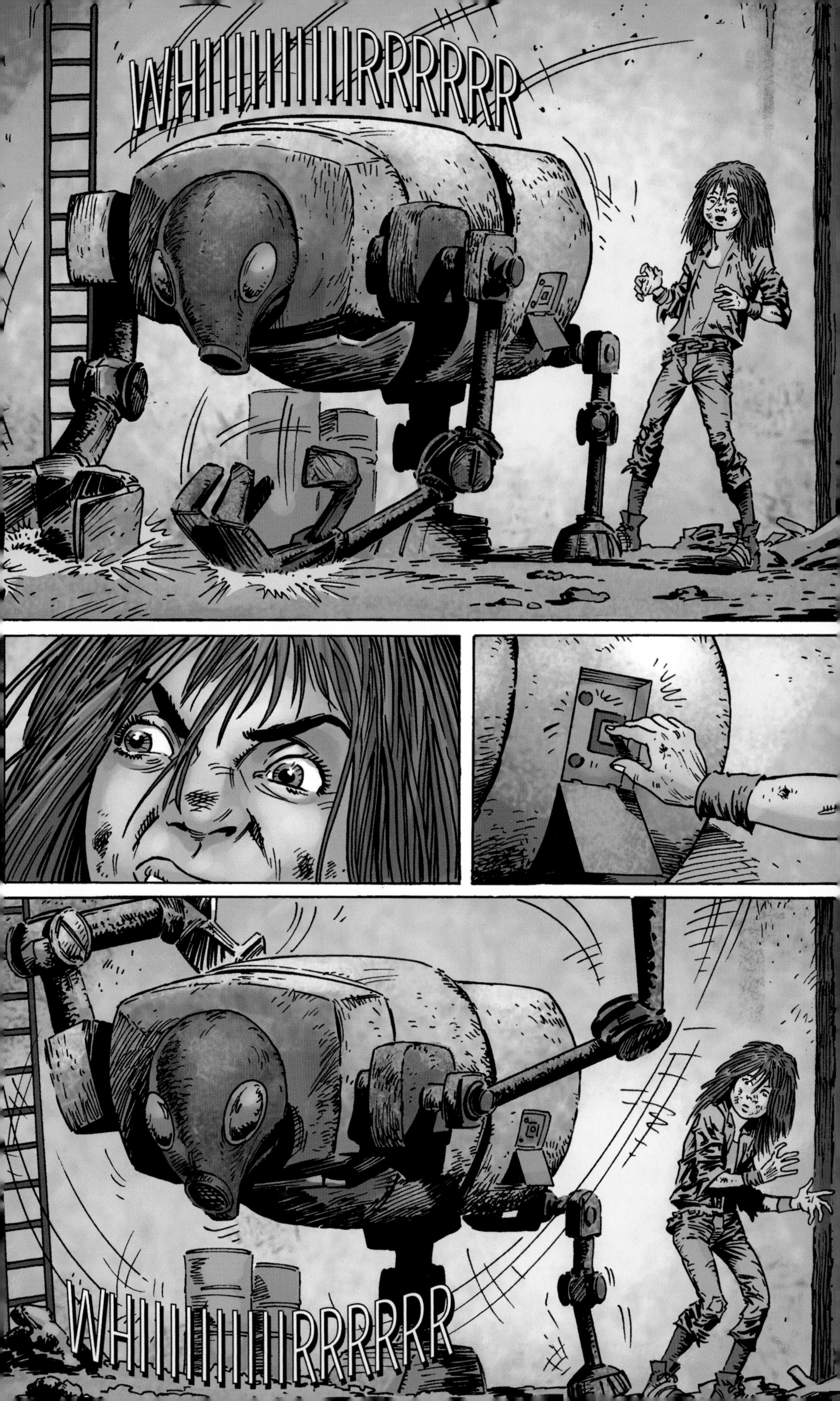
WHIIIIIIIIRRRRRR
WHIIIIIIIIIRRRRRR

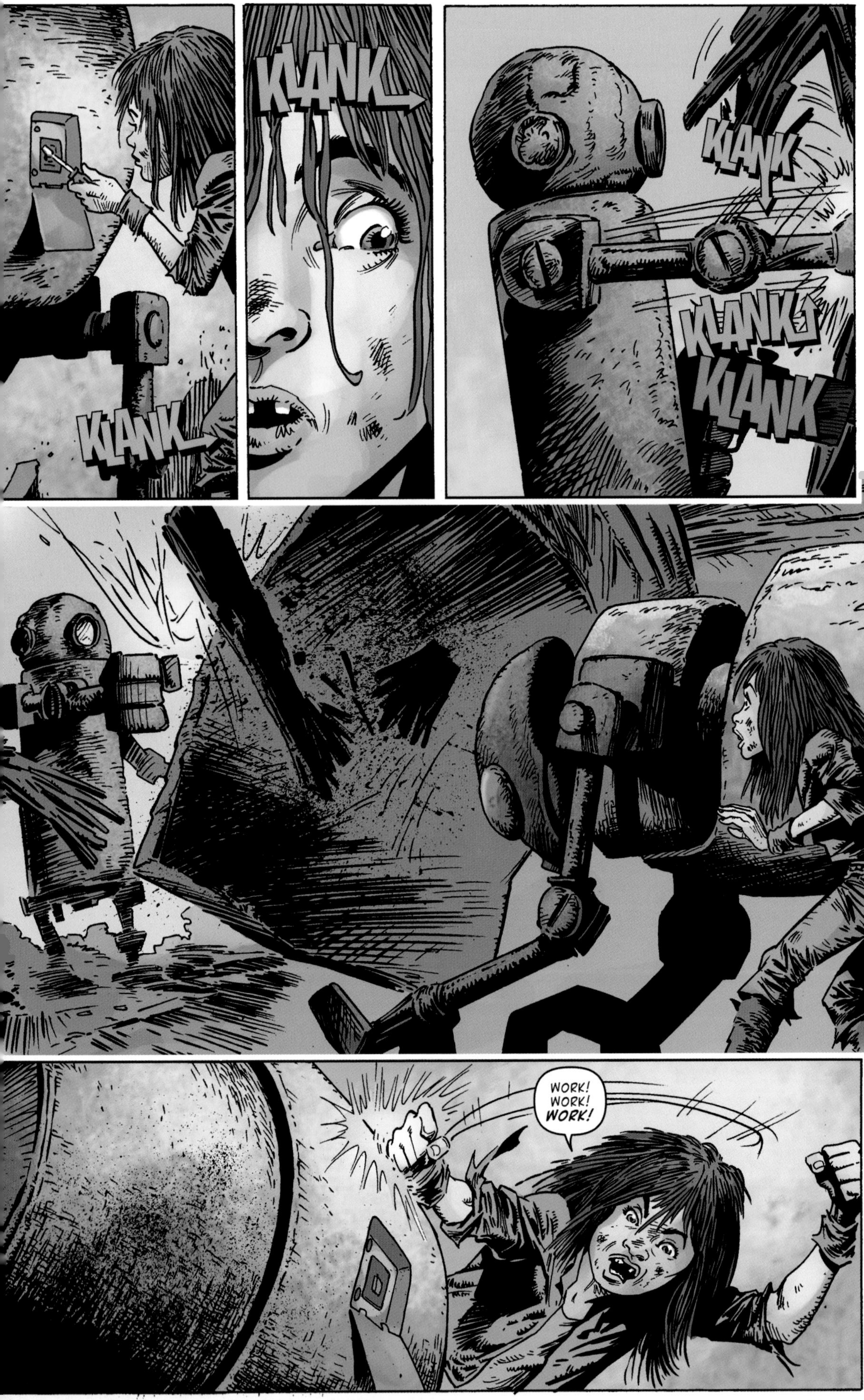
KLANK
KLANK
KLANK
KLANK
KLANK
WORK! WORK! WORK!

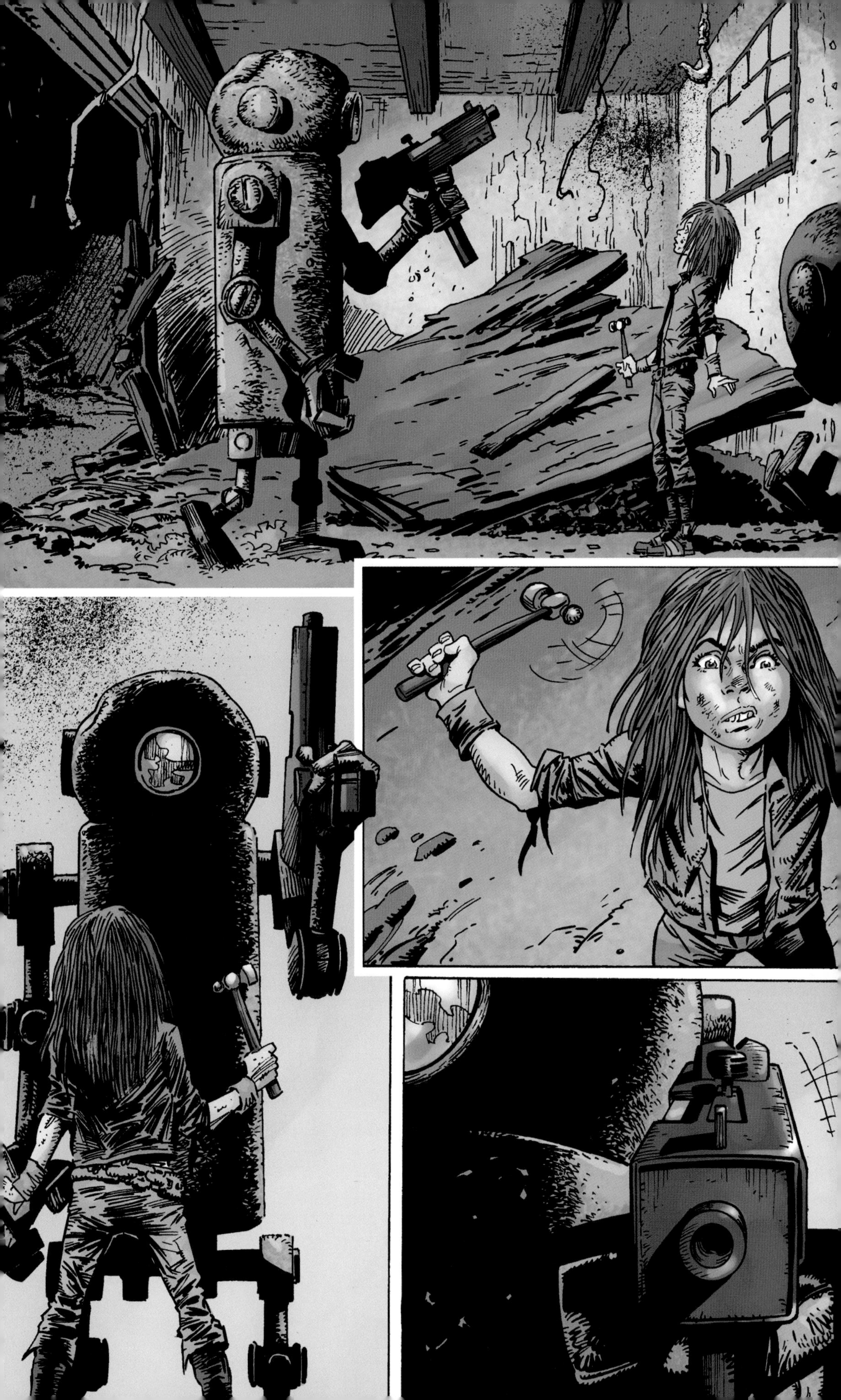

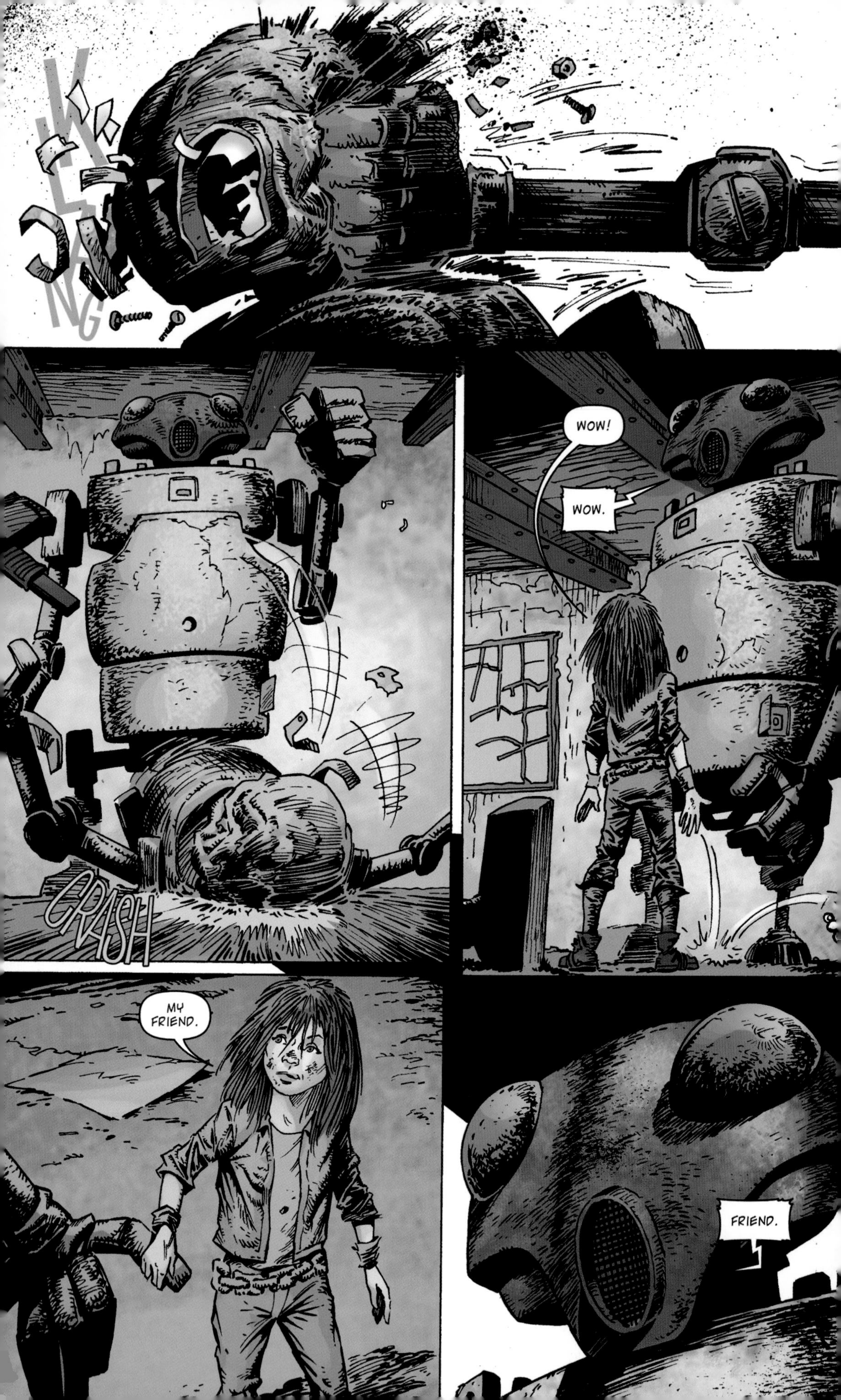
KLANG
CRASH
WOW!
WOW.
MY FRIEND.
FRIEND.

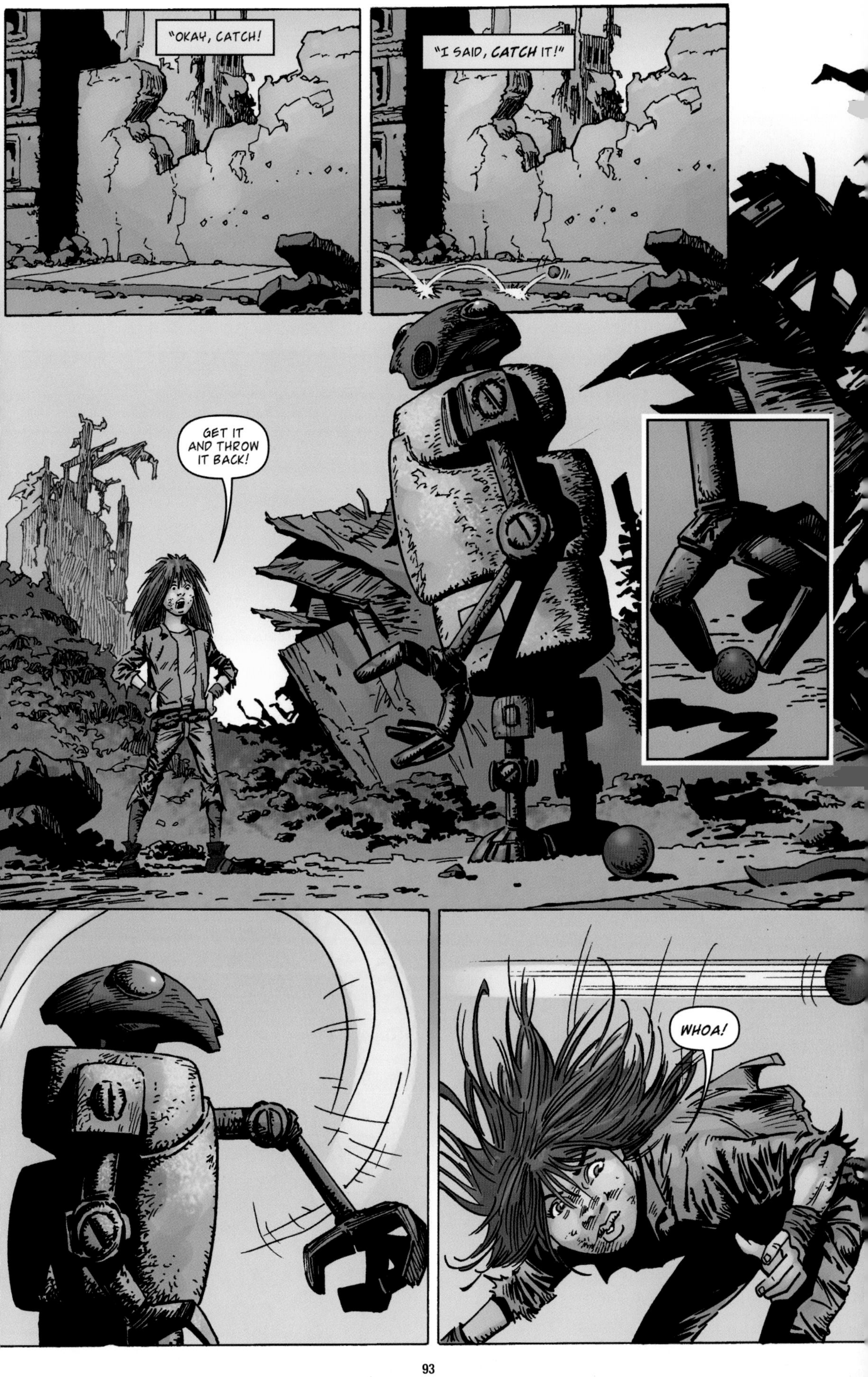
"OKAY, CATCH!
"I SAID, CATCH IT!"
GET IT AND THROW IT BACK!
WHOA!

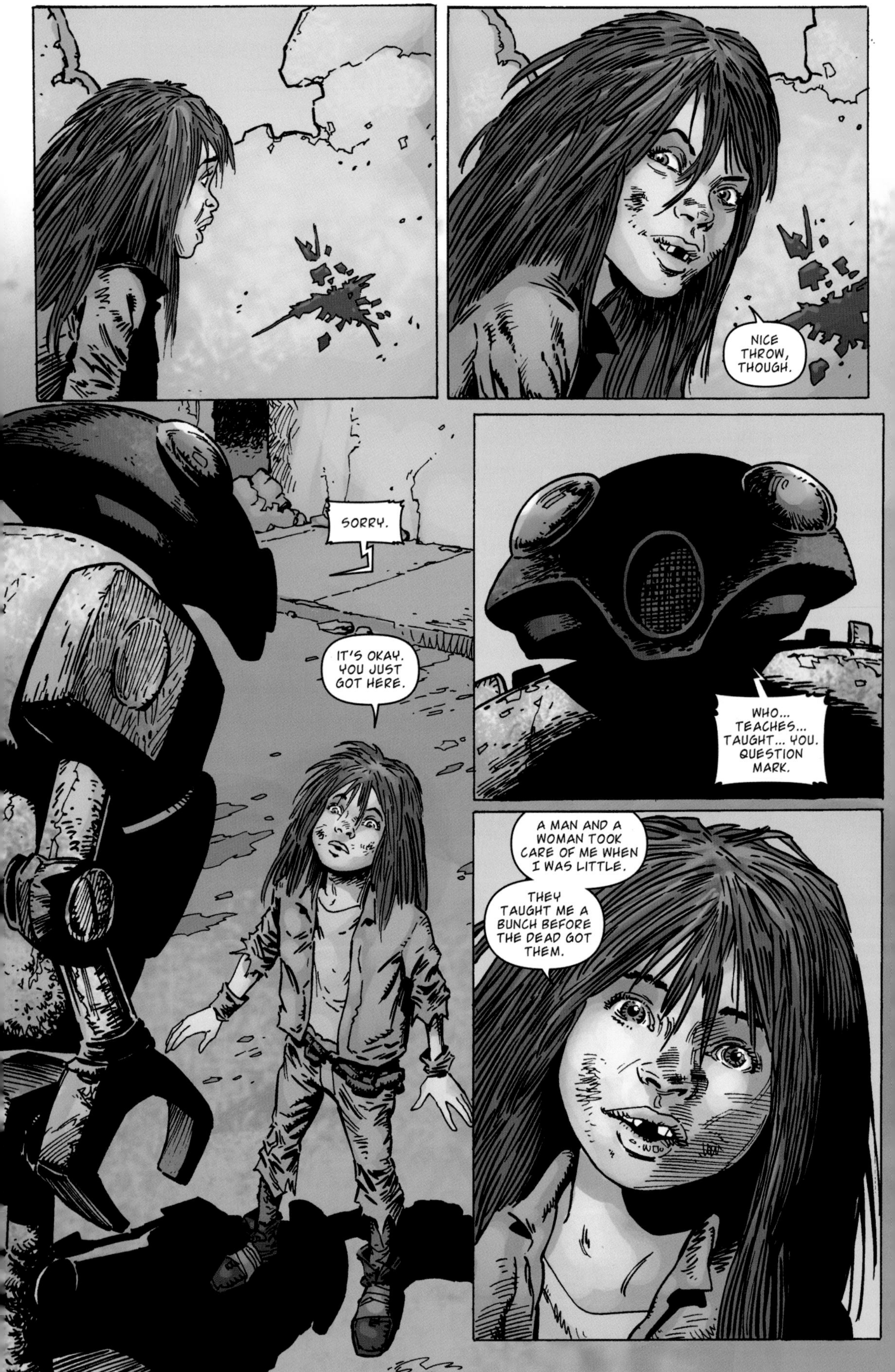
NICE THROW, THOUGH.
SORRY.
IT'S OKAY. YOU JUST GOT HERE.
WHO... TEACHES... TAUGHT... YOU. QUESTION MARK.
A MAN AND A WOMAN TOOK CARE OF ME WHEN I WAS LITTLE.
THEY TAUGHT ME A BUNCH BEFORE THE DEAD GOT THEM.

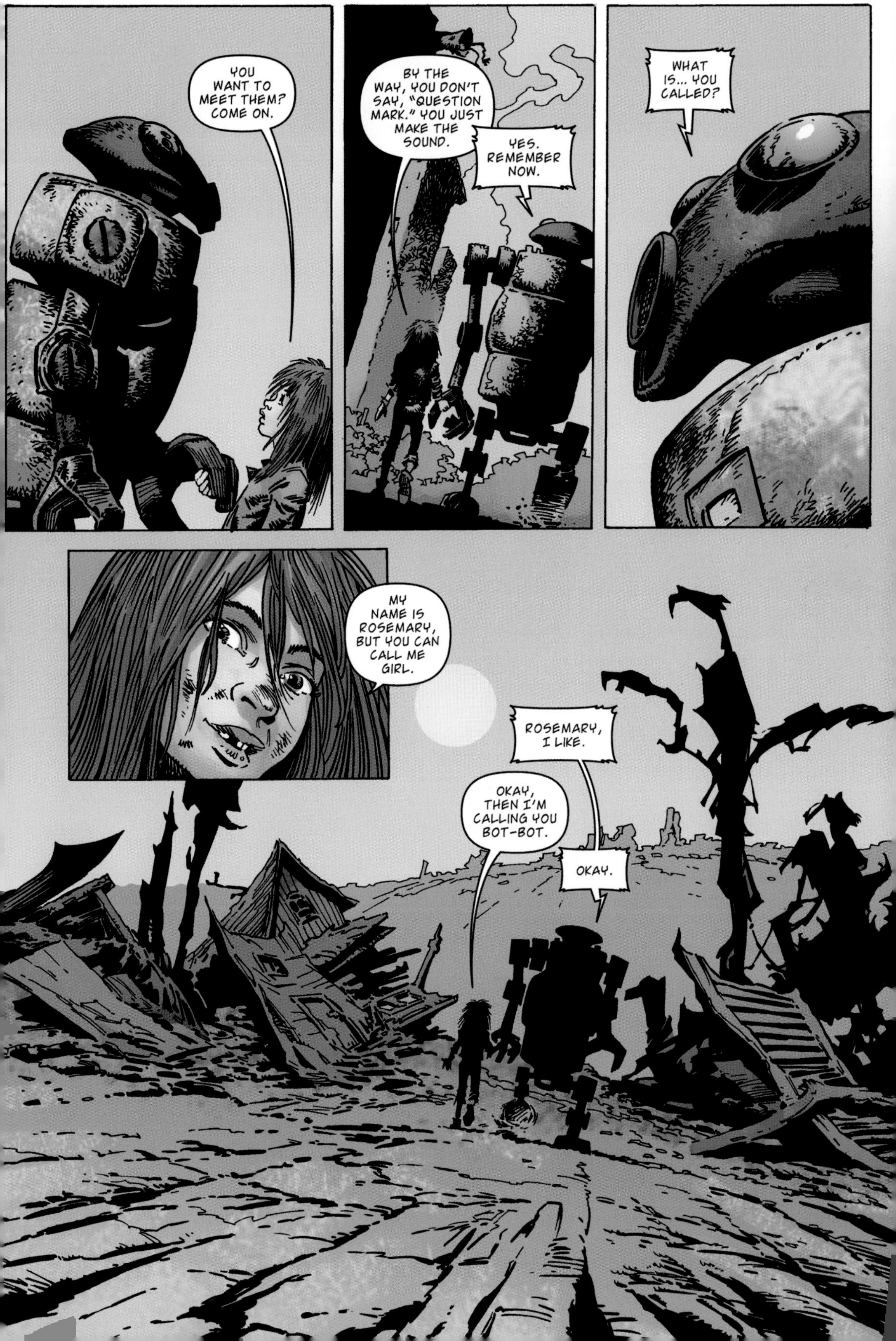
YOU WANT TO MEET THEM? COME ON.
BY THE WAY, YOU DON'T SAY, "QUESTION MARK." YOU JUST MAKE THE SOUND.
YES. REMEMBER NOW.
WHAT IS... YOU CALLED?
MY NAME IS ROSEMARY, BUT YOU CAN CALL ME GIRL.
ROSEMARY, I LIKE.
OKAY, THEN I'M CALLING YOU BOT-BOT.
OKAY.

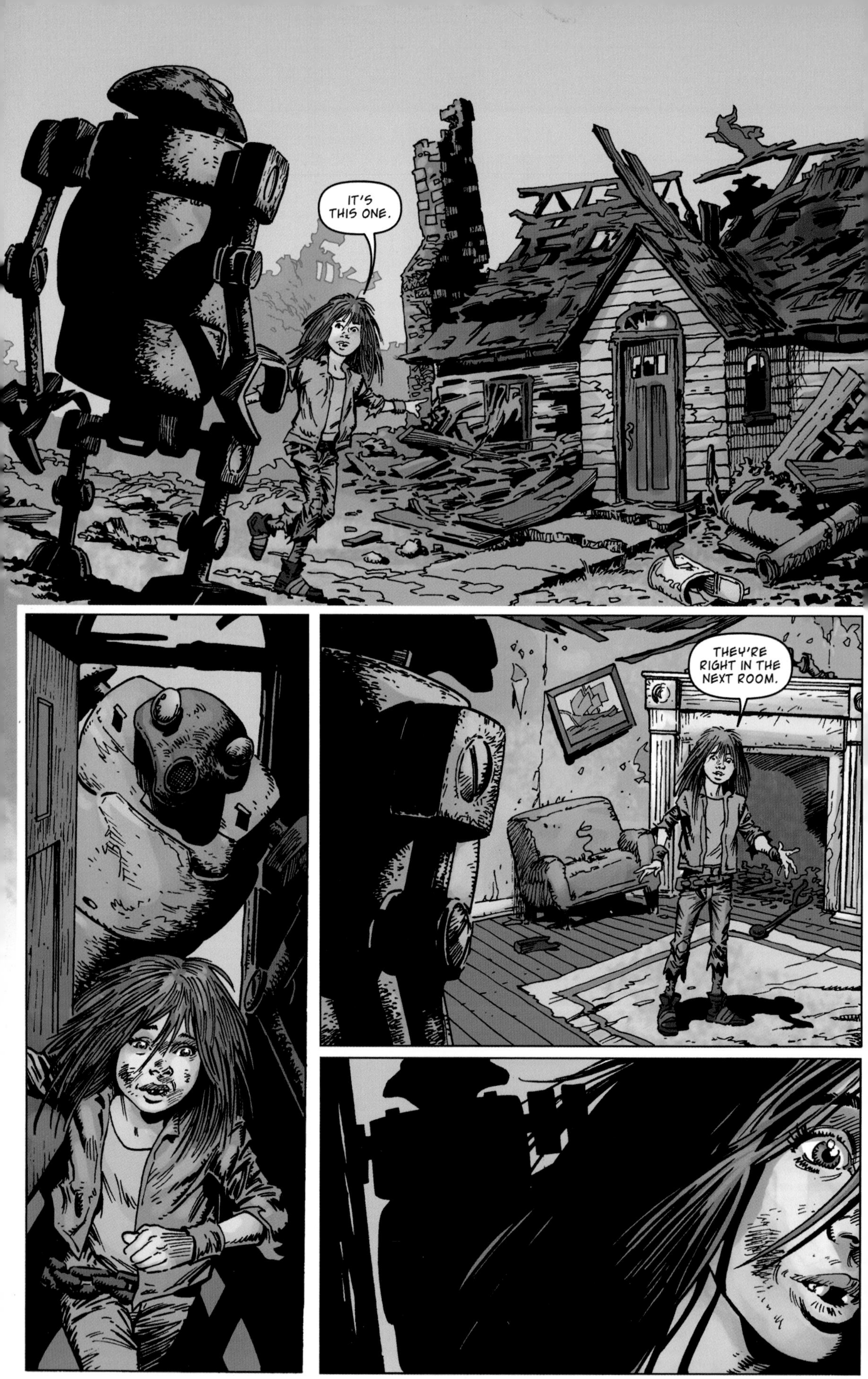
IT'S THIS ONE.
THEY'RE RIGHT IN THE NEXT ROOM.

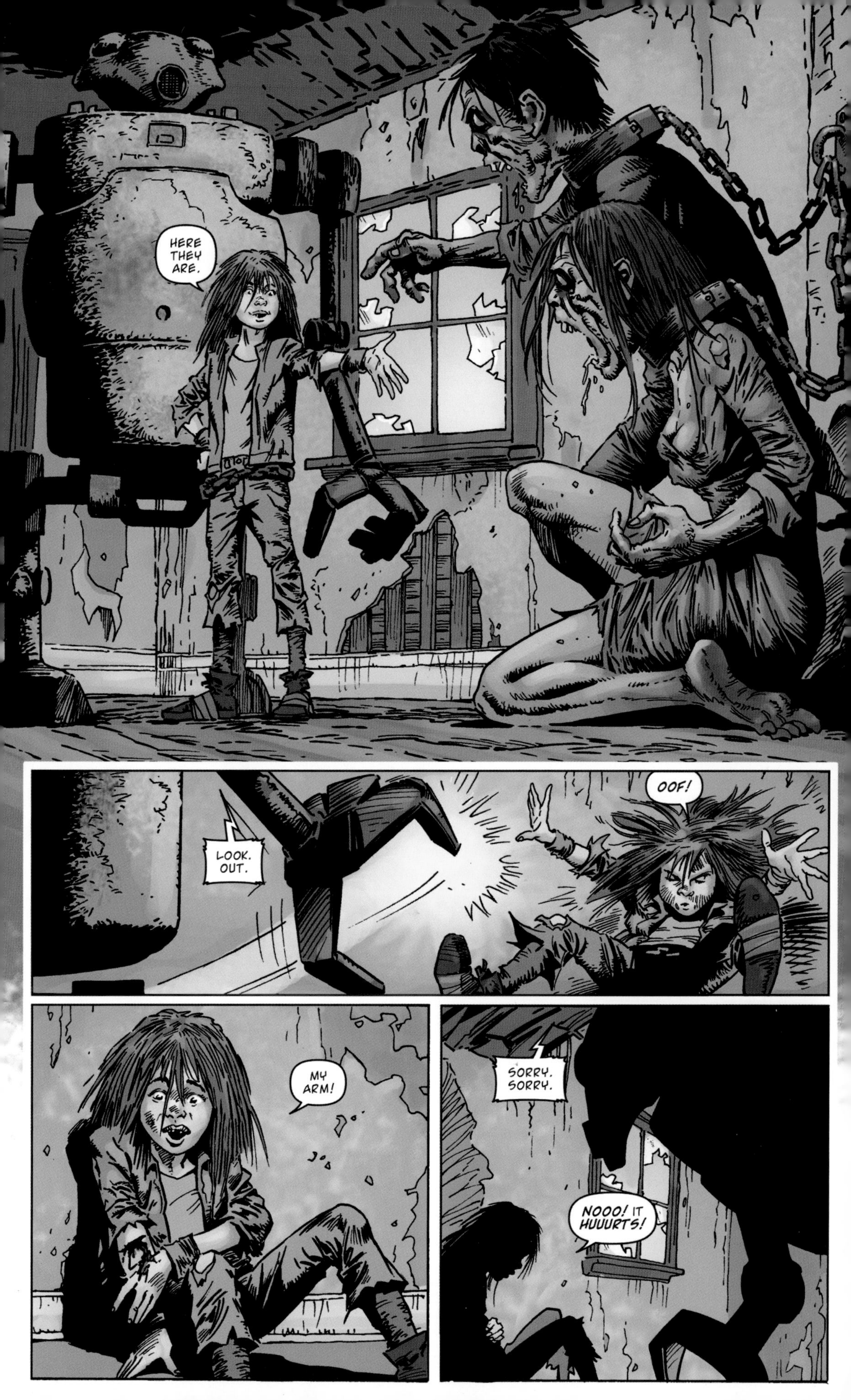
HERE THEY ARE.
LOOK. OUT.
OOF!
MY ARM!
SORRY. SORRY.
NOOO! IT HUUURTS!

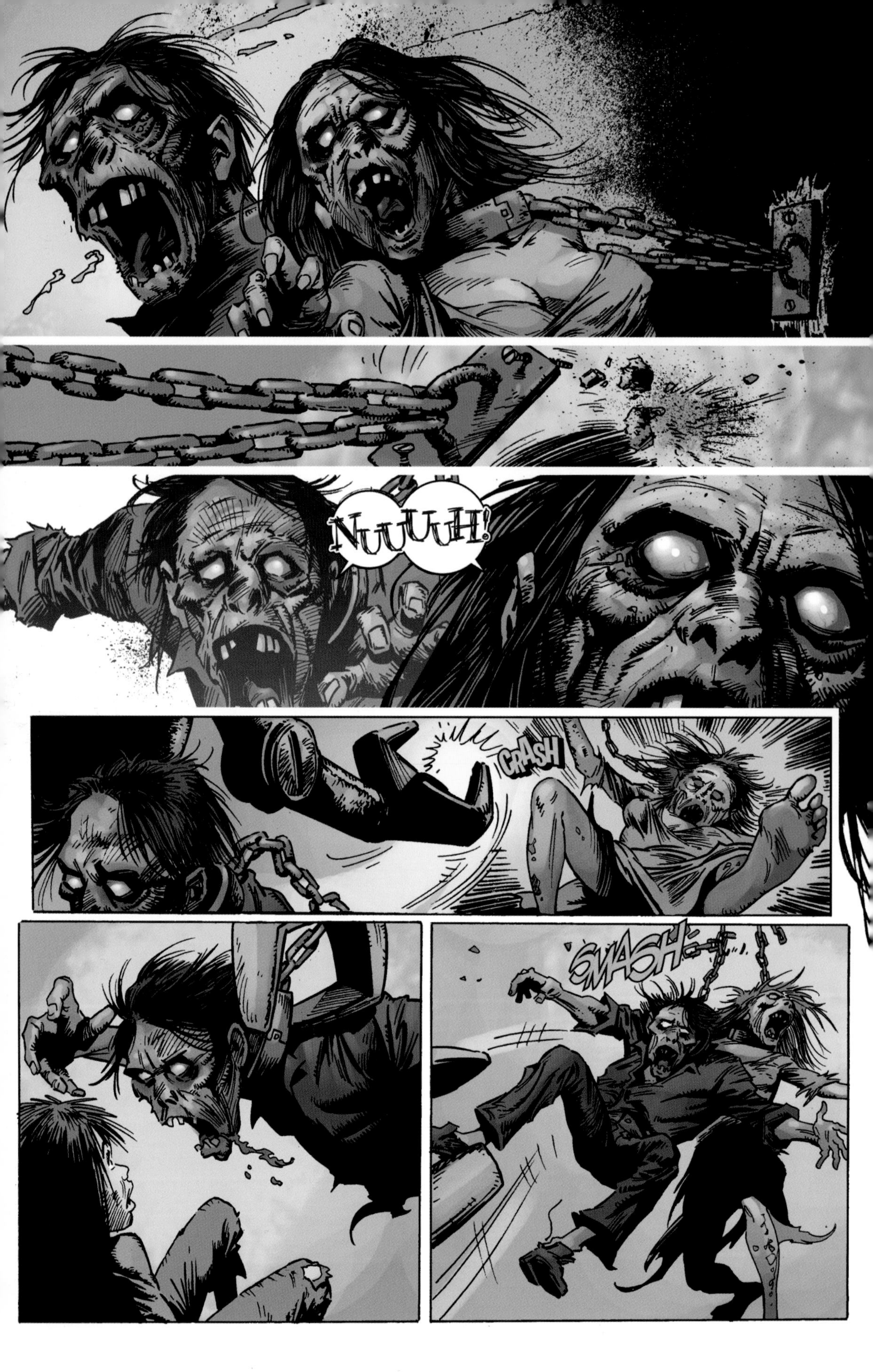
NUUUUH!
CRASH
SMASH

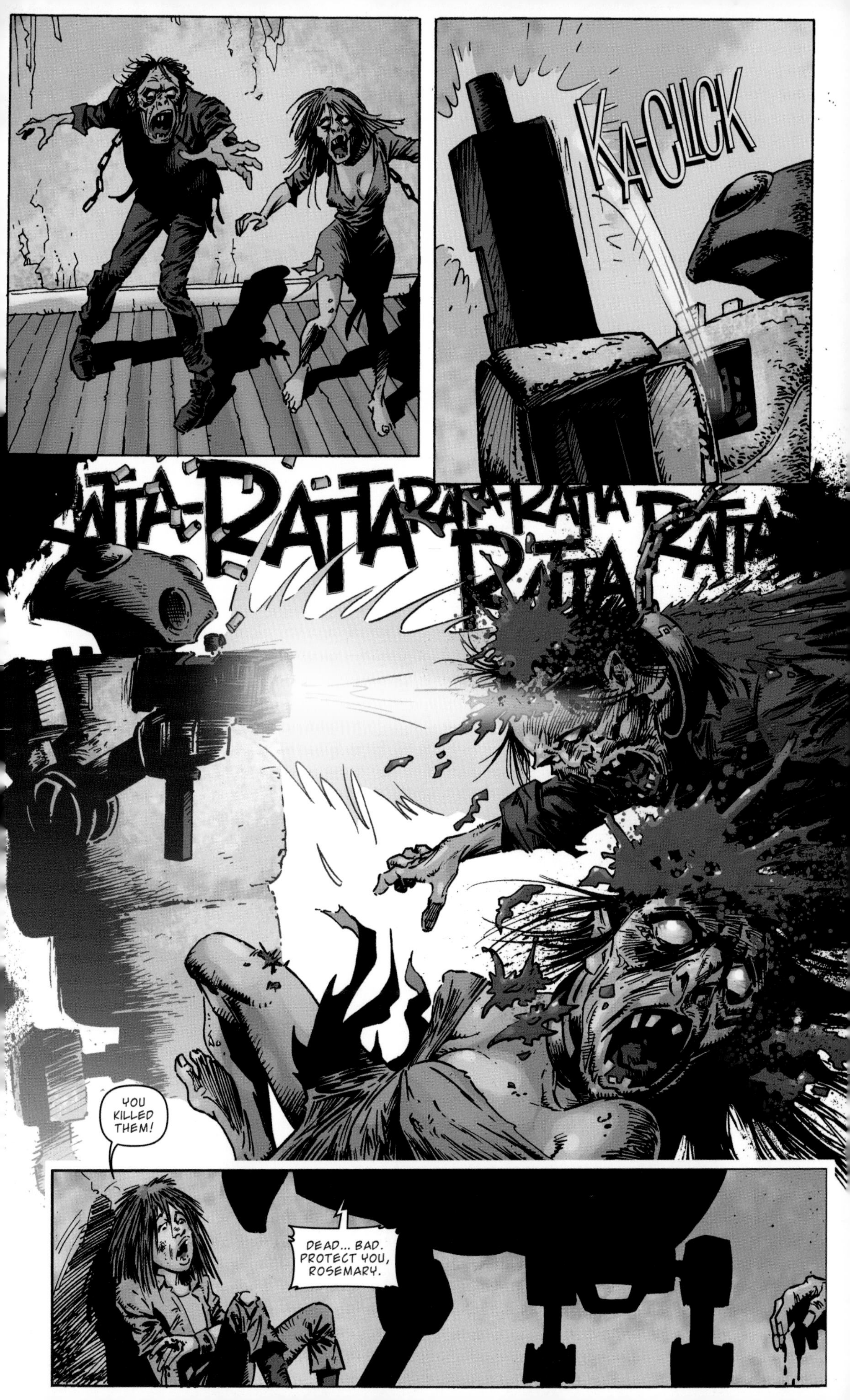
KA-CLICK
RATTA-RATTA-RATTA-RATA-RATA-RATA-RATTA-RATTA-RATTA
YOU KILLED THEM!
DEAD... BAD. PROTECT YOU, ROSEMARY.

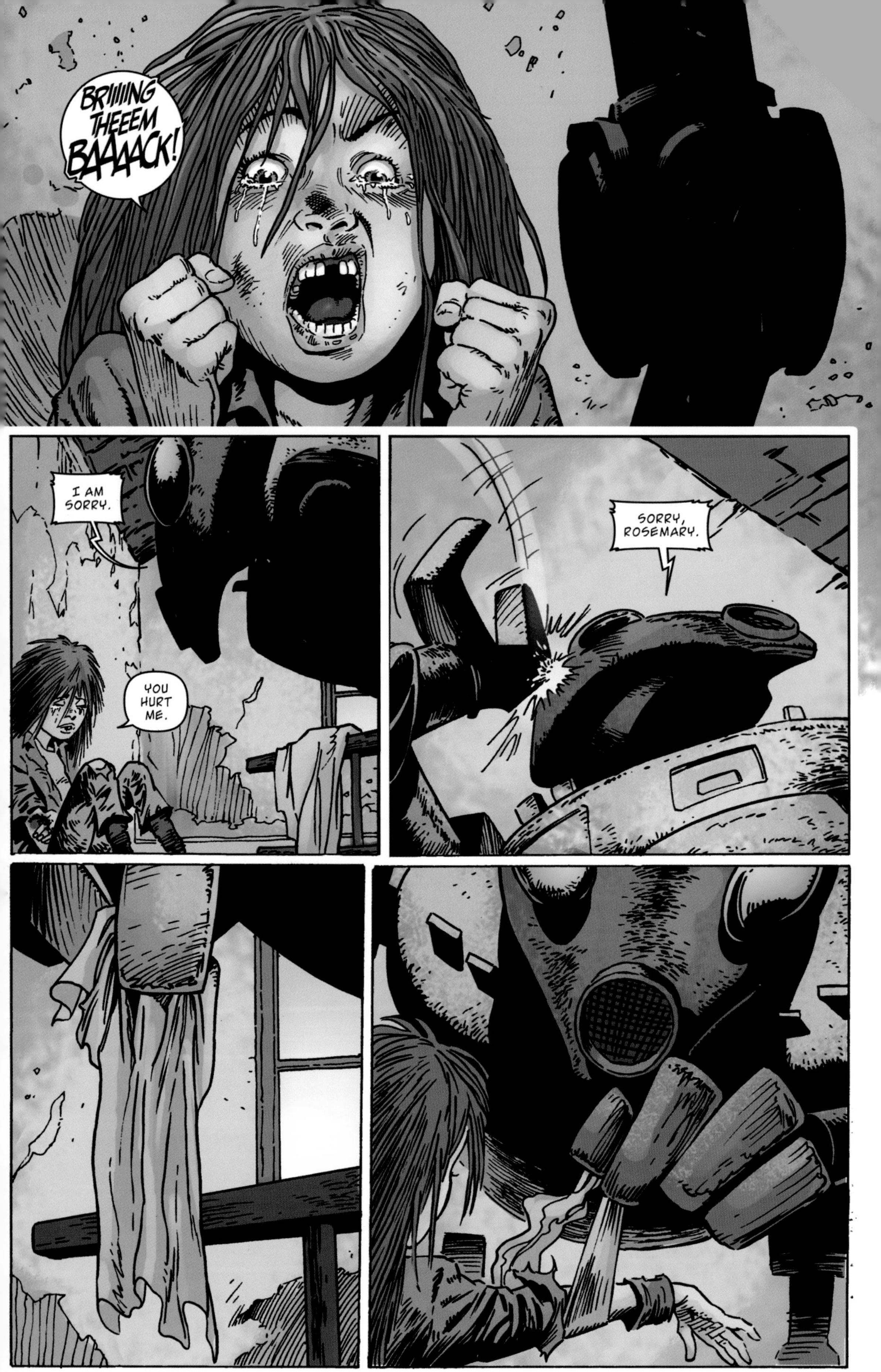
BRIIIING THEEEM BAAAACK!
I AM SORRY.
YOU HURT ME.
SORRY, ROSEMARY.

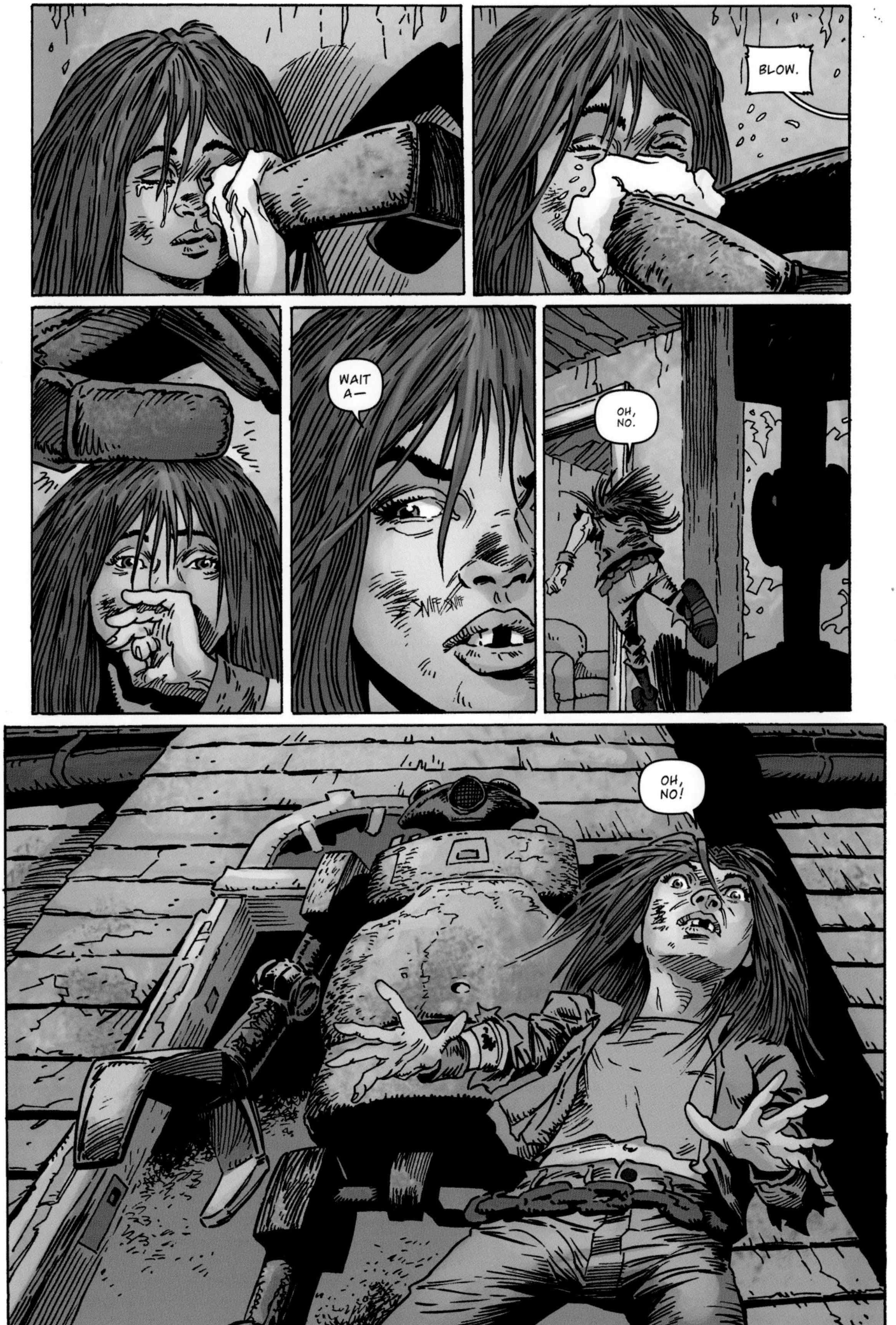
BLOW.
WAIT A—
SNIFF SNIFF
OH, NO.
OH, NO!

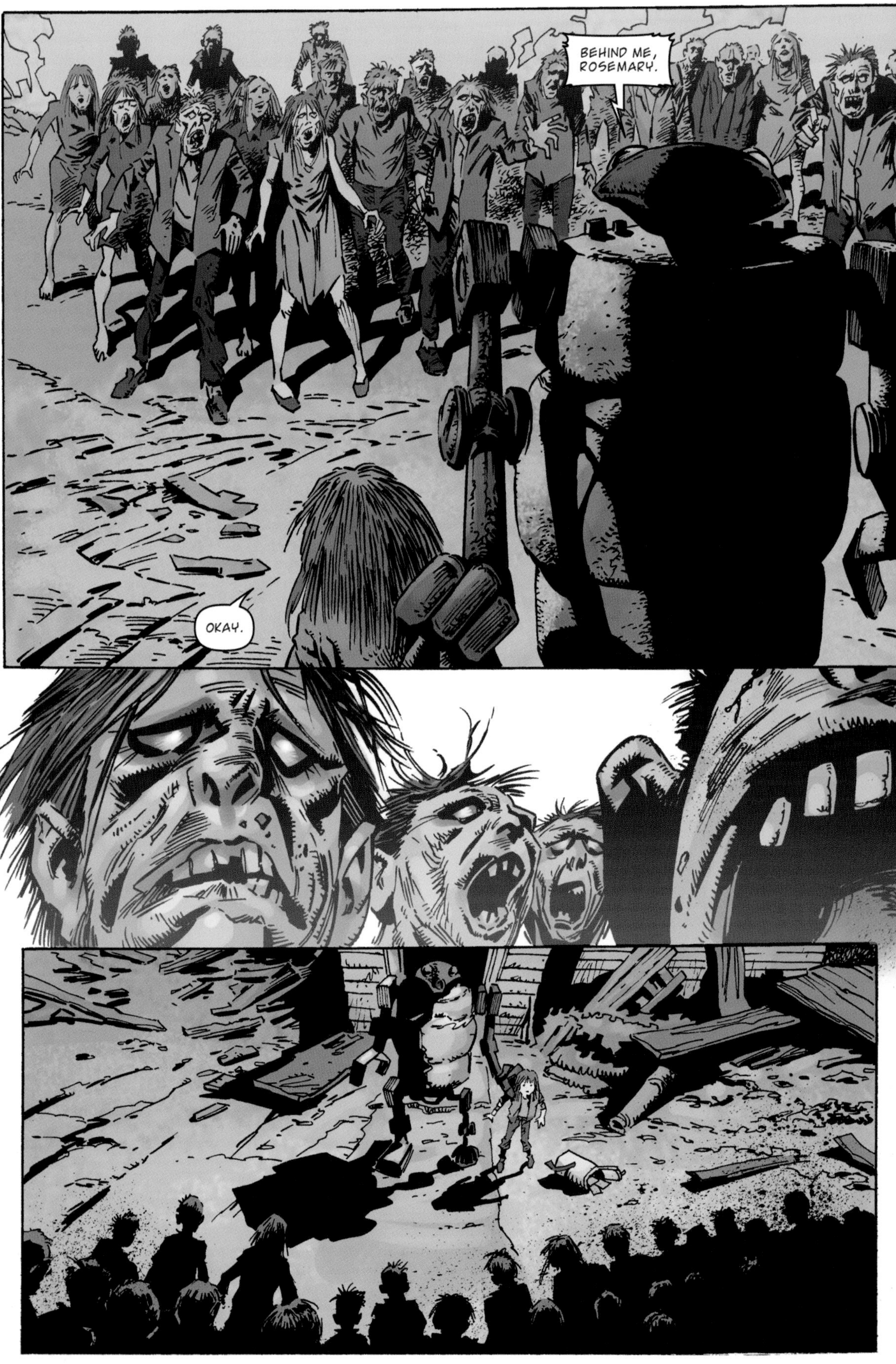

BEHIND ME, ROSEMARY.
OKAY.

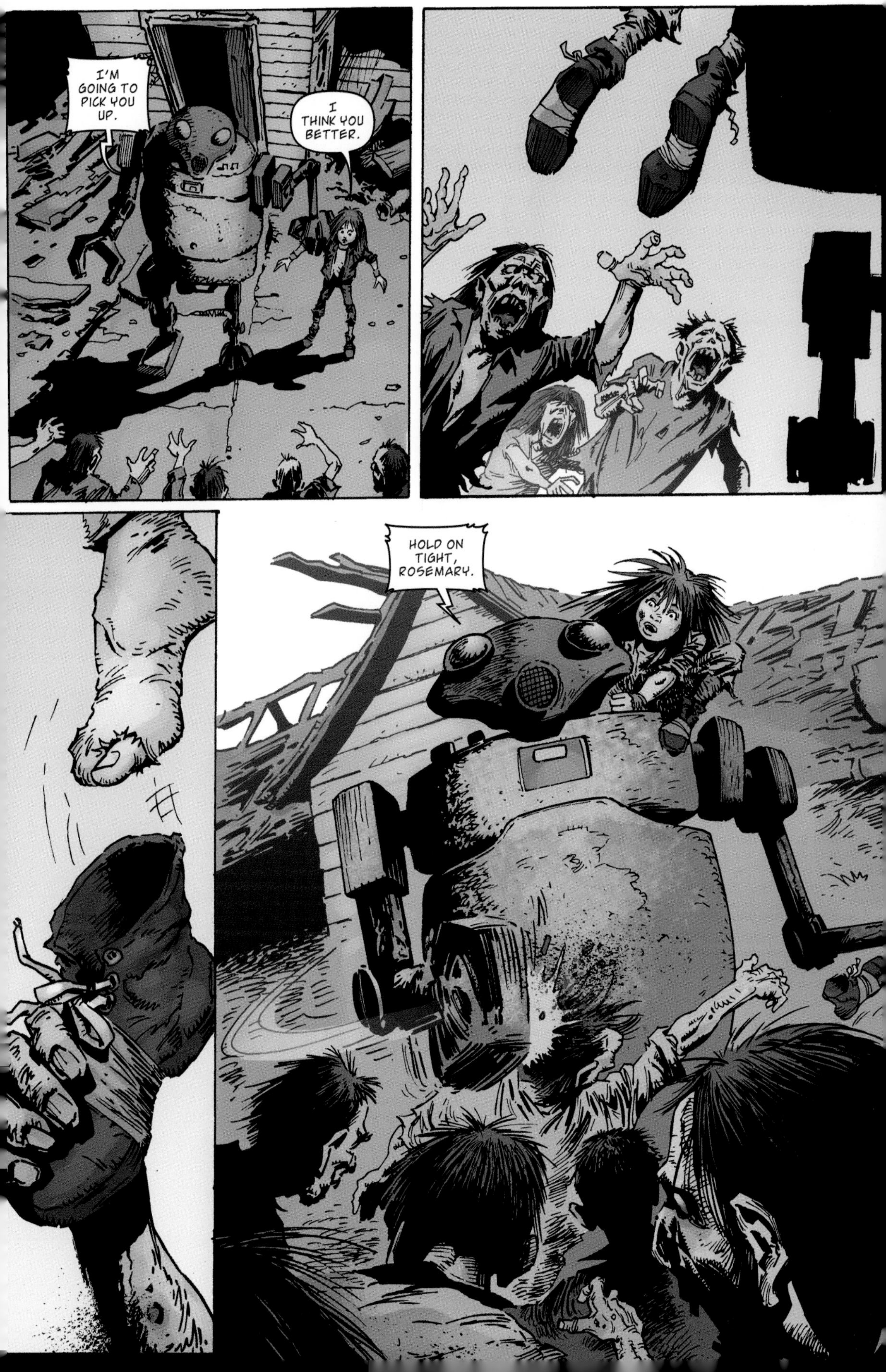
I'M GOING TO PICK YOU UP.
I THINK YOU BETTER.
HOLD ON TIGHT, ROSEMARY.

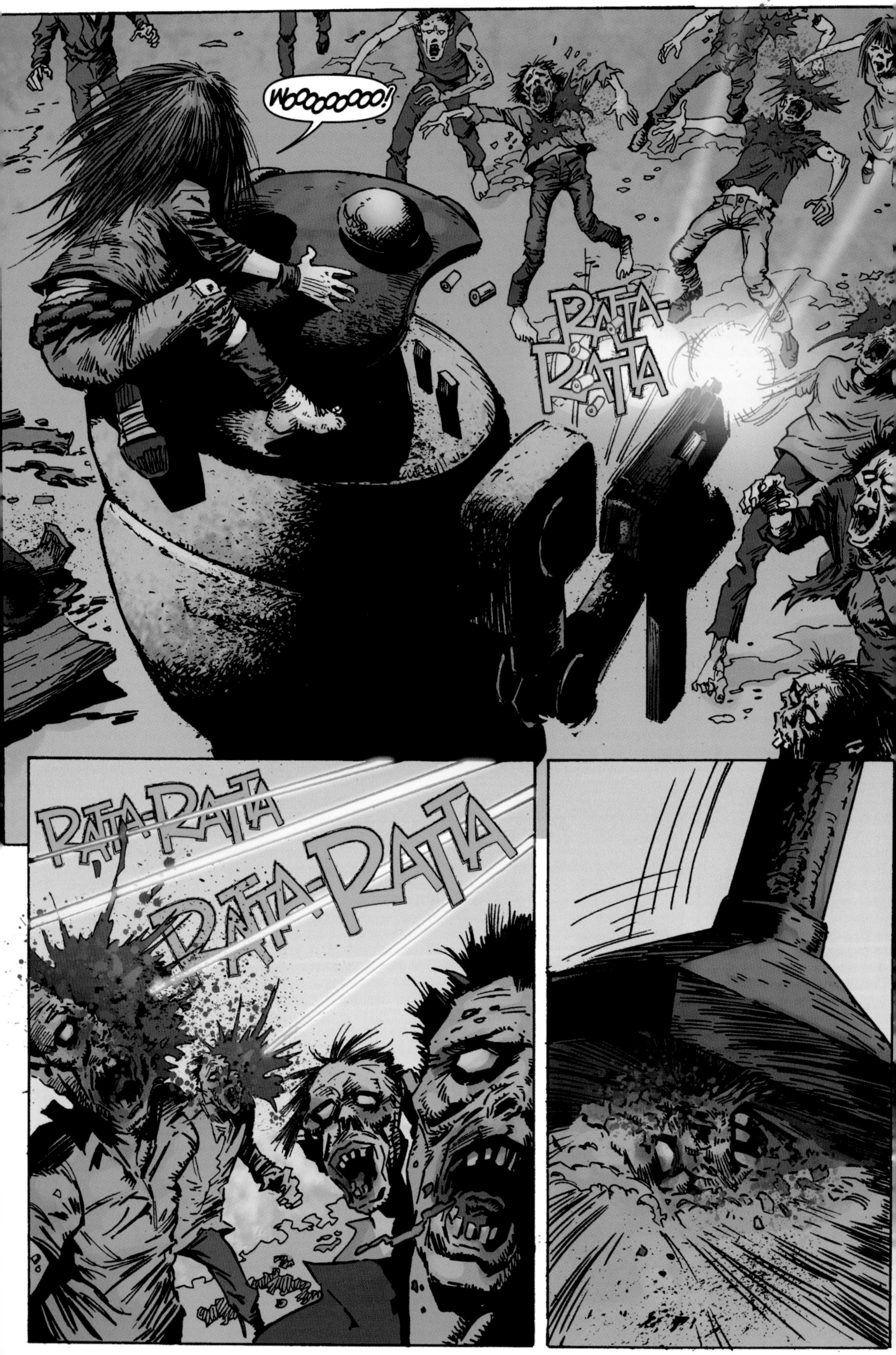
WOOOOOOOOO!
RATA-RATA
RATA-RATA
RATA-RATA

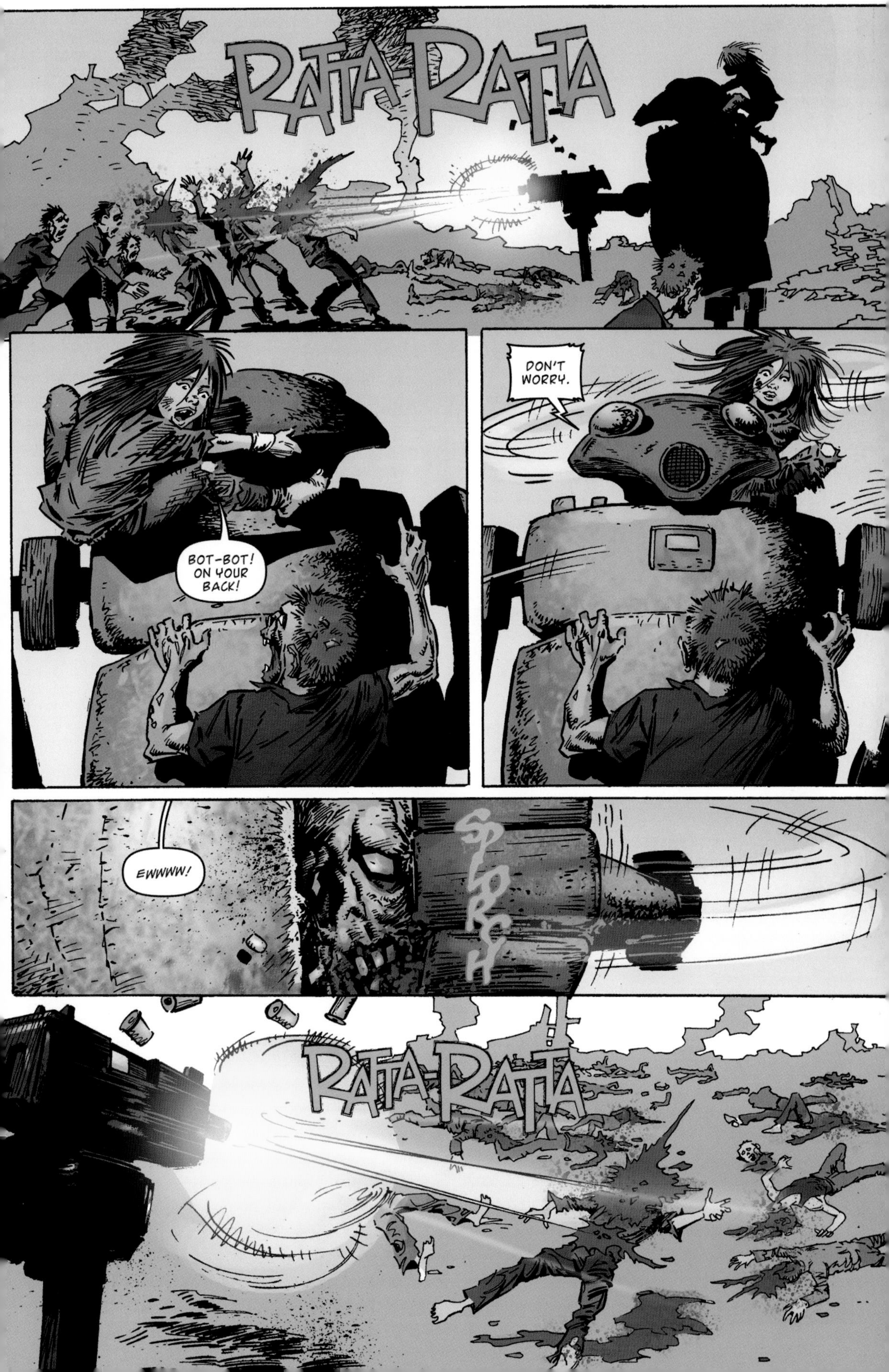
RATA-RATA
BOT-BOT! ON YOUR BACK!
DON'T WORRY.
EWWWW!
SPLORCH
RATA-RATA

I HAVE SOMETHING TO SAY TO YOU.

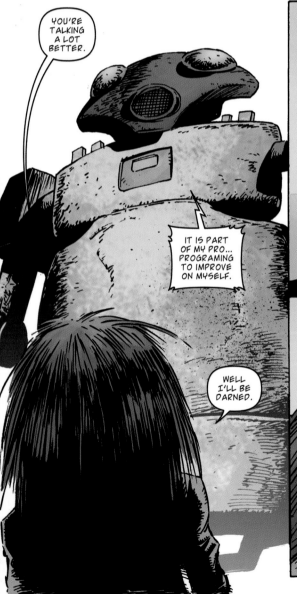

YOU'RE TALKING A LOT BETTER.

IT IS PART OF MY PRO... PROGRAMING TO IMPROVE ON MYSELF.

WELL I'LL BE DARNED.

I AM SORRY, ROSEMARY. I KILLED THEM. I KNOW THEY MEAN... MEANT SOMETHING TO YOU.

IT'S OKAY. THEY WERE KIND OF GROSS.

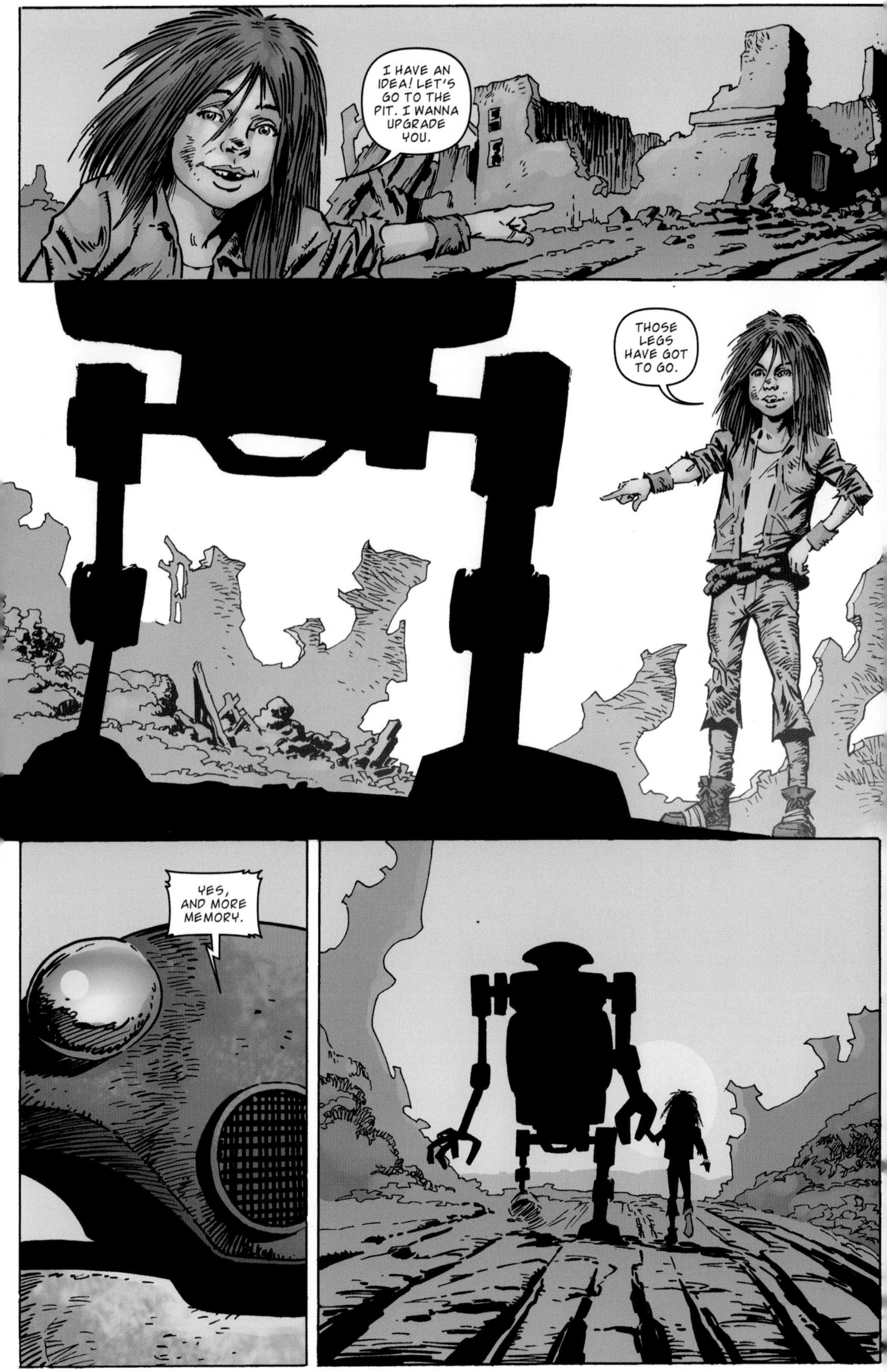
I HAVE AN IDEA! LET'S GO TO THE PIT. I WANNA UPGRADE YOU.
THOSE LEGS HAVE GOT TO GO.
YES, AND MORE MEMORY.

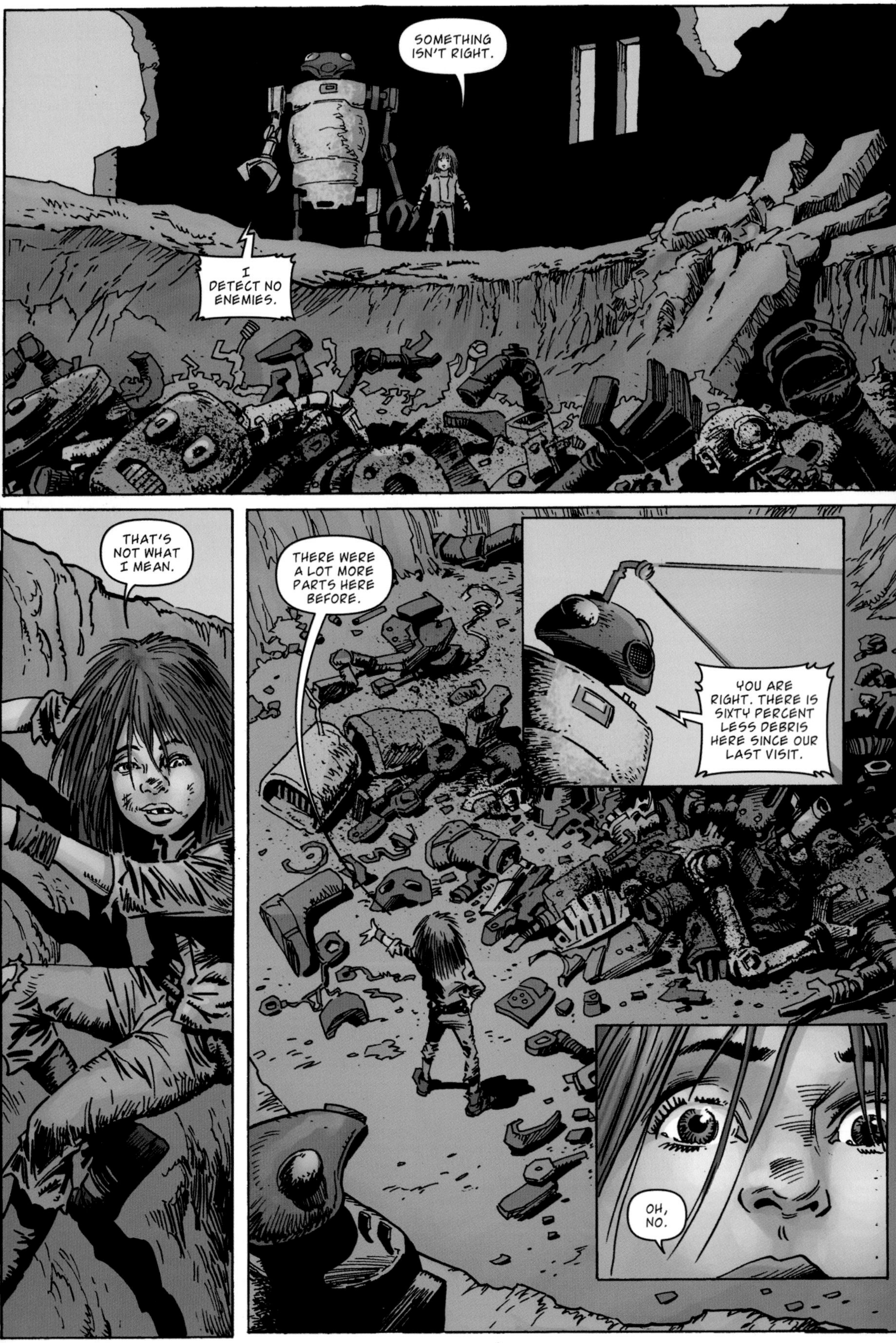
SOMETHING ISN'T RIGHT.
I DETECT NO ENEMIES.
THAT'S NOT WHAT I MEAN.
THERE WERE A LOT MORE PARTS HERE BEFORE.
YOU ARE RIGHT. THERE IS SIXTY PERCENT LESS DEBRIS HERE SINCE OUR LAST VISIT.
OH, NO.

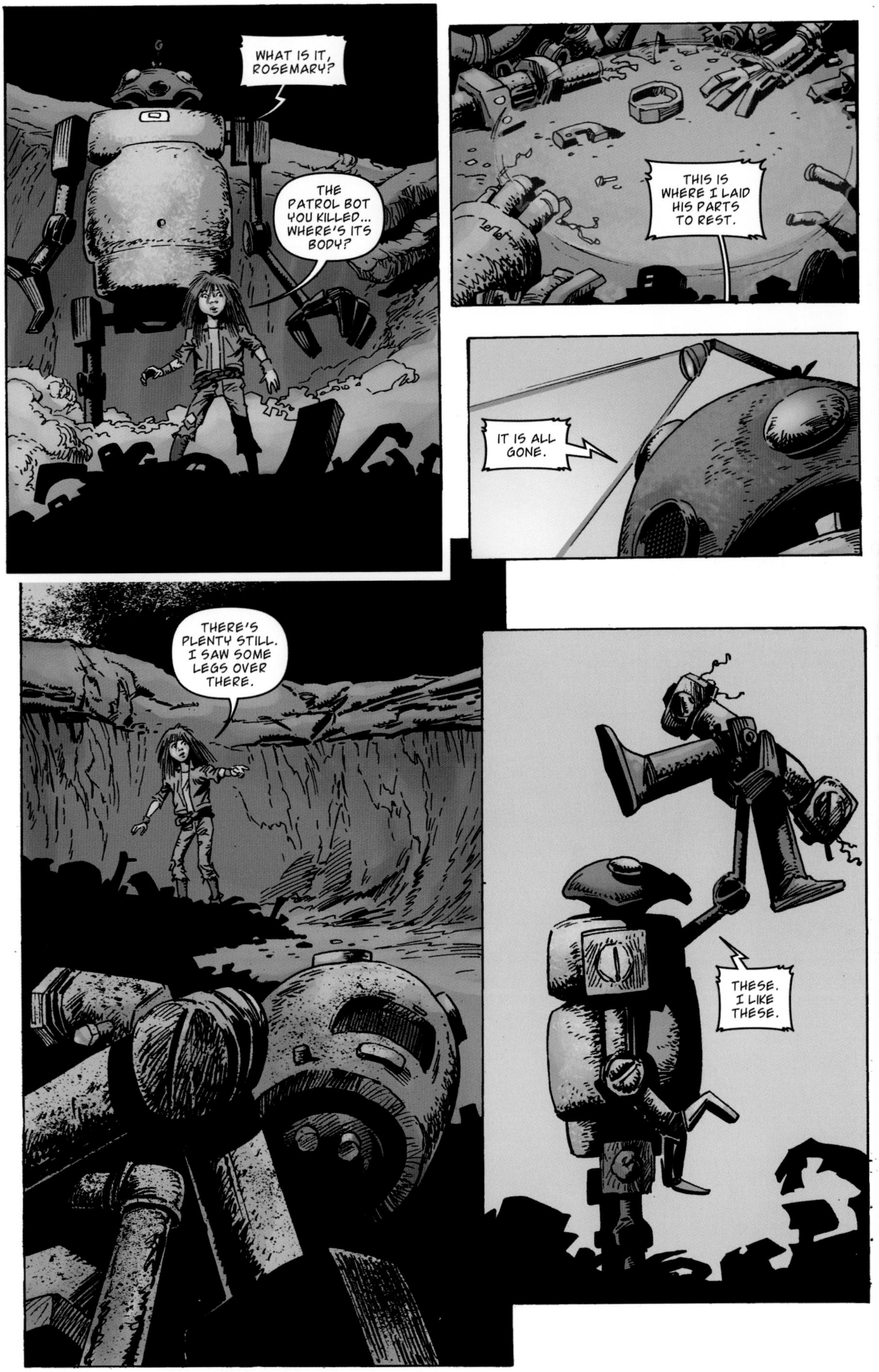
WHAT IS IT, ROSEMARY?
THE PATROL BOT YOU KILLED... WHERE'S ITS BODY?
THIS IS WHERE I LAID HIS PARTS TO REST.
IT IS ALL GONE.
THERE'S PLENTY STILL. I SAW SOME LEGS OVER THERE.
THESE. I LIKE THESE.

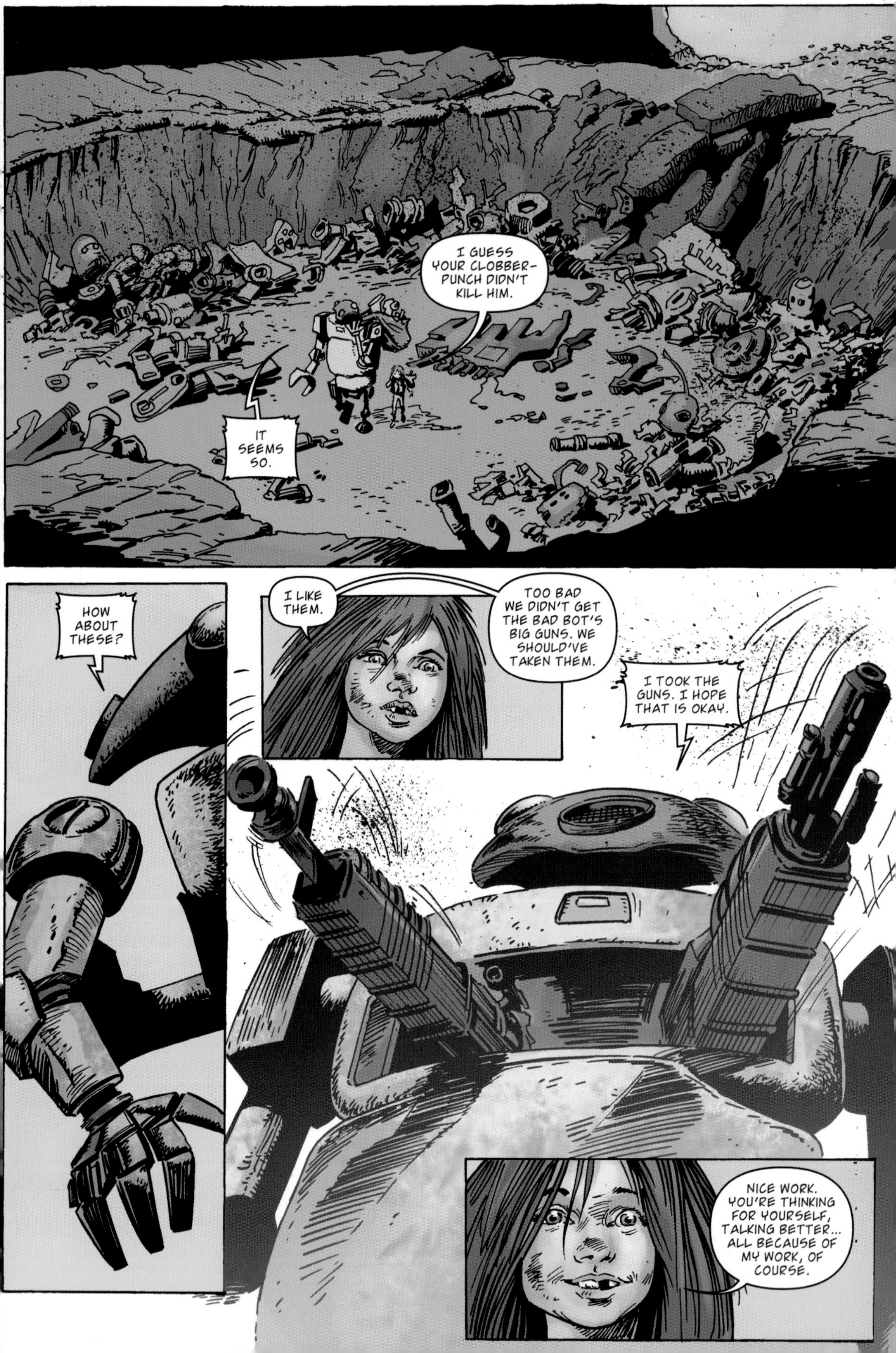
I GUESS YOUR CLOBBER-PUNCH DIDN'T KILL HIM.
IT SEEMS SO.
HOW ABOUT THESE?
I LIKE THEM.
TOO BAD WE DIDN'T GET THE BAD BOT'S BIG GUNS. WE SHOULD'VE TAKEN THEM.
I TOOK THE GUNS. I HOPE THAT IS OKAY.
NICE WORK. YOU'RE THINKING FOR YOURSELF, TALKING BETTER... ALL BECAUSE OF MY WORK, OF COURSE.

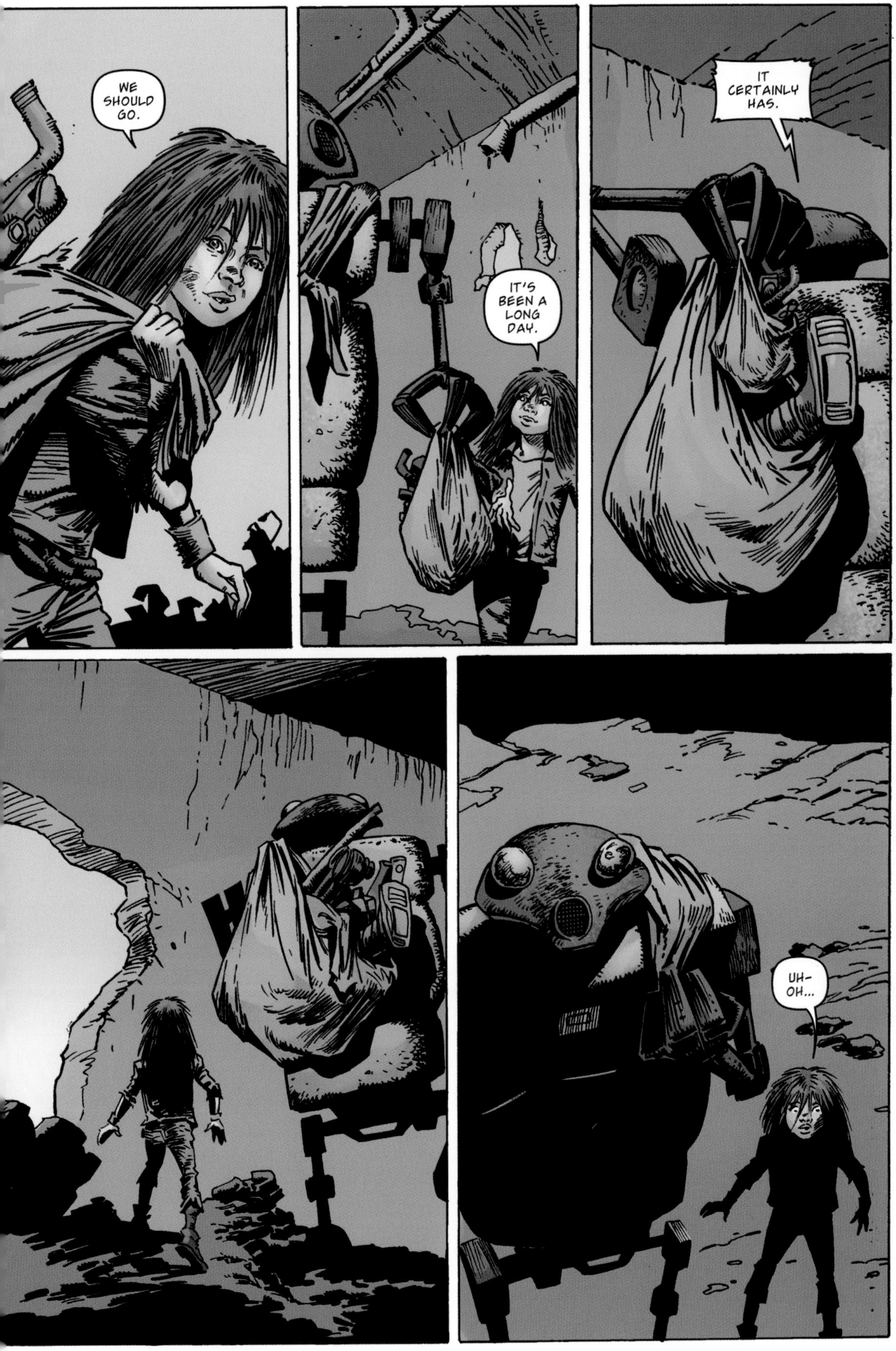
WE SHOULD GO.
IT'S BEEN A LONG DAY.
IT CERTAINLY HAS.
UH-OH...

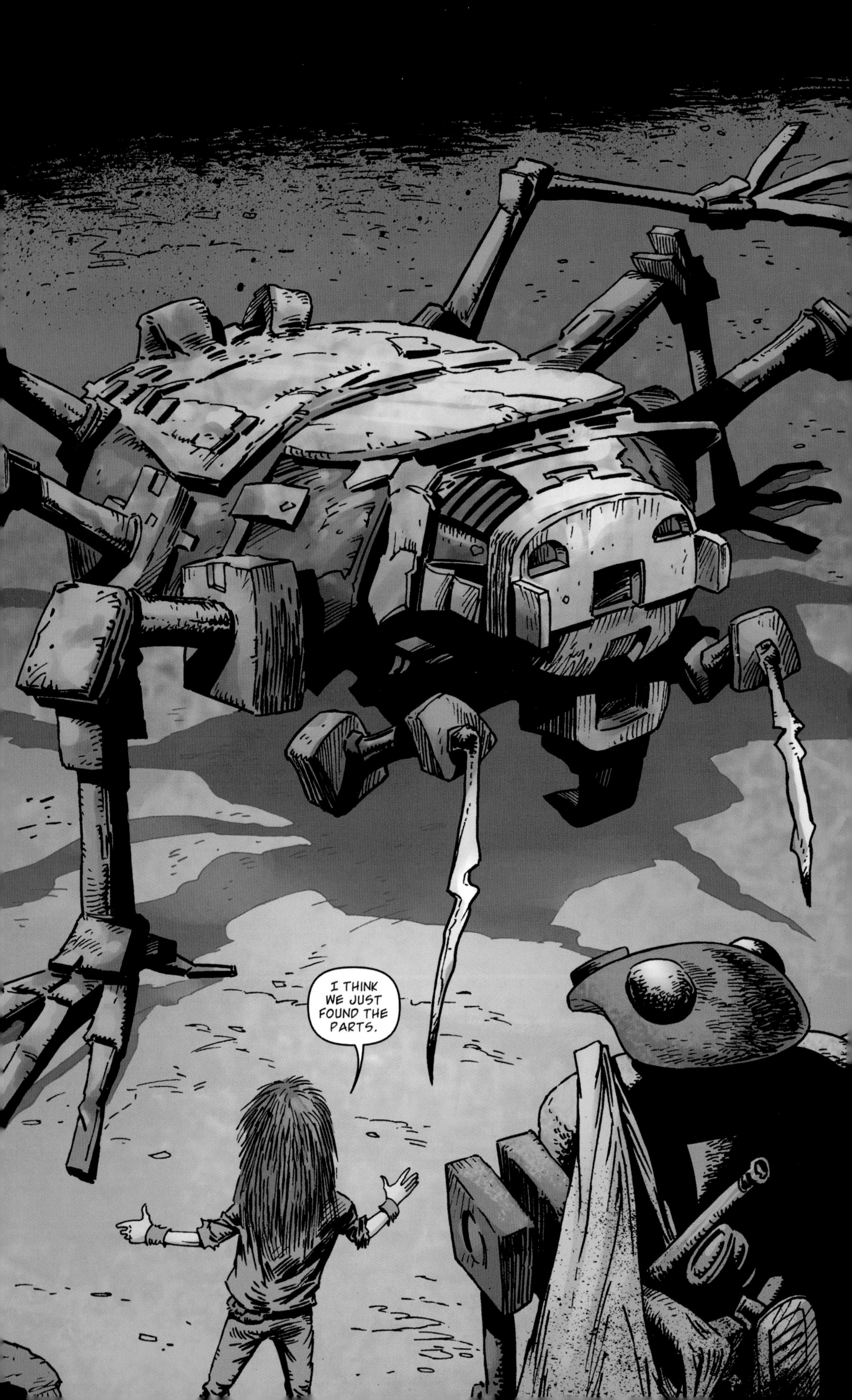
I THINK WE JUST FOUND THE PARTS.

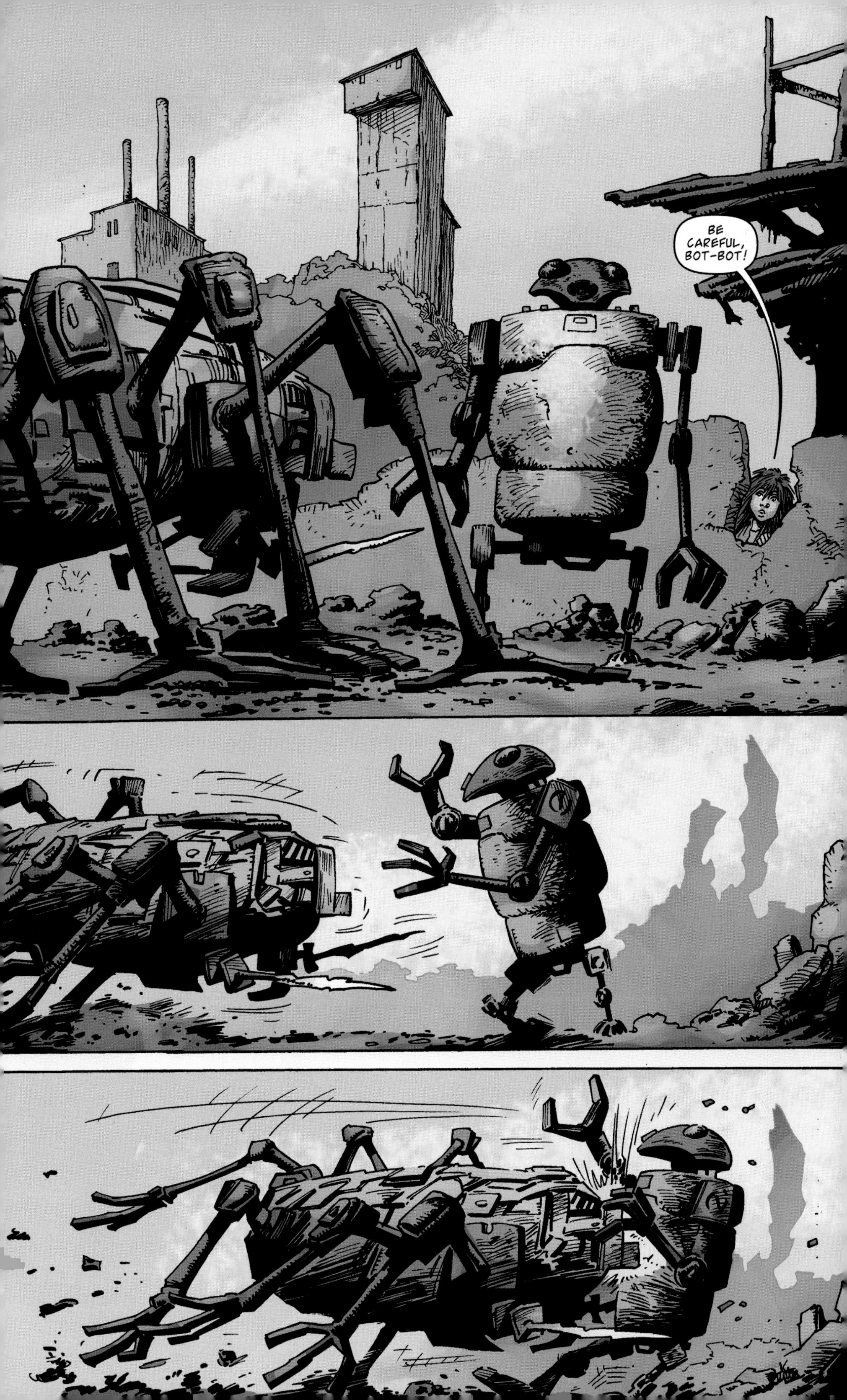
BE CAREFUL, BOT-BOT!

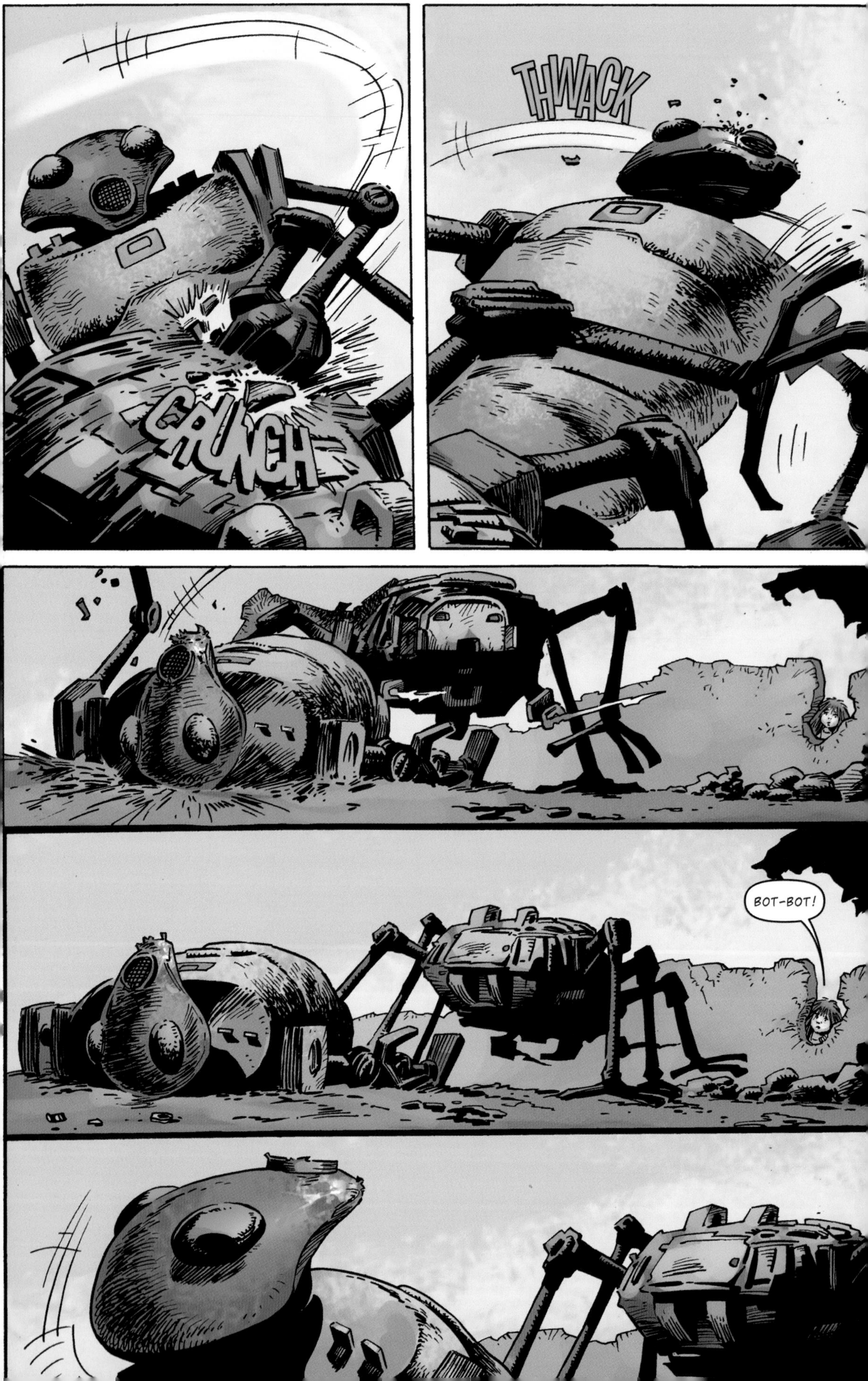
CRUNCH
THWACK
BOT-BOT!

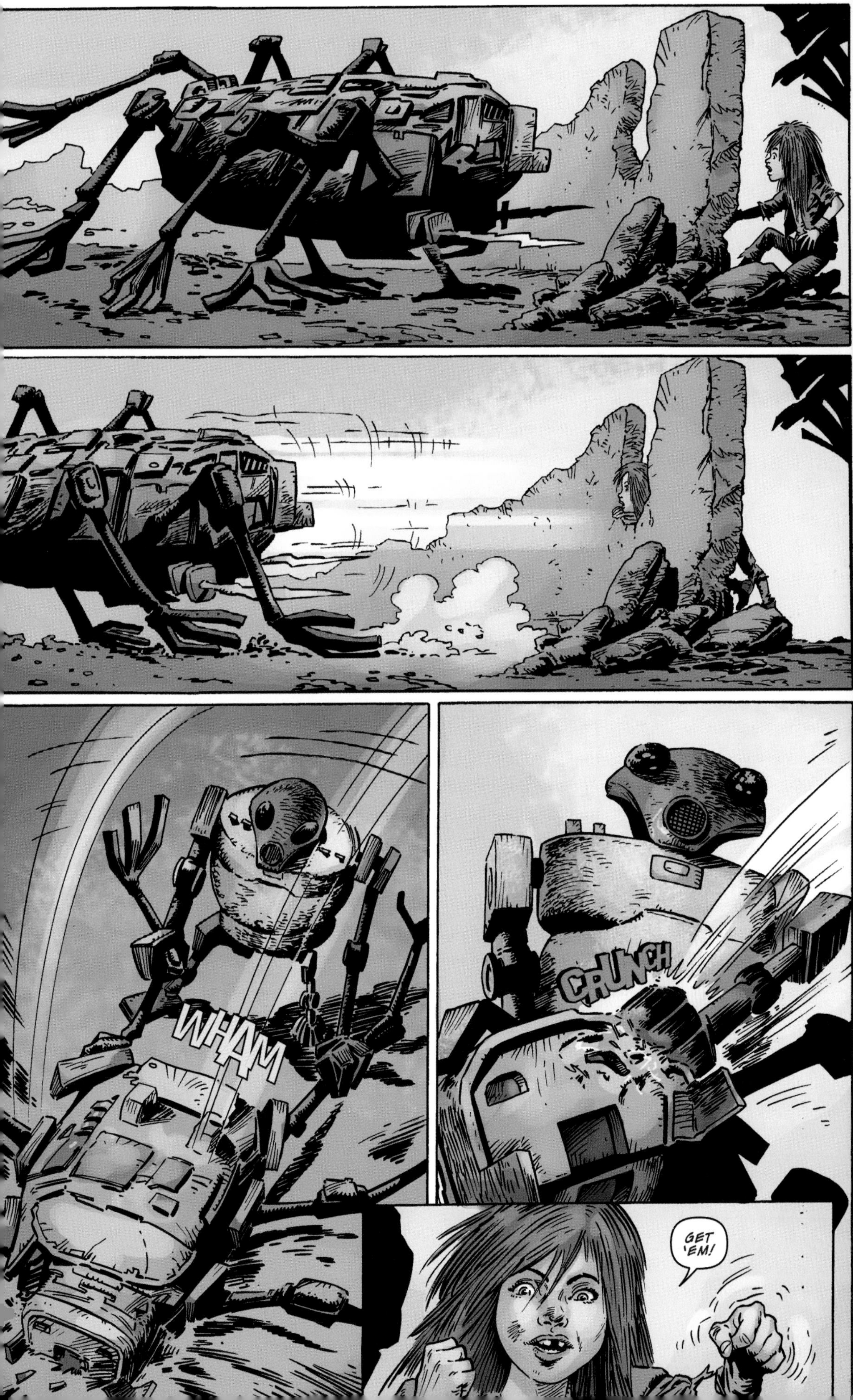
WHAM
CRUNCH
GET 'EM!

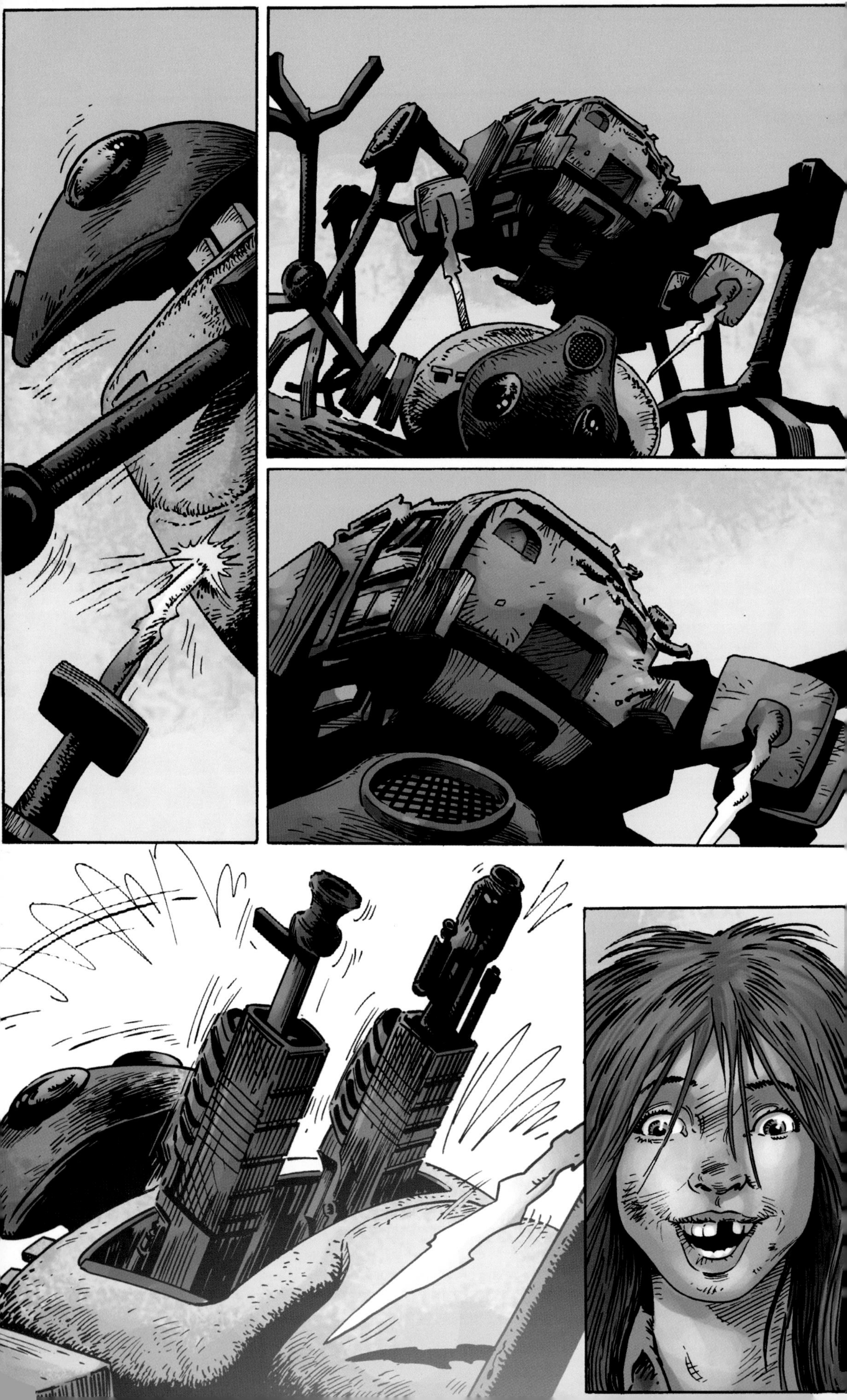

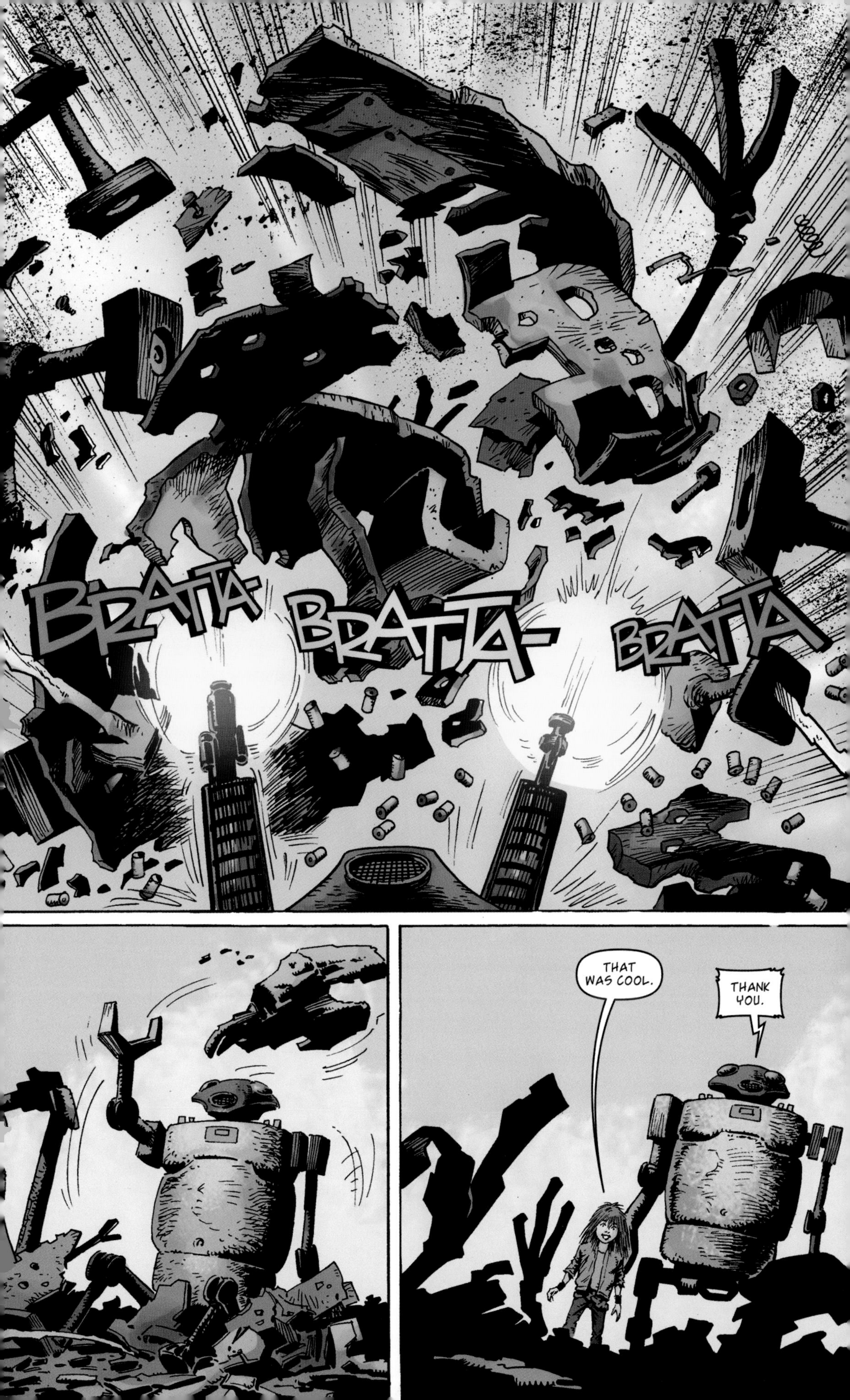
BRATTA-
BRATTA-
BRATTA
THAT WAS COOL.
THANK YOU.

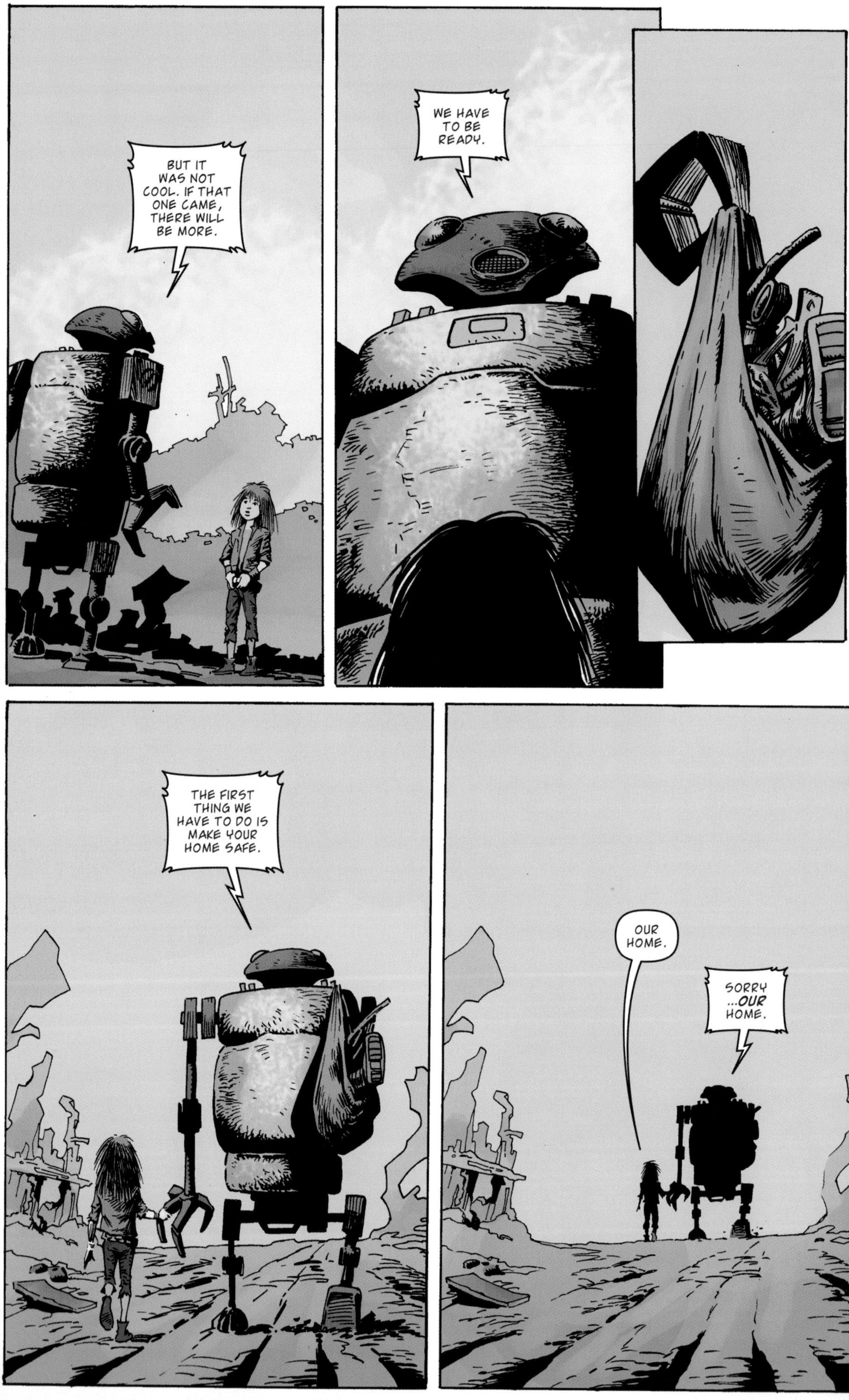
BUT IT WAS NOT COOL. IF THAT ONE CAME, THERE WILL BE MORE.
WE HAVE TO BE READY.
THE FIRST THING WE HAVE TO DO IS MAKE YOUR HOME SAFE.
OUR HOME.
SORRY ...*OUR* HOME.

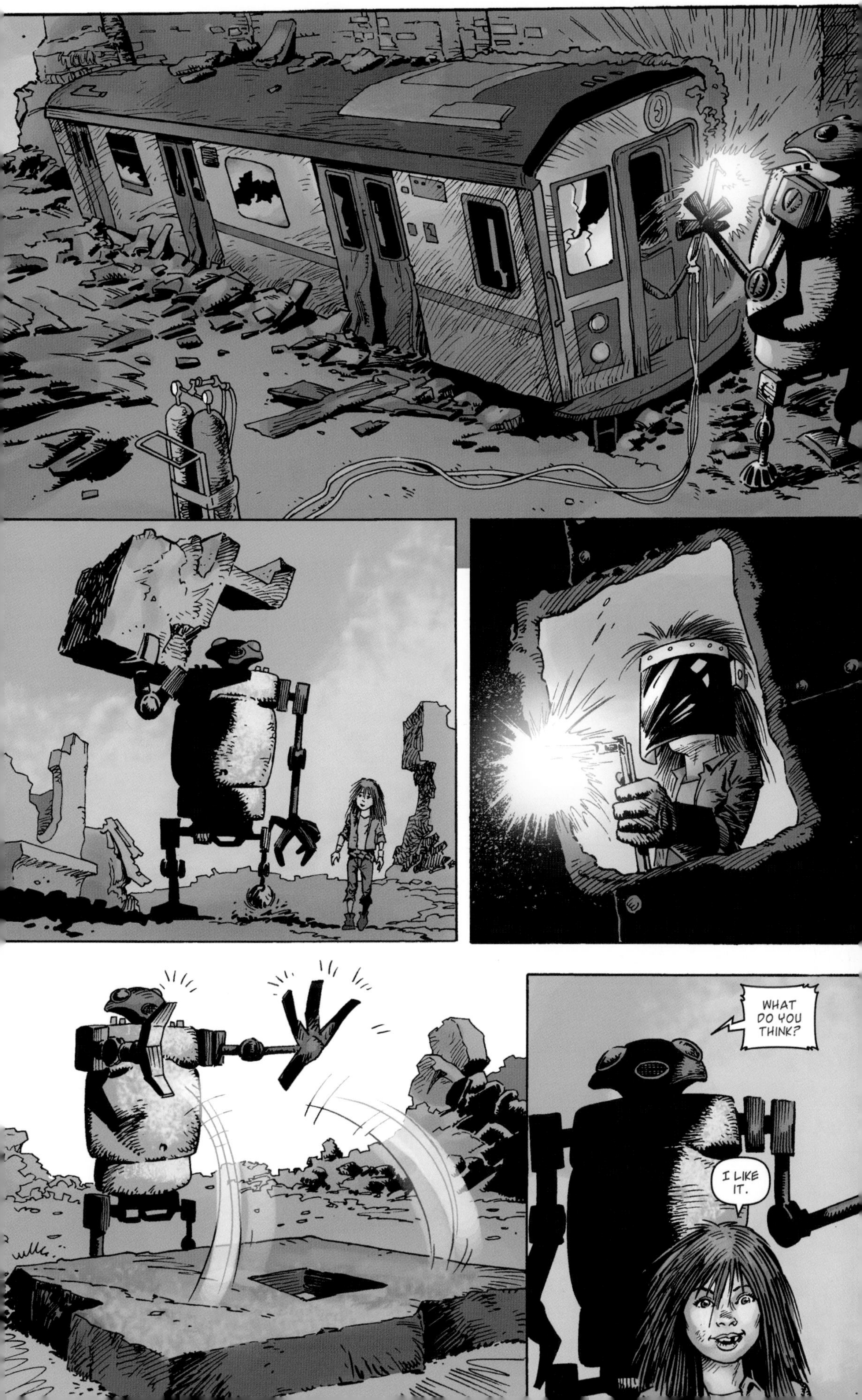
WHAT DO YOU THINK?
I LIKE IT.

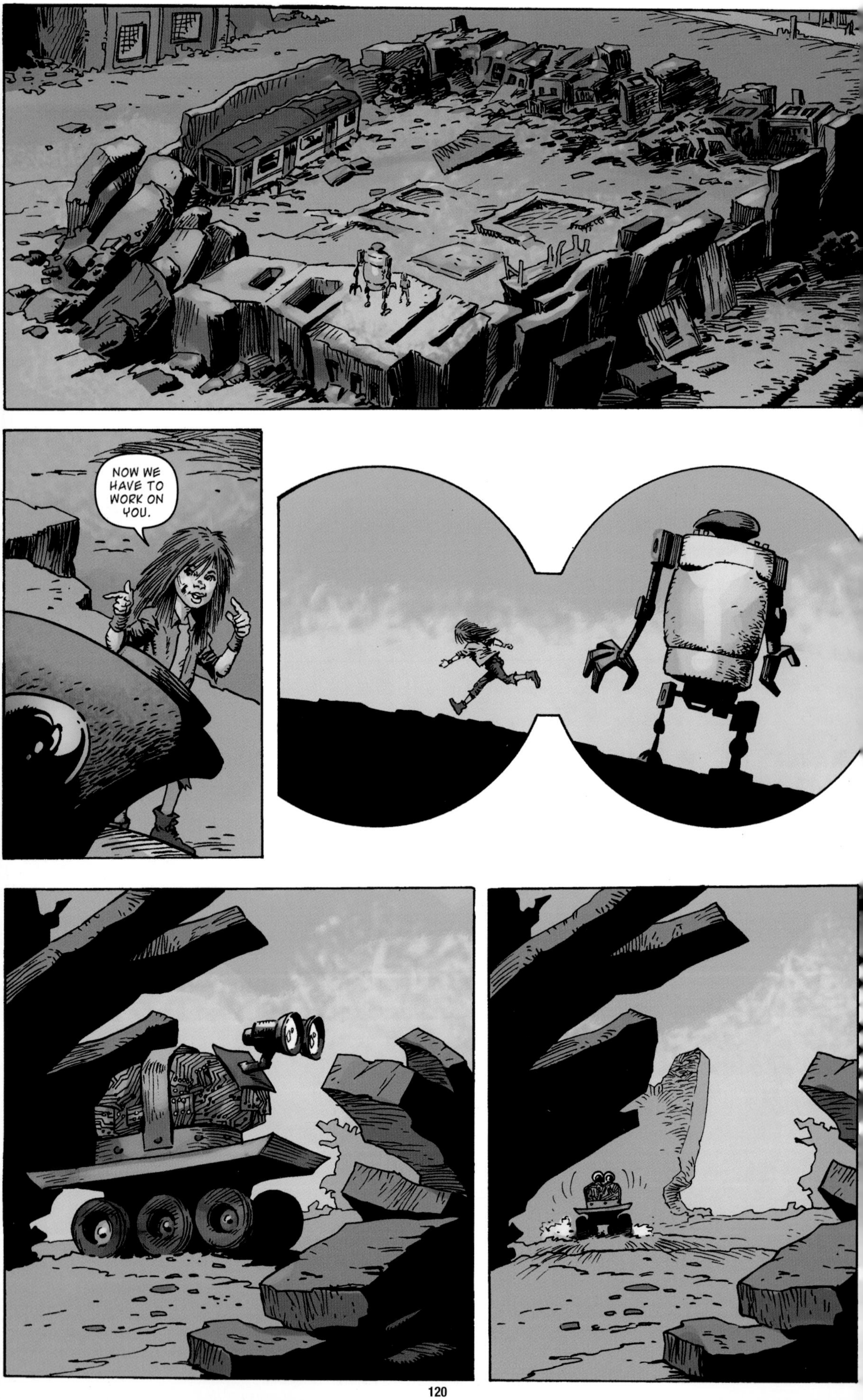
NOW WE HAVE TO WORK ON YOU.

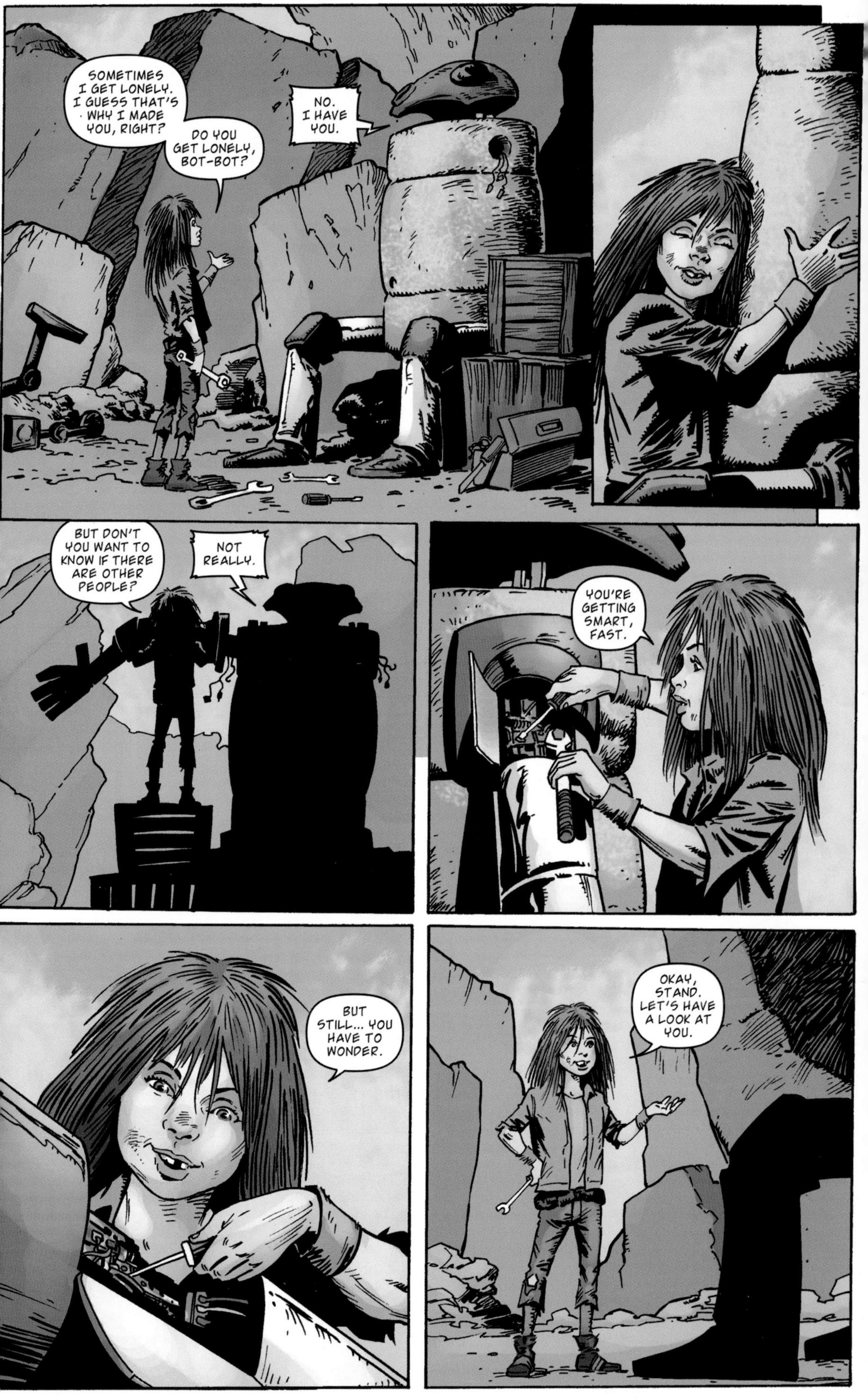
SOMETIMES I GET LONELY. I GUESS THAT'S WHY I MADE YOU, RIGHT?
DO YOU GET LONELY, BOT-BOT?
NO. I HAVE YOU.
BUT DON'T YOU WANT TO KNOW IF THERE ARE OTHER PEOPLE?
NOT REALLY.
YOU'RE GETTING SMART, FAST.
BUT STILL... YOU HAVE TO WONDER.
OKAY, STAND. LET'S HAVE A LOOK AT YOU.

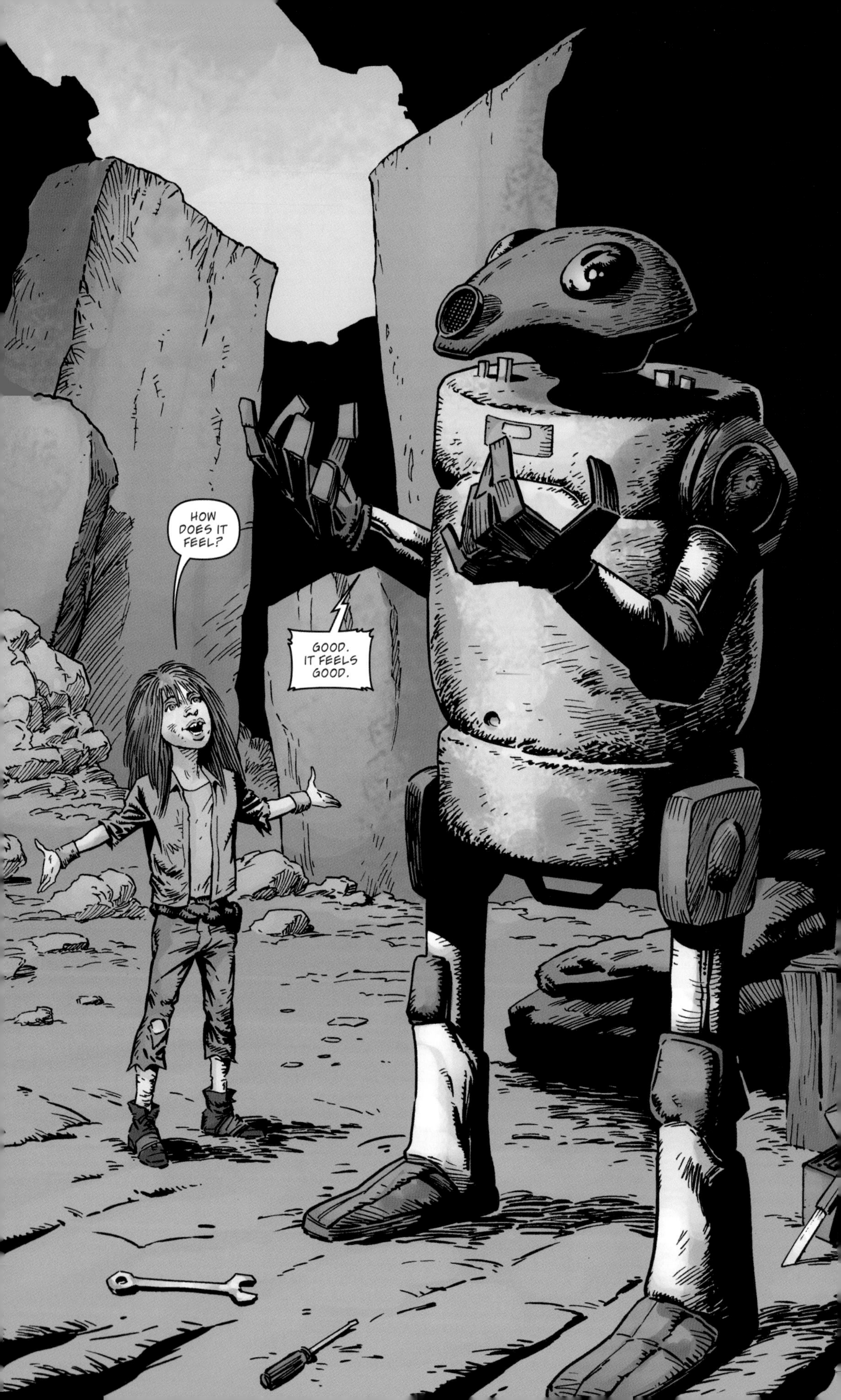

HOW DOES IT FEEL?
GOOD. IT FEELS GOOD.

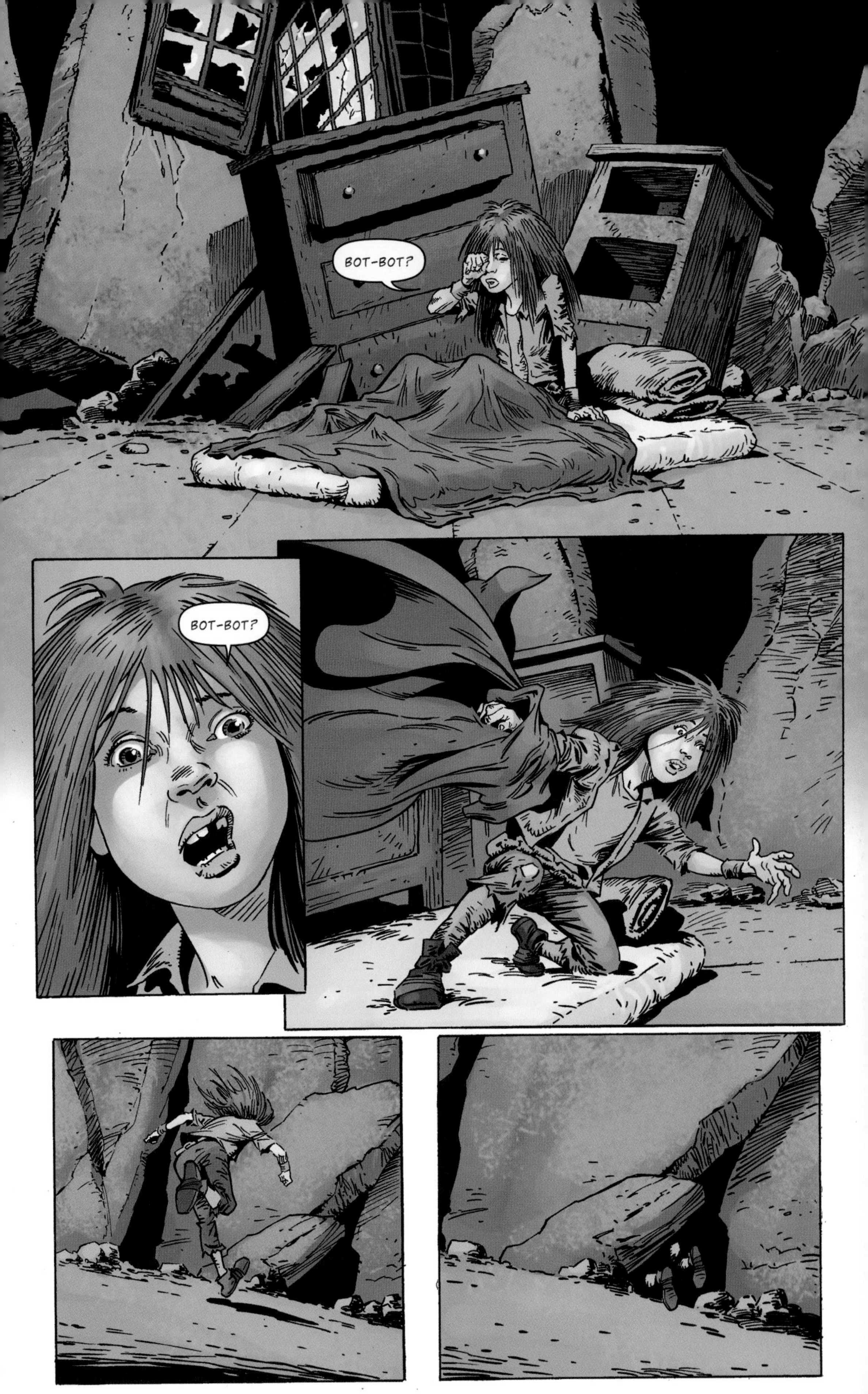
BOT-BOT?
BOT-BOT?

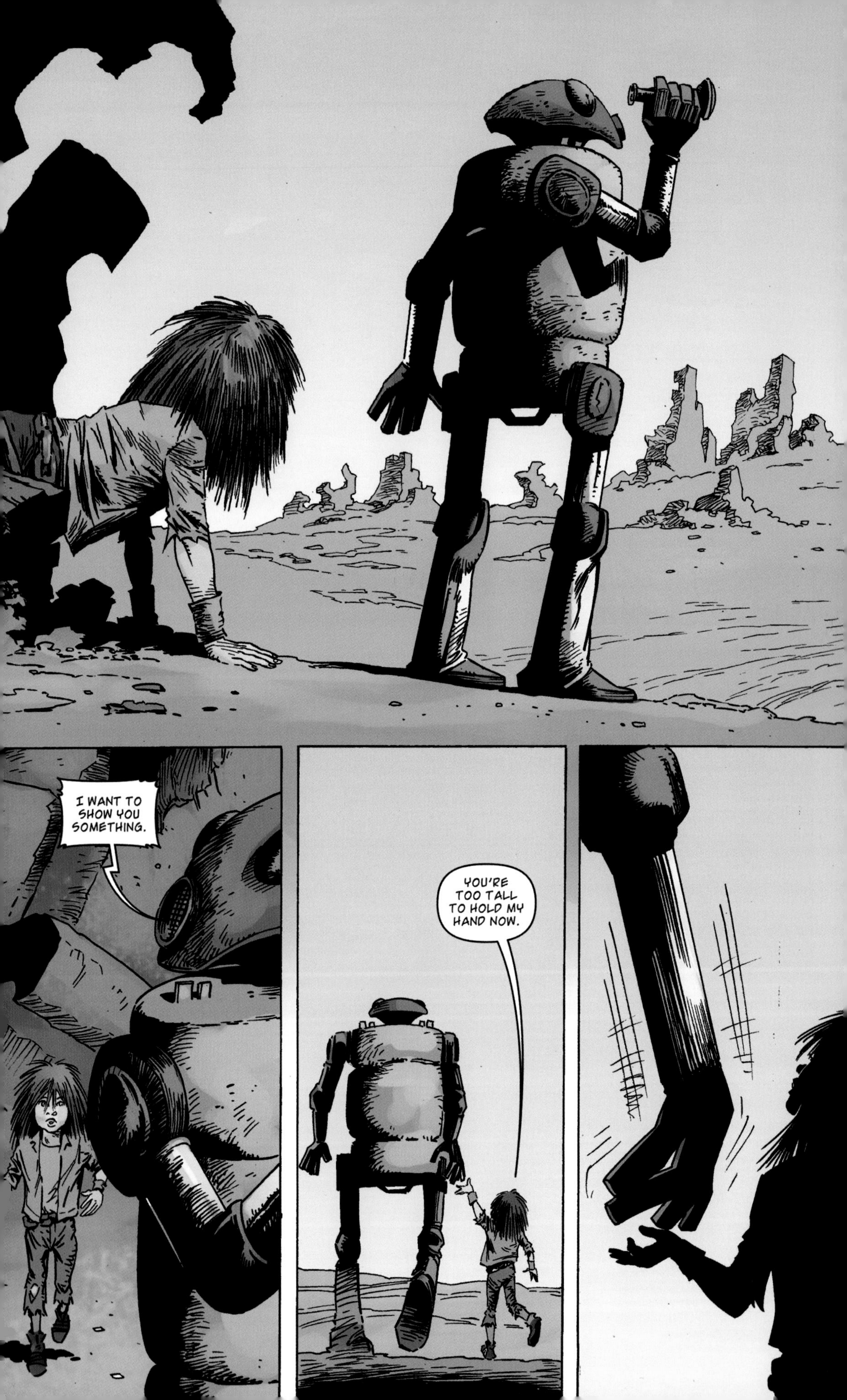
I WANT TO SHOW YOU SOMETHING.
YOU'RE TOO TALL TO HOLD MY HAND NOW.

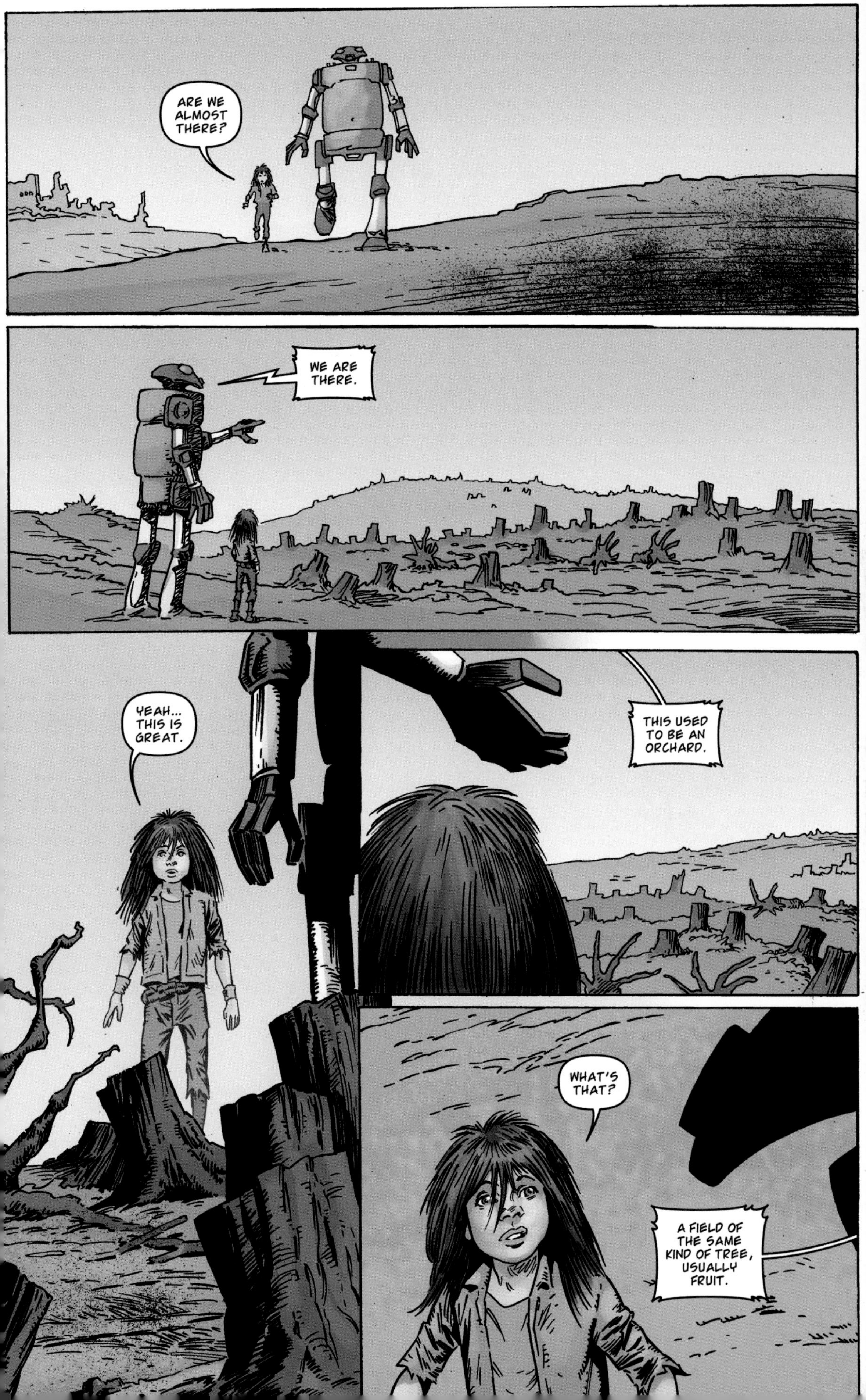
ARE WE ALMOST THERE?
WE ARE THERE.
YEAH... THIS IS GREAT.
THIS USED TO BE AN ORCHARD.
WHAT'S THAT?
A FIELD OF THE SAME KIND OF TREE, USUALLY FRUIT.

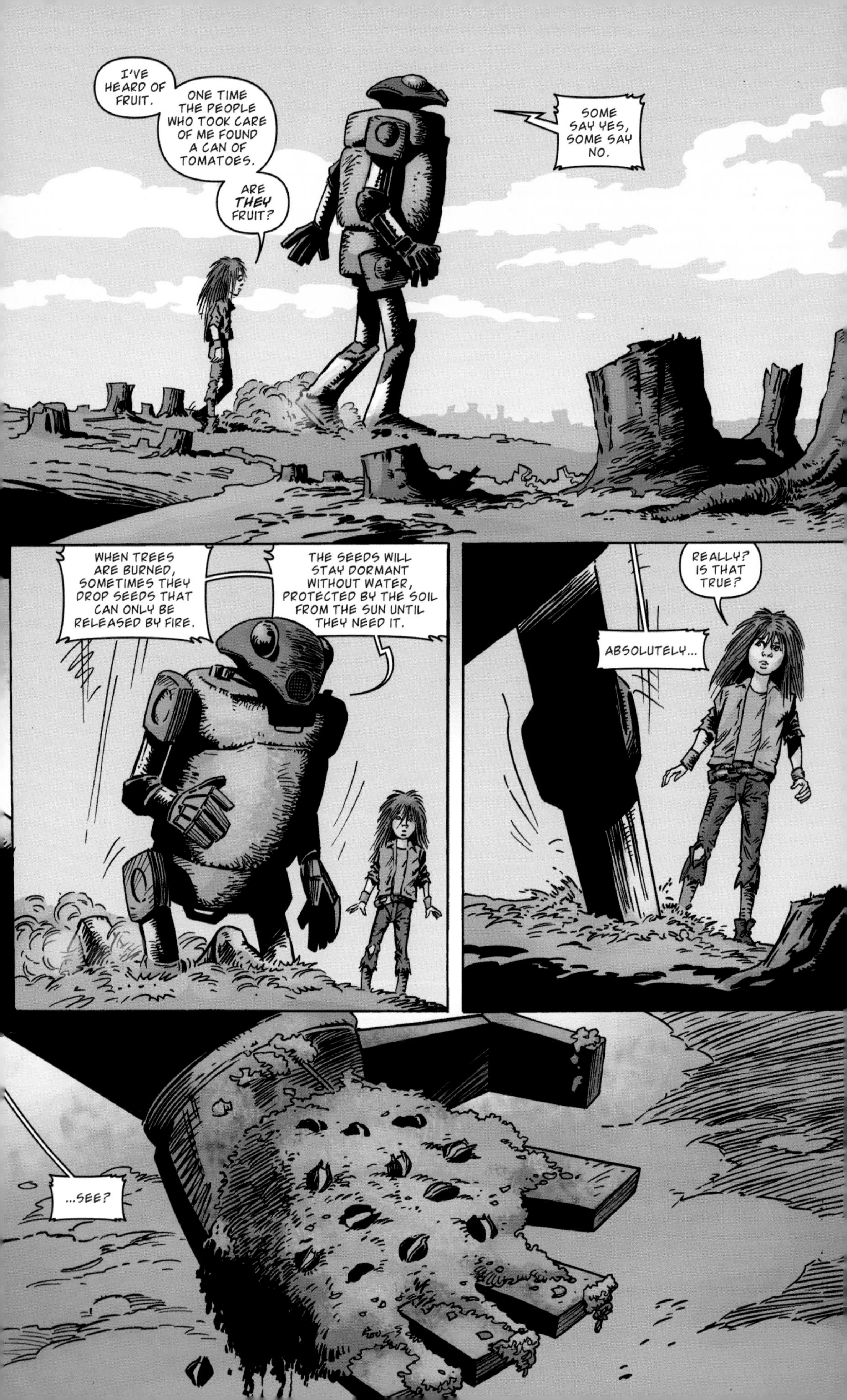
I'VE HEARD OF FRUIT.
ONE TIME THE PEOPLE WHO TOOK CARE OF ME FOUND A CAN OF TOMATOES.
ARE *THEY* FRUIT?
SOME SAY YES, SOME SAY NO.
WHEN TREES ARE BURNED, SOMETIMES THEY DROP SEEDS THAT CAN ONLY BE RELEASED BY FIRE.
THE SEEDS WILL STAY DORMANT WITHOUT WATER, PROTECTED BY THE SOIL FROM THE SUN UNTIL THEY NEED IT.
REALLY? IS THAT TRUE?
ABSOLUTELY...
...SEE?

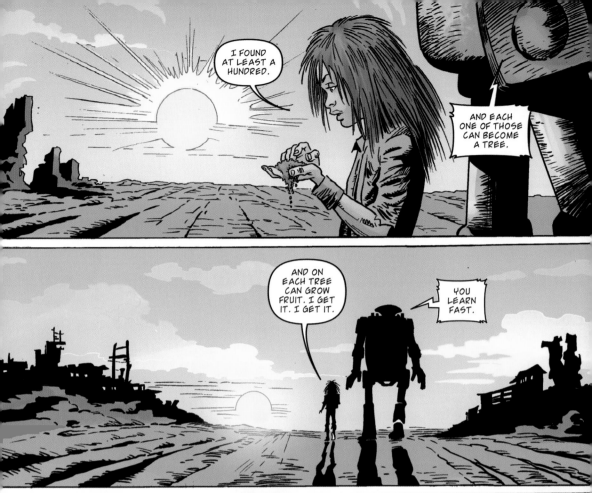

I FOUND AT LEAST A HUNDRED.

AND EACH ONE OF THOSE CAN BECOME A TREE.

AND ON EACH TREE CAN GROW FRUIT. I GET IT. I GET IT.

YOU LEARN FAST.

LOOK WHO'S TALKING.

WAIT, ROSEMARY. THERE IS SOMETHING AHEAD OF US.

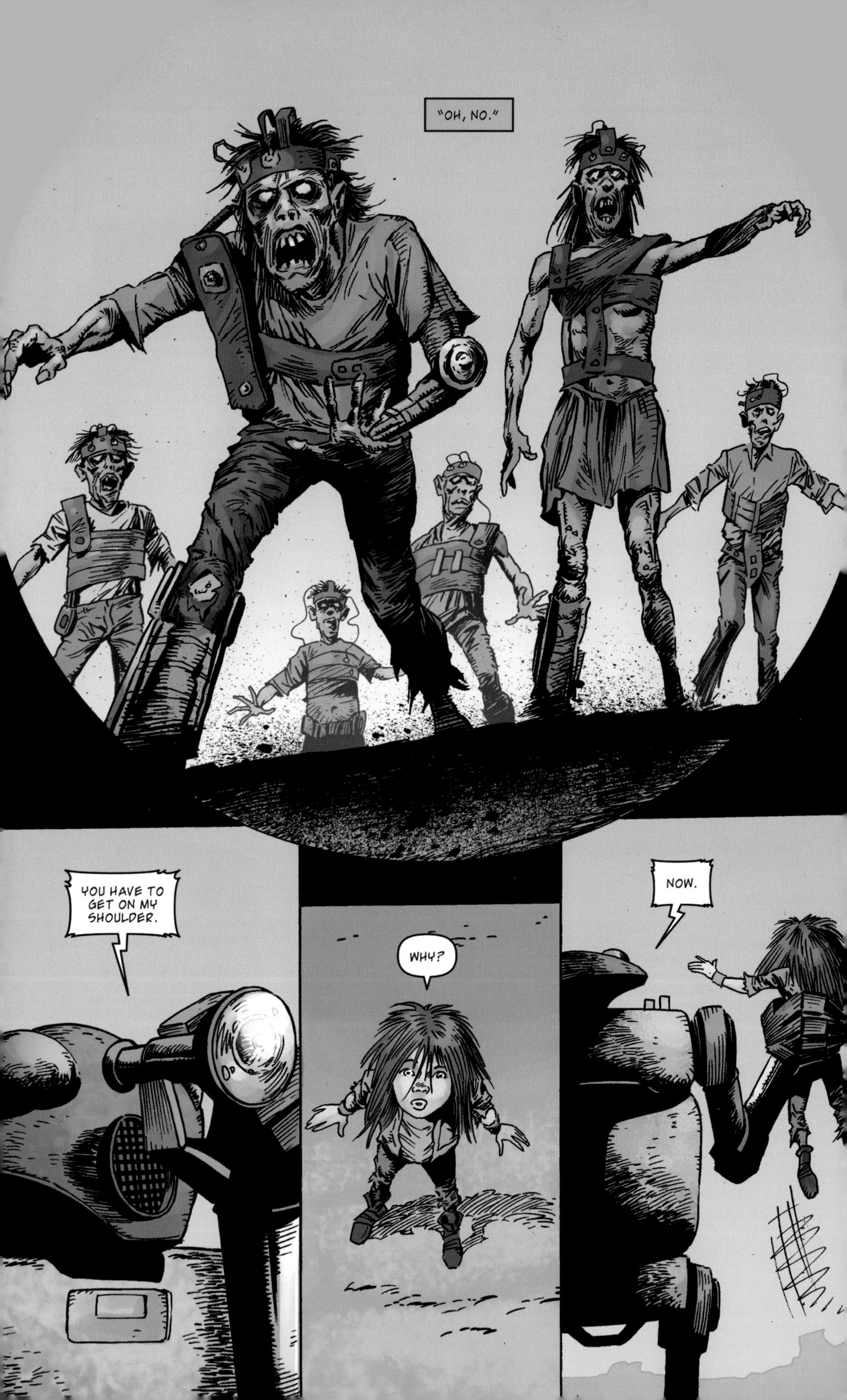
"OH, NO."
YOU HAVE TO GET ON MY SHOULDER.
WHY?
NOW.

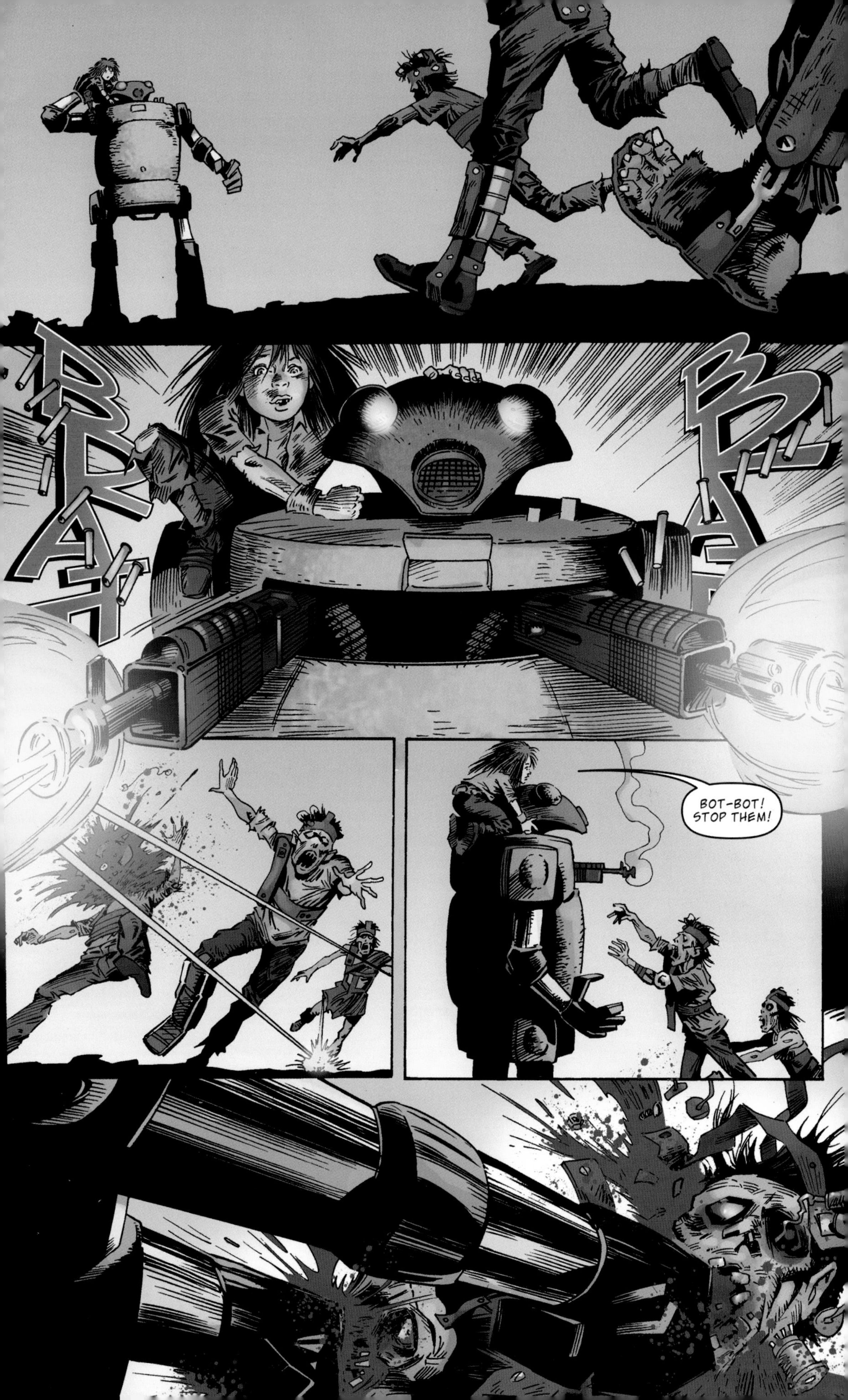
BRAT
BRAT
BOT-BOT! STOP THEM!

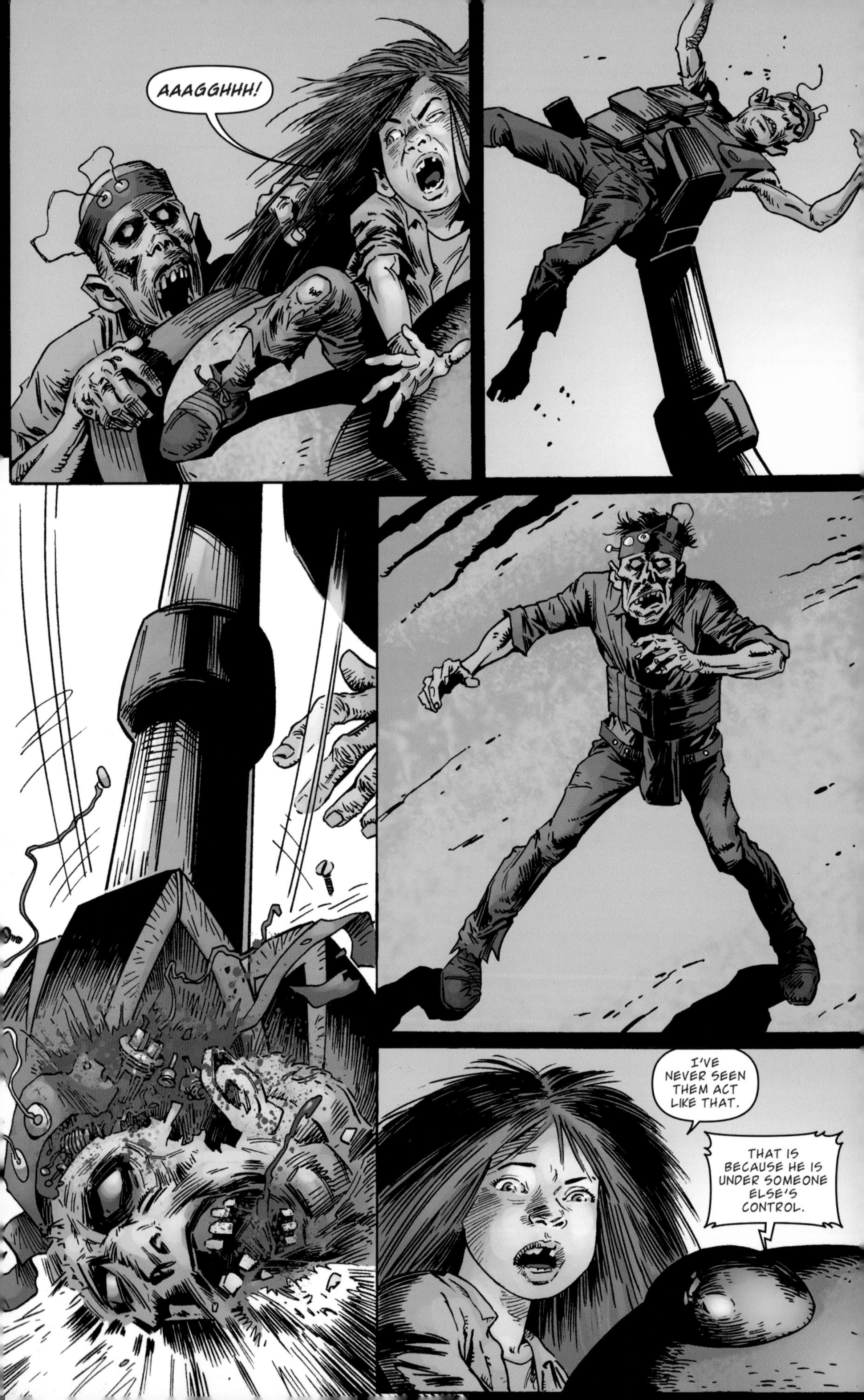
AAAGGHHH!
I'VE NEVER SEEN THEM ACT LIKE THAT.
THAT IS BECAUSE HE IS UNDER SOMEONE ELSE'S CONTROL.

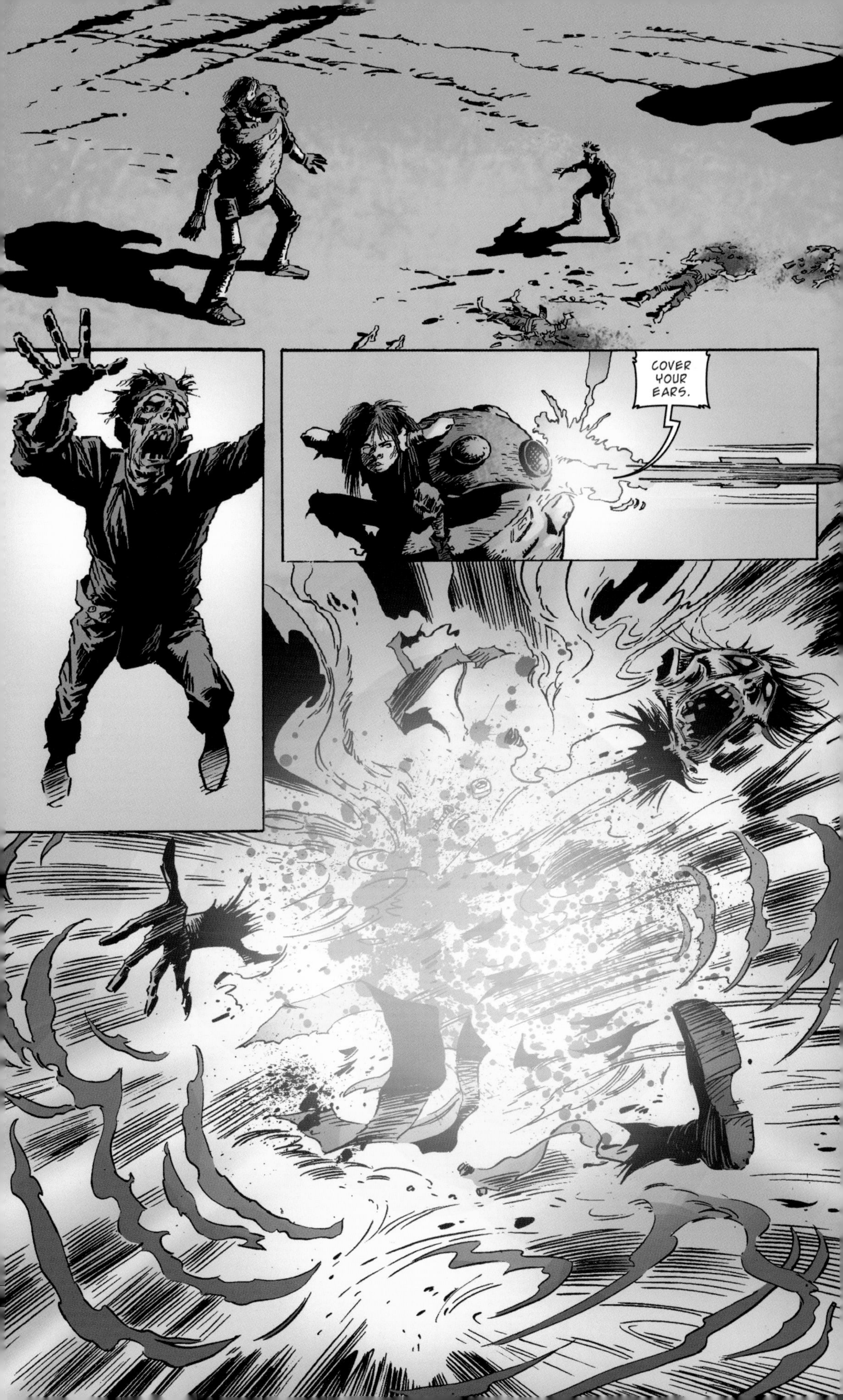
COVER YOUR EARS.

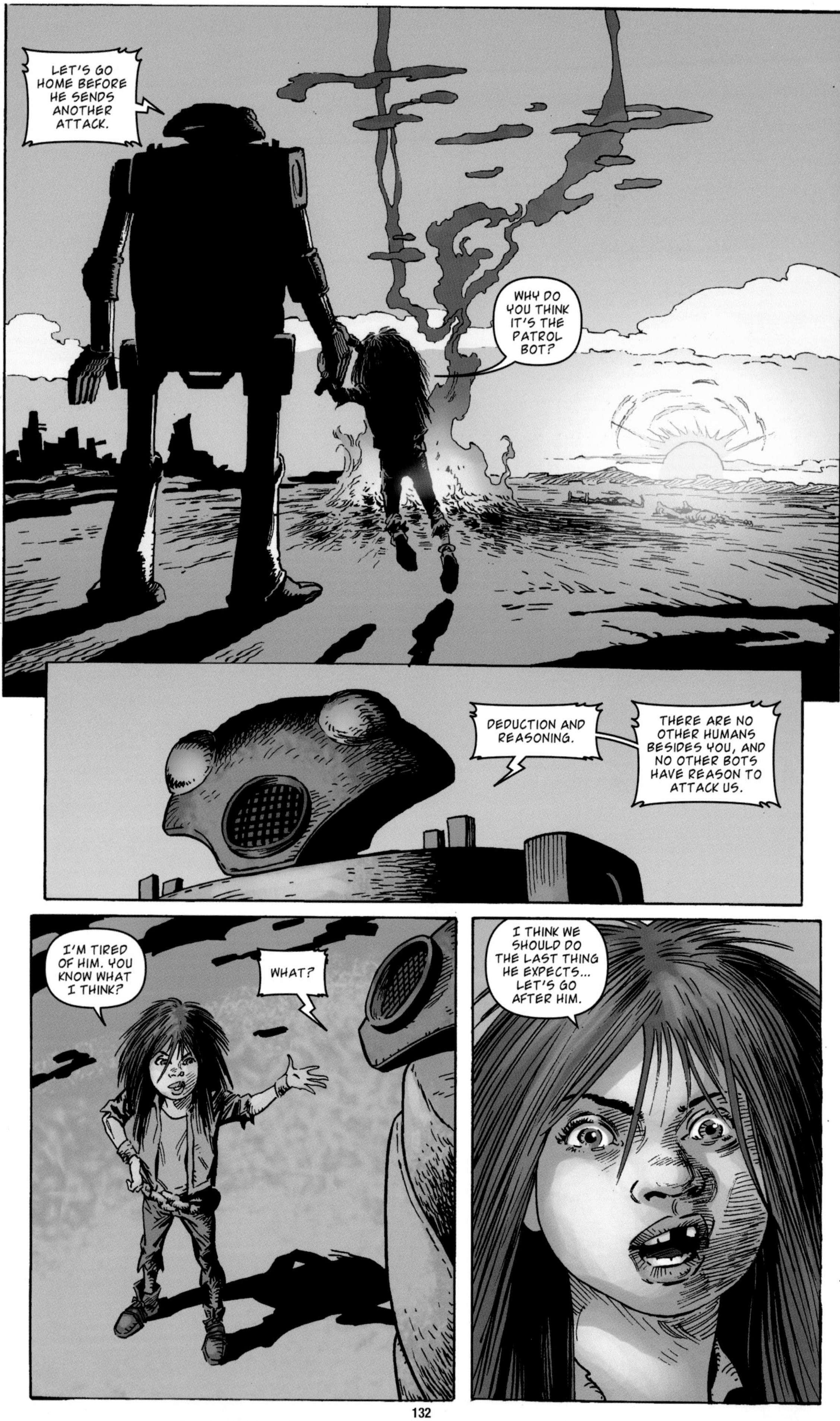
LET'S GO HOME BEFORE HE SENDS ANOTHER ATTACK.
WHY DO YOU THINK IT'S THE PATROL BOT?
DEDUCTION AND REASONING.
THERE ARE NO OTHER HUMANS BESIDES YOU, AND NO OTHER BOTS HAVE REASON TO ATTACK US.
I'M TIRED OF HIM. YOU KNOW WHAT I THINK?
WHAT?
I THINK WE SHOULD DO THE LAST THING HE EXPECTS... LET'S GO AFTER HIM.

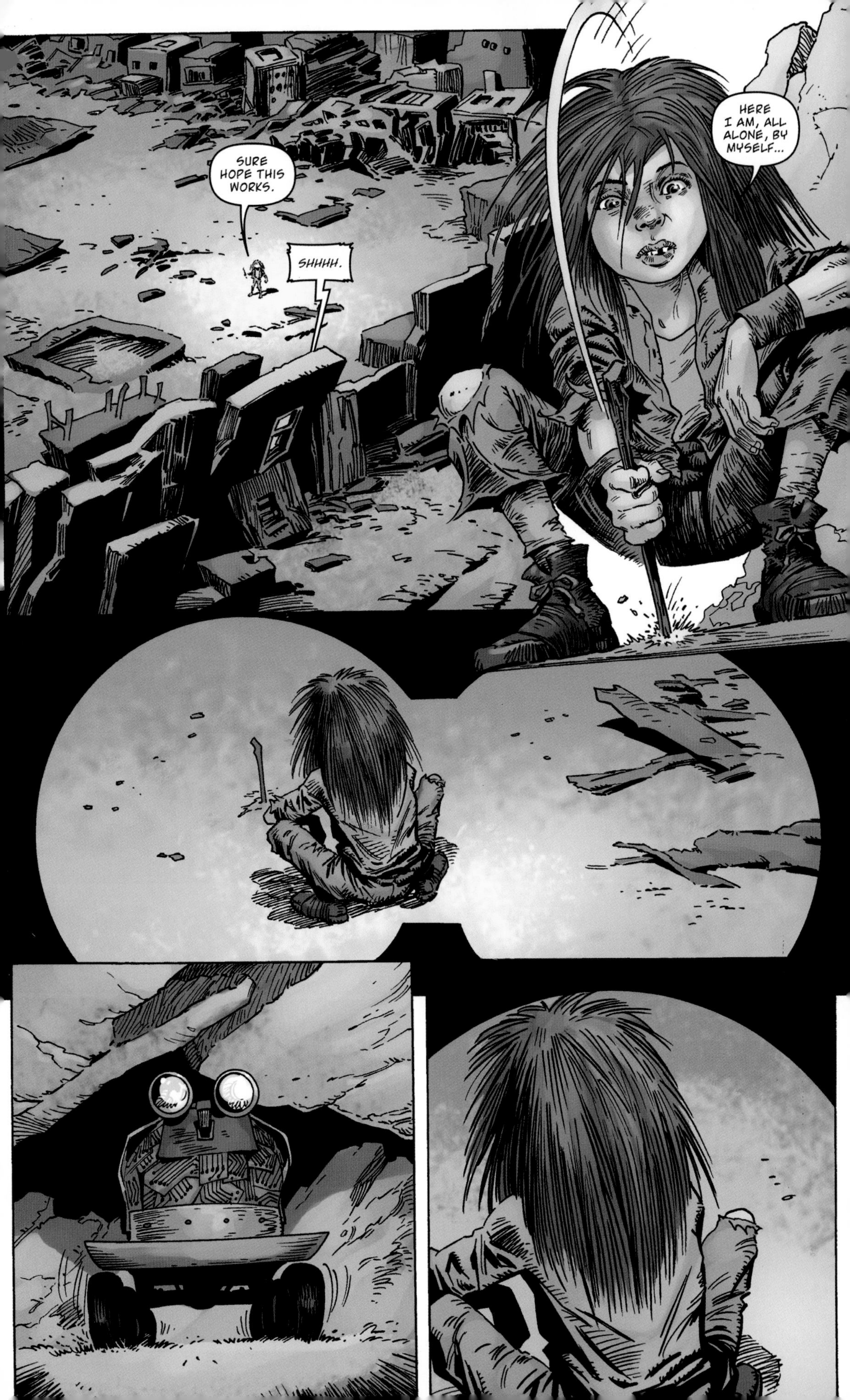
SURE HOPE THIS WORKS.
SHHHH.
HERE I AM, ALL ALONE, BY MYSELF...

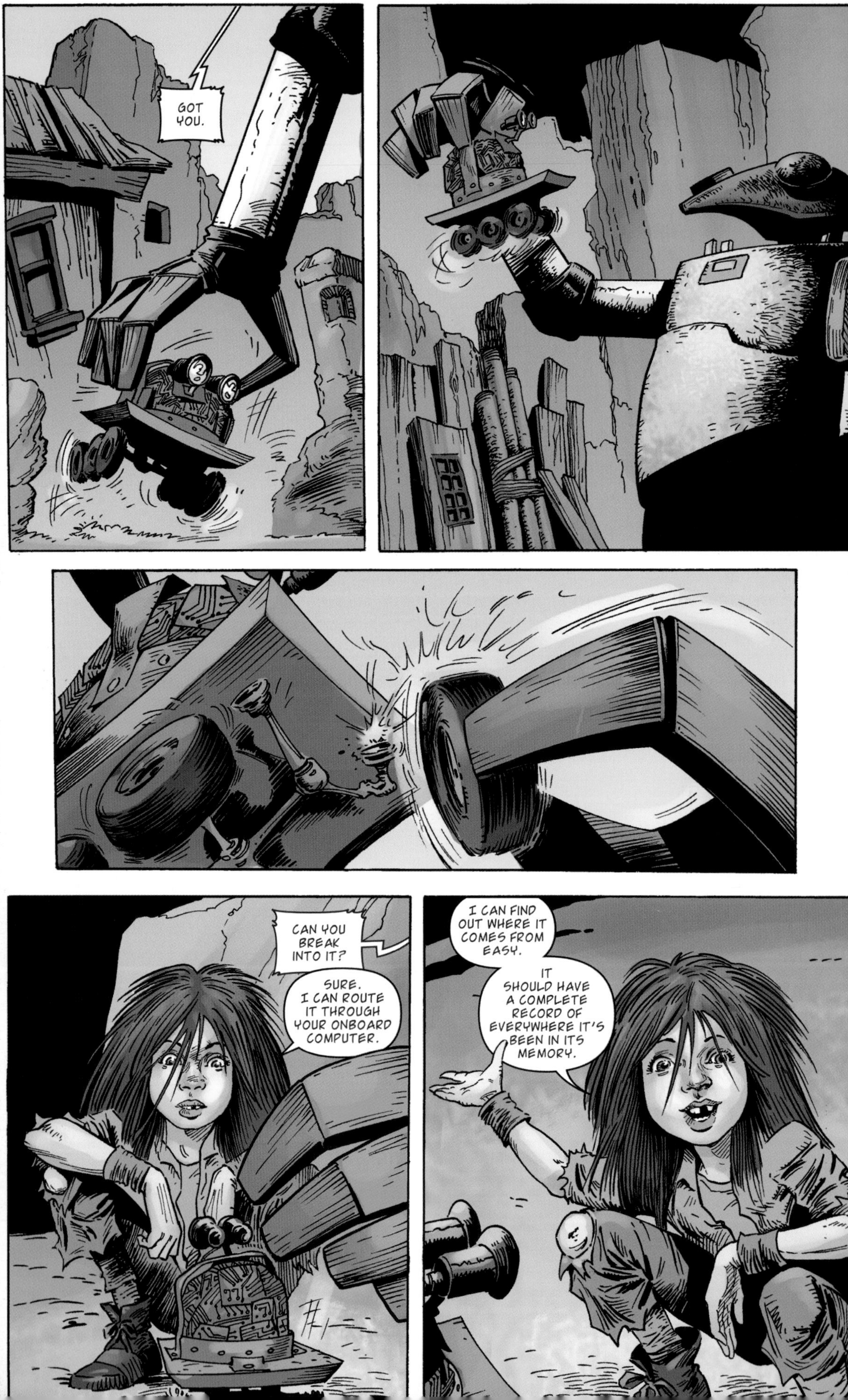
GOT YOU.
CAN YOU BREAK INTO IT?
SURE. I CAN ROUTE IT THROUGH YOUR ONBOARD COMPUTER.
I CAN FIND OUT WHERE IT COMES FROM EASY.
IT SHOULD HAVE A COMPLETE RECORD OF EVERYWHERE IT'S BEEN IN ITS MEMORY.

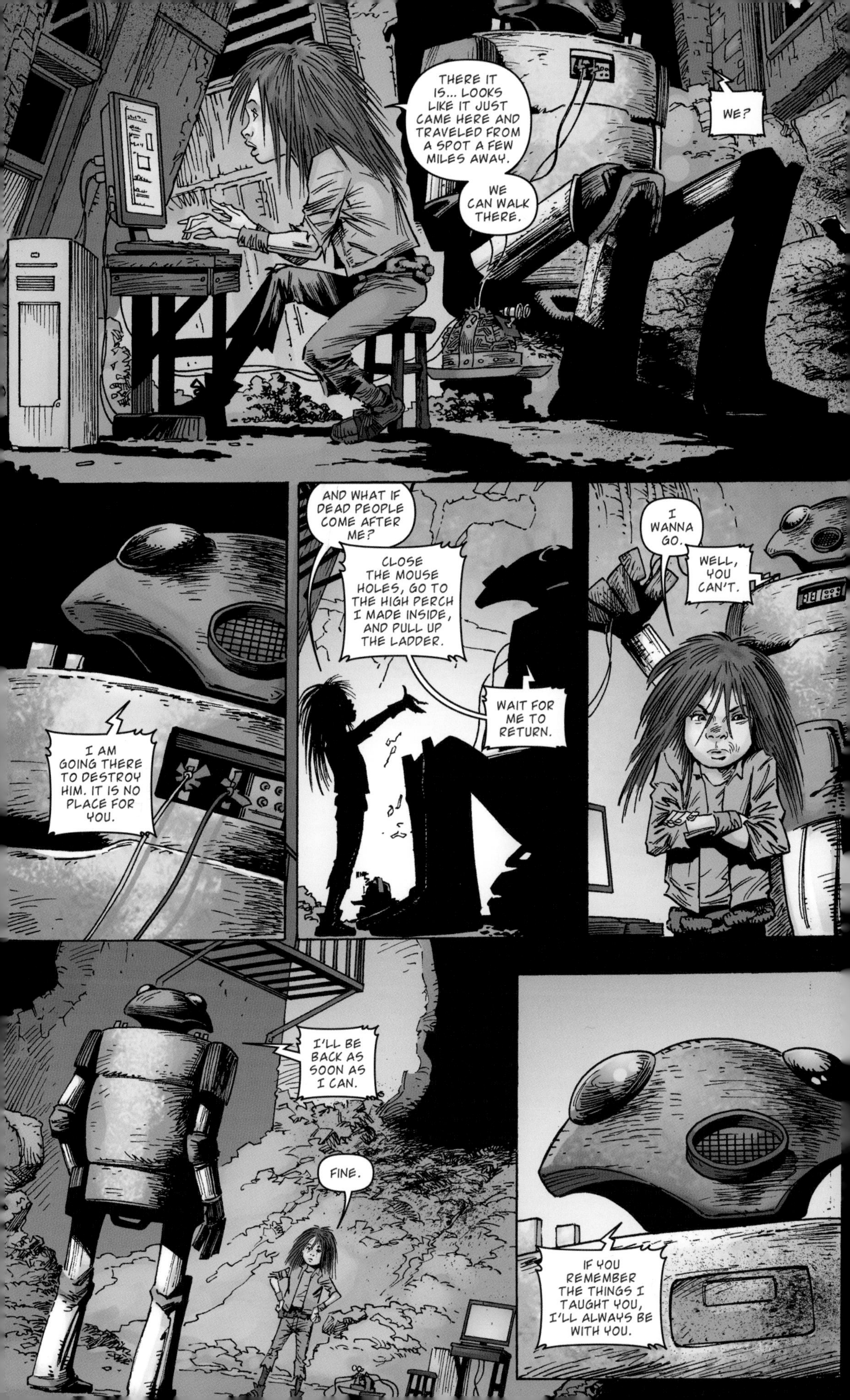
THERE IT IS... LOOKS LIKE IT JUST CAME HERE AND TRAVELED FROM A SPOT A FEW MILES AWAY.
WE CAN WALK THERE.
WE?
I AM GOING THERE TO DESTROY HIM. IT IS NO PLACE FOR YOU.
AND WHAT IF DEAD PEOPLE COME AFTER ME?
CLOSE THE MOUSE HOLES, GO TO THE HIGH PERCH I MADE INSIDE, AND PULL UP THE LADDER.
WAIT FOR ME TO RETURN.
I WANNA GO.
WELL, YOU CAN'T.
I'LL BE BACK AS SOON AS I CAN.
FINE.
IF YOU REMEMBER THE THINGS I TAUGHT YOU, I'LL ALWAYS BE WITH YOU.

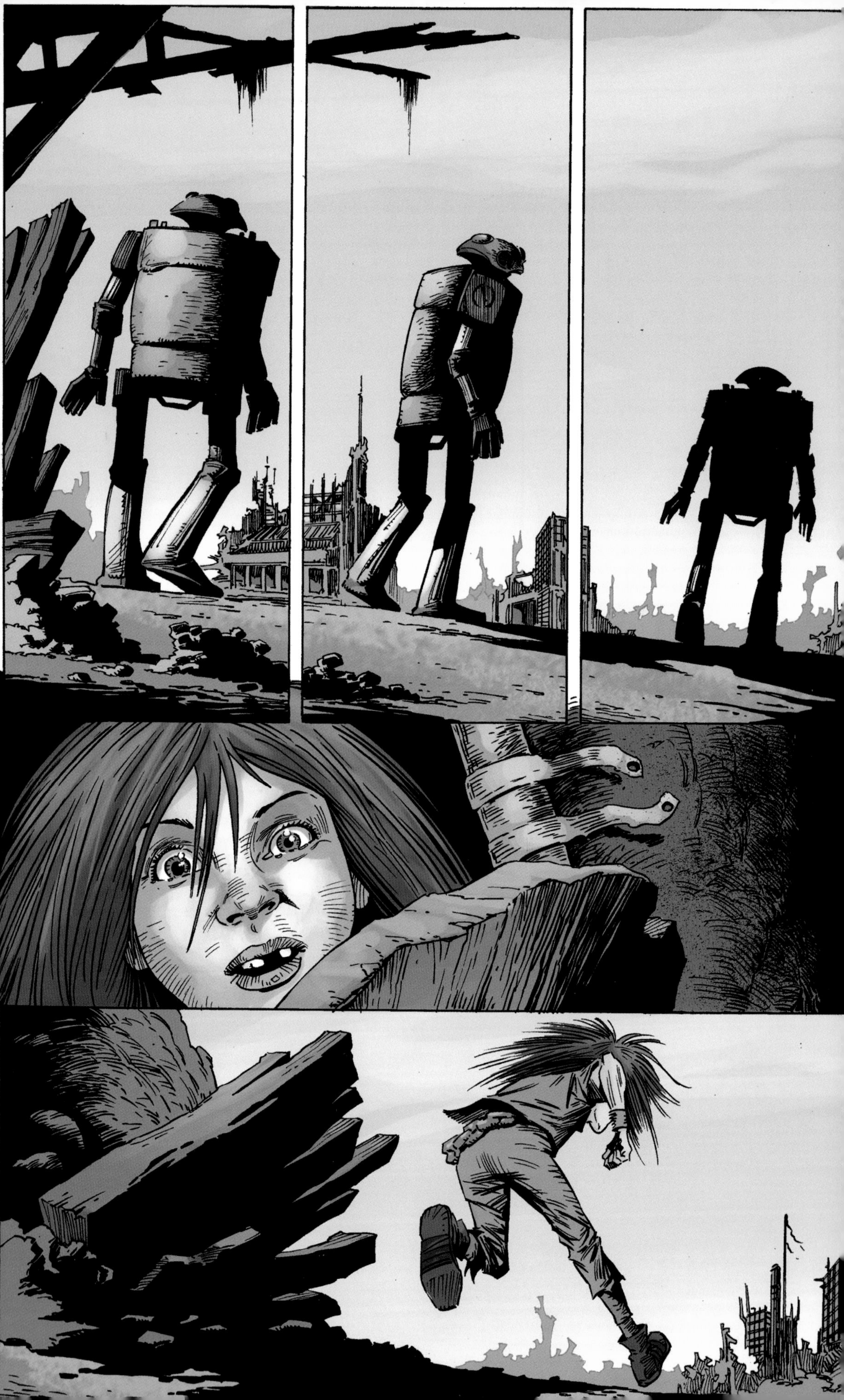

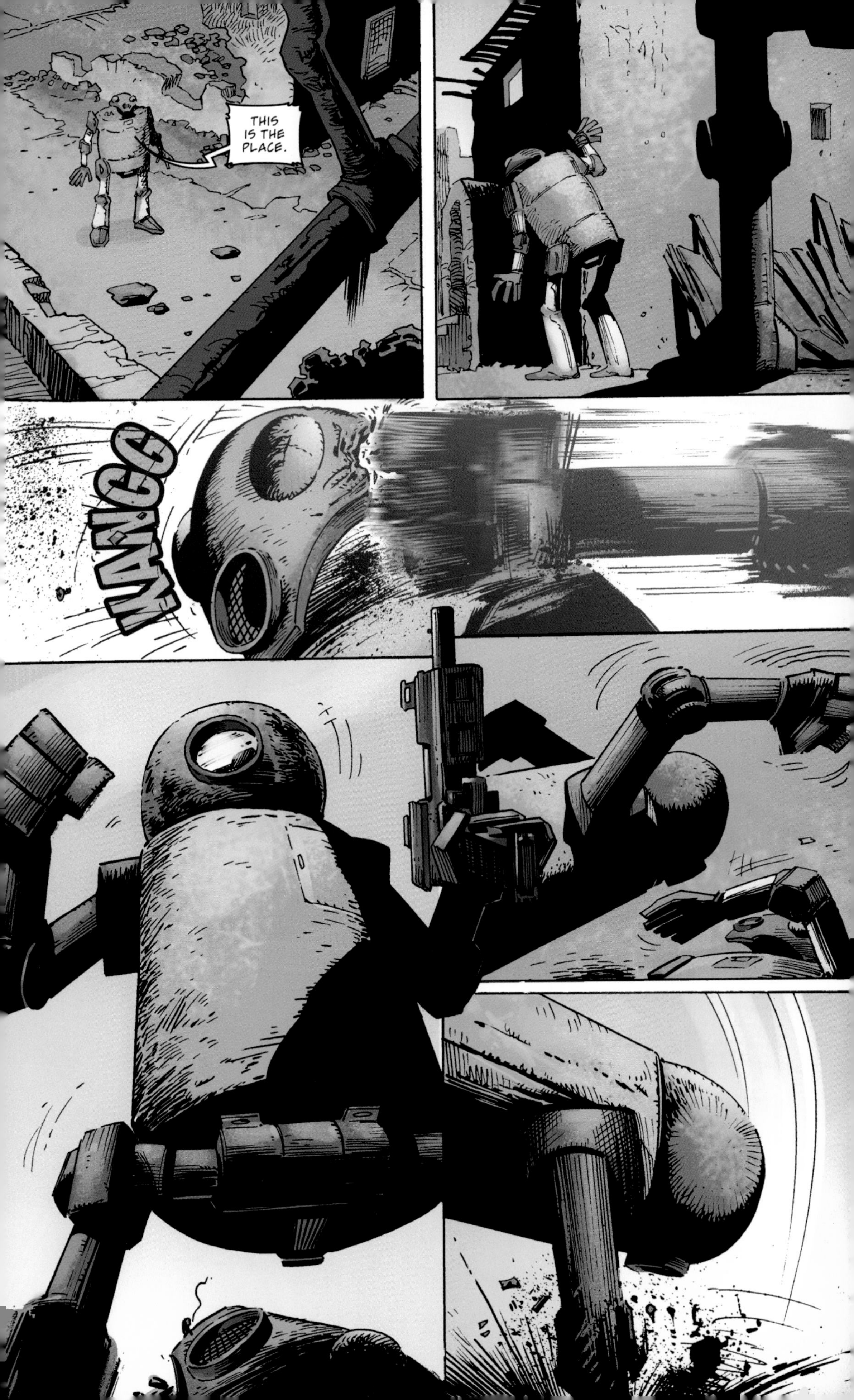
THIS IS THE PLACE.
KANGG

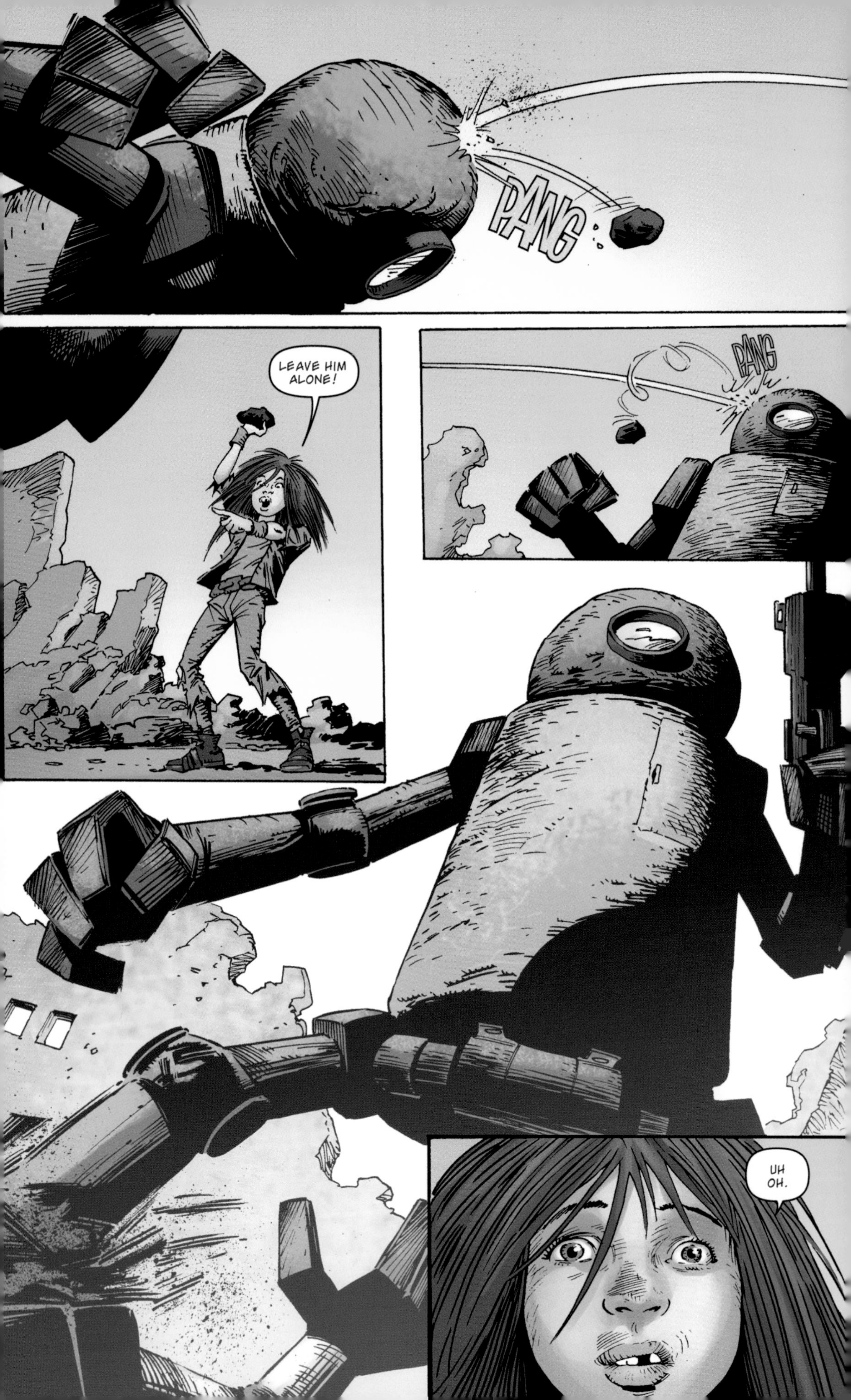
PANG
LEAVE HIM ALONE!
PANG
UH OH.

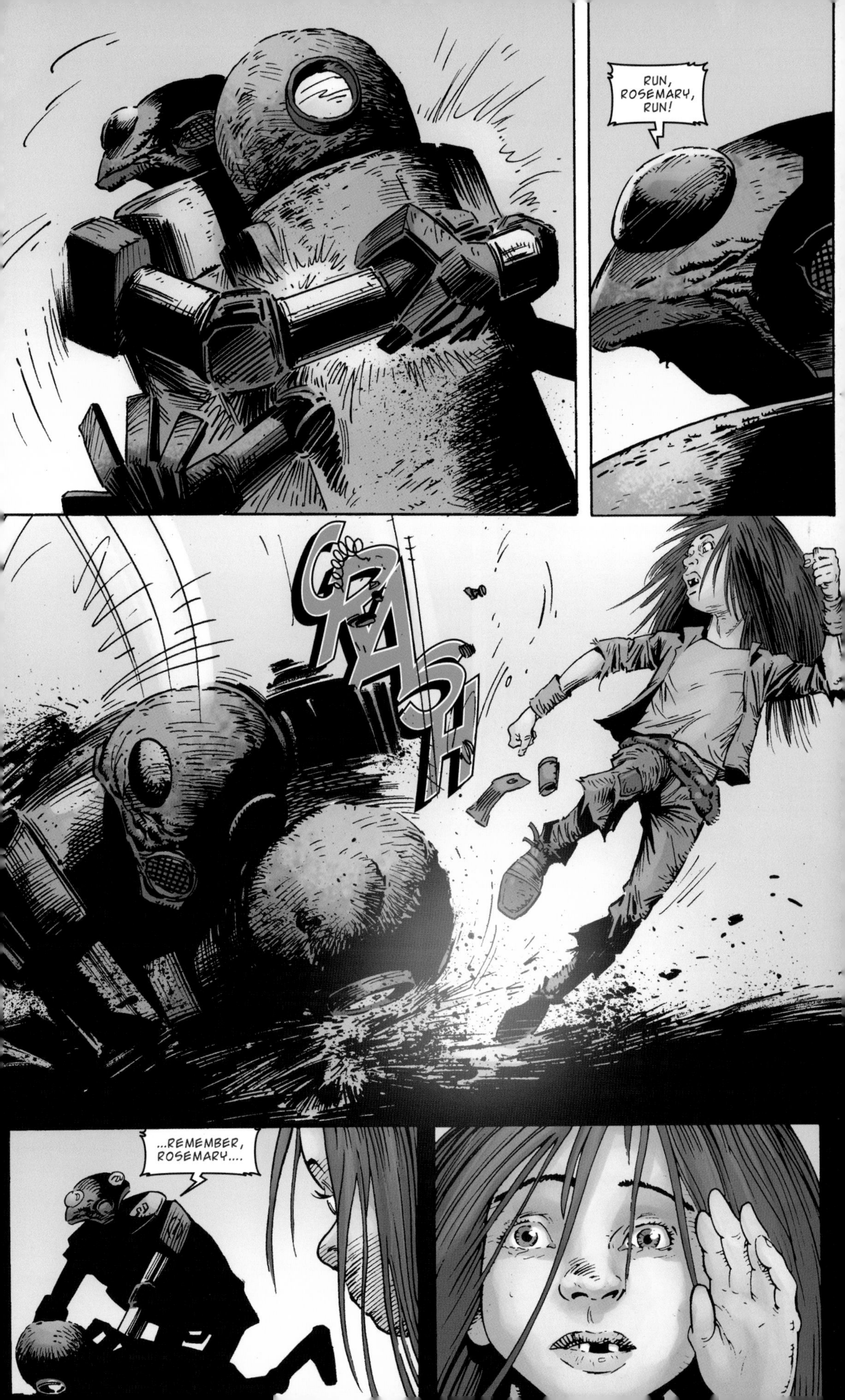
RUN, ROSEMARY, RUN!
CRASH
...REMEMBER, ROSEMARY....

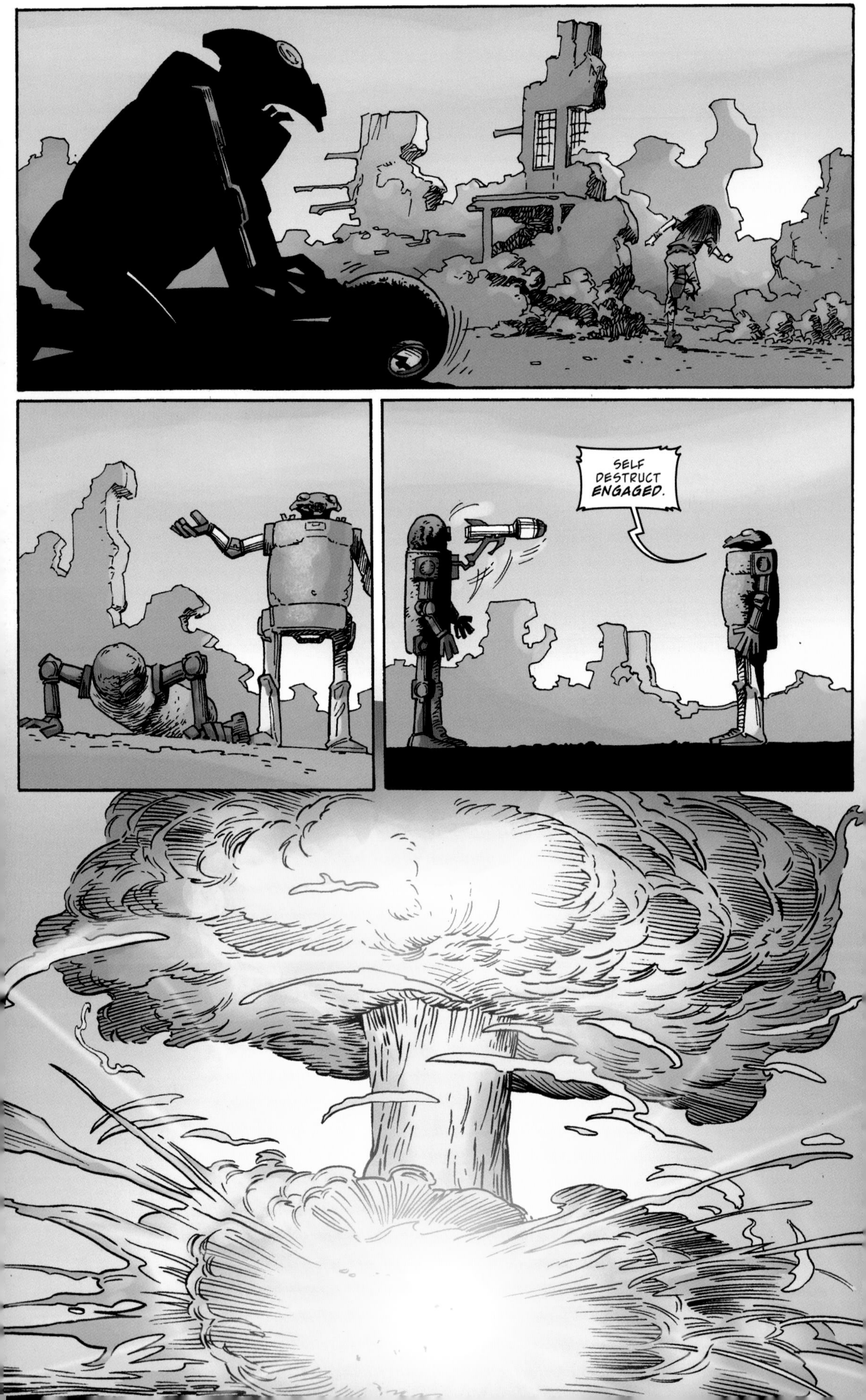
SELF DESTRUCT ENGAGED.

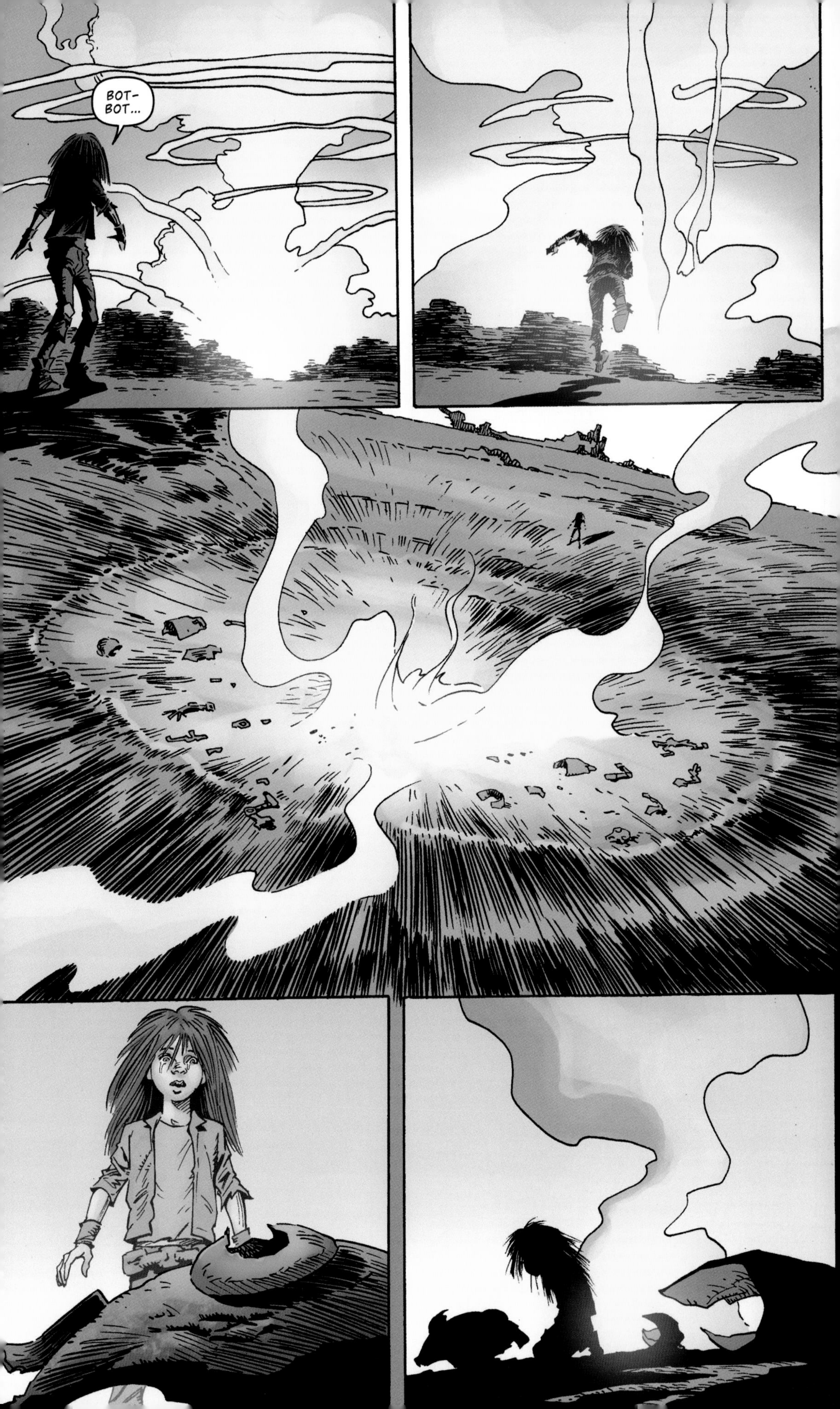
BOT-
BOT...

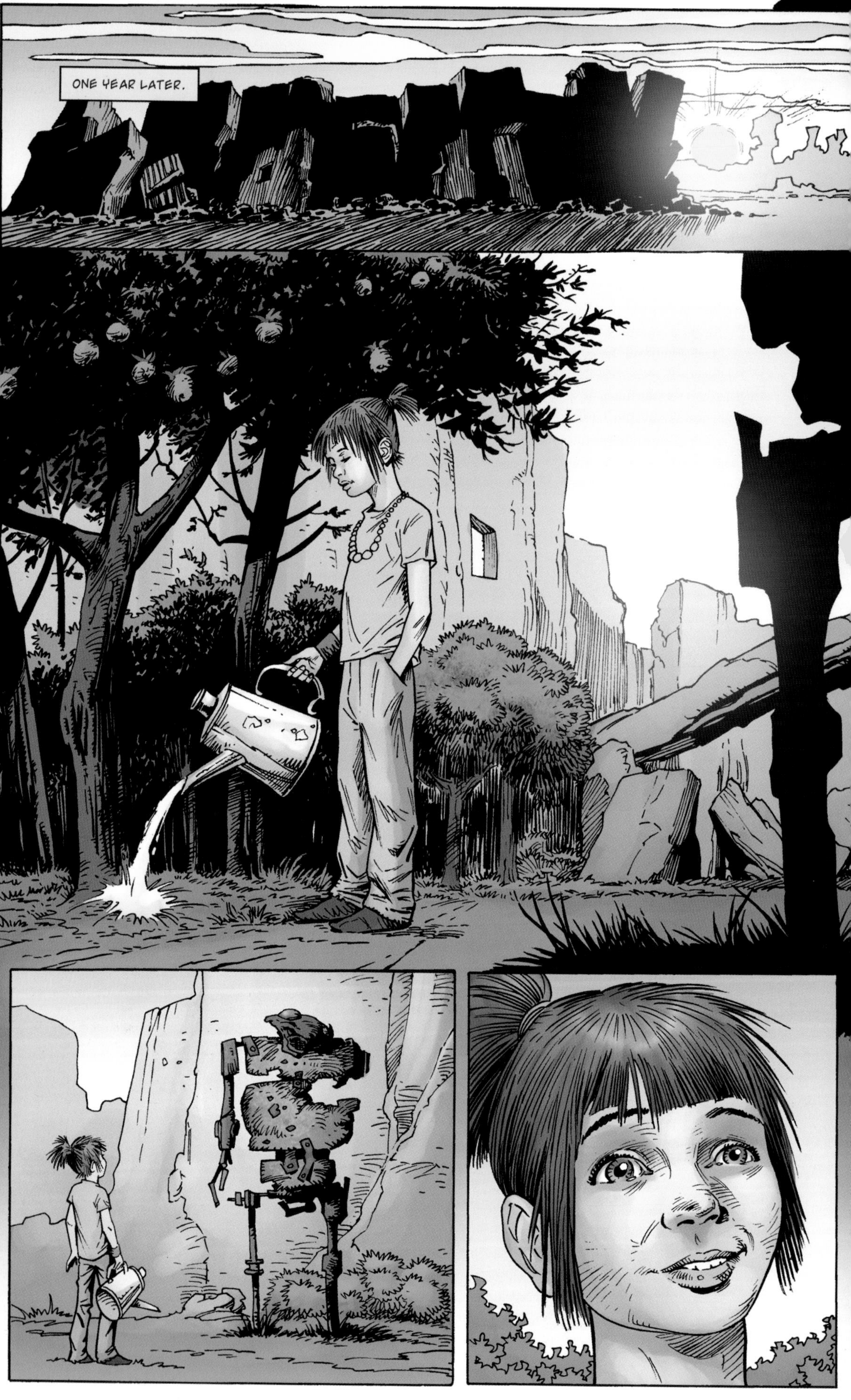
ONE YEAR LATER.

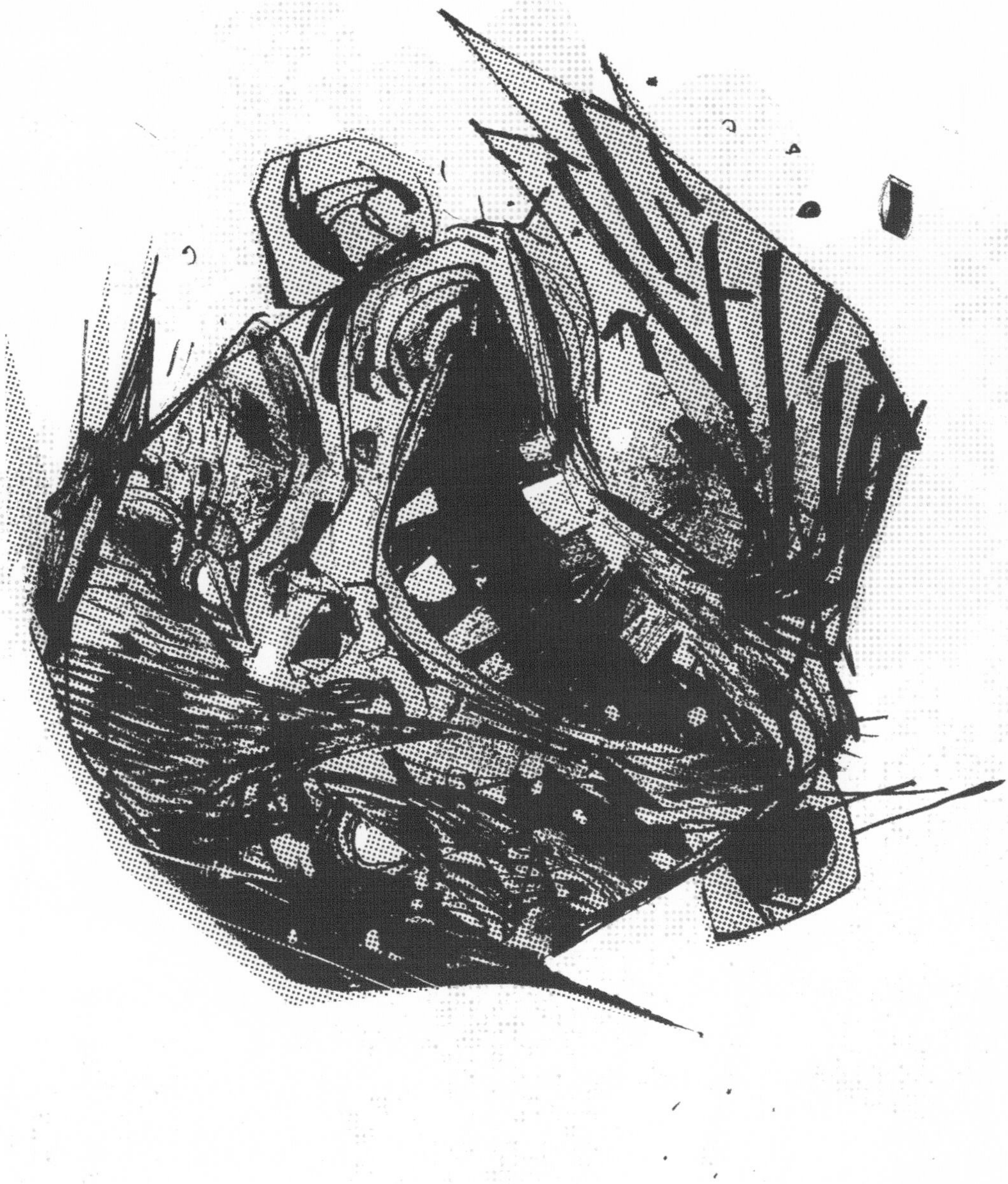

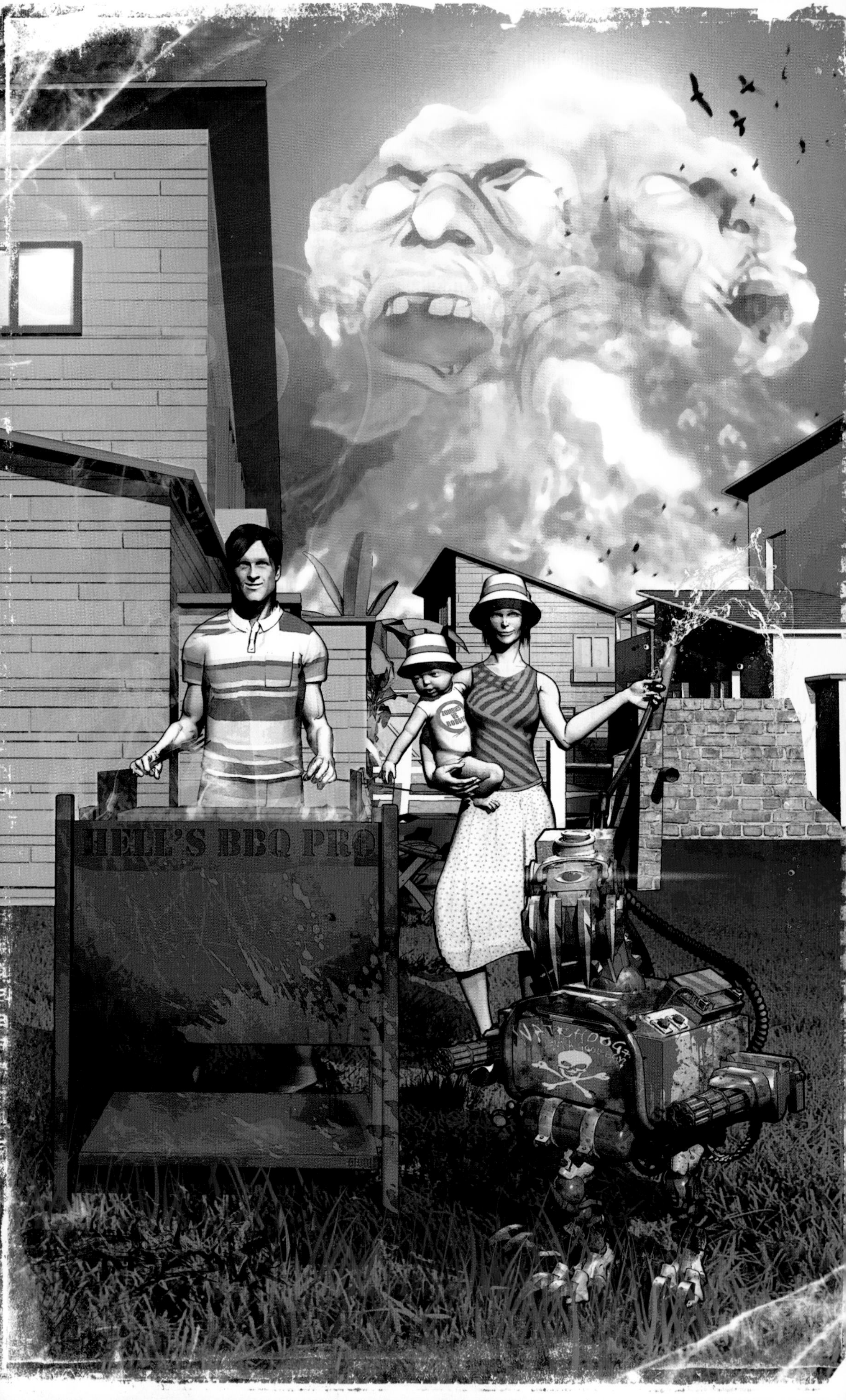
HELL'S BBQ PRO

MEANER THAN A
JUNKYARD DOG

by *Chris Ryall* / illustration by *Fabio Listrani*

"A chicken in every pot, and a Watchbot in every yard."
— *Update of the 1928 Republican National Committee*
Slogan often misattributed to Herbert Hoover

FOR PABLO CRUZ, the posh SoCal neighborhoods with their noise restrictions really took some of the fun out of hunting degenerates.

Which was a real shame, since the layout of communities like Hidden Acres offered the illusion of actual hunting to men like Pablo. The wooded greenbelts between the cul-de-sacs, not to mention the ample yard space around each of the large houses, provided nice faux-wilderness which attracted pests like raccoons, skunks, possums, coyotes, and the occasional meth-fried dumpster diver. All looking for scraps that didn't belong to them.

Pablo's team was on retainer to discretely sweep out all such undesirables.

Used to be that private security in nice neighborhoods was provided by an individual who armed himself with a nightstick and chemical stimulants and walked the grounds until the sun came up.

Pablo's employer, Maximum SeCUREity, traveled with considerably more manpower—and firepower—than that. The van transporting Pablo and the others to Hidden Acres was loaded for armed assault. Their job was to contain any security breach without alerting the residents to their presence.

Pablo fingered the Heckler & Koch HK33 in his lap. It was fitted with a custom suppressor, the kind of thing that'd allow Pablo to take the head off someone in their living room and not bother the person on the crapper down the hall. In theory—he'd never yet had cause to use the thing. Which was fine, since their firearms were intended as a last-ditch save-your-own-ass sort of solution.

"Think twice about what your job means to you before you pull that trigger," advised Pablo's supervisor, Kevin Schmidt. "These old folk get the name of the person who interrupts their cocktail hour and I can't guarantee you've got a job the next day. And you do not want to be cut loose in today's world, trust me on that one."

Schmidt rode shotgun tonight, sitting in the catbird seat next to Blount, their best driver. The Man didn't accompany them on many missions, but lately he'd been tagging along more often than not—and Pablo didn't know why. It sure wasn't because he was any good at field work, but at least Schmidt couldn't get any worse at it if he kept up this new routine.

Pablo looked around at the other men riding with him in back.

Directly behind Schmidt sat Peter "Red" Verdugo. Red spoke only when he had to, and it seemed he never had to. Pablo still waited for Red to speak his first full sentence to him.

The other two, Keyshawn Taylor and Mickey Kingfisher, often bickered about petty things but tonight, owing to Schmidt's presence, they too rode in silence.

Blount eased the van into a spot near the guard's station, empty this time of night, the residents opting for an after-hours keycard system rather than springing for full 24-hour sentry service. No one went anywhere after sundown now anyway, or so it seemed. Or if they did, they weren't coming back.

When the guard shack was closed Hidden Acres' main entrance was sealed by a pair of imposing black steel gates, which looked solid enough to stop any vehicle this side of a marauding dump truck. They were framed by a high stucco-faced perimeter wall that was being successfully overtaken by jasmine and wisteria. All around Hidden Acres, wooded land added to the sense of rural seclusion the residents desired.

Inside the gate there was more greenery, as well as a centrally located public pool featuring separate changing rooms with showers, sand-pit with slides and swings, and tables for the parents to gather while their kids worked off endless energy.

"Pull in and park this bitch near the pool," Schmidt said, trying but failing to sound like one of the guys. "Druggies like to hang out inside bathrooms, so that's as good a place as any to figure out what caused this latest noise complaint."

This central pool area was larger than any public park where Pablo lived. Never mind that each of the estates here also had their own backyard pools and sprawling acres of lawn. Pablo hoped the people living here appreciated their good fortune to the same degree that he lamented his paycheck-to-paycheck existence.

The park was quiet. It was late, and the residents here knew the value of a good night's sleep over the pursuit of a good time deep into the wee small hours of the night.

Pablo and the others stepped out of the van. He was the youngest man in the van by a few years—and more than a few in the case of old Red. He hoped someday he too might settle down in such a nice neighborhood as this but his general run of bad luck didn't inspire much hope in that regard.

Schmidt—"Robert" to no one at work (but quite often "Schmidt-head," "Schmidt-stain," or "Schmidt-for-brains")—loved to lord it over everyone in the company, no matter his or her age. He strutted around, talking up his previous time spent as an airport cop as if that gave him real authority. Keyshawn and Red, who actually had *real authority* in the form of Army and Navy time served, respectively, found him endlessly amusing. Yet they fell in line and followed Schmidt's orders, which only fed into Schmidt's delusions of grandeur.

Pablo didn't like the man either, but was much more content to follow Schmidt's orders on these bullshit "missions" than he would've been in actual military service. There was a lot of talk about conscription making a comeback, and he had no desire to get drafted. So he followed Schmidt's orders and hoped the military would never get desperate enough to come knocking on his door.

The news was full of disturbing reasons for a larger military force. Dissidents had sprung up here, abroad, seemingly everywhere. Malcontents and anarchists starting yet another revolution, Pablo assumed. He wished he felt strongly enough about anything to fight for a cause. Then again, reports were that the fighting was much worse than your average source of unrest. Bad, bloody and quite deadly things were happening, overwhelming the military in many regions. Maybe it was better not to care so much.

People were scared. And when people are scared, they look for strength in numbers, whether actual or just virtual. But the spreading of messages, both hopeful or hateful, across various social media platforms had been shut down. Cold. The all-powerful NSA at work?

Pictures had leaked out, and continued to, and information networks adapted, grew, and spread the word as best they could. But the pipeline had constant breaks, and the messages that came through were garbled at best.

"Zombies," many reports said. That's what they called the angry mobs that attacked anyone normal in their sightline. The crackpots shouted as loudly as possible that the Z-word wasn't just hyperbole, but Pablo kept a sane head about him. He didn't know why, or even how, the various uprisings the world over would take on a dead-man motif, but it was obviously all part of their message.

Whatever the case, people were frightened. And what that meant for Pablo and the Maximum team was much more frequent calls lately. He spent a lot of nights away from home checking out reports of lurching, shadowy figures outside windows. He felt bad for the homeless, which was a much more likely explanation for these intrusions than the anonymous slash-mobs reported elsewhere, but he had a job to do.

"Don't care what the problem actually is," Pablo said to Mickey.

"Huh?" Mickey scratched the side of his nose with the barrel of his rifle.

"Don't care. 'Zombies,' druggies, homeless, whatever. They pay me to check something out, I'm checking. Good soldier, man, that's me. They can count on that."

"I give a shit," Mickey said. "You and me both know we're here to provide visible peace of mind to these old bastards, and that's it. How many damn coons have we trapped after getting a panicky call about 'marauders'? People build houses on top of animal lairs and then get surprised when those critters show up—what a bunch of assholes."

Pablo looked at Red to his right. Red sauntered along, chewing a toothpick.

"That guy's got a bad attitude, huh, Red?" Silence.

"I know, I tend to run off at the mouth," Pablo said, "but that's no reason to lash out. I told him, he can rely on me, man. I tell you, I'm a good…"

"—good soldier?" Red spoke, looking at him hard. "During my service the better soldiers were the ones kept their mouths shut."

"Hey, I got you talking," Pablo smiled. "But, uh—point taken."

Up ahead, Schmidt stopped and turned to face everyone. "Gather round, dogfighters. Remember, whoever or whatever you see inside, do *not* come up shooting. Maximum SeCUREity lieutenants keep their composure. Contain and incapacitate, if called for, but stay holstered."

"You don' really think we're gonna mix it up with 'zombies,' do you, teach?" asked Mickey Kingfisher. He laughed a dirty little cough of a laugh.

Mickey was a tetchy little guy. Talked tough, but if anyone was apt to fire off a round, it was him. Pablo wasn't sure why he got assigned to this mission in the first place.

The other men laughed at the utterance of the Z-word, too.

"Reports said mysterious men were sighted prowling around. *That's* who we're looking for. What we do not do is talk like children and mention the boogeyman. Bueno, Mickey?"

"Just sayin'."

"*Bueno*, Mickey?"

"Yeah, yeah, I'm bueno, I'm bueno. I'd just like to see one of these zombies up close, take him down."

"Look," Schmidt said, "I know most of these are false alarms, and that can get tedious for a man of action like yourself…" The other men snickered at this as well. They were equally opportunity ball-busters.

"…but in my time as airport law enforcement, I saw how situations can go from calm to explosive in a flash. So stay mindful. The homeless love public bathrooms, to wash up or do drugs or play stink-finger. Whatever the case, they don't like being surprised in the act. So you come across some riff-raff, identify yourself to them. Do not go scaring them. Cornered animals lash out viciously, you know."

"Tread lightly but carry these big-ass guns, eh?" said Keyshawn. "Seems dicey to me."

"Guns are for appearances' sake, that's all. Use your pepper spray or Taser, if it comes to that. Now let's get to it. Kingfish, you and Cruz sweep the park near the swings. Check out both bathrooms and all stalls. Verdugo, Keyshawn, with me. We'll explore the yards and regroup in fifteen."

Pablo couldn't help notice that Schmidt the tough-guy leader chose to surround himself with the two former military men, while sticking him with the nervous live-wire.

"Blount just stays put while we doing all this?" asked Keyshawn. "Must be nice to chill in the van having a smoke while we're out here earning his pay for him."

"Dell Blount is one of the most prepared men we have," Schmidt said. "He knows better than to smoke while we're on mission. I'm sure he's at the ready now, if we have need for him."

As the men moved off in different directions, Dell Blount sat in the van, smoking his third American Spirit.

He rolled his window down and flicked out the still-smoldering butt. Into the night air the cigarette floated, its trajectory a smooth parabola until it bounced off a dark shape a few feet away. The shape moved forward in the direction of the van.

As he was rolling the window up, Dell sensed or perhaps heard movement nearby. A smile starting to curl on his lower lip. He caressed the revolver on his lap.

"Game on, druggie," he said, "game motherfuckin' o—"

Bony hands grasped either side of Dell's open mouth and pulled in opposite directions. His lips split, and then the flesh under his mouth, exposing teeth and gums in a flurry of blood spatter.

Even then, Dell could have gotten a scream off if the thing hadn't latched onto his tongue and likewise given it a good yank. Tendons tore as the creature's face came close, teeth gnashing in what seemed like orgiastic pleasure. The thing fed heartily on the mess that was Dell's shredded face.

The zombie took its time before releasing him. Tongueless, he could only gurgle and gush blood. His convulsing fingers grasped for the gun on his lap, but blood-slicked as his hands now were, it slid to the floorboards. Dell had no choice but to sit, still belted in, and be devoured far too slowly.

On the upside, he was finally cured of his nicotine addiction.

PABLO AND MICKEY stopped near the pool area, watching Schmidt and the others head toward the first secluded cul-de-sac. He didn't love the idea of checking out the darkened bathrooms (the lights inside were on timers set for 6:00 AM) but at least he and Mickey were spared the long trek up endless driveways, separating wooded areas, and other such terrains that were not a lot of fun to navigate in an area that frowned on bright public illumination. The sparse streetlights here issued only a small nimbus of low, burnished auburn.

Mickey tromped through the sandy play area toward the pool gate. The gate was low, three-feet high, but tall enough to keep out the curious tykes. No one wanted children to drown (or lawyers to descend on their set-up).

Pablo looked at the fence around the pool. It had areas of slickness on it that shined in the low light. Likely water from Earlier play-time. Or blood, he thought wryly, before pushing that thought away. Now he was just trying to scare himself.

The gate to the pool was left open, but that was likely just due to some neglectful parent. Pablo pulled it closed and moved toward the men's bathroom. Mickey entered the women's.

The walls in these locker room/showers were thick slabs of stone. The kind of material that prevented pervy guys from spying on naked women (never the other way around, Pablo mused). They were also dense enough to sufficiently muffle the cry that emanated from the ladies' locker room.

Pablo definitely heard the second noise, though—it was hard to miss. A deep, guttural scream from Mickey.

MICKEY ENTERED the women's shower area prepared to shoot anyone he happened upon. Zombie, transient, drunken teenager... it didn't matter to him. Mickey didn't particularly like people, not his co-workers and certainly not anyone who put him in a tense situation like this. Checking out strange locker rooms at night, using only the moon's radiance from the skylight for illumination, what kind of life was this for him to lead?

Mickey knew if he shot anyone, man or beast, he might lose his job. He wasn't all that worried about that. There were other jobs. Or there weren't. In this world, which seemed in a rush to implode, he could make do without steady income of his own. As long as others had wealth he could take, he'd be okay. He didn't require much. A simple man with simple means is never left wanting, his father used to say.

He less liked the idea of paperwork, or a possible inquest, if he pulled the trigger, but that was offset by the appeal of shooting some skel.

The adrenaline surged through him, sending waves of spiked heat across the back of his neck.

He moved deeper into the shower area, struck by the irony that, after all the times he'd thought of storming into a women's locker room with a rifle in hand, when it finally happened, the place was deserted.

Something made a scraping sound.

Mickey froze. He preferred to go in hot on these kinds of assignments, but this time, he followed orders. Kept his rifle on his back, and instead fingered a canister of pepper spray.

He looked around the corner, and in the back shower stall, he saw a darkened figure. The moonlight streaming down from overhead painted the room with faint yellow streaks, but not enough to illuminate the person standing back there.

Mickey didn't say a word, but he raised his pepper spray. He stood in place and peered through the gloom. The shadows toward the back were deep, distorted from the overhead light. He steadied his hand and took aim at the shadow.

Wait. Were those ... breasts?

Mickey couldn't be sure, but he thought the shadow had a definite protuberance in the pectoral area. A woman. Possibly drunk or high.

The thought of an inebriated woman hiding out in the shower gave Mickey a bit of a protuberance of his own. He took another step forward. He had the power here. He had the pepper, he had a gun. The woman was troubled, or stoned, or ... lonely?

The woman was *dead*.

She was also ravenous. That raw, desperate need gave her speed greater than Mickey expected. He barely got the can of pepper spray up before she reached him, blasting her in the face full-force. It never slowed her down, and she was upon him in an instant. The fumes from the spray, so close to Mickey's own face, burned his eyes, but that was the least of his problems.

The dead woman tore at Mickey's cheek and brow, raking her teeth across his right eyebrow before settling into the more accessible area under his chin. She chomped at his neck skin, catching it and tearing it a couple times.

Blood gushed down Mickey's hand. Dropped the worthless canister and reached for his gun, screaming in pain. He lunged back away from the dead woman, falling hard onto the cold tile floor.

She was on him as though connected to him, teeth gnashing, drawing skin and blood with each frantic bite. Her jaws had more power, and more viciousness, than any living person would have had. Her desperate hunger drove her forward again and again.

Even sightless, bleeding and in horrific pain, he managed to pull his gun loose. He pulled the trigger. Which may well have saved his life even then if only he'd remembered to disengage the safety.

Pablo rushed into the women's locker room. He stopped in horror at the scene in front of him—that of a shadowy figure leaning down over his co-worker, its jaws working through long, bloody ropes of his flesh.

The sounds were the worst. Such horrible noises. The sounds of someone chewing wet meat.

Pablo swung the heavy butt of his rifle into the attacker's face. There was a grisly *popping*. The momentum of the blow snapped the thing's neck. It fell to the tile floor but immediately resumed its frenzied scramble toward Mickey.

Mickey was also on the floor of the shower, whimpering and bleeding profusely. Still *alive*, for God's sake. Why did he have to still be alive?

Shocked and horrified, Pablo slammed his rifle barrel down on the zombie woman's face, one, two, three times. The eyes popped in a burst and, on the third blow, the face collapsed inward in a gush of red.

The thing's hands still clawed at the floor. At this point, that was probably just dying—or already dead—reflex, but Pablo wasn't taking any chances. He swung the rifle down again, shattering its right hand, and then the left. Finally, breathing too heavily and heart pounding at 100 bpm, Pablo backed away toward the door. The woman stopped moving.

He disengaged the safety on his gun. Firing in this tiled room at such close range would not only serve to wake up the neighborhood, it'd probably be deafening. But tough shit—that horrible gnashing *thing* was not going to get him like it got poor Mickey.

Mickey gurgled, trying to speak. Pablo paid him no mind.

"Plllkkkkkhh," Mickey managed. Which would've come out as "please kill me" if he'd still had lips or a tongue. Pablo couldn't make out the words (although the sentiment was pretty clear) and the effort of trying to speak caused more blood to pour down Mickey's throat. They were in the shit, now, weren't they? Yes, indeed they were.

Pablo glanced down at him, but then right back at the dead woman. "S-sorry, man. I can't... I can't help you now. Can't take my eyes off her. Just in—just in case."

Mickey tried again, but the wet sounds remained unintelligible. Pablo looked at him again. "Jesus Christ. What am I doing? Mickey, stay here, man. I mean, where would you... never mind, I... I have to... I'll go. Get help. Hold tight, you'll see. I'll..."

Pablo turned and hurried out of the shower. He didn't want to leave Mickey, but if he didn't get away from that scene immediately, he might never have found the legs to get up again. One of his co-workers was torn apart by another human being! God, the zombie stories were—they were *real*. Why did no one sit them all down and shake them until they believed the stories? Pablo couldn't process this. He needed to find Schmidt and the others, warn them that this was far beyond what they expected.

He didn't get that chance. Two more zombies came at him out of the shadowy night. He raised his rifle, which is when he heard Schmidt yelling for him from up the street.

"Jesus Christ, fucking shoot them, Cruz! Shoot them fucking all!"

Pablo backed up quickly, gun trained on the first one's head but not firing. They ambled forward slowly. Surely he could take them if he had to. He spared a second for a look at Schmidt, who was sprinting toward the pool area, waving his arms in the air. Red was right behind him. No Keyshawn in sight.

Pablo spun back and put a bullet into the head of the creature on his left. He turned toward the other thing (*Zombie. Just say it—accept it—admit it*) and it never broke stride, impaling itself on the rifle's barrel as it dove at Pablo.

"Shit!" he yelled, pulling the trigger. Back on his heels as he was, the rifle was unsteady in his grip, and the recoil, coupled with the zombie's forward momentum, knocked Pablo off his feet. This was the only thing that momentarily saved his life.

Pablo, near the pool now, landed hard on his tailbone. As the creature, still impaled on his gun, clawed at him, Pablo did a reverse somersault into the deep end of the pool to get away. But the creature was pulled right along with him.

The water wasn't deep, really—six feet at the most—but the zombie had no idea how to navigate it. No muscle memory, Pablo thought bitterly, as the thrashing creature sank to the bottom.

There was always a chance it could move along the floor of the pool, reach him that way, so Pablo quickly pulled himself out of the water. He stood in the dark, wet and shivering, as Schmidt and Red drew close, still yelling.

Pablo looked past the two men and saw nothing but dark. "Guys...where is Keyshawn? What the hell is happening here?"

Behind Schmidt, the darkness shifted. The shadows were alive, a veritable wall of non-humanity, moving closer.

Schmidt and Red leapt over the small fence around the pool.

"They... they're fucking everywhere, Pablo, everywhere! Dead, they're all—they got Keyshawn... we dropped our rifles...!" Schmidt was nearly hysterical.

"*Your* gun?" Red asked Pablo. "Where is it?"

Pablo looked at the darkened water in front of them, where the zombie still moved around underneath the surface, and nodded.

"Well, then. Guess we're all well and truly fucked," Red said.

The mass of zombies moved closer, pushing against the fence. The posts held.

If only any of the three men had thought to close the pool's gate. The zombies pushed around the fence, spilling into that opening and streaming forward.

"Mickey... guys, he was just—eaten. Right in front of me! What do we do?!"

Red ignored Pablo. He continued to look at the pool and the movement under the water. "Well, guess one gun wouldn't have done much good against all of these things, anyway."

Red sighed a large sigh. He drew a large pistol out from inside his jacket. He pulled back the trigger. "Survived three tours. But now this. Life—and death—is funny." He nodded to Pablo. "Welcome to use it after I do."

"What—no! We can use that, save ourselves—!"

"Clip holds twelve bullets, man. No way out."

The zombies closed in on them.

Red put the gun under his chin and pulled the trigger. The gun blast shattered the night's stillness as easily as it did the top of Red's skull. He dropped to the ground, the gun clattering on the tiles.

The zombies were ten feet away, coming at them from both sides.

Pablo looked at Schmidt. He looked down at the gun, and up at Schmidt's stricken face again. Schmidt nodded slowly.

Pablo reached for the blood-slicked weapon…

MASTER SERGEANT PHILLIPS watched the scene on a monitor in the vehicle parked a safe distance from the pool area. On the other screens arrayed around the motorhome's interior, he could see his men moving in to sweep through the zombies near the homes. After they finished with those, they'd move on to the couple dozen that had drawn close to the pool near the outside park. Not as much hurry there, they'd be feeding for a while, and were relatively penned in by the fence.

He looked up at the man standing behind him. Phillips hated it when people hovered over him.

"I'm not saying that these men were the best and brightest, but you can see how they went down without much of a fight."

"Despite their training and guns," the older man said. "Further proof why we have the legitimate military clean up the messes these wannabe paramilitary dummies can't handle."

On the screens, helmeted men cut a soundless swath through the zombies on the lawns. Phillips was very glad these monitors had no audio hooked up.

"And if armed jagoffs can't handle these creatures, what chance do the civilians in their little houses have?"

"Currently zero chance, based on what we've seen tonight."

"So…?"

"So… obviously we need to try something else." The older man sighed. You've got your field test, Mr. Phillips."

"Yes!"

"Don't get too excited," the older man said, turning one of the monitors toward him so he could better watch what was happening. "It's just phase one. Something needs to be done before the problem gets out of hand but I'm not convinced this is it."

"Let me convince you."

"By all means," the man said, putting his hands on Phillips' shoulders and smiling. "Let slip your dogs of war."

1—The Watchdogs of Robwood Circle

THE ATTACK HAPPENED while they slept. The way Helen Pasvar heard it, the invaders came in the middle of the night and found—or forced—their way into the residents' homes. The news reported sounds of screaming, of sirens and gunfire, and of heavy vehicle engines. But Helen slept right through it. She hoped the victims did, too, but realized that probably wasn't the case.

The report she heard said that the attack didn't last long. By the time the sun cast its pallid Early-morning glow over the houses on Loyola Plaza, all the people who lived there were hours dead. Quick and savage.

Assorted stains, spent shell casings, tire tracks, and burned and broken walls remained to tell the story of what really happened. Those things had to suffice, since not one person got out so much as a panicked call or text.

Home invasions weren't exactly a new invention, as man had been peddling that particular service as long as we'd been bipedal and living in domiciles. But the severity of the assault—the totality of it, with not one living thing, human or pet, left alive—was staggering.

Add to that the attack on Hidden Acres the month prior, and you had something out of the ordinary. As much as everyone acknowledges that random attacks can happen anywhere, no one ever assumes that randomness will actually ever hit close to home.

The assault on Loyola Plaza happened two weeks ago, only one mile away from the barbecue being held in Helen and Earl Pasvar's backyard on Robwood Circle. These neighborhood streets were not wide, the spaces between the homes not ample. Whereas Hidden Acres was comprised of large homes on larger lots with wooded land separating the blocks, Helen and Earl lived very close to their neighbors. They knew them, spent time with them, gossiped about them. And when problems that affected the whole cul-de-sac encroached, they got together to discuss it. Helen assumed similar barbecues were happening on many streets in their area.

As she set down the plastic tray on their old wooden picnic table, Helen noted with dismay that the paint job on the table had begun cracking and peeling. Earl would need to repaint soon. She tried to keep her focus on life's mundane details as a way to keep a sense of normalcy in her world. Didn't work.

The glasses of iced tea were sweating. So was Helen—it was bound to be another scorcher today, which wasn't helping her mood.

Joe Rovito sauntered over to the table and picked up a glass. "Helen," he nodded by way of saying hello, without actually looking at her. Joe hated Helen's tea, it was way too sweet. And she used that liquid sugar, not even the real stuff. Left him thirstier than before he started, but it was too hot to avoid it today.

Joe's wife Jan made him promise to mind his manners today. Like manners had any place in a world where neighbors were being wiped out en masse. There was a palpable tension in the air, Joe thought, gulping the too-sweet beverage. Which is bound to happen when a group of people gather to discuss a problem they're then all too gun-shy to face head-on.

Grady Binder and Bryce Clinkenbeard stood under the patio cover, away from Joe. Joe didn't have many friends on the block, and certainly not Grady, who'd had a couple run-ins with Joe over the years. Staying out of the direct sun wasn't helping them cool off.

Grady reached out for Bryce's hand, but he pulled it away. "Sorry, too hot for contact right now," Bryce told him.

"Fine," Grady told him, smiling. "I was only going to tell you that Chuck smiled at me earlier." Everyone seemed to be in denial mode about why they'd all gotten together.

"That'd really be something," Bryce said, "since I'm pretty sure our bedroom is the only one on the block that Chuck hasn't seen."

"Ooh, touched a nerve, I see."

"No, I love your sarcasm. I'm just less of a fan of that big caveman. He's so out of touch—thinks straight guys can still pull off that moustache."

Mustached firefighter Chuck Lyon was the big man on the cul-de-sac. He knew it, and he made sure everyone else knew it, too. Bryce was right, the scuttlebutt had it that Chuck's wandering eyes were advance scouts for his exploring hands. But his Debbie happily stood by his side, ignoring the rumors that had persisted over the years. Yet every time she turned her gaze away from Chuck, his head swiveled like a compass needle in Sharice Koerner's direction. Everyone knew it but Debbie, and maybe she did, too. Bryce always figured that if Debbie didn't think to react to the situation, why should he? He couldn't completely understand what Debbie saw in Chuck, but then again, he *did*.

Helen watched her party guests: the Rovitos; Grady and Bryce; Sharice Koerner without her husband Mitchell; the Putnam brothers, currently getting a walking tour of Earl's meager garden; and Chuck and Debbie Lyon. Helen had known all of them for years. Only Chuck and Debbie had lived on the small cul-de-sac longer than she and Earl.

Yes, Helen had known them all for years, she knew their tics and their quirks and their moods and *goddammit, why were they all acting like everything was still normal in their world?*

Helen was never overly assertive. She looked at Earl in the garden, hoping to catch his attention with her pleading expression, but he was too engrossed in talking about his spindly tomato plants. The Putnam boys looked on, unable or unwilling to mask their boredom, but Earl paid them no heed.

Without Earl to help her remind everyone the reason for this get-together in the first place, she weighed her options and decided on a different and more effective course of action.

She started crying.

For a second or two, Helen thought she might have to fake the tears. Turns out, no. The fear and panic and paranoia that had grown inside her these past two weeks manifested itself in the form of sudden, gasping moans.

Grady was the first to notice Helen, arms at her sides and tears breaking loose from under her closed eyelids.

"Helen?" he said. "Helen, what's wrong?"

Grady's emphasis on the word "wrong" was loud enough to catch peoples' attention. Even her husband looked up from his garden, a tomato worm wriggling between his fingers now.

"Honey? Honey!" said Earl, casting the worm aside and rushing to her side. "What is it, are you okay?"

People started to gather near Helen, although no one but Earl got within arm's reach.

"Is it the iced tea?" asked Joe Rovito.

Bryce regarded him with contempt. "Why would she be crying over the iced teas?"

"Well, they're a bit too sweet, you've got to admit," said Joe.

"Will you forget the fucking iced teas!" yelled Helen, which even took Earl aback.

"Honey, Helen, what—"

"All of you," Helen started, "you're all just going about your day as though everything were hunky-dory. When everything is so *not* hunky-dory!"

Helen tucked herself into Earl's arms and cried some more. The others looked at her.

Chuck decided to fill the silent air. "Helen's right. Hiding our heads in the sand isn't going to help anything." Sharice watched him talk, a smile curling up the right side of her mouth. He caught her eye. Time to put on a show, Chuck thought. He spoke louder.

"Let's get it out into the air. The residents of Loyola Plaza—not so far from our own little block here—were all wiped out in a brutal, senseless attack. Not to mention those rich fucks up on the hill. The cops came, cleaned up both and disappeared. No one was arrested, nothing was done. So we've all thought about what we would do if that horror made its way here …" He paused to take a drink of the iced tea, but really, it was for effect. "… but we're all still anxious. How can we defend against something we don't understand?

"None of us really believe that hungry bears or rabid dogs broke down doors and attacked all those people," he continued. "And news reports are increasingly concerning. So we're all nervous. All we have to lean on is each other."

Joe Rovito spoke up. "It's the drugs, man. Bath salts! PCP! Drugs that turn people into rabid freaks. We all watch the news. We assume it's all going on elsewhere, but time to stop that kind of thinking. There's crazy shit going on *right here!*"

"Alright, that's enough," said Earl Pasvar. He steadied Helen and then stepped forward.

"Crazy shit," Joe repeated under his breath.

Chuck figured it best if he deferred to Earl now that the old man had something to say. He was in the man's home, after all. Chuck respected some boundaries.

"Now, I think Chuck's right about one thing," Earl said, measuring each word carefully. He didn't want his neighborhood to go from quiet worry to overblown panic because someone like Chuck Lyon got them riled up. "And that is, we all don't know exactly what's going on. So I tried to find out. I went and talked to the cops over on Loyola."

"You—you did? When?" Helen asked. "You didn't tell me. The entire cul-de-sac is cordoned off, so how …?"

"Never mind how, my love," Earl smiled. "This old lefty wasn't going to just sit back and trust the government or the media to tell me the whole story. So I made my way up to the cops they had stationed there, and took a look around."

In truth, Earl took the afternoon off work, picked up a case of beer and the plate of Helen's cookies she'd given him for his office Earlier that morning, and approached the policemen guarding the site. Earl was an affable guy, and old enough to be afforded certain courtesies that the local cops might otherwise deny someone. He talked to them for an hour or so. They wouldn't show him the crime scenes inside the homes, but that was to spare him the night terrors they'd been having. They assured him that four-legged animals were not the cause, though. And they left him with a final message—arm yourself. *Arm everyone.*

Earl left the block haunted by what he'd heard, so he organized this get-together right away. He didn't want to worry Helen, and didn't want to see everyone go gun-crazy—mob mentality wasn't just a thing seen in old *Frankenstein* films—but his wife's safety was paramount.

"So what the hell did you see?" Joe Rovito fairly shouted.

"Doesn't matter," Earl said. He walked into the yard, over near the old picnic table. The assemblage followed him. "But what I left there knowing was that we should talk about how to defend ourselves from such an attack here, if it were to happen. No one is saying it will, but …"

"Jesus Christ," Bryce said, "you really think we're next, don't you?"

"I didn't say that," Earl said. "but I do think being ready is a damn sight better than being dead. Like… like maybe a more vigilant Neighborhood Watch, along those lines. Maybe a few of us get some shotguns. I think we can decide who—"

That was all Chuck Lyon needed to spur him on again. He liked Earl, but he'd be damned if he'd sit back and let "an old libertarian" be the one to tell him how to defend his neighborhood.

Chuck spoke up. "Earl, no offense, but I think I can better handle this part. I've got guns. I can run point here."

"Of course you can," said Raymond Putnam. Lower, he added, "you blowhard." Raymond was the closest thing this cu-de-sac had to a full-on sociopath, unless you counted his younger brother, Chris. And you should. He was the first one anyone on the block looked at if a fire started in the woods or a pet went missing. He hated guys like Chuck.

"Hey, a little respect here, kid," Chuck said. "I'm the closest thing this block has to law enforcement—"

"You're a fireman!"

"Exactly right. So if we end up going at it with some crazies, then you'd be smart to listen to a guy like me—someone who knows how to put out fires, not *start* them."

He liked that line. He smiled at Sharice. She smiled back, but then looked away at the loud rumbling sound that kicked up out front just then.

Chuck stepped up onto the picnic table on the lawn. His foot knocked over the pitcher of tea. Joe couldn't help but smile.

Chuck looked into the front yard and saw a half-dozen 16-wheeled transport vehicles coming down the street and parking in front of Earl and Helen's house.

"What are those …" he started. His command of peoples' attention was suddenly shot to hell by the screeching noise of hydraulic doors on the trucks opening.

There was a heavy knock at the back gate, followed by a booming voice. "Earl Pasvar, are you back there?" Earl started toward the gate.

"Earl, wait …" said Helen. "Don't go, it might be … it might …"

Earl reached out and grasped her by the hand. He lifted it to his mouth, kissing it lightly. "Don't worry, Helen. The invaders that took down Loyola Plaza didn't knock on doors and call out names. Something's up out front. Best go see what."

As he walked to the gate around the side of the yard, Sharice and Chuck's wife Debbie both stepped up to where he still stood on the table, gazing over the fence at the developing situation out front.

"Chuck, honey, what's going on out there?" asked Debbie, staring up and down at Sharice, who took a step back.

"Trucks," he said, almost under his breath. "Military trucks. *Lots* of them."

Earl opened the gate and stepped onto the side yard near his garage, closing the gate behind him. Standing in front of him was a man in a black suit. He was bald, with steel-grey eyes. Not hard eyes, though, that was good, Earl thought. Next to Mr. Suit waited a younger, shorter man with some kind of electronic clipboard gadget and a stylus in his hands.

"How can I help you gents?" asked Earl. "You really gave my gate a pounding. Makes me think this might be important." Earl looked past them to the street, where boxy transport vehicles were now parked, with doors open and loading ramps arrayed. Men in military fatigues walking up and down them, wheeling wooden crates.

"I am Mister George Jaxon, Department of Homeland Security. Apologies for the vigor with which we hit your front door, but it was important that we catch your attention."

"Pardon sir," said the other man, consulting his device, "but confirming that all the residents on Robwood except Mitchell Koerner are in the yard."

"Thank you, Mr. Alford. Like I was starting to say, Mr. Pasvar—"

"Wait a minute," Earl said, stepping forward and closing the gate behind him. "Just how do you know who I have in my yard at the moment? Who all lives on this street, for that matter?"

"Are those really the questions you should be asking right now, Mr. Pasvar? Earl—may I call you Earl?" The man called Jaxon smiled warmly.

"Perhaps you should tell me why you're here, for starters," said Earl. His wife knocked on the gate from the other side. "Earl? Is everything okay?"

"I think so, hon. Just confirming that now."

Jaxon said, "Is that Helen? Your wife? Earl, perhaps you'd be so kind as to let us into the yard. What I have to say is for everyone. If you're okay with that."

"Guess that all depends on where this conversation goes, but okay," Earl said.

He opened the gate and met his wife's worried gaze. "This is misters Jaxon and Alford. They're with Homeland Security."

"Ma'am," Jaxon said, before following Earl into the back yard.

Out front, the men by the trucks continued on with their unknown business.

"IT'S NICE TO have all of you together like this," the man in the black suit said. Many suspicious eyes were on him, but he seemed at ease. Polite and professional.

Jaxon took a seat on the picnic table in the backyard—Chuck Lyon stood nearby, a scowl on his face. Chuck didn't like to cede leadership to anyone, especially those actually in positions of authority.

Jaxon took a big pull of iced tea, making a pleasant sound of approval as he did. He looked at Joe Rovito as he wiped his mouth with the back of his hand and said, "Ahhh, perfect sweet tea, Missus Pasvar. Hits the spot on a warm day.

"My name is George Jaxon," he continued. "I'm here as a representative of the United States Department of Homeland Security. As you all know, there was an encroachment of zombies not far from here. What we know is—"

"An encroachment of *zombies*?!" interrupted Grady Binder. "You come here in front of us and tell us that the attack on Loyola was a *zombie attack*?! They were, what, eating brains? that's … that's …"

"Ludicrous," finished Joe Rovito. "Why don't you try talking straight to us and not just throw fairy stories our way?"

Jaxon took another long drink, pausing to savor it.

"Mister Rovito, you don't know me, but you should understand that no one is going to talk straighter with you than I am. So trust me when I tell you that the things that attacked and killed everyone on Loyola Plaza were, as close as we can determine, zombies. Real, flat-out, flesh-eating walking dead men, women and children. When I've said what I came here to say, I'll show you a few video clips that leave no room for doubt. They'll be hard to watch, but they will leave you no room for doubt. Believe me, zombies are regrettably *real*."

He was met with stunned silence.

"Now," Jaxon said, "before your imaginations run even more wild at the thought of this, a couple other things you should know. One, after the attack on Loyola, the zombies most likely just … left. Wandered off. From what we've been able to tell—and we're learning as we go, believe me—these creatures seem driven by hunger the way, say, a piranha is. When that hunger is sated, their bloodlust fades and they again start swimming in the forward direction. They don't linger. They don't reason. They're not out to get you personally. It's our postulation that a well-fed zombie could stand next to you and leave you untouched. Theoretically."

"*Theoretically.* Goddamn," Darren Putnam said, looking at his brother Raymond. Whether that was true or not, this was fucked up.

"We cleaned up the situation," continued Jaxon. "Meaning in straightforward terms, Mr. Putnam, that we tracked down those zombies, and blew the living shit out of them, the same way we'd put down, say, a rabid cougar that wandered into your yards and ate your children."

"All of them? And now you have bodies you can study and figure out how to stop this?" Joe Rovito asked.

"That would be nice, yes—but no. Their flesh is too decomposed for us to glean any real insights. As I said, we're learning as we go, and clearly more study is needed, which is on-going, I assure you. And these random attacks have revealed some glaring weaknesses in our capabilities to understand what we're dealing with. Not to mention the challenge of just keeping up with a threat that seems to keep growing. We're looking for the most effective way to stop it."

"It's a fucking zombie war," said Raymond. "We're at *war* with something none of us even knew existed until right now and you tell us you're hoping to someday cure it. It's like … like cancer that can walk. You have no clue how to stop it, do you? How could this even happen? What kind of bullshit lab experiment caused this?"

"The *hows* are indeed important, Mister Putnam," said Jaxon, "but less vital than the fact that this has signs of developing into a war to be fought on a worldwide front by every able body we've got. Which also means we are finding ourselves in short supply of proper troops to watch over every neighborhood."

Bryce Clinkenbeard: "So … you're telling us we're on our own?"

Darren Putnam: "Can't count on the authorities? Big fuckin' surprise."

Joe Rovito: "Maybe they've come here to tell us they're re-instituting the draft? Not a bad idea. Some of the younger punks in this world could use some discipline." He spat the word "punks" in the direction of the Putnam boys.

"Better to be young punks than an old dick," snarked Raymond.

"Keep it up. What better use then the army for your firebug tendencies? And your brother can move up from killing animals to killing humans—isn't that the natural progression for psychopaths, anyway?"

"Fuck you, man!"

Jaxon smiled a smile that Earl learned was his stock in trade, the reason he was sent here today: patient, calm, knowing.

"Please, Mister Putnam, Mister Rovito. We're not here to draft anyone. Or to leave you to your own devices." He motioned to Alford, who still stood near the rear gate. "Mister Alford, if you please? I think they're ready to see what we brought them."

Alford in turn signaled the men out front, waving them over.

"Like I said, if this situation explodes like it could, the military and your local police won't be able to be everywhere. Deep down, under your fear and frustration and mistrust, I hope you can understand that this is only because we're trying to end the problem before it moves beyond our ability to contend with. *We cannot be everywhere.* But no one thinks that arming a scared populace is a good idea …"

"Not 'no one,'" said Chuck. "I'm pretty damned okay with that very idea."

"Be that as it may," Jaxon continued, "it's not a realistic option. but there's… *something else.* Something we've been working on. Human soldiers are at higher risk when fighting zombies. These creatures can infect humans—through biting or scratching that is, not by an airborne virus—so we must limit our fighting forces' exposure to them. To that end—and this has been a top-secret initiative, but we're all well and truly through the looking Glass, eh?—we've been using robots on the front lines. They've got adaptive AI that allows them to make real-time battlefield decisions, so you can think of them as drone-soldiers. We call them *Warbots*, and they seem to be getting positive results, greatly reducing infection risk to our troops."

"*Robot* troops fighting *zombies*. I knew you guys kept secrets from us, but not science-fiction shit," said Joe Rovito.

Jan meekly asked "You're going to have these … killer warbots patrol our neighborhoods, too?"

"No, no," Jaxon said. "Warbots are big, slow, and very expensive. They're built for the front lines, for war. They're not suited for more than carrying supplies or firing weapons—rudimentary tasks, not the more nuanced work a civilian context requires. We could never build them in the numbers required for meaningful domestic deployment, anyway."

"Putting it another way," he said, "that would be like driving tanks up and down your streets."

"Bring it on," said Chuck.

"First thing you've said all day that I agree with," Joe whispered to him.

"However," Jaxon continued, "our robotics experts have split their focus—despite some higher-ups' complaints that we should only be building military weapons. They've made a possible breakthrough in the area of suburban residential defense—a small, security-minded bot keyed to the needs of civilians in their homes."

He paused for another drink of tea.

"These specialized robots have not been field-tested, nor are they built for battle. In light of recent developments, we're confident they're ready for a proper trial," Jaxon said. He drained the glass with a satisfied gulp.

"We know you're worried about your families, friends and neighbors. So I'm here today to ask you to be the most important beta-testers in history. We'd like the people of Robwood Circle to be the first in the nation to experience the residential defense provided by our newly-minted *Watchbots*." Jaxon finished.

Behind Alford were two soldiers carrying rifles, and *something else* walked alongside them. That something was a bipedal mechanism with what looked like a large car battery for a torso. Its "head" was a smaller box swiveling on hydraulic joints, red optic sensors mounted on all sides. Its "arms" were comprised of a gathering of rotating cylindrical tubes. The entire contraption stood no more than thirty-six inches high. It clanked and rattled as it waddled forward like a metallic penguin.

Its gait might have been bird-like but its overall appearance was more canine than anything. It was a metallic nightmare version of a dog.

On the front of its boxy torso, someone had stenciled "Watchdog #1." And, smaller beneath that, "I'm a good boy!" next to a skull and crossbones.

All was quiet for a moment as the boxy device shuffled toward them. "Oh my God, it's horrific," said Jan. Joe, next to her, spoke up with his usual tact.

"You've got to be kidding the fuck out of us!" he said. "What shit are you pulling here? You think you're going to foist these metal monstrosities on us? And then what, we tie 'em in the yard and let it chase down zombies like a hound goin' after the mailman?" He scowled at Jaxon. "Our goddammned tax dollars at work," he mumbled as a follow-up.

Jaxon made no effort to stand up from the picnic bench, and indeed, didn't react at all to Rovito's outburst. Instead, he reached into his inside suit pocket and pulled out a pair of darkened sunglasses. He put them on, crossed his arms and sat back to observe the others' reactions as the metallic beast approached.

Debbie Lyon said, "Let's all stay back from it until we know what this really is."

"We know what it is," Sharice Koerner said. "it's *false hope*."

Helen Pasvar eyed the metallic beast with a raised eyebrow. "We don't know that yet. But it *is* sort of hideous."

"One thing we do know is there's a lot of trucks on our street," said Chuck Lyon. "You're going to give us each a robot bloodhound to chase down those monsters before they kill us?"

"God, listen to yourselves," said Bryce Clinkenbeard. "Ten minutes ago he tells us that zombies walk the land and you all about piss yourselves with panic. Now you're shown that the military has built a defense system for us and you instantly crap on the idea? Why don't we all wait and see what … hey, what's it doing?"

The robot's head-mounted ocular devices began to glow. Its pulsating right arm extended.

Jaxon picked up his empty glass. He casually tossed it in the air toward the unoccupied back of the yard. The three large ice cubes in it tumbled into the air as it spun around.

Four quick bursts escaped the hose-like "gun barrel" on the robot. The glass itself exploded into tiny pieces that rained down on the lawn. The ice cubes likewise landed on the grass. Earl stepped over and picked one up, holding it out to everyone. It had a thin metal toothpick lodged in its center.

"God a'mighty," Earl said. He placed it back on the ground, careful not to let it slip from his grasp lest the robot fire more micro-spears at it. Or him.

Jaxon lowered his sunglasses onto his nose as though he were a college professor about to make a point.

"Apologies for the glass, Helen, and the shards now in your lawn. The glass was too thin to survive the dart blast, but these cubes tell a story, eh?" He held it up and slowly moved his arm around so everyone could study it, like a kid doing show-and-tell in class.

"The watchbot fired off four computer-targeted bursts faster than any of us could even cock a gun. Didn't miss once." He held the cube out to them again. "It *never* misses."

"Holy shit. Wow," said Darren Putnam quietly. No one else said a word.

"We didn't build a robot that is aesthetically pleasing. That's what real puppies are for. What we built is a device that will keep you *alive* no matter who or *what* might threaten you. Now, if you're all satisfied with that display, I'd like to move on to the next step of our little pet adoption program."

3—Man's best Friend

THREE HOURS LATER, everyone was back at their own homes, armed with a thick, illustrated owner's manual, as well as a dedicated communicator keyed to a military frequency, and their watchbot itself.

Each "dog" looked subtly different from the next. They all contained a base level of shared functionality but also had variable features designed the engineers hoped would give the residents a sense of proprietary ownership over their particular robot. Anything to help the residents bond with these boxy little killing machines, to the extent that was even possible. And each family took to their new charge in decidedly different ways.

The Putnams:

Ever since Darren's arrest a couple years back, Raymond and Darren preferred not to leave their house very often. So they loved the idea of a lethal defender keeping away strangers, and maybe even cops. What's more, Raymond and Darren were technologically adept, but thus far had only ever used their skills to hack credit cards or engage in petty phishing schemes. They were confident that they could customize their "dog" in ways the government hadn't intended.

"Like some kind of crazy door-to-door salesman," Darren was saying to Raymond. "'Here, watch this demonstration as our robot dog destroys your ice cubes. So, how many can I sign you up for?' God."

"I wasn't leaving there without one, and neither were you," Raymond replied. "Look at this thing—it's a work of art."

The robot stood motionless in their garage.

"You think it's something now, wait'll I crack open its motherboard and make it do some tricks they never intended."

"Think you can?"

"Know it. Just let me grab my tools."

Grady Binder & Bryce Clinkenbeard:

Grady Binder and Bryce Clinkenbeard stared at the robot sitting on their back porch. They loved the way theirs moved on tank-like treads rather than the clunky legs on the model left with the Pasvars. This one was quieter, could traverse their stairs without too much difficulty, and was overall more aesthetically pleasing.

"What do you really make of all this?" Bryce asked Grady.

"It's definitely weird," Grady said. "But, you know, so are zombies. Besides," he said, "we'd been toying with adopting for a while, so …"

"Now we have this robo-beast to fill that parental void in our lives," Bryce finished for him, smiling back at him.

Grady didn't smile back. "No, silly. What I was getting at is that having this horrid thing here helps give us the security to consider adoption in a world full of zombies. *Zombies.* For God's sake," he said more to himself than to Bryce, "the things that humanity does to itself."

Grady looked at Bryce now. "We agreed to never keep guns in the house, but here we are letting this death machine live with us now."

"It's not a gun, Grady," Bryce said. "I mean, Mister Jaxon even went so far as to say the teflon-coated claws on its feet won't leave as much as a scratch on our hardwood floors." Both their moods seemed to cloud over as they discussed the watchbot.

"It's a walking box that fires bullets, or blades, or whatever the hell it put through those ice cubes before we could blink," Grady said. "It might not be the textbook definition as used to exist, but Bryce, you better believe that that thing next to you is a gun."

Bryce looked down at the anti-zombie robot, which sat still at his feet. "Then I guess our rule about that has to change. I for one don't mind being kept alive, and if this eyesore can accomplish that, then I approve."

"I'm not saying I don't. I'm just saying that once we start compromising the things we agreed on together, where does it end?"

The question hung in the air. Both men stood in silence, their faces wearing matching scowls.

The Koerners:

Mitchell Koerner wasn't nearly as willing to accommodate the new arrival as his wife, Sharice. The Koerners' relationship had been strained for many months, and lately just about every conversation seemed to make it worse. The fact that Sharice accepted this metallic creature without his say-so was the latest bone of contention.

"Well, what did you want me to say? You couldn't be bothered to even come to the Pasvars' in the first place!" Sharice said angrily. She was pretty sick of Mitchell's accusations. Chuck Lyon might've been a blowhard, but when she was with him, he never made her feel like an idiot.

"You wouldn't think I'd *need* to be there to tell you not to bring a government weapon into our house. As defense against *zombies*, of all things. The government told one scary story about terrorists and frightens you into letting some piece of their hardware into our house? For all we know, the thing emits some kind of radon gas or has a secret camera on it or whatever else. The government can spy on or test its junk on a naïve citizenry. Well, I say *no!*"

Mitchell opened the front door and pointed at the open doorway. "In fact, I want this thing out of here now. Get!" Mitchell told it, but the bot paid him no heed. "How are we supposed to control this thing, anyway?"

"Why don't you read the manual and figure it out for yourself!" She said, thrusting the heavy book against his chest. "I've got to get ready for book club tonight."

"You're *still going out,* even with marauders or zombies or whatever in the area?"

"I'm still going out. I refuse to become a prisoner in my own home."

Mitchell sure could be pig-headed, she thought as she headed upstairs. Her back was tense. She was a ball of coiled tension right now. Yet another reason she was glad Chuck told her to come see him tonight.

The Rovitos:

Joe threw another stick across his yard. The mechanical oddity that had followed him home from the Pasvars just stared at him with its unblinking eye.

"So much for them programming this thing to act like a real dog," he said.

Jan walked up to him, putting a hand on his shoulder. "Honey? You've been outside throwing things for a while now. Why not let it go? They might have called this thing a *dog,* but it's not a pet, it's—"

"A goddamned engine of destruction with no soul. Yeah, pretty obvious. I just hoped that it might be good for *something* other than junking up my lawn. 'Least it won't be crapping everywhere."

Joe walked across the yard, to the accumulation of sticks, rocks, and tennis balls that he'd tossed over the last half-hour. He picked up a chunky, baseball-sized rock in his hand.

"It's frustrating, y'know? Every ape on this block fighting for primacy: Earl acting like he's old enough to have all his shit together, but meanwhile, his wife can't even figure out that outside of
Atlanta, iced tea doesn't need to be five parts sugar to one part tea. And then there's that blowhard fireman. Bad enough he's screwing his way through the neighborhood and his wife ignores it, we also have to deal with him trying to plant his flag on *this front*, too?"

"Honey," Jan said, "that's not fair. We all *suspect* Chuck of sleeping with Sharice, yes, but no confirmation. And there's been no one else I know of."

"Aww, for all I know, he'll come calling on *you* next, that dog." He tossed the rock in the air, caught it. "Yeah, he's the real dog here, not this stupid contraption." He kicked his foot out at the watchdog, but was careful not to make contact. He thought the thing was ridiculous, but it *did* shoot holes in those ice cubes earlier. unless maybe that Jaxon jack-off pulled some sleight-of-hand shit on them.

Jan laughed. "Oh, I doubt Chuck'd come calling over here, hon. I think Sharice is more his type. I don't think I'm …" She patted her considerable hips. "… the *color* he prefers." A small quiet part of her liked the idea of Chuck knocking on her door, but she kept that to herself.

"It makes me crazy, that's all," Joe said. "As far as I can tell, this thing that's supposed to protect us is beyond—" With a grunt, Joe hurled the rock as hard as he could, directly at the robot sitting thirty feet away. Instantly, the dog's optic sensor whirled, its left tube-arm extended and emitted a small gassy burp. The rock exploded into dust in mid-flight.

"—worthless …" Joe finished, his voice suddenly low, trailing off as he finished speaking.

Jan stared at the boxy metal beast. "Maybe … maybe not so worthless, after all? Geez, hon. I better, uh, I better go toss together a salad for Debbie Lyon, she called to say she's still planning to come by and chat tonight."

Joe stood in place, not ready to move closer to the robot just yet. He spoke slowly, at low volume. "Yeah, uh, yeah … good, um, idea. Good idea."

Joe continued to stand in the yard for another forty-five minutes. He never took his eyes off the robot dog.

THE LYONS:

"Did you *see* the way that thing put four perfectly placed holes in those ice cubes? I wasn't crazy about the idea at first, but this little baby might be a welcome addition to the family," Chuck said, patting the cold steel box on top of its head. The tubes connected to it released steam that could have been mistaken for a contented animal's sigh. For anyone who couldn't *see* the terrible machine that made the noise.

"It was pretty clear today that there was no way we were all going to mobilize into a good fighting unit on our own."

"'Fighting unit'?" His wife said. "Chuck, you heard that military man, and I agree with him—the last thing I want is for any of us to fight zombies ourselves."

"Yeah, I heard what he said. I could also tell that Earl was hiding something. I mean, really—if it was me who snuck into that housing tract after the attack, I would've made a stop at the gun store on the way home and dropped off rifles on everyone's porch. No delay. But what does Earl do? He's so upset that he … he schedules a damn barbecue a couple days later. The man knows as much about urgency as those Putnam kids know about religion."

Chuck kept rubbing the robot's "head" as he sat in his chair. A funhouse image of a man and his dog. Debbie wanted to laugh at the ridiculousness of the scene but she was afraid if she did, it'd turn to the crying fit she'd been suppressing all afternoon.

Instead, she said, "I just don't know about this. Are we all supposed to just sleep soundly now, knowing there's a killer robot sitting in our living room?"

"Well, you heard Jaxon—the zombies could well have moved on," Chuck said. "So we're probably instead being used to justify some military-spending budget line item. Makes them seem nice in our eyes. Turns loudmouths like Joe Rovito into a compliant little sheep."

He patted the thing's head again. "But one thing I do think," Chuck said, "is that we should be mindful to keep our lives as normal as possible. So I'd say if you still want to go visit with Jan Rovito tonight, by all means, do it. Me and ol' Junky here can hold down the fort. No reason one of us shouldn't have some fun tonight."

THE PASVARS:

Mr. Jaxon sat on the couch. Earl took a seat across from him, in his favorite chair, while Helen sat a zucchini muffin and a cup of tea on the ottoman. Jaxon's men had packed up and shipped out with Alford after unloading all the bots, but he stuck around.

Earl watched Jaxon take a bite of the muffin. He found him personable enough, but in that politician sort of way. Not sure he was being totally forthright, but he sold what he was saying in convincing fashion. "Well, Mr. Jaxon, what's your take-away from today? You came and shook up
everyone's worlds and outside of a couple of loudmouths, everyone accepted it without complaint. And you know why."

"No, why?"

"Wasn't a question," Earl said, sitting back in his seat. "You know why we all sounded so spooked earlier. None of us know how to react to Loyola Plaza."

"But *you* did, Earl," said Jaxon, biting into the warmed muffin. "You visited the block. You talked to those cops. Scary, wasn't it?"

"It was that, yes. Attacks done by something a lot harder to kill than a few innocent ice cubes, I'd say."

Helen was standing behind Earl, hands atop the high back of his chair. He reached up and grasped her right hand.

"Well, I don't agree with you there," Jaxon said. "These little bots might not look like much on the outside, but they're technological wonders. One of our best achievements."

Earl sighed. "Those zombies were created by man, too."

"That's my point, Earl," said Jaxon. "While we don't know exactly *how* these zombies were created, or possibly by *whom*, we do know that we can stop 'em with *these*." He touched the immobile robot seated on the area rug under the couch. "Man breaketh, and man fixeth and saveth, or some such. Earl, I know everyone is on edge—"

"As much by these little bundles of shrapnel sitting in our houses as by the zombies, I'd imagine." Earl leaned forward to stare at the watchbot.

"—and I'm telling you, we're here to help."

"What about the folks over on Woodsboro Drive? or Ladoga Avenue? You drop off these bundles with all of them, too?"

Jaxon stood up and stretched a slow, deliberate stretch. "One thing—one *street*—at a time, Earl. We've got to build more watchbots. This is a test, remember. It's also the start of something great, we think."

"Not sure I love the idea of us being your guinea pigs," Earl said, sitting back in his chair, resigned.

"Guinea pigs are a damn sight better than victims in my book, Earl. And like I mentioned before, we haven't seen any zombies creeping about in this area for a while now. You may well turn these doggies back to us in three months' time with nothing to report."

Jaxon bent over, took his tea and drank the entire cup before setting it back on the table. "I think you're all going to be fine. It's one more appliance to have in your house. Only this one, you don't have to ever *use* it, but it'll still be there when you *need* it."

"Will it, now?"

"It doesn't sleep on the bed, Earl," Jaxon continued, "and it won't mess on the floor or eat off your plate. But it will sure as hell *save all your lives*, if that becomes a necessary thing. We'll check back in tomorrow and see how night one goes. Sorry again for the long intrusion today."

With that, Jaxon stood and reached out to shake Earl's hand by way of a goodbye. The older man stayed in his seat but extended his hand to Jaxon.

Helen walked Jaxon to the front door and opened it for him. "Earl's not big on change," she said. "Neither am I, not this kind."

"Then it's fortunate you won't have to change at all. The watchbot will see to that. Forget about it while it's here and just live your life, Helen. Live it *without fear*."

Jaxon walked out into the damp night. Helen closed the door and locked both the door and the deadbolt behind him.

4—These Dogs *Will* Hunt …

It only took three hours for it to all start going wrong.

THE PUTNAMS:

That evening, in the garage, Raymond crouched down and looked over the watchbot. He was searching for any kind of panel that might open and give him access to its robotic guts.

Darren sat in an open lawn chair, a laptop perched on his knees and a beer in his hand. He looked over, smirked at Raymond's futile search and then went back to his laptop. "Anything yet?" he said, typing away, not really caring if Raymond replied or not.

"Goddammit, no," Ray said. "Really, it's like this thing came out fully formed—no panels, no wires, no openings, nothing. Not even any welding marks anywhere. How'd they even build it? How much ammo does it have in there?"

"Dude, it's a lethal, government-built robot," Darren said, half-listening and typing at a frantic pace. "What'd you think, you could just open it up and grab a handful of bullets? They probably have 3D printers that fabricate these things whole cloth. Whole metal. Whatever."

"I'm telling you, dipshit, I think I could re-program this thing if I could just mess with its motherboard. Trust me—I was cracking smart phones before you stopped pissing your pants. I could make this bot-dog our bitch."

Darren finished his beer and let out a hearty belch. "I still piss 'em now and again! Anyway, I keep telling you that re-wiring hardware's an ancient art. You crack, but I hack. And—hey, hey. looky there. Do me a favor and step away from it, I got something to show you. Right about … *now*."

He made a grand gesture of punching "Enter" on his laptop with his index finger. The robot's red "eye" illuminated. Then, on the computer's touchpad, he drew a circle with his index finger.

As he did, the robot turned in a circle.

"Holy shit," Ray said, jumping back from the robot. "*Holy shit*, dude."

"I am *in*, baby," Darren said excitedly, moving forward in his seat. "They thought they could Deepnet the interface, but I know how to navigate that dark road."

"But … how … where …" Darren stammered as the robot mirrored Ray's finger-moves on his laptop.

"Magic fingers, dickhead," he said, twirling his fingers in the air. "Ask your old geography teacher Mrs. Barnes if you don't believe me on that. Now watch this. Hey, Rin Tin *Can*, can you fetch me another beer?"

He drew a straight line on the touchpad. The robot moved in a straight line toward the cooler.

"That is damned amazing. What kinda range you think it's got?"

"I dunno," Darren said. "But the back door I found goes right into somewhere called Kirtland, which seems to be point of origin. Nice security, eh?"

"You rock."

"Yep, I do. I tell you, the Wi-Fi signal linking me to this robot got some kind of huge boost when I connected. It's way stronger than anything I've ever seen—I wouldn't be surprised if they could control these things by satellite. I think I could send it on beer runs to the liquor store. *In Arizona.*"

A big smile spread across Ray's face. "So … can you access its weapons systems, you think?"

Darren's fingers moved across the keyboard. "Sure, just another … ho-ly shit. Shit! The arsenal inside the fucker looks crazy-huge," he said. "Hah, check this out—there are all kinds of combat-sims in there, too. It'll let me simulate all kinds of shit for this bot to play around with. Like, in

some zombie-attack scenarios, it looks like this bitch has a stealth mode that can take the zombies' heads off with little more than a whisper—"

The top third of Darren's head came off with little more than a whisper, not even a second after he clicked on that particular zombie-attack scenario. It landed with a loud squelch against the garage door, where it splattered and then slowly slid to the ground. Blood and brains streaked down the door. The robot's paper-thin blade disappeared as quickly as it appeared. A fine mist of blood settled on the robot as it retracted.

"FuuuuCK!" shouted Raymond. "Shi—"

Raymond met a similar end to that of his brother, a micro-thin blade slicing through skin, bone and sinew. This time, his entire head was separated from his body at the neck. It was only when his body fell to its knees that the head was jarred loose upon impact, rolling across the cement floor and coming to a stop against Darren's foot.

Two whisper-bursts from its arm, two dead brothers.

The hacked zombie-sim executed perfectly. The robot returned to rest mode, its glowing eye dimming to black.

Grady Binder & Bryce Clinkenbeard:

Over the past two hours, Grady and Bryce's discussion had grown into a full-blown fight. Grady sat on their front porch step and stared at the sky, blinking back tears of anger. Bryce could be so goddamned thick-headed at times.

Grady knew Bryce was scared about the recent murders, and so was he. But did that mean they just instantly drop everything they both cared about? Bryce was a vegetarian—if the broccoli crops all went bad, would he instantly start biting the heads off live chickens?

Grady half-smiled at the visual of Bryce as an old-time circus geek. It occurred to him then that they'd get through this. They'd gotten through so much already.

He pulled out his cell phone and walked into the street to call his mother. Perhaps because their house sat on a lot next to a wooded greenbelt, the cell signal indoors sucked. But it was fine in the middle of the cul-desac street. So the neighborhood had gotten fairly used to Grady standing in the street to make calls.

Grady, standing over the manhole cover, punched his mother's name on the phone. Nothing. He noticed he had no cell signal at all, even outside. It was then that he noticed dark figures moving near tree-lined greenbelt. He stared at them, trying to make them out in the darkening night. He never noticed the others, the zombies who shuffled toward him from the opposite direction. They grabbed him from behind, the suddenness of the assault stealing the air from his lungs with just a gasp, inaudible to Bryce or anyone indoors.

Grady died then, violently but quickly. Which meant he would never see the horrible things about to be done to his still-flailing body. Dinner was served in vicious bites and tears.

Minutes later, Bryce opened the front door. "Grady? Grady, I've been thinking about things while we both pouted. And, well, you're right. I don't want that robot in our house any more than you do. So how about if we tie it up out back like a real dog? That way, it can still keep watch over things and … Grady?"

He stood in the open doorway. The moon was a sliver in the sky, the shadows pooled on the street in front of their house. Bryce really hated the fact that this street still had no streetlights. No streetlights and all telephone lines hard-wired underground—as if the residents of this neighborhood really loved to stargaze with no obstructions. Grady wondered if anyone younger than Earl ever even looked up at all. And God help you if you dropped something and needed to find it by starlight.

The watchbot came to animated life behind Bryce, whirring over to the doorway, bumping into Bryce's calves with surprising force. Damned thing almost knocked him over from behind.

He regained his balance and kicked backward at it. "Screw you!" he said. The thing had already caused Grady to storm off in anger, and now it was going to act up on him?

Bryce turned around and pushed it with his foot. "Get back, dammit." The robot was heavy—he barely moved it. Its center eye was whirring back and forth, back and forth. A low hum in all three of its cylinder-like arms was building, like a whining in Bryce's ears.

"Oh, this is stupid. Where did Grady put that owner's manual? I'm shutting you down tonight, pooch. Not in the mood."

He turned and again stood in the center of the doorway. Behind him, gun barrels extended from the tubes on the robot. "Grady? Are you out there? Come back, hon! All is forgiven. Besides, I need the booklet to tell me how to turn this lousy robot—"

Bryce saw three shuffling shadows step onto his porch. One of them, the one closest to Bryce, the one reaching out for him with a rotted, clawlike hand, was chewing on a severed arm wearing a scrap of the same shirt that Grady was wearing when he left. No sooner had this fact registered

with Bryce than the watchbot behind him fired multiple projectiles up and down the height of the doorframe. Each one struck its mark—the zombies that had shambled onto the porch.

One of the zombies stood directly in Bryce's sight line. The robot's projectile hit its mark there, too, despite the slight change in trajectory caused by the spike first entering and exiting Bryce's head before moving on to its intended victim.

Bryce wavered on his feet for a moment, and then fell forward, landing on his face but fortunately past the point of feeling pain as he made hard contact with the ground.

Another zombie wandered up the driveway, driven forward by the commotion and hot blood steaming into the night air. The robot fired one more time. And then, once again, all was quiet at the Binder/Clinkenbeard household, except for the humming of the watchbot.

THE KOERNERS:

Mitchell stretched out on his couch. He was enjoying the silence now that Sharice had gone out for her little book club meeting or whatever she got up to some nights. Who could keep track?

He glanced over at the metallic thing that Sharice brought home from the barbecue. He wasn't crazy about her happily accepting some government contraption, but maybe it could become her pet project, no pun intended. She could focus her attention on it instead of him. Yep, that would suit him just fine.

She'd become a real pain in the ass of late. She was always a talker, but her voice had taken on a shrill tone that it never had before. Or that he'd noticed before, anyway. That was *before* he had to listen to all of her yammering about the neighborhood slaughter that happened recently, too. She'd gotten even worse since those killings. She wanted him to get a gun; she wanted a security system; a dog; she wanted them to consider moving. On and on and on. He just wanted her to be quiet.

The fact is, Mitchell was well aware that the world was going to hell. Moving to a different location would just mean a different view from which to watch things burn. The rumors of fighting, of… *zombies*, and troops being lost to unknown threats overseas, it was all just sounding like the beginning of the end.

The last thing Mitchell wanted was to listen to other panicky neighbors kvetch about all of this. He had his own views about what was going on but didn't feel the need to share them with the local busybodies.

So he'd stayed inside with the shades down while Sharice went to the Pasvar's party. He barely shrugged when he'd looked out his window and saw all the military vehicles stopping at Earl's.
Additional confirmation that the end was rapidly approaching.

He glanced at the robot again. The thing seemed to stare right at him with its big, unblinking lens. He stared back. Then he closed his eyes and fell into a good dreamless sleep.

THE ROVITOS:

Joe grabbed a golf club out of the bag in the garage. A two-iron.

Upstairs, the sound of breaking glass. He heard Jan—or was that Debbie?—scream. He ran back up the stairs three at a time, the club handle slipping a bit in his sweaty hands. He gripped it tighter.

He burst through the door back into the house. He could hear signs of struggle. He also heard the robot firing round after round into… something.

Some *things*.

The zombies had come without warning, right through the big family room window. There wasn't time to figure out how they got into Chuck's yard in the first place. The robot was doing what it could, but Chuck could swear he saw a dozen or more shapes in his yard. He ran off to get a weapon, any weapon, before they overran his house.

Rushing into the living room, he noted the half-dozen dead (dead-*again*?) bodies on the floor, on his couch, their blackened blood staining his furniture and floor.

Debbie and Jan were cowering behind the TV as two zombies moved toward them. Joe raised the club, charging. *Finally* he'd be able to hit something properly with this damned two-iron, he thought. The watchbot moved in the same direction. Joe smiled. Together, he and this killing machine could stop these things. He always came out on top, whether he got the credit that a guy like Chuck Lyon got or not.

But Joe's streak of coming out on top came crashing to an end with the next swipe of his club. He swung the two-iron at the zombie, but his foot slipped on the blood pooled on the tile floor and he came down hard, the club head jamming into the watchbot's neck joints.

Instantly, the bot's defense systems kicked in, sending a lethal jolt of electricity up through the club shaft— and right into Joe. His heart exploded even as his hair caught fire.

Jan had no way of knowing how much electricity was coursing through her husband's smoking convulsing body, but she knew something was very wrong. In her panic, she jumped up to try to pry the club out of Joe's hands. She absorbed a dose of electricity powerful enough to ignite her eyelids. The Rovitos were down for the count, both falling into a smoldering heap on the floor.

Debbie, eyes wide with terror, followed survival instincts very different from Jan's. She made sure not to touch either body, a decision made easier by the fact that both were smoking briquettes now. She beat feet for the front door. Behind her, she heard the robot-dog firing away. there was nothing she could do here now, and she wanted to get home and warn Chuck. He'd be alone and would need warning.

A zombie on the porch grabbed at her as she ran by, its index finger nail shard gouging her arm. She pulled away and kept moving, losing a little skin as she did. It could have been much worse, so she blinked back the pain and tears and ran. She needed to get home.

THE LYONS:

Chuck told Sharice he needed a few more minutes of rest, only a few, and then he'd be ready to do her again.

He really loved having sex with her but sometimes their age difference was noticeable. It was only seven years' difference but still, Chuck's need to go more than once in a session had largely subsided while hers had grown.

He looked at her lying on the bed as he stood drinking a glass of water, her caramel-colored skin gorgeous in the low light.

He supposed that bringing Sharice into his conjugal bed wasn't the smartest or most decent thing to do, but Debbie truly seemed oblivious to whatever he did. He took it as tacit approval, something they just would never speak of. And if banging Sharice in the same bed where he occasionally rolled on top of Debbie gave him a memory he could conjure when he was bored, well, Debbie would
benefit from that in the long run, too, he reasoned. A win-win, really.

Chuck glanced at the clock, mindful of the time so as not to take longer than he should while Debbie was just a few houses down. He knew he needed to wrap this up soon so there wouldn't be any surprises.

He heard a noise downstairs. Was that breaking glass? Jesus, was Debbie already home?

Breaking things wasn't her way, but if she actually acknowledged what everyone else seemed to know was going on between Chuck and Sharice, who knew?

"Sharice," Chuck hissed, "get dressed! Someone's downstairs!"

She was up and out of bed and grasping at the undergarments she'd placed on the nightstand without saying a word. Her eyes were wide, though. She wasn't worried about Mitchell finding out, but she did actually like Debbie. She didn't want her hurt by their affair.

"Shit, she's coming up here!" He whispered. "Into the bathroom!"

The stairs fairly groaned under Debbie's footsteps and… wait. There was more than one person downstairs. It wasn't just Debbie. God, had she brought her whole book club here?

Sharice closed herself in the bathroom. Chuck went to the double bedroom doors and peaked through them. He put a hand on the two knobs to steady himself. The door shook from the outside, someone trying to push it open.

He tried to peer through the crack between the doors. Then they pushed inward, one of the doors knocked partially off its hinges by the weight of whatever was shoving from the other side.

Chuck fell backwards onto the ground. "Debbie, come on, don't do—" he started. Then the bodies fell on top of him, biting at his face and shoulders. So many of them, too many to focus on. And definitely not Debbie. Chuck just saw a shapeless mass of arms, heads, and gnashing teeth. As far as last sights go, it was pretty horrific.

Sharice cracked open the bathroom door to see what all the commotion was. Which proved to be a bad idea. The last one she'd ever have.

Debbie heard a shrill scream as she ran toward the front door. Those things were here, too?

She ran inside the house through the already-open front door. "Where's the robot?!" she yelled to no one in particular. "Chuck!"

She saw the watchbot then, heading up the stairs, firing away at the zombies on the top stoop.

Debbie suddenly felt bad, truly bad inside, her stomach cramping and her blood boiling. Maybe it was her extreme panic, she thought. A heart attack? She touched the gouge on her arm as she moved with great effort now toward the bottom of the stairs. The pain was concentrated there, but spreading up and down her arm. When she touched the wound, her finger sunk deep, too deep, into it.

It was already infected and blackening around the edges. And it was growing, the torn flesh opening like a black rose taking bloom. Debbie wasn't a person who had ever seen a zombie movie in her life, so being caught in the throes of a zombie virus took her entirely unaware.

But not the watchbot. It stopped halfway down the stairs—it seemed to have already quieted down whatever scene had transpired on the second floor.

The robot's boxy head spun in her direction.

"Please," she whispered. "Have mercy, I'm *huuuuman*."

She wasn't, actually, not any longer. And mercy? Not a part of the robot's programming.

The robot fired one more time.

THE PASVARS:

Earl and Helen stood huddled together behind the watchbot as it fired. The zombies were streaming in from multiple entrance points. There looked to be dozens upon dozens, Earl noted, an endless stream of them.

He pulled Helen closer. He would protect her to the end, but he knew that end was likely to come painfully soon.

Looking wildly around the room, he noticed that every zombie that shuffled indoors was met with a debilitating head shot from the watchbot. It methodically kept its three arms whipping in all directions, firing away and dropping bodies left and right.

Earl doubted that whoever got stuck cleaning up this mess would find any errant spikes stuck in the walls, either. Every shot hit its mark. The watchbot really was an amazing creation, Earl thought. It somehow, impossibly, had an endless supply of spikes inside it, as well as its unerring aim. If a zombie tripped over some furniture, the watchbot auto-corrected its aim almost before the zombie moved, taking it out with a single killshot.

"Helen!" Earl shouted over the din, "Move toward the front door! Stay tight behind the robot!"

"But where… where can we go?!" She screamed back, tears streaming down her face.

"Anywhere *it* goes! but we need to get outside. We're too pinned down in here."

He pushed her toward the front door, the zombies moving toward them from the rear of the house. Although it never once looked in their direction, the watchbot kept earning its keep—so much for the "dog" aspect that Jaxon described. Clearly this robot was made to kill zombies, period—it wasn't much concerned about any humans that might stray across its path.

Throwing the front door open, Earl was grabbed by a bony claw of a hand. The zombie came at him, teeth gnashing. It smelled of spoiled meat, giving off a sweet putrid odor. Earl couldn't get his hands up to stave off the attack.

"Nooo!" screamed Helen.

The zombie clamped its jaws shut right in front of her husband's face. Earl wasn't sure what had stopped it from biting his face off, but then it became apparent—something had pulled it away from him at the last second.

That something was Mr. Jaxon. He had the zombie by the collar of its torn shirt. He spun it around and thrust it down onto the walkway. It went at Jaxon's ankle, but Jaxon fired a round into the thing's head before it could get too close. Blackness from within its skull splattered across Earl's feet.

"Didn't want to shoot it so close to your face," Jaxon said calmly. "If blood splatter had gotten into your mouth or eyes, well, you'd be *next*. Now come with me, let's get you both cleaned up and away from here."

"What… what…" Earl stammered.

"The zombies, Earl," Jaxon said, "the watchbot will clean up here, so let's get moving."

Earl pulled away. "The hell, you say!"

"Earl, what—?"

"A bit convenient that we get attacked the same day you deliver us these robots! We're not going anywhere with you!"

Earl planted his feet on his lawn, keeping Helen behind him with his outstretched arm.

Slowly, as his eyes focused to the dark, he became aware of the chaos all around the street. Soldiers fired silent rounds at groups of zombies in every yard. He heard screams from within some of the homes. bodies lay on the ground—hopefully zombie bodies. Additional soldiers were leaping out of trucks and running toward the fighting.

"Earl, you're not wrong," Jaxon said. "As I told you before, there was always a chance that zombies might remain in the area. And I was also truthful about the fact that we can't watch over everyone. We're fighting a war that's not going well. Globally, we're struggling. The *human race* is… losing."

"But…what can you do?" Helen asked. "How can you stop them?"

"We're working on that." Jaxon motioned to a man near a motorhome painted with military colors. "We're also testing other new robotic defense systems, as well as these home units. We need to know what works and what doesn't—so we're field-testing, and hopefully protecting people as we go."

The man, Alford, ran up to them.

"Alford, this is Earl and Helen Pasvar. You remember them from this morning. Let's get them inside and cleaned up. Earl's feet have been splashed with zombie muck, take special care there in case he has any open wounds on his feet."

"Yes, sir. Please come with me, folks."

Around them, chaos reigned.

"What of everyone else? Will you get them out, too?" Helen asked.

"Helen," Jaxon said, "we're getting everyone alive out of here. *You two.* Now please, go with Mr. Alford. He'll take care of you. You'll be okay."

"Will we?" Helen asked him, staring right at him. "Will *any* of us?"

Jaxon stared back. He was silent for a minute, and then he said something in a low voice. Something that Helen always remembered, even though she never saw Jaxon again.

He said, "Frankly, I'm starting to doubt that. But I'm an optimist, you never know, maybe the world will surprise us all."

After the vehicle holding the Pasvars backed out of the cul-de-sac and drove away, Jaxon stood in the middle of the street, looking around him. His men had contained the zombies on the street and moved into the houses to clean up the rest.

He walked over to one of the bodies lying on the street. A zombie with its head shot off. How many of these had he seen over the past two months? More than he could ever block out when he shut his eyes at night, that's for sure. But far fewer than he knew he'd see next week, or next month.

He looked at the zombie. It had carried out its task admirably. These undead monsters were impossible in so many ways, but they were easy to lead, that was for sure. Feed them an accessible human scent and they'd lock in like a hound dog tracking a coon.

Jaxon's men had helped funnel the creatures through the greenbelt that separated this cul-de-sac from the other streets in the neighborhood. They could move in relative secrecy and shadow by staying among the trees. That was one upside of people not really leaving their homes any more. From there, the zombies began the beta test of Robwood Circle.

The watchbots, for the most part, performed admirably. The scientists cataloguing their actions were pleased with certain aspects of the defense systems. For starters, their aim was indeed infallible. Human losses were still at a high level, but as the zombie problem had grown, so had the number the military considered an "acceptable loss."

Two of the twelve residents here survived, but they might not have without Jaxon's help there at the end. Not stellar performance perhaps, but not enough to send the dogs to the scrap heap either. Up to four of the residents were killed because of the watchbots' actions. They still seem to have a difficult time distinguishing between humans and zombies, unable to make proper distinctions to safeguard lives at a necessary level. But the robots were processing information as they gleaned it, learning as they went. Adapting. That was the important thing. Especially against an enemy that never learned, never changed, never grew in any way except for sheer numbers.

Jaxon was confident they could manipulate the reports to continue funding for the Watchbot initiative. one good thing about a looming, all-encompassing war was less oversight. The next test would net better results, he was sure of it.

The Pasvars' watchbot rolled up silently next to Jaxon. He noticed it had black blood caked on it. Of the six models deployed on this street, this one had performed the best. Jaxon just needed more like it; he'd "put down" the rest.

"Good dog," Jaxon said, patting a clean spot on its head. The machine had already gone into rest mode and did not respond at all to its master's touch.

Art by Ashley Wood

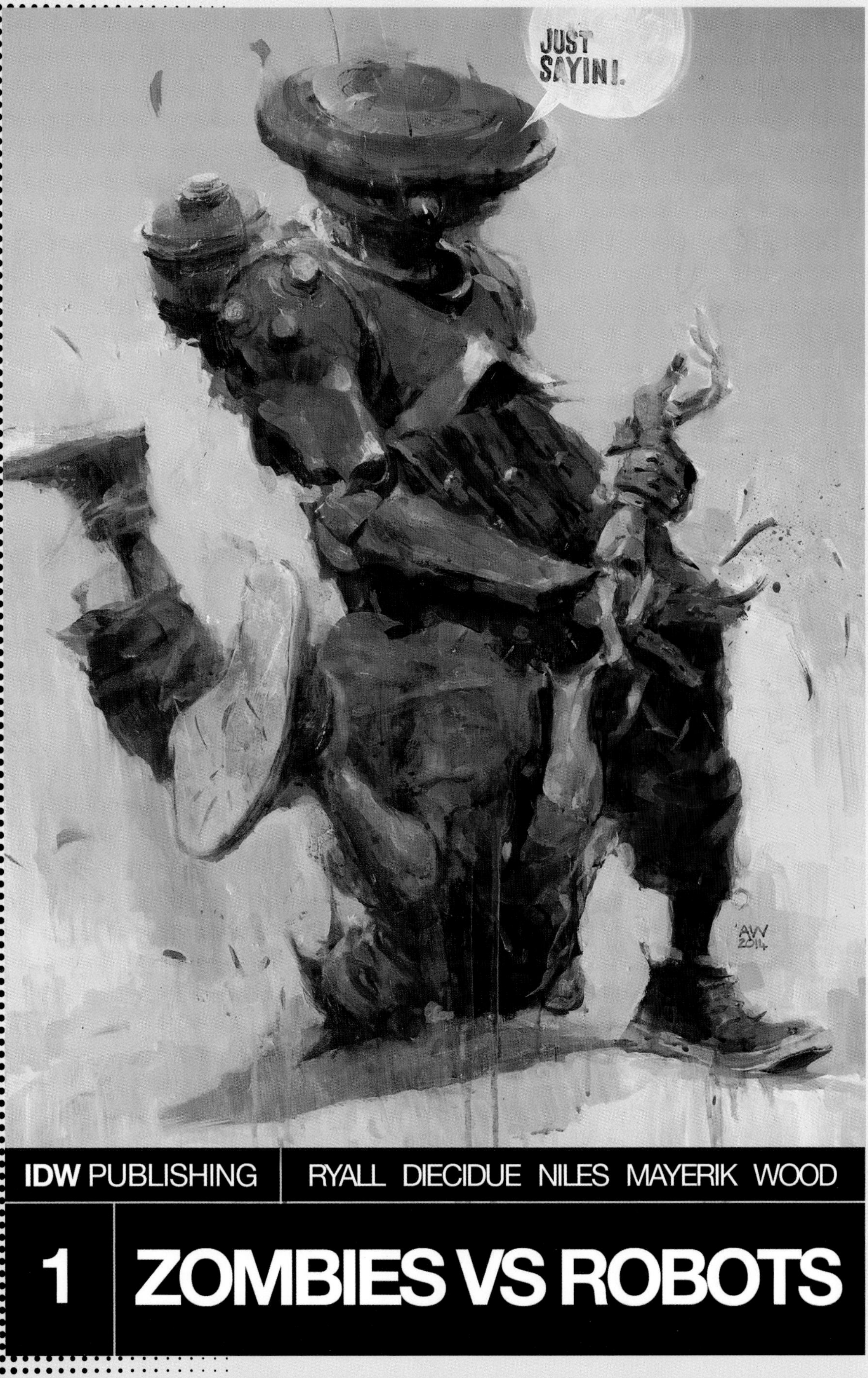
JUST SAYIN'.
AW 2014
IDW PUBLISHING
RYALL DIECIDUE NILES MAYERIK WOOD
1
ZOMBIES VS ROBOTS

Art by Gabriel Rodriguez

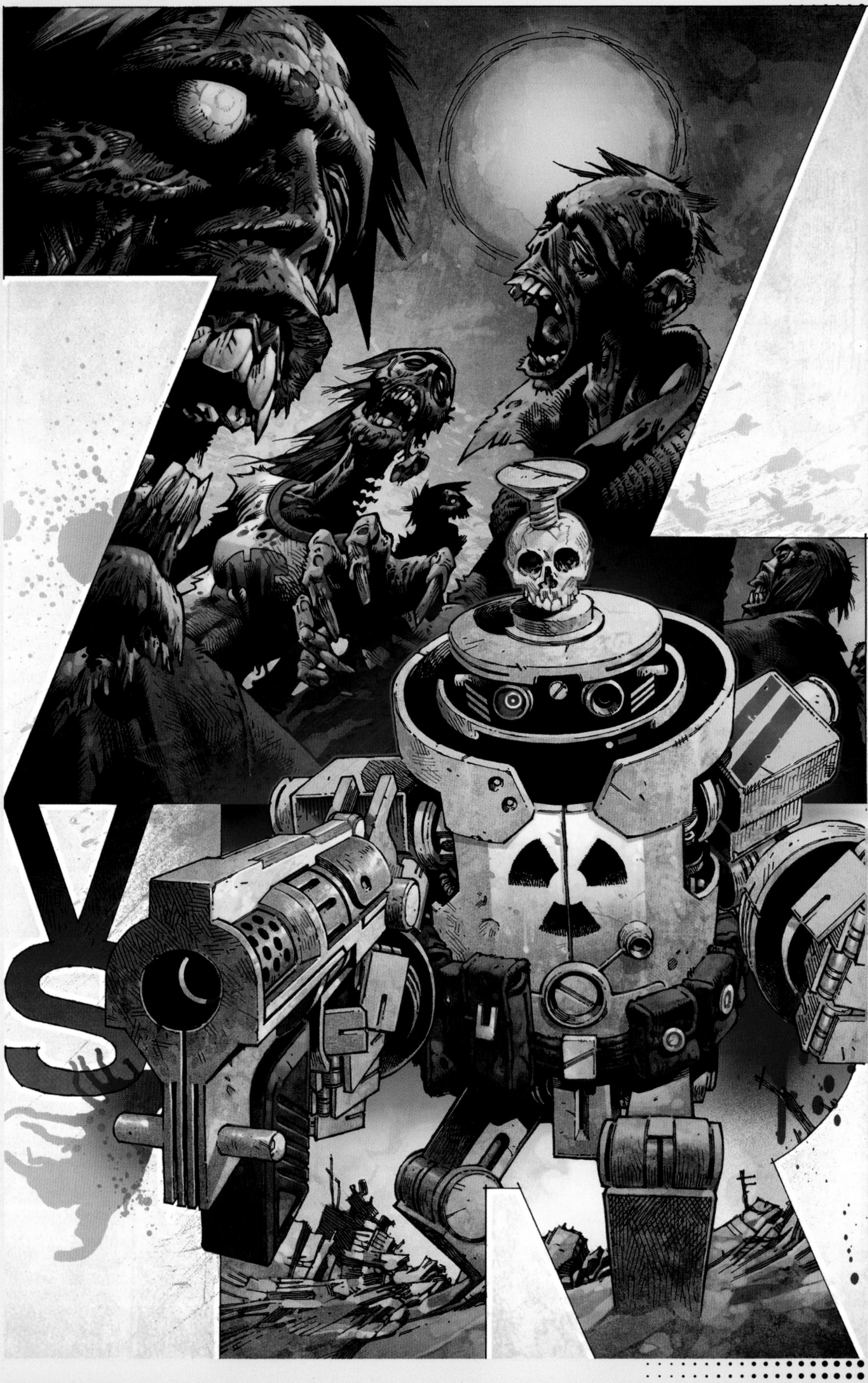

Art by Ashley Wood

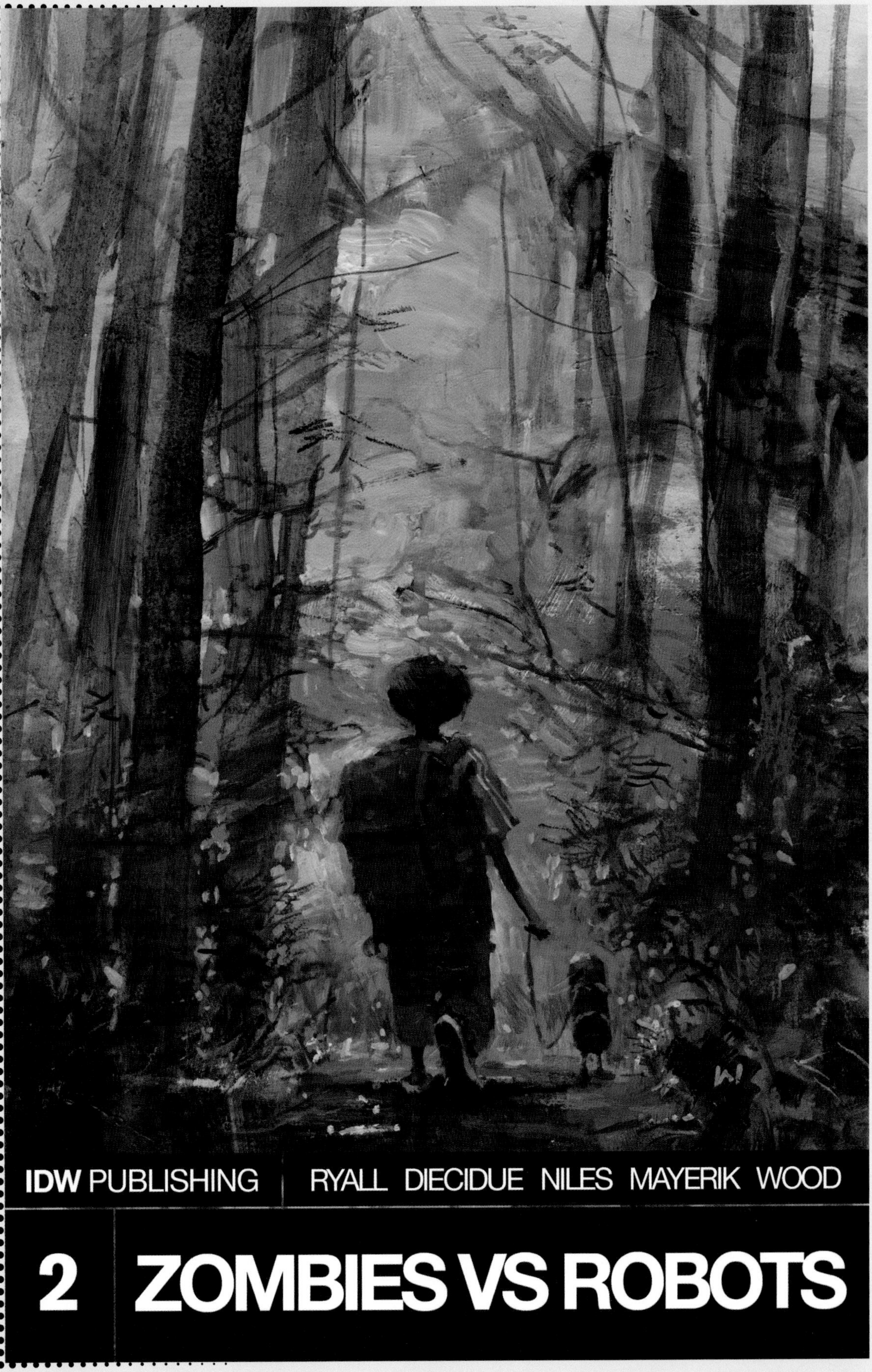
IDW PUBLISHING
RYALL DIECIDUE NILES MAYERIK WOOD
2
ZOMBIES VS ROBOTS

Art by James Stokoe

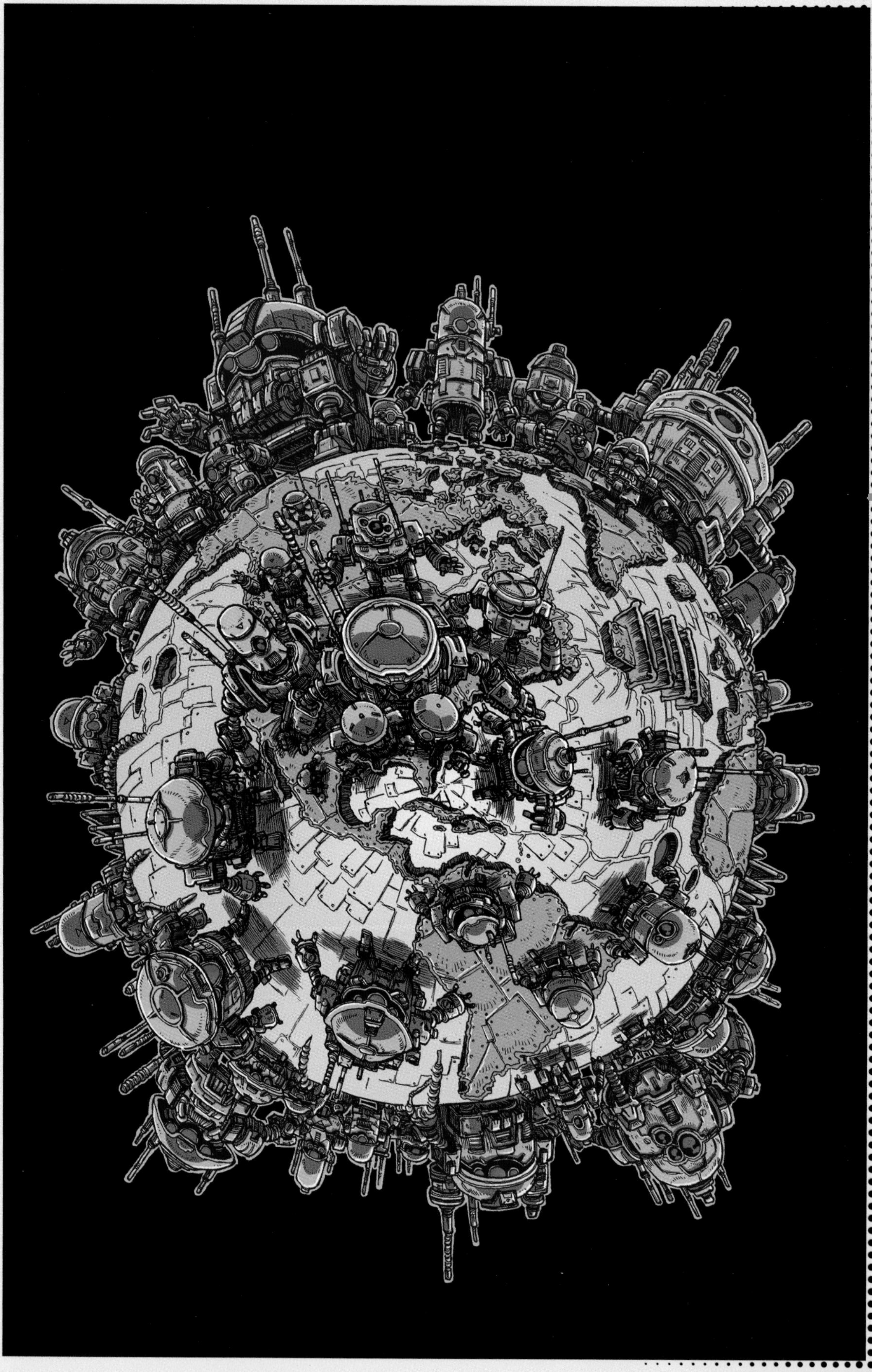

Art by Ashley Wood

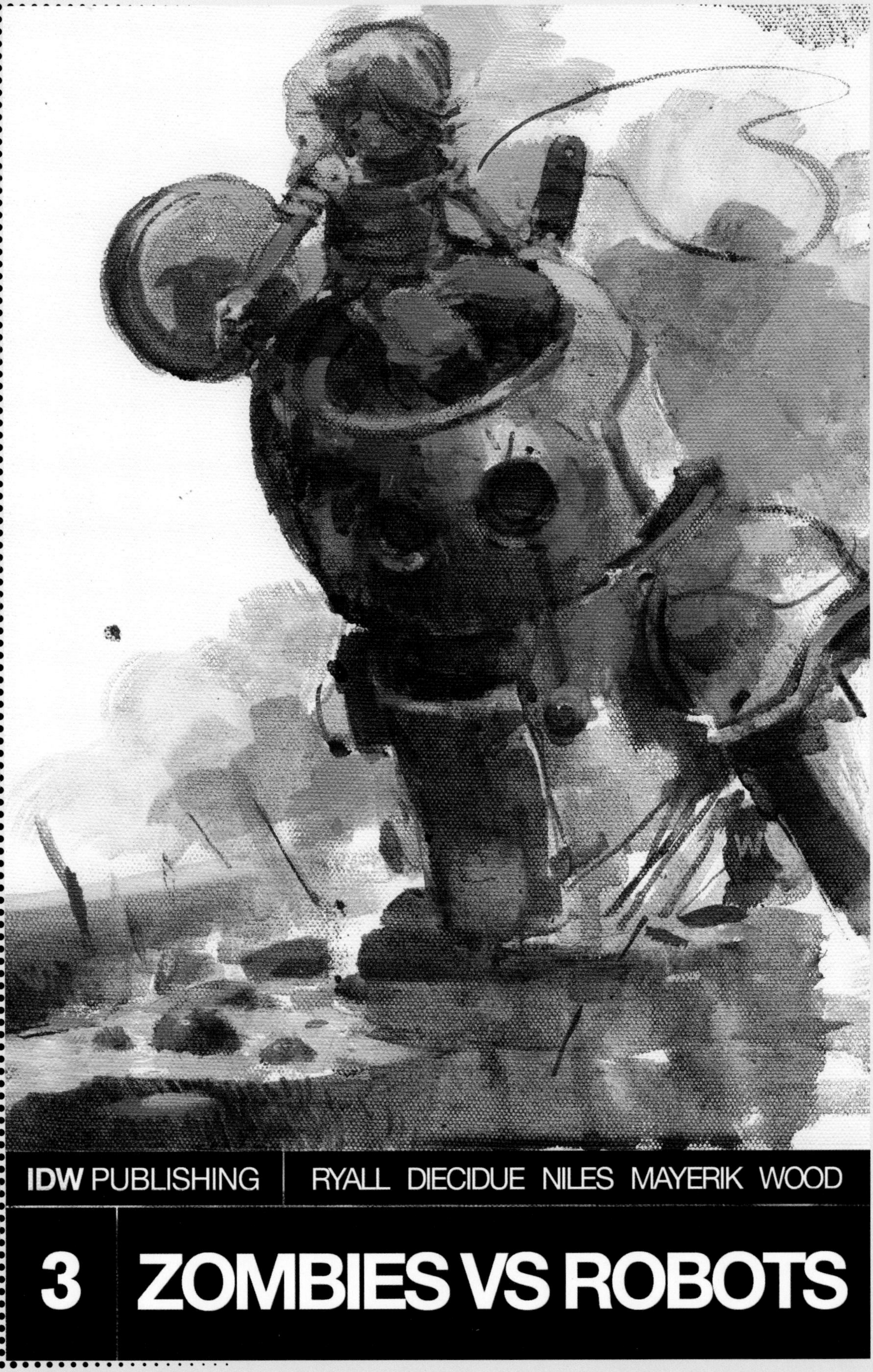
IDW PUBLISHING
RYALL DIECIDUE NILES MAYERIK WOOD
3
ZOMBIES VS ROBOTS

Art by James Stokoe

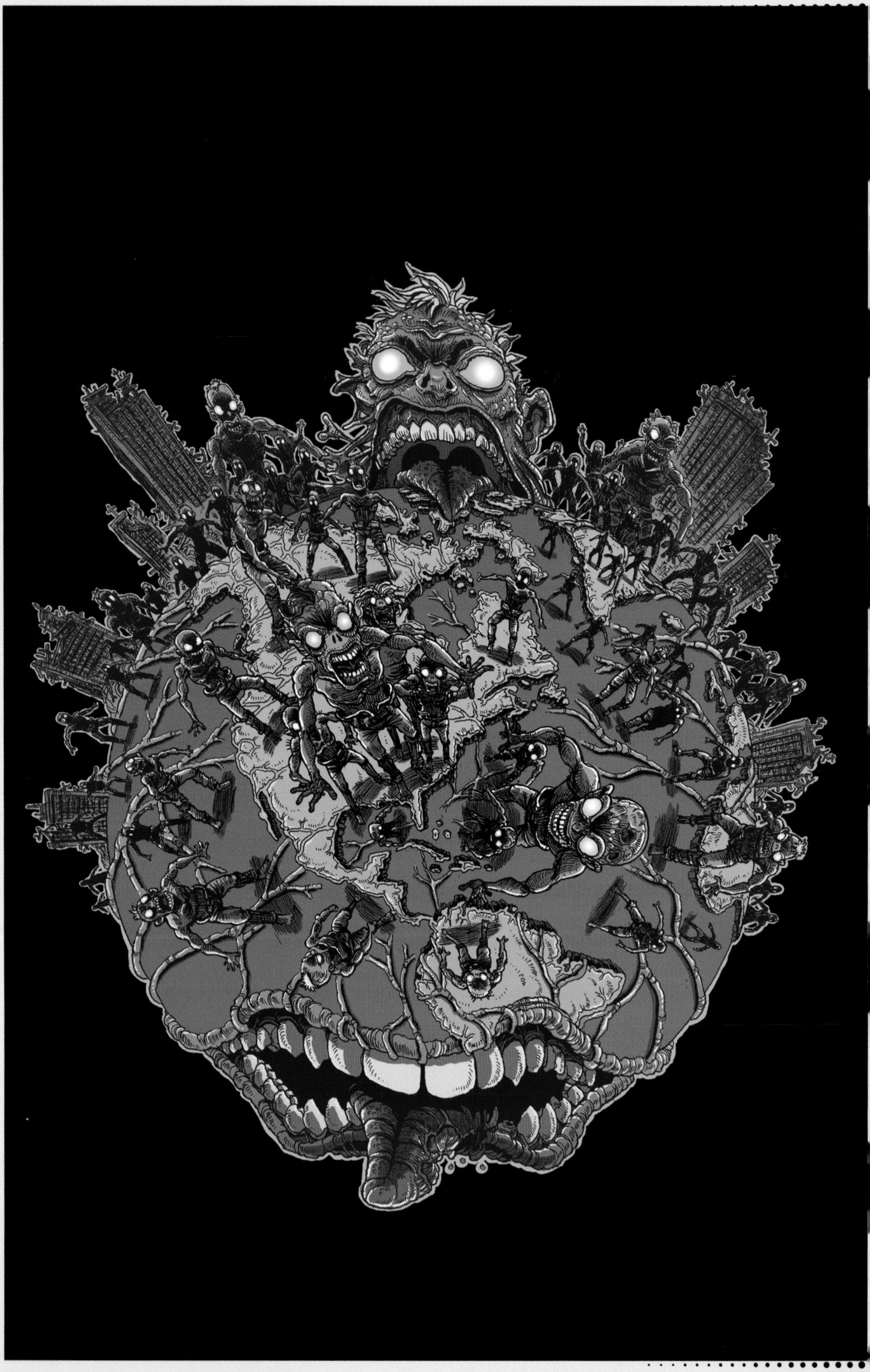

Art by Ashley Wood

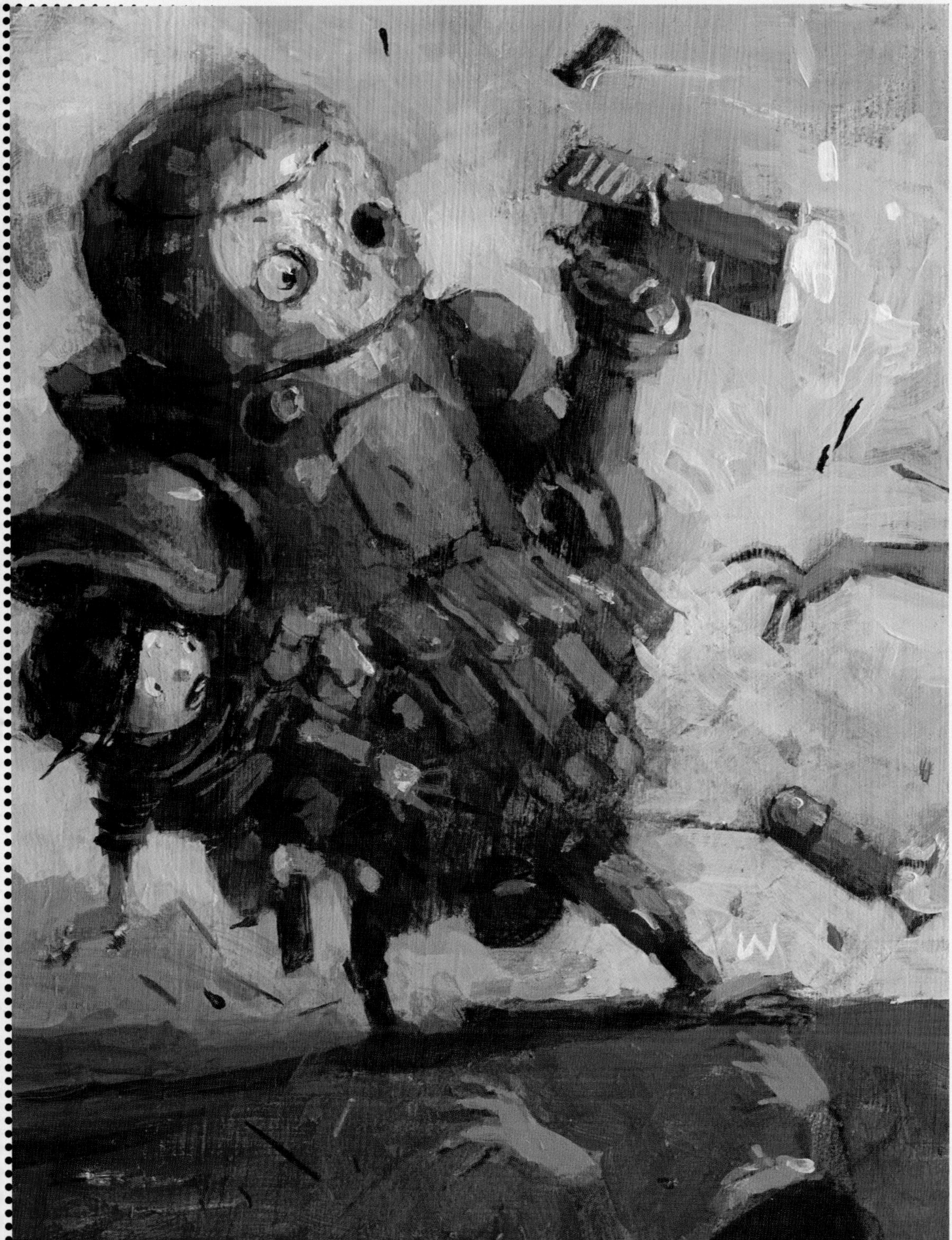

IDW PUBLISHING | RYALL DIECIDUE NILES MAYERIK WOOD

4 ZOMBIES VS ROBOTS

Art by James Stokoe

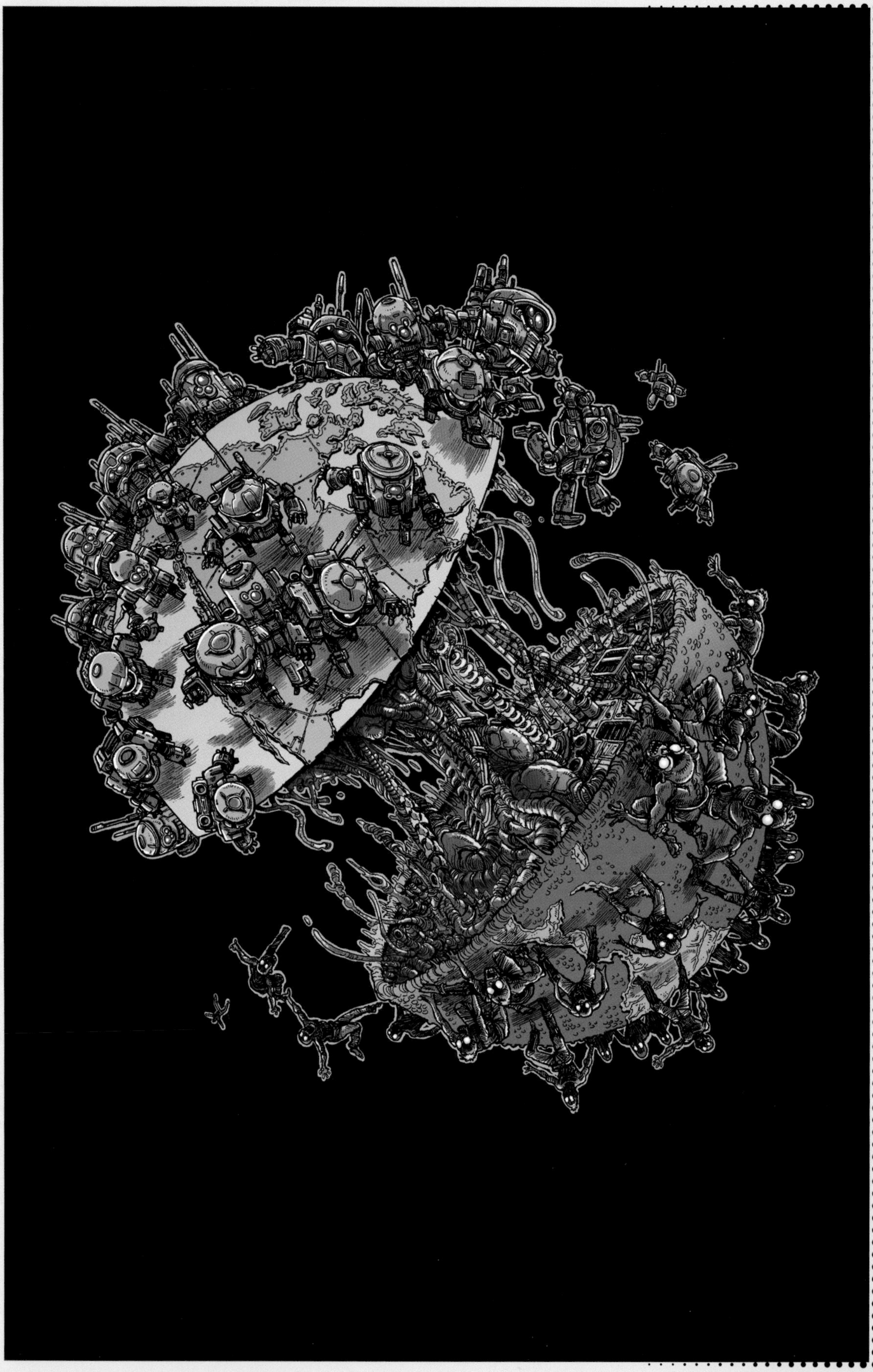

Art by Ashley Wood

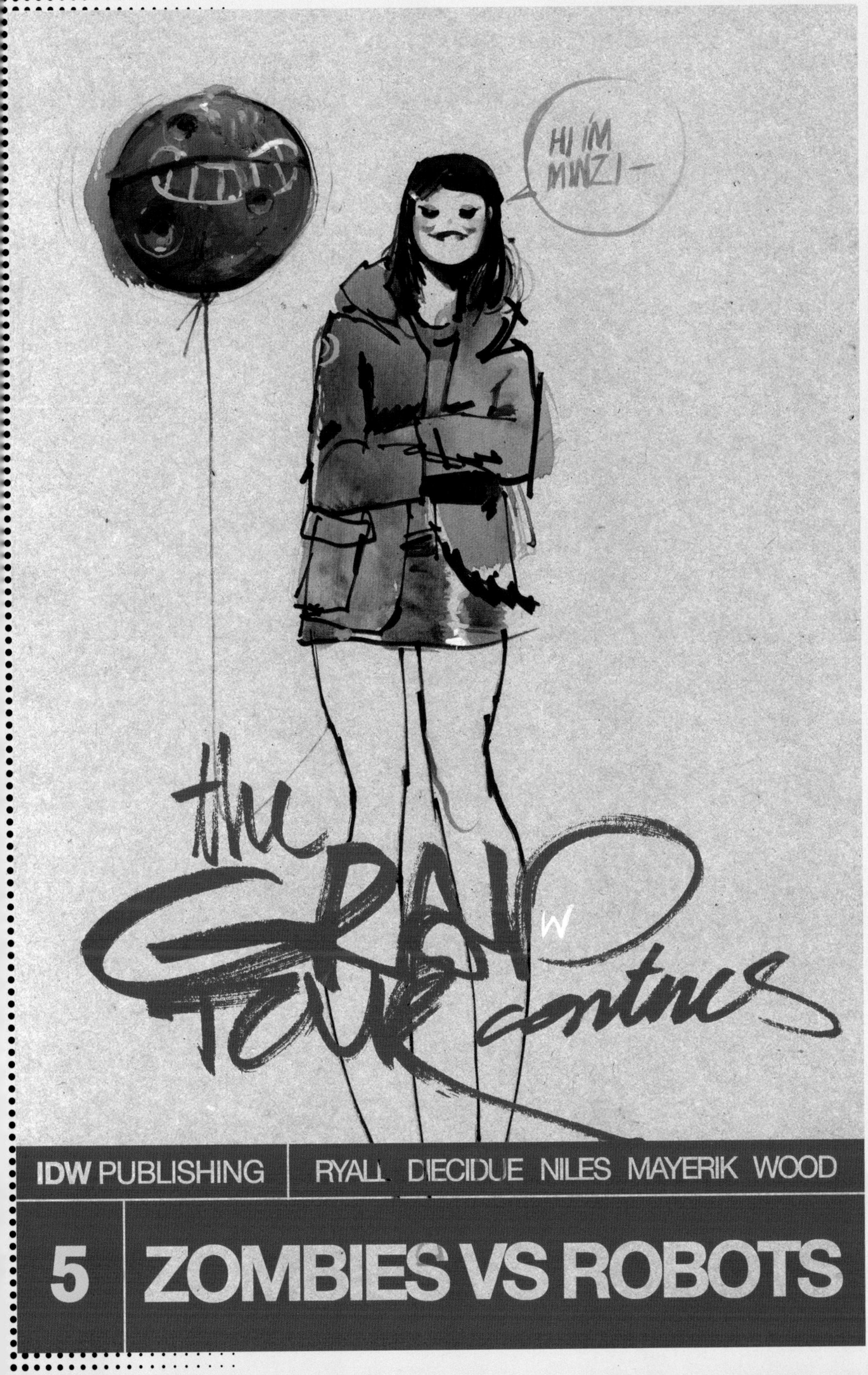
HI I'M MINZI-
the Raw Gravy Centres
IDW PUBLISHING
RYALL DIECIDUE NILES MAYERIK WOOD
5
ZOMBIES VS ROBOTS

Art by Mark Torres

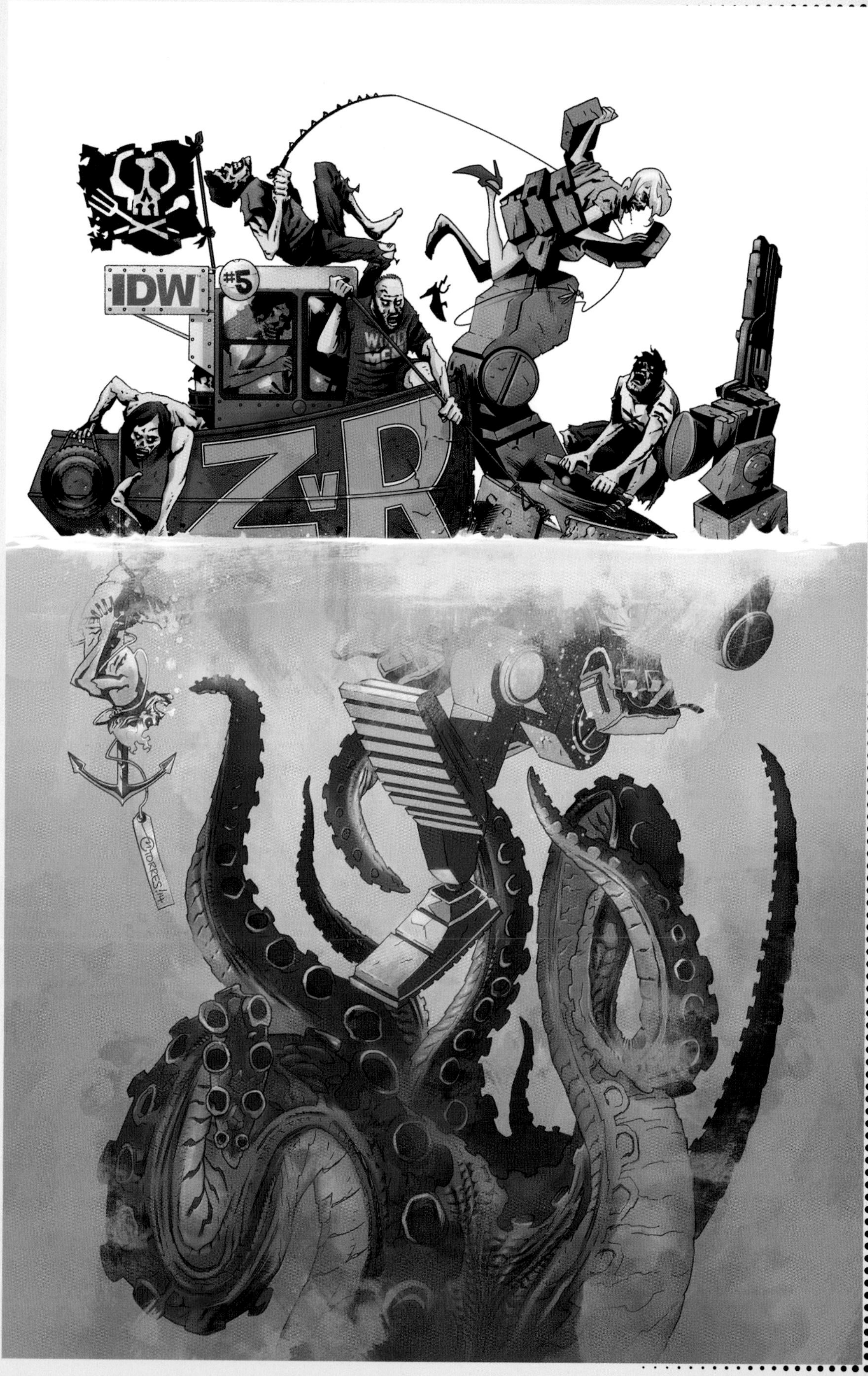
IDW
#5
ZvR
TORRES/14

Art by Ashley Wood

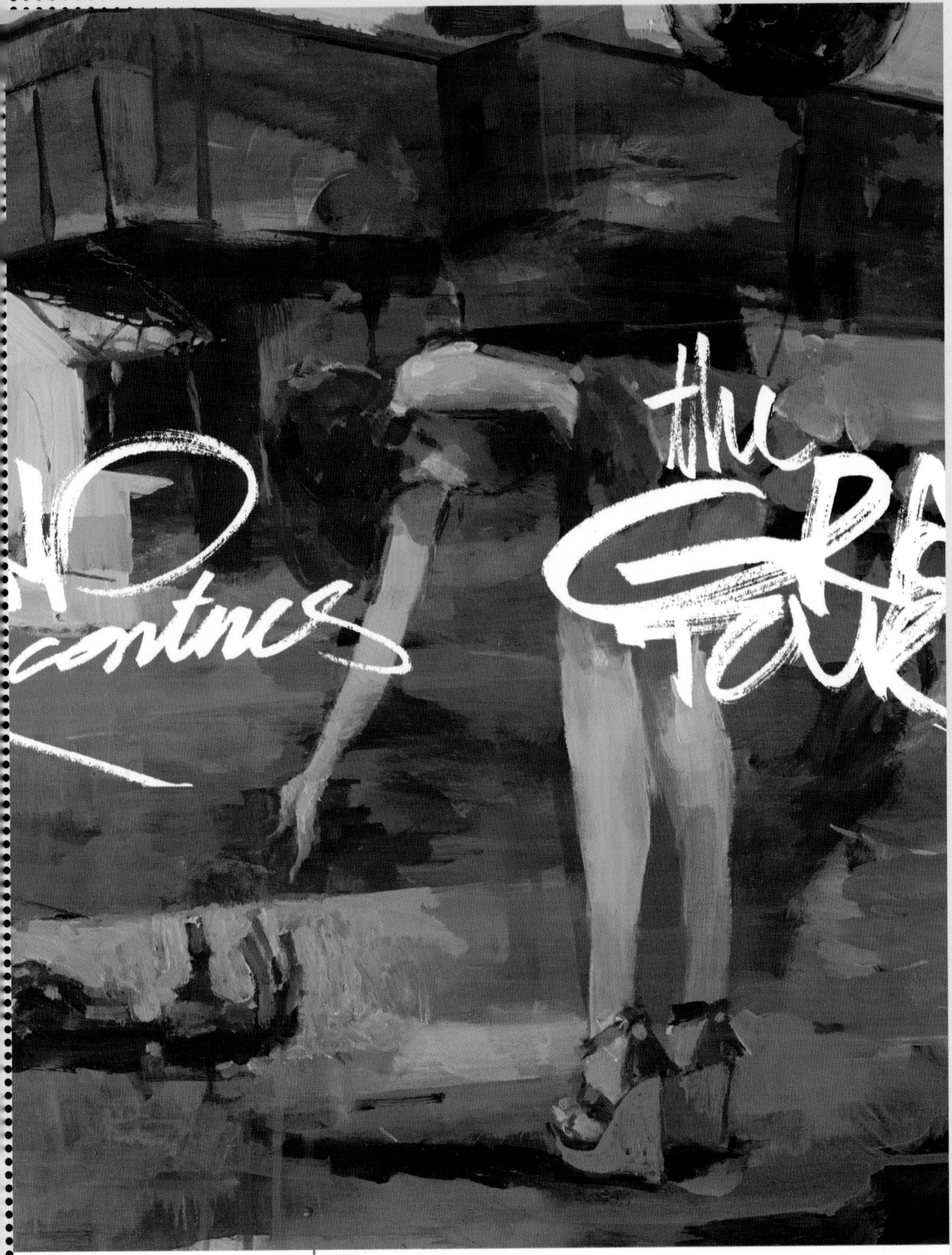

IDW PUBLISHING | RYALL DIECIDUE NILES MAYERIK WOOD

6 ZOMBIES VS ROBOTS

Art by Mark Torres

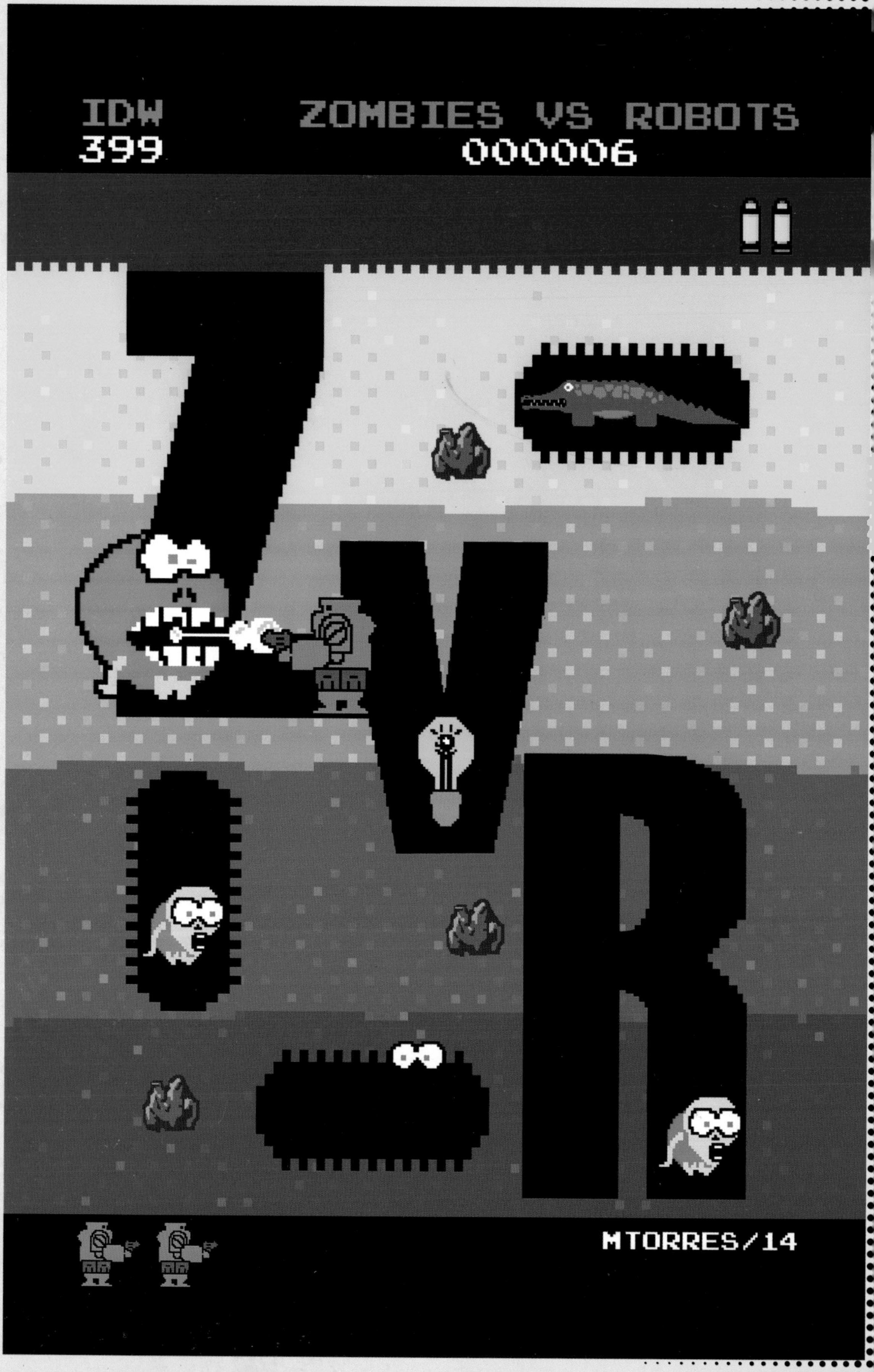

IDW
399
ZOMBIES VS ROBOTS
000006
MTORRES/14